LUTHERAN QUARTERLY BOOKS

Editor

Paul Rorem, *Princeton Theological Seminary*

Associate Editors

Timothy J. Wengert, *The Lutheran Theological Seminary at Philadelphia*
Steven Paulson, *Luther Seminary, St. Paul*
Mark C. Mattes, *Grand View University, Des Moines, Iowa*

Lutheran Quarterly Books will advance the same aims as *Lutheran Quarterly* itself, aims repeated by Theodore G. Tappert when he was editor fifty years ago and renewed by Oliver K. Olson when he revived the publication in 1987. The original four aims continue to grace the front matter and to guide the contents of every issue, and can now also indicate the goals of *Lutheran Quarterly Books:* "to provide a forum (1) for the discussion of Christian faith and life on the basis of the Lutheran confession; (2) for the application of the principles of the Lutheran church to the changing problems of religion and society; (3) for the fostering of world Lutheranism; and (4) for the promotion of understanding between Lutherans and other Christians."

For further information, see www.lutheranquarterly.com.

The symbol and motto of *Lutheran Quarterly*, VDMA for *Verbum Domini Manet in Aeternum* (1 Peter 1:25), was adopted as a motto by Luther's sovereign, Frederick the Wise, and his successors. The original "Protestant" princes walking out of the imperial Diet of Speyer in 1529, unruly peasants following Thomas Müntzer, and from 1531 to 1547 the coins, medals, flags, and guns of the Smalcaldic League all bore the most famous Reformation slogan, the first Evangelical confession: The Word of the Lord remains forever.

Lutheran Quarterly Books

Living by Faith: Justification and Sanctification, by Oswald Bayer (2003).

Harvesting Martin Luther's Reflections on Theology, Ethics and the Church, essays from *Lutheran Quarterly,* edited by Timothy J. Wengert, with foreword by David C. Steinmetz (2004).

A More Radical Gospel: Essays on Eschatology, Authority, Atonement, and Ecumenism, by Gerhard O. Forde, edited by Mark Mattes and Steven Paulson (2004).

The Role of Justification in Contemporary Theology, by Mark C. Mattes (2004).

The Captivation of the Will: Luther vs. Erasmus on Freedom and Bondage, by Gerhard O. Forde (2005).

Bound Choice, Election, and Wittenberg Theological Method: From Martin Luther to the Formula of Concord, by Robert Kolb (2005).

A Formula for Parish Practice: Using the Formula of Concord in Congregations, by Timothy J. Wengert (2006).

Luther's Liturgical Music: Principles and Implications, by Robin A. Leaver (2006).

The Preached God: Proclamation in Word and Sacrament, by Gerhard O. Forde, edited by Mark C. Mattes and Steven D. Paulson (2007).

Theology the Lutheran Way, by Oswald Bayer (2007).

A Time for Confessing, by Robert W. Bertram (2008).

The Pastoral Luther: Essays on Martin Luther's Practical Theology, edited by Timothy J. Wengert (2009).

Preaching from Home: The Stories of Seven Lutheran Women Hymn Writers, by Gracia Grindal (2011).

The Early Luther: Stages in a Reformation Reorientation, by Berndt Hamm (2013).

The Life, Works, and Witness of Tsehay Tolessa and Gudina Tumsa, the Ethiopian Bonhoeffer, edited by Samuel Yonas Deressa and Sarah Hinlicky (2017).

Preaching from Home

The Stories of Seven Lutheran Women Hymn Writers

Gracia Grindal

Fortress Press
Minneapolis

PREACHING FROM HOME
The Stories of Seven Lutheran Women Hymn Writers

Copyright © 2017 Fortress Press. All rights reserved. Except for brief quotations in critical articles or reviews, no part of this book may be reproduced in any manner without prior written permission from the publisher. Email copyright@fortresspress.com or write to Permissions, Fortress Press, PO Box 1209, Minneapolis, MN 55440-1209.

Interior contents have not been changed from prior editions.

Paperback ISBN: 978-1-5064-2717-1
eBook ISBN: 978-1-5064-2718-8

Contents

Preface	vii
Introduction	1
1. Dorothe Engelbretsdatter (1634-1716), Bergen's Deborah	15
2. Birgitte Hertz Boye (1742-1824), Falling Star	75
3. Berthe Canutte Aarflot (1795-1859), Bride of Christ	113
4. Lina Sandell (1832-1903), Young Preacher of Grace	163
5. Britt G. Hallqvist (1914-1997), A Twinkling in God's Eye	215
6. Lisbeth Smedegaard Andersen (1934-), Bringing Heaven to Earth	271
7. Gracia Grindal (1943-), Homemade World	319
Index of Names and Subjects	354
Index of Books and Hymns	359

Preface

The book that follows is a modest attempt to give English speakers a taste of Scandinavian Lutheran hymnody by women. Each one exerted a force on succeeding hymn writers whether or not they are still well known. The literature of the Lutheran parsonage, really women's literature, began in the hymns written by women, mostly pastors' wives, daughters, mothers, or preachers themselves. Dorothe Engelbretsdatter (1634-1716) of Bergen, Norway, wrote hymns of interest mostly to literary scholars, and feminists in Scandinavia, who admire her as a person, find her Baroque Lutheran piety hard to take. As I studied her and began to understand the persistence of the woman's voice from the parsonage, especially in hymnody, it was clear to me that the other women hymn writers of great moment in Scandinavian letters and sacred literature, most all of them from the parsonage, were also addressing their audiences as preacher, even though the notion of being pastors and preachers had probably not been an aspiration they had felt, at least until the twentieth century when women could be ordained in the Lutheran church. By examining the earliest Lutheran hymns, beginning with those by Martin Luther and probably his first student of hymn writing, Elisabeth Cruciger, we can see this tradition at its earliest. This book of parsonage literature dips into the past five centuries of Lutheran women hymn writers to see how they had absorbed the lessons of their fathers about preaching and hymnody, and how they thought of themselves as writers of hymns. I also see my role as one of introducing English speakers to their work, especially Lutheran women who do not

Preface

have many resources where women appear in their own right and are successful in their own careers. To do this I have, after briefly discussing Cruciger in the book's Introduction, chosen six more hymn writers, two from Denmark, two from Norway, two from Sweden, with a concluding chapter reflecting on their influence in my own work as an American Lutheran woman hymn writer who also grew up in the parsonage.

To do this, such hymns need to be translated into workable English so as to give readers some sense of the original. This means getting the language appropriate to the tradition and particular hymn writer into usable forms, usually the ones the authors originally suggested for their text. Fully aware that poetry is what is lost in the translation, I began, hoping to give the English reader some sense for the original. To do this I have reluctantly abandoned some of the literary forms of the original with their intense rhyming schemes, easy for those who write in the Scandinavian languages. Although these languages are thought to be word poor, they are rich in rhyming words, even two- or three-syllable rhymes that are impossible to find in English without making the work seem trivial or silly. So, unless it seemed necessary to do so (especially for Dorothe Engelbretsdatter, the most distant in time and sensibility), I tended to use metrical versions, with fewer rhymes, that could be sung to the intended tune, regrettably lacking the wonderful closures and wit that rhymes give in the original. The loss is significant, but if I had to twist the syntax around to get all those rhymes it would also do violence to the original. On occasion, I was able to give some sense for the original by rhyming some of the verses.

The original music for the hymns has also been provided as accurately as could be done, so the singer can also hear the sounds of the epoch in the singing of the hymns. Dorothe Engelbretsdatter was highly praised by musicians for her choice of tunes well regarded during her own time. Birgitte Boye (1742-1824) also used tunes for her texts from older hymnals, as did Berthe Canutte Aarflot (1795-1859). This common practice begins to fade with Lina Sandell (1832-1903) whose friend Oskar Ahnfelt pestered her for texts so he could write new hymns. These hymns, text and tune, swept the north with their particular Swedish sound. Britt Hallqvist (1914-1997) wrote texts that were so different and new they seemed to require new tunes, which were quickly provided by composers such as Egil Hovland, Norway's great church musician in the twentieth century. Together, they created a new sound and movement that in many ways have changed the sound of hymnody in the north. Lisbeth Smedegaard

Andersen (1934-   ) began by recommending old tunes, but now has attracted contemporary composers who have given her texts a contemporary feel and ambience.

The older tunes, however, are not well known in America or among their heirs in Scandinavian America partly because the old tunes with their modal sounds, unfamiliar to the American ear, seemed too grim in the new world. The prejudice against things Scandinavian among Lutherans in this country can be seen most clearly in American Lutheran hymnals where the rich traditions of all the Nordic countries were passed over in favor of English and American texts, because of both the tunes, and also the rather wooden translations of the texts. The second generation of immigrants made valiant efforts to produce suitable versions of their old favorite hymns in English. Their work was greeted by later generations and those not familiar with them as being inadequate for the use of contemporary Lutherans in this country. It is somewhat different with the new hymn tunes written in the latter half of the twentieth century. Although one can tell that most of them arise from the soil of Scandinavia, their sound is more contemporary and attractive, perhaps, to American singers. These new tunes should help to give the reader a sense for a very different kind of sound from Scandinavia than one is used to, especially in those tunes from the twentieth century.

In addition to providing translations for these very interesting works, I have also attempted to provide biographical materials that will give my readers a glimpse into the life, piety, and times of each author. Since these come from small countries where the need to preserve and protect such treasures is part of the history and tradition of the culture, they are, understandably, the object of much attention and intimate acquaintance. Over such, there can be much scholarly controversy that is sometimes rigorous and helpful, but often arcane to people outside the culture. I have not thought it necessary to consider much of that conversation, since such debates, while very learned and vigorous, would not be edifying to readers who are most interested in getting some sense for the lives and works of women in another culture and tradition. Rather, I have attempted to give a context for the writing of each woman's hymns, her life's work and interest. There is not very much available on most of these writers since they have suffered the fate of many women whose work was easily set aside by the next generation of male hymnal compilers. In some cases, I have relied heavily on resources that are only available in the original lan-

Preface

guages, especially in the chapters on Lina Sandell and Britt G. Hallqvist. For the life and work of Lisbeth Smedegaard Andersen, who is still an active writer and participant in the church of Denmark, I have had to gather up her works and life from her own writings, as well as our own personal contact as friends and colleagues. This working relationship has been a richness of considerable worth to me, personally, both as a writer of my own hymns, and as a scholar of Scandinavian hymnody. She has taught me much about the craft of writing hymns that has been fruitful to me in my own efforts. All told, then, this is a modest attempt to convey to Americans something of the treasures in which I have immersed myself over the past forty years.

One does not do this kind of work alone. First of all, I am grateful to Luther Seminary for its generous support of my sabbaticals over the years, and especially this last one. Without the luxury of time that I could devote solely to this one topic, I would never have been able to write what I have. Craig van Gelder, my department chair, worked to assure that I would have adequate support on my travels, for which I am most grateful. Furthermore, without the help of individuals both at Luther Seminary and also in Scandinavia, I would never have been able to prepare the work. Thanks to Sally Sawyer and Karen Alexander of the Luther Seminary library who were always eager to find obscure articles and books on these topics from far-off places. Victoria Smith, Faculty Secretary of Luther Seminary, was very helpful and consoling as she found images and created maps that would be suitable for the chapters. In Norway, Laila Asklesen generously met with me to speak of her work with the poets Petter Dass and Dorothe Engelbretsdatter. Her insights into the rhetoric of the two poets was a revelation to me that I have not fully understood yet but which was very helpful to me, as were her two books on the subject. Vigdis Østensø gave me invaluable advice on this chapter as well. Thanks also to Bishop Andreas Aarflot who read my chapter on his great-grandmother, Berthe Canutte Aarflot. Stig Wernø Holter, of the Grieg Academy in Bergen, proved to be a valuable consultant for me on the difficult and obscure Norwegian of his fellow Bergenser, Dorothe Engelbretsdatter, as well as on Norwegian American hymnody. Thanks to him for his warm and good-humored help.

I am also grateful for the help of the Danish bishop of Roskilde, Jan Lindhardt, for his help with my translation of Birgitte Boye's churching hymn. Marianne Tiblin from the University of Minnesota Special Collections advised me on resources and several translation issues, as well as helped me read the old-fashioned script of Birgitte Boye. That was invaluable and helpful.

Then, to the staff and professors and administration at Løgumkloster in Denmark, where I spent six weeks in October and November 2004, especially the librarian Helle Kjeldsen, I owe my gratitude for their typically Danish gracious hospitality in their lovely little town on the heaths of western Denmark. Spending time in the region of one of my favorite hymn writers, Hans Adolf Brorson, walking the meadows, woods, heaths, and beaches of western Denmark, was restful and refreshing for me, a time never to be forgotten. It was through the recommendation of my good friend Lisbeth Smedegaard Andersen that I was able to find a place there, and for that I am grateful.

Finally, thanks to my colleagues and family for hearing me out on some theological and historical issues that I needed help with, given the wide stretch of the periods represented here. Most of all, thanks to Paul Rorem, the *Lutheran Quarterly* editor, who took my proposal and helped shape it into the book you have before you. His editorial advice and sharp blue pencil helped immensely. Thanks also to the patient and careful eye of Eerdmans' Managing Editor Linda Bieze, to whom I introduced the mysteries of Scandinavian orthography along with some of its hymn treasury. Thanks also to Mark Granquist, who did me the favor of reading the entire book through and provided excellent comments and suggestions. John R. Christiansen, Senior Research Scholar at Luther College, an old friend and colleague, helped me a great deal with the Boye chapter. Mary Jane Haemig helped me clarify the Cruciger material, for which I am most grateful. My long-time friend and mentor Professor Mary Hull Hohr of Luther College, a scholar in her own right, read and helped me especially with the chapter on my work. Then, too, my young niece and nephews suffered with good humor as they traveled with their crazy aunt to remote villages all over Scandinavia in search of hymnological trivia on "my guys" as they called them. My friends and my family were also a support as they helped with my travels and work, as I studied and wrote. Thank you to them and to the memory of our mother and especially our father, who would have been able to speak knowledgeably about many of the questions I had. I missed him a great deal, but felt his spirit with me as I worked on these hymns, many of which he knew and loved. The others he would have come to love had he had the chance.

Introduction

According to legend, Elisabeth von Meseritz Cruciger, wife of Martin Luther's student Caspar Cruciger, and writer of the hymn "The Only Son from Heaven" ("Herr Christ der eynig gots son") dreamed that she was standing in the pulpit of the city church of Wittenberg preaching. When she told her husband about the dream, he assured her that when they sang her hymn in church, she was, in fact, preaching.[1] The story, which cannot be traced back before 1693, has lived in Lutheran hymnological circles for years. He is also said to have commented that perhaps God wanted to honor her by having the songs that she sang at home also sung in church.[2] Implicitly he (and the legend) recognized that hymns preach. While we remain uncertain whether the story is true, we do know now that Elisabeth Cruciger was indeed the author of "The Only Son from Heaven." In the seventeenth and eighteenth centuries a number of sources cast doubt on Cruciger's authorship and instead credited the hymn to Andreas Knoepken (1493-1539). Sixteenth-century authors credited her with the hymn, a judgment affirmed by nineteenth-century historical scholarship. Mary Jane Haemig has argued that sixteenth-century people had little trouble

---

1. Allen Arvastson, "Elisabeth Cruciger, 'den evangeliska kristenhetens första psalmförfatterina,'" *Svensk Teologisk Kvartalskrift* 62 (1986): 111.

2. Simon Pauli, *Auslegung der Deutschen Geistlich Lieder*, 1588, as quoted in Mary Jane Haemig's "Elisabeth Cruciger (1500?-1535): The Case of the Disappearing Hymn Writer," *Sixteenth Century Journal* 32, no. 1 (2001): 41-42.

crediting her with the hymn because of the apocalyptic thinking of that century. Haemig cites early Lutheran theologians (Simon Pauli and Gregory Strigenitz), who discussed Elisabeth Cruciger's hymn writing activity as proof that Joel 2 had been fulfilled.

> Your sons and your daughters shall prophesy, your old men shall dream dreams, and your young men shall see visions. Even upon the male and female slaves, in those days, I will pour out my spirit. (Joel 2:28-29)

Pauli saw Cruciger as one who is "moved and enlightened" by the Holy Spirit, proving that the Holy Spirit can speak through women as well as men. For Strigenitz, Cruciger was like New Testament women who were inspired by the Holy Spirit. Strigenitz also commented that in his time one could also "find among women and girls many who through the grace of the Holy Spirit, understand scripture better and can speak from it more wonderfully than a doctor under the papacy."[3] We do not know whether Luther saw her hymn writing as fulfilling apocalyptic expectations. We do know that he approved of her hymn because he used it in his first hymnals, the *Erfurt Enchiridion* and Johannes Walther's *Gesangbuch* published in 1524.

Whether or not the legend is true matters little for my purposes. What is clear in the anecdote is the commonplace Lutheran understanding that a hymn is a sermon, or proclamation of the gospel, and anyone who writes a hymn is a preacher. This is what Luther seems to have thought as he cast about for hymns that were suitable for evangelical worship. By the time of the writing of the Augsburg Confession in 1530, this understanding had been clearly stated. The Augsburg Confession of 1530 noted that "German hymns" were "added for the instruction of the people." German was important so the people would understand this new thing since "ceremonies are especially needed in order to teach those who are ignorant."[4] In Melanchthon's *Apology to the Augsburg Confession*, written in 1531, with much help from Luther, the statement expands on the topic. Not surpris-

---

3. Haemig, pp. 36-37.

4. The Augsburg Confession 24 in *The Book of Concord: The Confessions of the Evangelical Lutheran Church*, edited by Robert Kolb and Timothy J. Wengert; trans. Charles Arand, Eric Gritsch, Robert Kolb, William Russell, James Schaaf, Jane Strohl, and Timothy J. Wengert (Minneapolis: Fortress Press, 2000), p. 69.

ingly, Melanchthon, a classical scholar steeped in ancient rhetoric, is more interested in the rhetoric of the hymn: "We also use German hymns in order that the [common] people might have something to learn, something that will arouse their faith and fear."[5] Although there is a strong emphasis on instruction in this note, there is the clear notion that German hymns should function like the preached word — *viva vox* — that arouses faith and fear.

That Luther thought of the hymn as a way to *teach* the new evangelical faith is commonplace among hymnologists and theologians. Nearly everyone knows that Luther wanted worship resources in the language of the people so that they could understand the faith he was teaching. In the "Order of Mass and Communion," 1523, he expressed the need for "as many songs as possible in the vernacular which the people could sing during mass."[6] He lamented, however, that "poets are wanting among us, or not yet known, who could compose evangelical and spiritual songs, as Paul calls them, worthy to be used in the church of God."[7] We read in Luther's letter to his friend, the court chaplain George Spalatin, that he thought the new evangelical hymn needed to be in the vernacular in order to communicate the Word of God to the people. "Following the example of the prophets and fathers of the church, I intend to make German Psalms for the people, i.e., spiritual songs so that the Word of God even by means of song may live among the people."[8]

These words of Luther have been understood by many who have looked closely at Luther's hymn texts to mean that his hymns only *taught* the pure evangelical doctrines of the Reformation. I do not think this fully comprehends what Luther meant to do when he wanted hymns to *be* the "Word of God."[9] What he meant is that the rhetorical function of the Lutheran hymn is to preach the Word of God, and thus *be* the Word of God, preached to the gathered assembly by those singing it to each other. Luther's hymns, like most classical Lutheran chorales, are, for the most part, sermons.

---

5. The Augsburg Confession 24 in *The Book of Concord*, p. 69.
6. Martin Luther, "An Order of Mass and Communion," *Luther's Works* [hereafter *LW*] 53 (Philadelphia: Fortress Press, 1958), p. 36.
7. Luther, "An Order of Mass and Communion."
8. Martin Luther, *The Hymns*, trans. George MacDonald, in *LW* 53, p. 221.
9. Luther, *The Hymns* in *LW* 53, p. 221.

It is difficult to find Luther reflecting much on his work as a hymn writer, but the hymns themselves are evidence enough for us to infer what he intended them to be. Like all of the Reformers, Luther's theology of preaching, over against the medieval custom, elevated the proclaimed word above the sacraments. The preacher's voice was the voice of God. Thus, for Luther, there was no higher office than that of preacher.

> Whoever has received the call to . . . preach has the highest office in Christendom imposed on him. Afterward he may also baptize, celebrate mass, and exercise pastoral care. If he does not wish to do so he may confine himself to preaching and leave baptizing and lower offices to others as Christ and the apostles also did.[10]

Since every passage in the Bible pointed to Christ, the preacher was to preach whatever in the text "drove Christ." Luther believed the preacher's call was to be like John the Baptist — to make his hearers into sinners, and then point to the Christ as the one who takes away the sins of the world. This was a heavy responsibility where one needed help from God. Luther advised preachers to preach and "pray to God and leave all the rest to him."[11] The preached Word of God was fundamental to Luther's reform.

Fred Meuser in his book *Luther the Preacher* noted that most of Luther's discourse, from "treatises, doctrinal writings, commentaries on Galatians, lectures on Genesis and John, expositions of Psalms, devotional and pastoral writings, correspondence and sermons," had the quality of a sermon.[12] Meuser's fairly exhaustive list of what one might consider homiletical works, surprisingly, does not include Luther's hymns. They, of all of Luther's writings, are most clearly sermons. Thus, for Luther and his early followers, the hymn should contain the classical Lutheran hermeneutic of Scripture: Law and Gospel. "A Mighty Fortress Is Our God" is not a paraphrase of Psalm 46, but a sermon on the psalm, with its images updated from ancient Palestine to medieval Saxony, and its direct address to

---

10. Martin Luther, "That a Christian Assembly or Congregation Has the Right and Power to Judge All Teaching and to Call, Appoint, and Dismiss Teachers, Established and Proven by Scripture" in *LW* 39, p. 314.

11. Martin Luther, *Table Talk*, 2606-2607, cited in Roland H. Bainton, *Here I Stand: A Life of Martin Luther* (New York: Abingdon-Cokesbury Press, 1950), p. 350.

12. Fred Meuser, *Luther the Preacher* (Minneapolis: Augsburg Publishing House, 1983), p. 39.

the congregation concerning their enemy and God's intervention to defend them against the ravages of Satan. People singing it learned it easily because of its poetic form and tune. By using meter, rhyme, and a good tune, Luther assured that the people would learn the faith and be able to use it to preach to one another. Most of Luther's hymns address the fellow member of the congregation with the good news, after which he admonishes the congregation to "thank, praise, serve, and obey him."[13]

If it is true that Luther used his hymns to preach the Gospel, several clichés about Luther's hymns fall by the wayside. Richard Massie, one of Luther's better translators, noted in his preface to his book *Martin Luther's Spiritual Songs*, that there was "no originality of thought, no splendid imagery, no play of fancy to attract the reader, whose taste has been formed on the productions of the nineteenth century."[14] While there is a hint of condescension in Massie's comments, Luther's own words indicate that he is not interested in the "play of fancy" in his hymns. His art had an evangelical rhetorical purpose: to preach the Word of God. We can read in his correspondence with his colleague George Spalatin that Luther wanted hymns simple enough so the people could understand them, be moved by them, and be brought to faith. In a letter to Spalatin asking him to help with the task of writing new German hymns, Luther wrote, "I would like you to avoid new-fangled, fancied words and to use expressions simple and common enough for the people to understand, yet pure and fitting."[15] In the same way that Calvin feared the innovations of hymn writers who were not using the Bible directly, Luther did not want his teaching to be anything but the pure evangelical faith as found in Scripture expressed without straying into topics that were not the Gospel.

Scholars who have examined Luther's hymns closely have tended to look at the forms or sources Luther used for his hymns much as the historical-critical scholar of the Bible examines its texts. They have looked at the sources and content of the hymn and what it means, not what it is trying to do rhetorically. Ulrik Leupold, editor of volume 53 of *Luther's Works*, did so in his work, looking to discover the sources of Luther's texts

---

13. A common phrase for Lutherans, taken from the last line of Luther's *Small Catechism* and his explanation of the First Article of the Creed.
14. Luther, *The Hymns* in *LW* 53, footnote 34.
15. Luther, *The Hymns* in *LW* 53, p. 221.

and tunes and his choice of Germanic poetic and musical forms.[16] While there is an impressive amount of learning in Leupold's work, he does not consider, explicitly, the rhetoric of Luther's hymns.[17] Finally, not many of these scholars appear to have noted Melanchthon's tantalizing statements in his *Apology of the Augsburg Confession* about the rhetorical purposes of ceremonies and the German hymns in the service: they were to cause people admonished by the Word "to experience fear, faith, and even to pray."[18]

That these ideas are explicitly understood by Luther and his followers can be shown in an examination of the hymn by this young woman, Elisabeth Cruciger, present at the creation so to speak. Her hymn is one of the first Lutheran hymns to be written. It appeared in two of the earliest Lutheran hymnals in 1524, the *Erfurt Enchiridion* and Johannes Walther's *Gesangbuch*. The time between the late fall of 1523, when Luther's *Formula Missæ* appeared, and the summer of 1524, was a period of intense concentration on hymnody by Luther and his friends. Leupold estimates that during this time, Luther and his friends wrote more than two-thirds of the twenty four hymns that appeared in these early hymnals.[19] They are said to have worked around a table in Luther's home, writing and singing and trying out their work. It would have been impossible for anyone near Luther to have missed this or his conversations about what an evangelical hymn should be.

About the time he was finished with this first collection, Caspar Cruciger (1504-1548), a friend and student of Luther and Melanchthon, married Elisabeth on June 14, 1524. Luther felt warmly toward the couple and performed the ceremony. (Caspar's daughter, also called Elisabeth, by his second wife, would later marry Luther's son Johannes.) Caspar served as rector and pastor in Magdeburg and then returned to Wittenberg in 1528 to become professor in Wittenberg, where he completed his doctorate in 1533. He often served as secretary to Luther and sat at the table in Luther's home many times, as did Elisabeth, apparently, for there is record of her

---

16. Leupold in his notes and prefaces to Luther's works in volume 53 of the *LW* series carries on a quiet battle with the regnant liturgical crowd of his time (and ours!), which I have always found refreshing.

17. Leupold does note, in his commentary on "Ein feste Burg," that Luther wrote his hymns to comfort his people but says no more.

18. Philipp Melanchthon, *Apology of the Augsburg Confession*, in *The Book of Concord*, p. 258.

19. Luther, *The Hymns* in *LW* 53, p. 193.

asking Luther a question about the mass. As a former nun she showed herself to be theologically acute in the hints we can read in this conversation. The Weimar edition of the *Table Talk* records a question she asked Luther concerning what a pious and Christian person should do if he or she came into a Catholic church and found the priest elevating the sacrament. Luther's answer, while not to the point, shows that he cared about her. "Dear Els, don't take the priest from the altar and do not put out the light."[20] This cryptic glimpse into her relationship with Luther shows his regard for her, and that she had rather important theological questions and understood one of the central issues in the liturgical reforms of Luther: the elevation. Whether or not she was at the table as Luther and Walther worked on their hymns is another question. The hymn that she wrote reveals a keen theological acuteness as well, even if the hymn, to some, begins like a German version of the Latin hymn by Aurelius Clemens Prudentius (348-413?), "Of the Father's Love Begotten" ("Corde natus ex parentis"). Luther himself used this method of invention in several of his most famous hymns such as "To God the Holy Spirit Let Us Pray" ("Nun bitten wir"), the first stanza of which was a popular medieval hymn that Luther loved and to which he added the next three stanzas.[21] A shrewd student such as Elisabeth could have figured out how to do this simply by listening to the reformer talking about his work, as well as reading and singing from his works with his guests at the table. Imitation is, after all, a fundamental way to learn how to preach or write. Luther himself might even have assigned the task to her, saying, "Dear Els, take Prudentius' hymn and do what I have done with these." While this is pure speculation, it would be hard to imagine that this gifted young woman would not have been influenced by Luther at this time.

We can certainly see his influence in the rhetoric of Elisabeth's hymn. It follows clear Lutheran homiletical practices, beginning with a theological and Scriptural assertion about the incarnation, much as we have it in the beginning of the Gospel of St. John, along with the images from Matthew's story of the wise men following the star.

---

20. In *Luthers Werke: Kritische Gesamtausgabe: Tischreden* [hereafter *WA TR*] 1 (Weimar: H. Böhlau, 1912-21), pp. 382, 803.

21. It is the preferred hymn in the Danish service of 1685, which remained in force until the late nineteenth century in Norway and Denmark.

1. Lord Christ, from God forever,
   The Father's only Son,
   From his heart, ceasing never,
   As prophets had written
   He is the Star of Morning,
   Whose beams afar are soaring
   Above all other lights.

This is from the traditional translation by Richard Massie. The rest of Massie's translation only vaguely hints at the theological themes of the hymn. The following is from Timothy Wengert's translation with some of my more literal renditions of the text:

2. For us, he was incarnate
   Now in these latter days
   So we were not abandoned
   Before eternity.
   For us death's power was broken,
   The courts of heaven opened
   That life may bloom again.

3. Let us imbibe your mercy,
   Of wisdom take our fill,
   And stay within faith's limits,
   To do the Spirit's will.
   For in our hearts so broken
   We long to taste your sweetness,
   Thirst only for your grace.

4. Creator of all creatures,
   With fath'rly pow'r and right
   You rule through all the ages,
   Alone in all your might,
   O, turn our hearts to serve you,
   Our senses toward your mercy
   So we will never stray.

5. O kill us with your goodness
   And raise us to your grace,

> Make ill our old sick natures
> And turn to us your face,
> So here we may adore you
> With all our being praise you,
> And sing our thanks to you.[22]

The second stanza takes off from the first statement of the theme and context, biblically, of the hymn. Here she preaches the Law: only Jesus can save us from the power of death and open up the heavens to us.

She continues exhorting her hearers — those who are singing and hearing the hymn — to pray with her to God, whom she now addresses.

> 4. Creator of all creatures,
>   With fath'rly pow'r and right
>   You rule through all the ages,
>   Alone in all your might.

Then she moves to describe the glories of the faith to the congregation — living in God's love and wisdom and faith in service to the neighbor. Now she instructs us in what will be the results of the relationship, not prescribing it, but describing it, so that we can taste the sweetness of the gospel in our hearts.

The last two stanzas continue the prayer, even as they teach about the Creator and his works:

> O, turn our hearts to serve you,
> Our senses toward your mercy
> So we will never stray.

The prayer that God will turn us to himself is standard-issue Lutheran prayer language, addressing and praising God for all his power. Asking that God use his power also for us is the classic rhythm of Luther's explanation of the Lord's Prayer: "God's kingdom comes indeed without our praying for it, but we ask in this prayer that it may come also to us." In addition, the hymn has, deep in its center, the sense that we can stray and will, without

---

22. This translation is a reworking based on the work of Timothy Wengert as quoted in Haemig, p. 24.

the power of God's work in us. Everything comes from God. This is stated most clearly in the last stanza with its surprising language (to this generation) asking God to kill us with grace — the *coup de grace.* Scripturally there is warrant for such language. In Deuteronomy 32:39, Yahweh describes himself as a God who both "kills and makes alive" which less robust translators have changed to "put to death." A safer translation might be "slay." Elisabeth had obviously heard the theologians speaking of the radical nature of grace, and the necessity to kill the old Adam so Christ can be raised up in us, or in another paradox "Make ill our old sick natures." This stanza is the most Lutheran of the entire hymn and uses a trope directly from Luther: Christ is the death of death, sin to sin, and Satan to Satan. Although it is a prayer, it teaches those who are singing it, or listening to it, the essence of the evangelical faith: the killing nature of grace, the believer as saint and sinner, the absolute dependence of the person on the grace of God, and the daily life of faith, which her hymn preaches.

> O kill us with your goodness
> And wake us to your grace,
> Make ill our old sick natures
> And turn to us your face,
> So here we may adore you
> With all our being praise you,
> And sing our thanks to you.

In her work, Cruciger shows a precocious theological sensibility for the new faith, as well as a shrewd sense for how the Lutheran hymn was to cause "faith and fear" before there were many other evangelical models of hymns for her to use.

About the time that Elisabeth and her husband were getting ready to establish a new Lutheran parsonage, Luther was beginning to realize that he needed to prepare not only German hymn resources, but a version of the liturgy for the "uneducated laity" that came to be called the German Mass. Elisabeth, as a former nun, must have felt the need for devotional resources in German that would help families with their devotions. Most of the new evangelical pastors and their wives came out of monastic traditions which practiced the seven hours of Lauds, Matins, Tierce, Sexts, Nones, Vespers, and Compline, so they were accustomed to a regular cycle of prayer during the day, which worked for monastic communities where there were no children. Families could not adapt to such a rigorous schedule of prayer, but they could blend prayer into their daily activities. As priests and nuns began to marry and have families, among them Luther himself, they very soon began to realize that materials needed to be provided for the daily services at home as much as for the Sunday service. Although Luther had been preaching catechetical sermons from the pulpit at St. Mary's in Wittenberg since 1518, he did not prepare a catechism for another ten years, although it was clearly on his mind. In 1526, he noted the need for a good, serviceable catechism in his preface to the German mass: "First the German service needs a plain and simple, fair and square catechism." He then described how the catechism should work: instructing heathens in how to become Christians, especially by teaching them the Ten Commandments, the Creed, and the Lord's Prayer. "This instruction," he continues, "must be given, as long as there is no special congregation, from the pulpit at stated times or daily as may be needed, and repeated or read aloud evenings and mornings in the homes for the children and servants, in order to train them as Christians."[23] He then went on to provide a short model for the questions and answers he thought necessary for catechization of the young.

It was not, however, until 1528, that he prepared the *Small Catechism*, not long after he realized how urgent was the need. When he finally published the *Small Catechism* in January 1529, which many consider to be the classic text summing up the Western church's teaching begun with Charlemagne's requirement that all the empire had to know the Lord's Prayer, it contained several suggestions for family devotions, including prayers for morning, noon, and evening. To conclude the devotions, he added, "After singing a hymn perhaps (for example, one on the Ten Commandments) or whatever else may serve your devotion, you are to go to your work joyfully." Each part of the catechism began with the note "In a simple way in which the head of a house is to present them to the household." While "head of the household" implies father, mothers, older siblings, aunts and uncles were also empowered by this statement to take charge of the teaching of the faith in the home if and when the father was absent.[24]

From these instructions an entire tradition of family devotions developed that would flourish among Lutherans for many generations. Pas-

---

23. Martin Luther, "The German Mass" in *LW* 53, pp. 64-65.
24. Wengert et al., trans., "The Small Catechism," in *Book of Concord*, p. 351.

tors' wives like Elisabeth Cruciger and Katie Luther and others who followed after them, were quick to take up the charge to teach the faith in the home. While the form for daily devotions may have been obvious — Scripture, catechism, and a hymn, with prayers — it is of interest that Elisabeth and those pastors' wives and daughters who followed after her felt that it was possible to preach the gospel, not simply by teaching it to the children, but by providing hymns that could be used at home, but more surprisingly, in church at the public service. Hymns, such as this one by Elisabeth Cruciger, preached the gospel as the apocryphal legend made quite clear. In that way, although they did not hold a public office of a pastor, Lutheran women preached until they were actually able to take up the office in the twentieth century.

While the number of Lutheran hymn writers who are women does not approach the number of men who wrote hymns for public worship, there is a significant number. Many of them were either pastors' daughters or wives, and now, when women can receive the call to preach, pastors themselves. It is clearly the parsonage that has been the source of most Lutheran hymns. It is a significant historical fact and worth examining with some attention to the lives and work of at least a small number of them because they show us how a tradition developed and flowered as the place of women changed with the time and culture. The freedom women had from the first to write hymns for public edification set them on the road toward writing of all kinds. It is no secret that in Protestant lands some of the first published women writers grew up in the parsonage — Camilla Collett, for example, the first woman novelist in Norway grew up in a parsonage, as did Harriet Beecher Stowe in America.

While there are numerous women hymn writers in the Lutheran tradition, I have chosen to limit what follows to the work of six from the Scandinavian traditions. All of them are pastors' daughters, wives, mothers, or, in the case of Lisbeth Smedegaard Anderson, a pastor in her own right. Their work spans the past four centuries and gives a good picture of the various pieties important in the development of the Lutheran tradition, as well as revealing some interesting things about the parsonage life of each period. While I will focus mostly on the work of women authors, they did not appear in a vacuum: they had pastor fathers, brothers, husbands, friends, and others who influenced them. The first hymn writer I will consider will be Norway's most famous woman hymn writer of the seventeenth century, Dorothe Engelbretsdatter; the second, Birgitte Boye from the Danish Enlightenment; the third, Berthe Canutte Sivertsdatter Aarflot of the Haugean movement in Norway; Lina Sandell, daughter of a Pietist Lutheran Swedish pastor from Småland; then Britt G. Hallqvist of modern Sweden; and finally, Lisbeth Smedegaard Andersen, one of Denmark's most accomplished hymn writers in the post-modern period.

CHAPTER 1

Dorothe Engelbretsdatter (1634-1716)
Bergen's Deborah

Ludvig Holberg (1684-1754), one of the great figures of the European Enlightenment, and the first great dramatist of the Twin Kingdoms of Denmark and Norway, remembered that when he was a young boy in Bergen he would see Dorothe Engelbretsdatter, the well-known poet and hymn writer, walking around the town in old-fashioned Bergen clothes. For him it was a matter of pride that his home town had produced a woman poet thought to be unique in her ability to write such spirited poetry. No other Danish or Norwegian city could make the same boast.[1] While he agreed her work was exceptional, it did not ultimately appeal to him. Holberg was a man of the Enlightenment. By the time he wrote about her, her poetry, like her dress, was already old-fashioned, wedded to a penitential piety to which he was not attracted. He did, however, know she was significant and mentioned her with high praise in his writings about Bergen.

Who was this strange old lady in the old-fashioned clothes who called herself "Bergen's Deborah," and what kind of a legacy did she leave? It is surprising to discover how highly regarded and famous she was in her own time, and how she broke through many barriers to take her place in the early pantheon of Dano-Norwegian hymn writers such as Thomas Hansen Kingo (1634-1703).

---

1. Ludvig Holberg, *Den Berømmelige Norske Handel-Stad: Bergens Beskrivelse* (Copenhagen, 1737; reprinted ed. Bergen: Joh. Nordahl-Olsen, 1920), p. 70.

Figure 1 Posthumous copperplate print of Dorothe Engelbretsdatter, 1780, from her book *An Offering of Tears*.

Dorothe's Early Life

Norway's first published woman poet, Dorothe Engelbretsdatter, was born in Bergen, Norway, on January 16, 1634, to Anna Wrangel and Engelbret Jørgensen (1592-1659), rector in the Bergen school, and later head pastor (*sogneprest*) at the cathedral in Bergen. He was reputed to be a "pious, quiet, God-fearing man."[2] A typical member of the clergy class of the day, he was the son of a pastor, Jørgen Hanssøn, and his wife Anna Engelbretsdatter. Dorothe, probably named for her father's first wife, Dorotea Due, grew up in Bergen, a lively trading port in the Hanseatic League, where merchants from Europe came to buy the dry salt cod from Lofoten, coveted by Catholic Europe for the Friday fast. Given the lifestyle of traveling men streaming in and out of its harbor, Bergen became known as Norway's Sodom and Gomorrah.

In addition to its reputation as a wild port city, Bergen also had a lively spiritual tradition, with its cathedral, bishop's palace, and school, central for many in the small city and the region around it. Well-known clergy and theological professors worked together in the town to carry out their duties of passing on the Lutheran faith. This was the social circle where Dorothe spent her youth imbibing Lutheran theology, culture, and piety. In addition to her learning, her poetry reveals her attachment to Bergen, its people, its location in the harbor between mountains, and its history of devastating fires. When she was only four years old, in 1638, almost the entire city burned down, taking with it several hundred homes, the Cathedral, Cross Church (Korskirken), the city hall, and the Latin school, buildings she knew well even as a young child. During her lifetime she witnessed three other great fires, one in 1660, another in 1675, and finally in 1702, when she lost her own home to fire, which she summed up in a poem ("Medlidig Trøst til Jndvaaneren i Bergen") typical of the many religious poems on the same topic:

> O Bergen, where I was born, you have been tried
> In fires which my pained eyes saw
>   Happen four times.[3]

---

2. Michael Hofnagle, quoted in J. N. Skaar, *Norsk Salmenhistorie*, II, 1880, p. 581.

3. Dorothe Englebretsdatter, "Medlidig Trøst til Jndvaaneren i Bergen over den Jammerlige Jldebrand som Aar 1686, d. 27 Sept. Lagde en stor deel af Byen i Aske," *Dorothe Engelbretsdatter Samlede Skrifter*, ed. Kristen Valkner (Oslo: Aschehoug, 1999), p. 276.

The young girl also experienced the close and special relationship Bergensers had with Copenhagen, the capital of the Twin Kingdoms of Denmark and Norway. Copenhagen was not too far away by sea, and those in the official classes, the clergy and other government officials, moved easily between the two cities. We know that Dorothe's family lived in Copenhagen on several occasions. She may have been in Copenhagen when she was a young child, around 1640.[4] We know for certain that when Dorothe was a teenager, she and her parents moved to Copenhagen for about three years, from 1647 to 1650, an exciting time in the life of Denmark, marking as it did the end of the Thirty Years' War with the Treaty of Westphalia in 1648; the death of Denmark's greatest king, Christian IV in 1648; and the accession of King Frederick III to the throne that same year. Dorothe must have followed these events closely.

Her stay in Copenhagen, however, did not change her very strong identification with Bergen and Norway. She was Norwegian, she made clear in a poem to a supposed lover.

> I am Norwegian born, of clergy folk,
> My father's name was Engelbrect,
> He lived in Bergen's city,
> And there he had a pastor's calling,
> Where I was made and born
> When the times were good.[5]

In addition to the Norwegian culture around her, she also soaked up the German influences in the Hanseatic city. One of Bergen's oldest churches, Maria Church (Mariakirken), became known as the German church that the merchants from Lübeck and Rostock attended. They came to Bergen with crews of masters and journeymen to manage the prosperous fishing trade occasioned by the rich cod runs in the North Sea. The German dominance created some resentment among native Norwegian Bergensers; at the same time, in what was really a small town of about eight thousand, the cultures mixed freely.[6]

---

4. See Valkner, p. 549.

5. Engelbretsdatter, "Till een der drømte vi hafde Lagt Kierlighed sammen Gamle dage, uden tvill 1520 d. 31 April," in Valkner, p. 424.

6. A tour through the Hanseatic buildings on Bergen's wharf, one of the world's

We do not know when she began writing her poetry, but her birth into the Lutheran parsonage culture of the Dano-Norwegian kingdom makes it likely she began as a teenager. Dorothe fits the model of a precocious pastor's daughter writing in her time. In a chapter on the history of women in Scandinavia, Marianne Alenius describes the educational profile of a young woman like Dorothe. First, she would have probably learned to read from her father, in Dorothe's case, a teacher and later pastor at the Bergen cathedral. Second, Alenius notes, biographies of these women would remark on a precocious ability to write, as the girl often began writing her own poetry about the time of puberty. These poems would be dedicated to a high official, such as the king. Although we do not have such a record for the young Dorothe, we can assume, like most people who make a name for themselves as writers, she began writing while a teenager. Third, she would be known for her singing voice and other musical accomplishments. In one of her poems, "Till Mag: Laurs Thura . . .", she indicated that she understood singing, "Now the tongue has sung *ut re mi fa sol*."[7] In another poem she described her musical evenings with Ambrosius Hardenbeck, her husband, who played the lute, showing that she played the keyboard.

> When Hardenbeck's lute gave many Joyful sounds,
> And my own fingers sprang over the keyboard *(clavicordiummet).*[8]

Fourth, she would be a fine seamstress and painter, accomplished in hand work, and the other fine domestic arts. She might know a little Latin and, less likely, some Greek. There is no evidence that Dorothe knew Greek, but she uses Latin phrases frequently in her poems; phrases that were in the air of the church life in which she was raised — Latin phrases such as *Claratum probatum quis negat* — appear frequently in her poetry.[9] Since there were no schools for girls her age, the library of her father, and husband, would have been crucial to her education. Without such a resource, it would have been difficult for her to acquire learning. Dorothe was fortunate enough to be in a family where she could learn

---

treasures, gives one a good sense for the high-handedness of the German merchants and their treatment of the fishermen coming from the North with their bounty.

7. Engelbretsdatter, "Till Mag: Laurs Thura, Rector i Kiøge," in Valkner, p. 430.
8. Engelbretsdatter, "At jeg for ingen Deel . . . ," in Valkner, p. 417.
9. Engelbretsdatter, "Till Præsid: Dyseldorph," in Valkner, p. 467.

Figure 2 Ambrosius Hardenbeck, a pastor, was Dorothe Englebretsdatter's husband.

easily. Lutheran pastors' daughters were expected, at least, to be able to read. As a member of the Lutheran parsonage tradition, especially as it developed in the Dano-Norwegian kingdoms, she benefited, as did other young women who became quite learned because of their father's teaching, from Luther's suggestion that girls be taught to read so they could study the Bible, and other edifying works such as Luther's Small Catechism, in order to teach their own children the faith.[10] In addition, young women preparing to marry clergymen had to learn how to manage a household economy, no small task in the great homes or parsonages of the time. Her vocation as a pastor's wife involved knowing how to run the parsonage, which in those days in Europe was usually a farm, or at least large acreage. This meant she had to master horticulture: how to grow

10. See note 5.

crops, fruits and vegetables in particular, preserve them, know the medicinal values of the herbs and the nutritional value of various foods; the husbandry of animals: how to breed and raise them, get milk, yarn, and hides from them, how to kill, butcher, preserve, and store the meat — not so she could do these tasks, but manage her servants as they did them. Furthermore, she had to do this on a schedule appropriate to the seasons and the local conditions of the farm. Dorothe probably learned much about these skills at the bishop's parsonage in the area of Bergen in which she grew up, with its full garden and farm. Her mother, Anna Wrangel, a woman of substance, gave Dorothe and Ambrosius some land beside the bishop's meadow near the cathedral. It is probably where she and Ambrosius lived or at least gardened. From her middle years until her death, she lived near Bishop Randulf's garden, one of the finest in Bergen with fig trees, grape vines, chestnut trees, coriander, bay leaves, and many rare plants not usually found in the north, imported from Holland and other places in the south.[11]

In addition, when she married, she had to see to the education of her children, either teaching them herself or finding someone to do so. She was also to care for the sick and dying in her family and in the neighborhood, using the women's lore she had accumulated from her aunts and mother, the knowledge she had of herbs from medicinal books, and her own observation for the curing of diseases or lingering conditions.[12] These skills, from learning how to teach the faith, to keeping the parsonage running smoothly, had been modeled by Katie Luther over a century before as she established the Lutheran parsonage tradition that lasted until the mid-twentieth century. Dorothe grew up in this tradition and understood it in her bones. Learning to manage these domestic duties had the effect of putting Dorothe in touch with the servants of the house, especially women, from whom Dorothe gained, by her own confession, an acquaintance with the folk culture of Norway and the oral culture of women, in contrast to the written culture of her father. She clearly understood that she was part of the women's culture of the time as she noted in one of her epistles to the poet

---

11. Kristian Bjerknes, "Dorothea Engelbretsdatter og huset in Kong Oscarsgt," *Gamle Bergen, Årbok 1963* (Bergen: John Griegs Boktrykkeri, 1963), p. 18.

12. Marianne Alenius, "Kvinder er ikke mennesker: Den europæiske debat om de lærde kvinder i 1500–og 1600 tallet," *I Guds navn: Nordist kvindelitteraturhistorie*, vol. 1, ed. Elisabeth Møller Jensen (Copenhagen: Rosinante/Munksgaard, 1993), p. 211.

Jens Sthen Sehested: "I keep house near the mountains among the geese and Norwegian servant girls."[13]

On October 24, 1652, when she was eighteen, like many in her class, Dorothe married a pastor, a young man with whom she had grown up in Bergen, Ambrosius Hardenbeck (1621-1683), her father's vicar. Ambrosius was the son of Maria Church organist Lucas Hardenbeck, originally from Lübeck. Like many of his contemporaries who felt called to become pastors, Ambrosius attended school in Bergen and then the University of Rostock, which was preferred by theological students from Scandinavia and the Baltics because Northern European Lutheran parents considered it to be a safe place for their sons to study.[14] When Ambrosius attended Rostock, in 1637, the university was undergoing reforms pressed by the increasing strength of spiritual movements sweeping Europe that would ultimately become the Pietist movement. However, after only a short time in Rostock, when he was twenty-four, because of an outbreak of the plague, Ambrosius moved to Copenhagen to study for his master's degree *(magister)*, which he received in 1645. In 1642, he took a position as a teacher for a Danish family, after which he was appointed teacher at the Sorø Academy in northwestern Zealand. However, that same year he returned to Bergen, "out of love for his fatherland,"[15] to be co-rector at the Bergen Latin school. He was ordained in 1650. His career took him from teacher to pastor *(kapellan)* in the Cathedral, to head pastor *(sogneprest)* of the Cathedral in 1659. In 1671 he became Dean in Norhordland, the region between Bergen and the Sognefjord. By all accounts he was a God-fearing and learned man who was considered to be an especially fine preacher and conscientious pastor.[16]

Like many in the Dano-Norwegian upper-class, especially in Bergen, with its many international connections, Dorothe had German, Danish, and Dutch blood; she felt connected to the continent through personal attachments as well as education. She could read German, a little French and

---

13. Engelbretsdatter, "Er Spurren end Vndshcyldt at holde Dantz med Tranen?" in Valkner, pp. 422-23.

14. Janis Kreslins, "A Safe Haven in a Turbulent World: The University of Rostock and Lutheran Northern Europe," *Reformation and Latin Literature in Northern Europe*, ed. Inger Ekrem, Minna Skafte Jensen, and Egil Kraggerud (Oslo: Scandinavian University Press, 1996), p. 32.

15. Bjerknes, p. 18.

16. Skaar, p. 583.

Latin, and probably some English, which we can infer from her poetry with its frequent catch phrases from these languages, especially when she wanted to show her command of the language and establish her credibility as a learned woman. Being able to read these dominant European languages meant that she could readily access the documents of the current spiritual movements flourishing in Germany, Holland, and England.

Dorothe was born during the brutal wars over religious dogma. Although Norway escaped the killing fields of Germany, she and her family knew men involved in the fighting and certainly understood the theological debates at stake. She did, however, probably experience the shelling of the Bergen cathedral by a British flotilla chasing a fleet of the Dutch East India Company in 1665, which left a cannon ball that can still be seen in the Cathedral wall. Her command of German helped her follow the explosion of orthodox hymnody pouring out of Germany during this time. Dorothe, as a budding young hymn writer herself, soaked up the work of German poets and hymn writers of the day, digesting the work of Martin Opitz (1597-1639) whose *Book on German Poetry (Buch von der deutschen Poeterey)*, printed in 1624, had introduced to German baroque writers lore about various metrical and poetic forms, especially the Alexandrine couplet from classical Greek poetry. Although Opitz wrote many hymns and poems, he is best remembered for his metrical and poetic handbook used by some of the greatest German Lutheran hymn writers of all time: Paul Gerhardt (1607-1670), Johann Heerman (1585-1647), and Johann Rist (1607-1667), pastor in Hamburg. Dorothe learned from them how to write her own hymns. Anders Malling, in his seven-volume handbook on Danish hymnody, suggests that Dorothe was more influenced by German poetry and prosody than by Danish poetry, in its infancy at this time. Denmark's poetic theory was only coming into being through her contemporary and friend Thomas Kingo (1634-1703) and his mentor, Søren Paulsen Gotlænder, who thought much about it.[17] Although she knew Kingo well enough to have become his friend during her residency in

---

17. Anders Malling, *Dansk Salme Historie VI, Digterne, A-K* (Copenhagen: J. H. Schultz Forlag, 1971), p. 164. Kingo's mentor Søren Poulsen Gotlænder, *Synopsis prosodiæ Danicæ eller kort Extrakt af Rimekunsten*, 1651, and *Prosodia Danica eller dansk Rimekunst*, 1671, and Hans Mikkelsen Ravn, *Rythmologia Danica*, 1649, were developing a particularly Danish prosody at the time, and Dorothe could have learned those forms as well, but it does not seem that she did.

Copenhagen from 1684 to 1685, she seems not to have learned much from him about the Danish poetic meters and forms he or his contemporary secular Danish poet Anders Bording (1619-1677) used. We can read proof of Malling's contention in an exchange of epistles she had with Iver von Ahnen (ca. 1659-1722), who notes that one could find in Dorothe's laurels the names of "Catz, Opitz, Flemming, and Bul," two Dutch and two German writers, clear evidence that her poetic influences were not particularly Danish.[18]

By the time Dorothe began to write her hymns and poems in the 1670s, the accents in the orthodox piety and theology of the Lutheran church were shifting. In 1675 Philip Jacob Spener (1635-1705) published his epochal work, *Pious Desires (Pia desideria)*, an introduction to an edition of Johan Arndt's *True Christianity*, the founding document of the Pietist movement. This work changed the direction of much of Lutheran thought for the next generations. As she began writing her own devotional poems and hymns, Dorothe was well aware of the spiritual movements popular in sixteenth- and seventeenth-century Europe, but she does not seem to have been influenced much by the Pietists. She made extensive use of Johann Arndt (1555-1621), the English writer Lewis Bayly (d. 1631) — about which more later — and some of the more popular devotional resources from Germany, especially Rostock's professor Heinrich Müller's *Tears and Spring of Comfort (Thränen- und Trostquelle)* (1675), and Peder Møller's Danish translation of it, *Taare og Trøstekilde* (1677), along with *Scholæ Crucis* (1627) by the pastor and hymn writer in Hamburg, Valentin Wudrian (1584-1624). Ambrosius, her husband, would have also been a fund of information and conversation as she read and discussed these works of devotional literature with him as she began writing her hymns.

We can glean details about Dorothe's life from her poems, especially the epistles *(rimbrev* — poetic epistles) she wrote to her contemporaries, which give us glimpses into her life, particularly her later life. We know that she bore her husband nine children in less than fifteen years — five sons and four daughters, seven of whom had died young — by the time

---

18. See Engelbretsdatter, "Von Ahnens Replique til D," in Valkner, p. 566, where Dorothe is considered to be the equal of these Dutch and German poets and hymn writers: Jacob Cats (1577-1660), a well-regarded Dutch poet; Nicolaas Boele; and Paul Flemming (1608-1640), a Saxon hymn writer of great note, considered next to Opitz as a poet and hymn writer.

she published her first book in 1678, *The Soul's Offering of Song (Siælens Sang-Offer)*. At forty-four, after twenty-six years of marriage, her book made her an instant celebrity of Dano-Norwegian letters. As Malling notes, she was "praised to the skies by both ecclesiastics and poets for her work and she won, to a high degree, the love of the common Norwegian people. Which she still has."[19] She became known as the Tenth Muse of Dano-Norwegian poetry. "The Tenth Muse," a common sobriquet for women poets ever since Plato called Sappho the Tenth Muse in the *Anthologia Palatnia*, was also used of Mistress Anne Bradstreet (1612-1672), America's first published woman poet, whom Dorothe may have known about.[20] In any event, the publication of Dorothe's book in 1678 made an impression on her society, and her contemporaries used the highest form of praise they knew in order to honor her. Many said at the time that she was the greatest poet in the north.[21]

Soon after this triumph, however, her sorrows multiplied. Ambrosius died on June 13, 1683, after taking ill in November of the previous year. This was a blow for which she grieved the rest of her life, and it gave her the topic for her next book, *Tear Offering* (1685). Her elegy for Ambrosius ("Sidste Ære-Mindis . . .") in the Alexandrine couplets recommended by Opitz, indicates, even beyond the conventions of poems of this kind, that she had been happily married.

> I am a widow, and my husband now is dead,
> Dead is half my life, dead my earthly gladness,
> Inside the grave, my husband with all my worldly joy is buried,
> Oh, my Ambrosius! My treasure, half my soul,
> Delightful Hardenbeck, my virtuous marriage partner.
> With me you lived these thirty years while your spirit moved,
> Peace loving, mild and kindly, like God's angel lived,
> Only pious deeds and good. With your eyes I saw

19. Malling, p. 164.

20. See Anne Bradstreet, *The Tenth Muse, Lately Sprung Up in America*, 1650. The awareness European and American divines had of each others' works is astonishing to us today. The Danish hymn writer and bishop, Hans Adolf Brorson, had a book in his library by Cotton Mather.

21. Laila Akslesen, *Norsk Barokk, Dorothe Engelbretsdatter og Petter Dass i retorisk tradisjon* (Oslo: Landslaget for Norskundervisning: Cappelen Akademisk Forlag A.S., 1997), pp. 139-40.

You thought the dust too hard for me to walk.
My heart is your grave, where you will never rot away.[22]

Part of a much longer poem, these lines give a picture of her love for Ambrosius and his spiritual character. In that same poem she speaks of the difficulty of drinking from "A bitter widow's cup" and concludes the poem with a tribute to her husband, praying that Jesus, her heavenly Bridegroom, will hurry her to heaven where she can meet both her husband, her children, and her father, concluding with thanks "for every minute" of their life together.[23] In a later poem to King Christian V, she wrote again of her fate as a "pastor's widow" appealing to him to help her or else put her in a cloister where she could pray "her Lutheran *Pater noster*" and forget all men whom she repeatedly calls "trouser-folks."[24] Her one complaint against Ambrosius was that he had left her "free of riches."[25]

After the death of her husband, she still had some hope of her two surviving sons. In a note to Mester Iens Pedersen, who probably knew her older son, Lucas, she noted that he "had not written."[26] Later, she heard that Lucas had died in a battle in the protracted Venetian Turkish Wars, some time in 1685, fighting as a second lieutenant in the regiment of Baron Ulrik Frederick Waldermar Løvendal's (1660-1740) cavalry. About the same time, to her great distress, her only surviving son, Engelbret, who had left Bergen in June of 1681 to study in Germany, seemed to have disappeared without a trace at the age of twenty-six. Dorothe referred to him as her "angel," as he was named "Engel." She wrote in an epistle to Madam Povlsøn, "Honorable Greetings in God's Name," that she had prayed God would look after her sons, comparing herself to Monica, St. Augustine's mother, and her prayers for her son.[27] In another poem she spoke of Engel "her angel" as a youth who left for foreign lands in order to learn. "God

---

22. Engelbretsdatter, "Sidste Ære-Mindis smertelig Dict/Over min allerkiæriste salig Hoßbond/Den Guds Mand/Ambrosius Hardenbeck/Skreved med en angstbevrende Haand af Dorothe Engelbretz-Datter," in Valkner, p. 404.

23. Engelbretsdatter, "Som den Taareful Jød-Jinde," in Valkner, p. 406.

24. Engelbretsdatter, "Som den Taareful Jød-Jinde," in Valkner, p. 409.

25. Engelbretsdatter, "At jeg for ingen Deel skal Regnis blandt de nj," in Valkner, p. 418.

26. Engelbretsdatter, "Svar til Mester Iens Pedersen," in Valkner, p. 427.

27. Engelbretsdatter, "Ærbødigst Hilsen med Gud," in Valkner, p. 458.

strengthen him," she prayed.[28] Later in "Oh, Father of mercies" ("Ah! Miskunds Fader . . .") she wrote

> You know that pale death with his murderous gnawing,
> Has thrown my husband and my children in the grave;
> Here I sit abandoned, in grief and left behind.
> Anxiety, unrest, sighing, and tears are mine both day and night,
> O! this divorce smothers me, I am torn up, uprooted,
> Crushed [mør] by hard blows from my head down to my foot.
> My last virtuous Son has fallen in a foreign land,
> I waited for the good, but see! The evil came![29]

Despite her sorrows, or maybe because of them, she continued writing poetry and her reputation increased.

Although some considered her the greatest poet in the north, she did have her detractors who did not believe that a woman could have written such elegant verses on her own and maintained that she had plagiarized her work either from her husband or some other man. Especially repellent to her was a group of students in Copenhagen, one of whom she addressed as Christen Skræp, perhaps a moniker she gave a critic meaning "babbler" or "boaster," or, ironically, "genius," who she heard had suggested that her work was not her own. This she contested with a poem called "A Prescription for a Babbler" ("Recept for en Ord-Gryder").

> He said in *Eugenspils House* postil
> that I warmed up old hymns
> that had been written long ago.[30]

For that, she says, "he can shit gold and piss cinnamon water," concluding that he should be castrated for such a lie, rather surprising language for us today, especially from a pious woman. What mattered the most to her, however, was her faithfulness and God's judgment, not the student's: "My work before God is revealed for the world to judge it."[31]

---

28. Engelbretsdatter, "Laus Deo von Bergen," in Valkner, p. 403.
29. Engelbretsdatter, "Ah! Miskunds Fader," in Valkner, p. 378.
30. Engelbretsdatter, "Recept for en Ord-Gryder," in Valkner, p. 447.
31. Engelbretsdatter, "Recept for en Ord-Gryder," in Valkner, p. 447.

Preaching from Home

Dorothe Engelbretsdatter as a Public Figure

The Soul's Offering of Song (*Siælens Sang-Offer*) (1678), her most enduring work, was first published in Christiania (Oslo) by Mickel Thomesøn, who printed only a few copies, so there are no extant copies of that edition.[32] She continued revising it and adding to it until 1699. All told, it was reprinted thirty times over the next two hundred and ten years, attesting to her popularity with those who bought hymnals and books of folk songs. Her work sold well enough so that she was able to support herself with her writings, a singular achievement for a woman anywhere in the world at the time.

In her poems we also see her struggling with her publishers, revealing herself to be something of a shrewd businesswoman, able to earn her own living despite the very small inheritance she had received from her husband, a signal accomplishment for a woman at this time. She is constantly issuing complaints against those who illegally printed her work for their own profit. After her husband's death and her obligatory year of mourning, Dorothe showed her continuing interest in her business affairs by setting sail for Copenhagen to see to the publication of her second book, *Tear Offering*, which had been inspired not only by her mourning, but also by the book *Tears and a Source of Comfort by Example from the History of the Great Sinners . . . in Twenty Examples* (*Thränen- und Trost-Quelle bey Erklärung der Geschichte von der grossen Sünderin . . . , in 20 Betrachtungen*) (1675), by Heinrich Müller (1631-1675). While in Copenhagen from 1684 to 1685, she lived in the home of her publisher, Christian Geertsøn, who published *Tear Offering* in 1685 along with a revised edition of her first volume, *The Soul's Offering of Song*.

During this time she participated fully in the life of the Danish capital city. She came to know Thomas Kingo fairly well, who had been appointed Bishop of Funen (Fyn) in 1677. Three years before Dorothe arrived in Copenhagen, he had published his second book of hymns, *Andelige Siunge-Kor, Anden Part (Spiritual Choir: Part II)*, and was beginning to prepare what he hoped would become the official hymnal of Denmark. We

---

32. Dorothe writes in a note "To the Favorable Reader" that there were only a few examples of the first edition, which she distributed among "Friends both poor and rich," p. 212. The scholars can not be certain about it since there are no copies extant. See Valkner, p. 505.

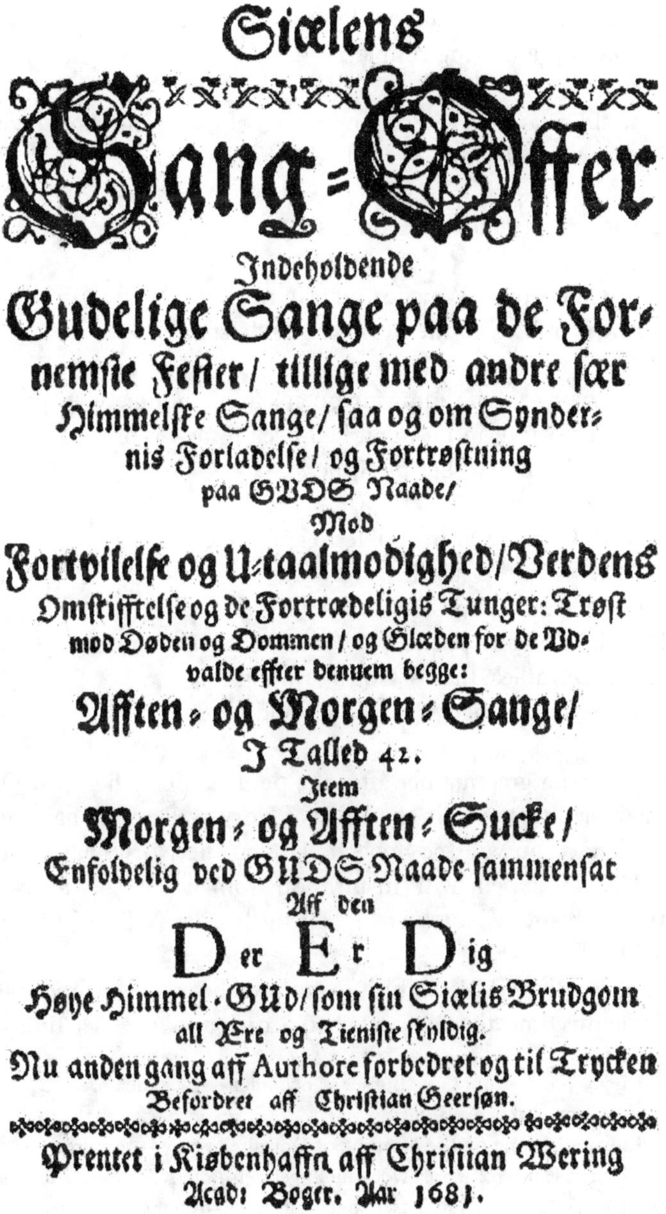

Siælens Gang-Offer

Indeholdende

Gudelige Sange paa de Fornemste Fester/ tillige med andre sær Himmelske Sange/ saa og om Synder-nis Forladelse/ og Fortrøstning paa GUDS Naade/

Mod

Fortvilelse og U-taalmodighed/Verdens Omskifftelse og de Fortrædeligis Tunger: Trøst mod Døden og Dommen/ og Glæden for de Udvalde effter dennem begge:

Afften- og Morgen-Sange/

J Talled 42.

Item

Morgen- og Afften-Suck/

Enfoldelig ved GUDS Naade sammensat

Aff den

D_{er} E_r D_{ig}

Høye Himmel-GUD/ som sin Siælis Brudgom all Ære og Tieniste skyldig.

Nu anden gang aff Authore forbedret og til Trycken Befordret aff Christian Geersøn.

Prentet i Kiøbenhaffn aff Christian Wering Acad: Boger. Aar 1681.

Figure 3 Title page of *The Soul's Offering of Song*, Royal Library, Copenhagen.

can see the easiness with which she mingled with Kingo, for example, in this exchange of poems, supposedly written as they dined together. First Kingo wrote this admiring couplet:

> I should have versified for you before, but knew not how I could,
> For the mistress of poesy sat beside me on my arm.[33]

Her reply is appropriately blushing:

> O matchless poet! Why do you call me that,
> For he is master, all the world can understand![34]

Kingo continued to write admiring poems in her honor, one a poem to be set under her portrait in 1685 that had been done for one of her publications by Cassuba, one of her publishers.

> Who will wonder at the politesse and honor?
> We can see in this face her ingenuity;
> One sees in the pupils of her eyes
> That the woman's poetic pen earns the laurel branch.
> This is Dorothea, that is, God's own gift[35]
> Just now on an angel wing, how could it better be![36]

In a longer poem greeting her after the publication of her *Tear Offering*, Kingo marveled that even in the wilds of Norway, Dorothe has found her Helicon. "Here you will see how she among the Norwegian mountains has her Helicon, a vein with inspiration from heaven" ("Her skal I see hvordan hun blant de Norsk Field, Har hit [trodtz Helicon] en Himmel-Aaris Veld").[37]

Kingo's official duties as bishop required he come to Copenhagen often. During this time, the two poets had occasion to meet. He finished The

---

33. Kingo, "Lever-Riim Over Bordet til Schiøller," in Valkner, p. 432.
34. Engelbretsdatter in Valkner, p. 432.
35. Kingo is playing on the meaning of Dorothe's name — gift from God.
36. Thomas Hansen Kingo, "Dorothe Engelbretsdatters Portræt," *Samlede Skrifter* vol. 1, ed. Hans Brix, Paul Diderichsen, and F. J. Billeskov Jansen (Copenhagen: C. A. Reitzels Boghandel A-S, 1975), p. 231.
37. Kingo, "Gaar nu, gaar hen i Ni berømeste Gudinder," in Brix et al., pp. 256-57.

Winter Part of his hymnal in 1689 and presented it to the King in 1690, where it suffered delay and revision from the royal committee. In 1699, when it was finally published under his name, it bore little resemblance to his original work. It must be noted with some regret that although Kingo seemed to admire Dorothe's hymns and poetry, her work was not included in the hymnal that finally came out in his name. Although one can speculate it was because she was a woman, or her hymns did not fit the very strict organization of the hymnal around the Sunday service, there is not much evidence as to why her work was not included.

After she left Copenhagen, most likely for the last time, on August 27, 1685, she received several farewell epistles from her friends there. In answer to an epistle from one of Denmark's better-known poets, Ahasverus Bartholin (1653-1710), she replied("Til Ahasverus Bartholin . . .") "Welcome, Danish skald, to the Norwegian grey mountain land."[38] Through the years she continued a lively correspondence with these friends. In an epistle to a Danish officer, Jens Sthen Sehested (1635-1698), a poet who wrote in Danish, German, and Dutch, she described her situation as a widow living in Bergen, which she paints as remote but still, however, able to produce a poet.

> I keep house near the mountains among the geese and
>   Norwegian servant girls
> So there is frost in my compliments.
> Forgive me, then, *monsieur,* that I am so direct,
> The linen is coarse where coalfish have their home,
> It is not exactly on the Top of Parnassus
> Whereof a simple poor creation boasts . . .
> In this country not a drop of water flows
> From Helicon's well for anyone who wants it.
> Though one can find freshwater fish in salty water,
> This Ducas lies salted *perfecht* in my head [*pand*]
> [a pun on *pand,* both forehead and frying pan].[39]

While she is a bit defensive about her place as a Norwegian poet, she gives a picture of Bergen's topography, its fishing industry, and her own position

---

38. Engelbretsdatter, "Til Ahasverus Bertholin," in Valkner, p. 449.

39. Engelbretsdatter, "Er Spurren end Vndshcyldt at holde Dantz med Tranen?" in Valkner, pp. 422-23.

in Norway and Bergen, admittedly far from the Muses of Helicon and Parnassus! Even though Bergen is remote and would not be expected to produce poets, one can still find a poet there, as one can occasionally find "freshwater fish in salty water."

Kingo was not her only hymn-writing colleague: she also became acquainted with the legendary life and work of Norway's poet and pastor, Petter Dass. Dass, a character whose personality comes through in both his hymns and the apocryphal legends about him, served the parish of Alstahaug north of Trondheim. Dass wrote many catechetical hymns, not published until after his death, and the first great poem from that region of the world, *The Northland's Trumpet (Nordland's Trompet)*. Over the years he amassed a fortune, profiting from the rich fishing trade between Nordland and Bergen. He had heard about this gifted woman very soon after she began her career. Not surprisingly, on one of his trips to Bergen, he came to visit her and get her book, probably sometime in the summer of 1680. She had not been home at the time. The following epistle is her answer to his request written August 2, 1680, only two years after the publication of her first book.

> To Hr. Petter Dass, when the book could be sent with this letter attached as per his request
>
> Salute, beloved Man of God,
> With happy wishes on sea and land
>
> I got poems well done and precious
> From a learned skillful priest.
> Oh, be happy with my poems,
> So he can be honored next.
> *Grand merci, mein lieber, Frater,*
> Honorable Hr. Petter Dass,
> We will be good *Camerater,*
> If it suits his own desires.
> I am just a youthful poet
> Giving just the best I write
> In a simple woman's language,
> Nor in very high *Discurs.*
> Though between us [zwischen uns] I can tell you

Figure 4 Petter Dass, one of Dorothe's colleagues in hymn writing.

Preaching from Home

> I know more than the Lord's Prayer,
> Yet I must yield to the learned;
> Trousers always must go first.
> But the songs that I have written
> Are quite simple, and direct,
> Though to God they're dedicated,
> For he helped as I had hoped.
> It is for me joy and gladness
> That my book has pleasured those
> Standing in for the Apostles
> And it drives the words of Jesus forth.
> I am sorry I am reft of copies
> Which I've shared so many times.
> All my shelves are bare and empty,
> All around the house I look
> For this book I borrowed from them
> Who had sweetly given thanks
> But now almost have ignored me
> Weeping when I came to them.
> Honorable and high-born friend,
> Take this book as my thanksgiving.
> If the others try to hook me
> I will give them one again,
> Afterwards when more are published
> Which I have revised a bit.
> Our good publisher will provide it
> After I have signed it.
> No more rhymes without some money
> In that I am *uperfect*,
> Travel well and live forever,
> Underneath the Lord's own watch.

She concludes with a wish that his honor may come home safely and happily and find his own with joy.[40]

We can hear in her ironic, teasing humor how she regards the youn-

---

40. Engelbretsdatter, "Til Hr. Peter Dass, da Bogen følgede med efter Begiering," in Valkner, pp. 398-99.

ger poet. Her praise of him, next to her modest but ironic self-portrait, is effective in its self-disparaging tone. Reference to herself as a "simple woman" and a "youthful poet" who does know something more than the "Lord's Prayer" is persistently part of her rhetoric. Within the boundaries of her feigned modesty, she is confident about her gifts, expressing her joy that her songs, simple and direct, and able to "drive Christ," have helped pastors, "those standing in for the Apostles."

We see also the frustration, which she shares with him, about how publishers treat writers, alongside her continuing irritation with male poets and those who could not regard her poetry as worthy since it did not come from a man. Already in one of her first hymns, she had referred to herself as a "She poet" *(hun poet)*. Her poem to Dass contains an early but recurring complaint against male poets, whom she consistently refers to as "trousers" or "trouser folk" *(buxefolck)*. Her note that, of course, "trousers always go first" sounds not a little bitter. The tone and language of these references can be rather bracing for those accustomed to her pious hymns and penitential poems. In her epistle to Ahasverus Bartholin she struck out at those who wished "that my poems have a whiff of trouser cocks in them."[41] If, she continues, once again wryly,

> knitted trousers make people so wise,
> I would have borrowed a pair,
> if only they did not smell so bad of old farts.[42]

In an epistle to another pastor, "Downward totters our Mother," she writes that she felt like a nun in a cloister, a recurring image in her complaints about her estate as a widow.

> Sorrow took over in the North
> when the supporter of her house went cold,
> all my joy upon this earth
> rests beneath the black dirt;
> I am like a nun in a cloister,
> going single in and out,
> Filled with pain in many letter

---

41. Engelbretsdatter, "Til Ahasverus Bartholin," in Valkner, p. 450.
42. Engelbretsdatter, "Til Ahasverus Bartholin," in Valkner, p. 450.

> with water-colored pale cheeks;
> No one to chirp the *pater noster*,
> no one can sing my wedding service
> even if it was the Pope's ruling
> that only men could sing the mass:
> O, no, away with trousered folk!
> I await my heavenly Bridegroom![43]

Is she reacting to someone who suggested that she marry again? She knew the Pope would not allow women to sing the mass. We also get the sense that even if she had the chance to remarry she preferred to await her heavenly bridegroom.

In a poem to another friend, she writes from the point of view of "We trouser folk" ("Vi buxe-folck tyckis").[44] We can see it again in an epistle addressed to a Madame Bladt as she shares her friend's outrage against trouser folk.[45] She repeats the same irritation in her exchange with Ivar von Ahnen, an old friend, as she sighs, "I am nearly a *Monsieur*, though created like other women, while more than excused from being among the goddesses."[46] Her weariness with the way she has been treated by those who do not believe that she, a woman, could write such poetry, is a constant in her work.

Her frustration with many of the criticisms she had gotten shows through very clearly in a funny poem she wrote entitled "To one who dreamt that we had made love in the olden days, without doubt April 31, 1520." In the poem, dated with a completely impossible date, since there is no April 31 and she was not alive in 1520, she responds sarcastically, "Just in the year I have put down, was I a babe of fifteen years, and just leaving my childhood? That is [the reason for] my short answer that I was never bound to him in love."[47]

Her loudest complaint, however, is over what she describes as the estate of widowhood. "So hard falls the estate of widowhood/Help, O Sav-

43. Engelbretsdatter, "Ned ad helder onse *Mater*," in Valkner, pp. 454-55.
44. Engelbretsdatter, "Paa same Maneer frem Kommen," in Valkner, p. 435.
45. Engelbretsdatter, "Tack til Madame Bladt for Bindebrevet," in Valkner, p. 439.
46. Engelbretsdatter, "Dorothe Engelbretsdatters Responsorium til von Ahnen," in Valkner, p. 461.
47. Engelbretsdatter, "Till een der drømte vi hafde Lagt . . . ," in Valkner, pp. 424-26.

ior!"⁴⁸ As a pastor's wife she had enjoyed a life of privilege in both the men's and women's worlds, but the condition of being a widow brought a radical change in her status, which she noted in a poem dedicated to the Queen. "I don't have more to bring her/Than a handful of black on white/ To honor God and the Queen,/Woman's power does not amount to much,/A widow's mite is laid down in God's chest."⁴⁹ In a poem to Madame Povlsons, probably one of her friends whose son had also died fighting the Turks, she gives us a clear picture of her own situation with some details of her life, not only as a widow, but also as a mother who had lost all of her children. She wrote it on March 16, 1686, after she had returned from Copenhagen but clearly before she had heard of Lucas' death.

> The Savior had set her in the painful state of widowhood with each arrow of anxiety, her husband with seven children are resting in the grave, my two surviving sons are spread out, the older of a mild humor, is in Italy, the younger with a little too much courage on his way. Only I am sitting here like an owl in a unquiet place.⁵⁰

In her concluding poem, intended to be sung over her coffin, she asks her soul's bridegroom to take his "tested Widow Bride," a phrase she frequently uses to describe herself.⁵¹ Even though her epistles and encomia are filled with pictures of her as a weeping sorrowful widow, in these poems we also see a saucy, lewd, tough, defensive, funny woman all at the same time, typically Baroque.

Old Age

Dorothe seemed to grow increasingly aware of herself as a public figure, however, maybe even as something of a character, with more and more sense for her role upon the stage of Bergen's civic life. Toward the end of her writing career, Dorothe had begun to make various acrostics of her initials, so many of her poems end with DED, standing not only for her own

---

48. Engelbretsdatter, "De rette Enckers Flugt til deris Naadige Dommer i Himmelen," in Valkner, p. 272.
49. Engelbretsdatter, "LJffsens Første Ærens Konning," in Valkner, p. 315.
50. Engelbretsdatter, "Ærbødigst Hilsen med Gud," in Valkner, pp. 456-58.
51. Engelbretsdatter, "Effterfølgende Grafskrift," in Valkner, p. 500.

initials, but other phrases beginning with DED, which in some sense tell us what she is thinking about herself at that moment, for instance, *Det Er Det* (that is that), *Denne Enfoldige Dicht* (that simple poem), and *Disse Eenhendig Documenter* (these one-handed documents).

In 1698, when she was sixty-four, Dorothe published a final volume, *A Farewell from This World and a Longing for Heaven* (*Et Christeligt Valet fra Verden og Længsel Efter Himmelen*),[52] several poems in which she reviewed her life, stating clearly that she understood herself to be writing devotional works for her public that would help them in their own spiritual journeys. "I now must bid farewell to those/who showed me favors/and visited the widow, faithfully,/and now and then let good works be seen,/ My book, like their lantern,/the devotions that increased their delight" (Barmhiertighedes Fader . . .).[53] This appreciation of those who had carried out the biblical injunction to care for the widows and orphans in their midst shows that she is aware of her advancing age and approaching end, but it also expresses her clear sense for her own public vocation. She was, by her own description, someone who was to provide light for her readers, in her way filling the office of a preacher or teacher of the faith. "Now has ended my anthem speech/now Dorothe bids farewell,/She hurries home, and is prepared/To travel blessedly forward in peace./The art of Prayer, hardened her weary/hands, and scuffed knees."[54]

In 1702, Dorothe lost everything in a great fire that swept through Bergen. For the next few years, until 1711, we are not quite sure where she lived. Like many of her neighbors, she had to rely on the help of friends and colleagues. In 1711, however, she was able to buy a house, near the cathedral, on what is now known as Kong Oscars Street, Number 42.[55] We know very little of her life after 1705. One of her last poems is an elegy for her friend Thomas Kingo who had died on October 4, 1703. Almost her exact contemporary, his death called forth some of her best poetry, which gives us a sense that she wanted to contribute something to the public expression of grief that the great hymn writer received:

---

52. Engelbretsdatter, *Et Christeligt Valet fra Verden og Længsel Efter Himmelen*, in Valkner, pp. 375-89.
53. Engelbretsdatter, "Barmhiertigheds Fader, og Trøstens Gud," in Valkner, p. 384.
54. Engelbretsdatter in Valkner, p. 384.
55. In 1963 it was moved to the Old Bergen outdoor museum, where it now stands as a private dwelling.

Ack! Kingo is gone back to dust,
Who wrote such lovely psalms.
Now he, for his praiseworthy pen,
Is in heaven bearing palms![56]

In 1704, when she was seventy, she used the moniker "Bergen's Deborah," claiming for herself a rather high position indeed. Deborah, one of the great judges of Israel, was also a singer, and Dorothe must have gotten some fun out of the title. Several of her poems show that Deborah had interested Dorothe from the first. In the introduction to her first book she referred to Deborah as one of the holy women whom God in his grace allowed to sing praise. Deborah appears again in Dorothe's revision of her first poem to the reader, this time with biblical women she had not used before, Mary and Judith, as well as Deborah and patient Anna. All are described as "Eve's daughters." In the poem intended for her burial beside Ambrosius she also noted that in heaven she is going to "sing with Deborah."[57]

Her closing poem in this collection of 1704, "Following the Burial Song,"[58] tells her survivors what she wants read at her burial, as she is lowered into the grave, "the Lord's servant woman in the vineyard." Signing it DED "*D*en *E*ensam *D*agløner-Inde" (The lonely laboress), she bids her public farewell. The Bible passage at the beginning of the poem is 2 Timothy 4:7-8, "I have fought the good fight. . . ." The poem begins "Now has Bergen's Deborah without any sorrow to see, sat in her Bethany and cooed like a dove." The dove, in addition to being the bird of Pentecost and peace, was the bird Noah sent out. This poem is what she calls her "Swan Song," or her entry into heaven: "In the Swan Song, which death received, and with useful devotional thoughts, she climbed up to heaven."[59] After describing her difficult life, she concludes with a *Te Deum nos Laudamus* that she is now singing with the angels, as well as Deborah! Her final stanza contains the normal exhortation to those left behind to listen to what she is saying, preaching from heaven on the necessity of repentance.

56. Engelbretsdatter, "Ach! Kingo blev til Jord igien," in Valkner, pp. 492-94.
57. Engelbretsdatter, "Nu har den Bergens *Debora*," in Valkner, p. 385.
58. Engelbretsdatter, "Efferfölgende Liig-Sang," in Valkner, p. 384.
59. Engelbretsdatter in Valkner, p. 385.

> Think, sheep I've left behind,
> With tears of regret, eternity
> Is at hand and death is ready.
> Farewell! My sisters, strew
> but a few leaves on her grave,
> In heaven she's bearing palm branches.[60]

The final stanza addresses her followers as her "sheep," clearly implying that she understood her office as shepherd. These are the words of a preacher, if not a pastor. It confirms that she is aware of her public role in the spiritual life of Norway. Once again she acknowledges that she had many followers who came to her for spiritual advice.

That same year, probably as one of Bergen's public figures, maybe even unofficial poet laureate, she wrote a poetic greeting to King Frederick IV who had come to visit Bergen in 1704, after the great fire of 1702, the worst ever suffered by the city, in which most of the old city had been destroyed, including her own home. These are among the last writings we have from her. Although she had twelve more years before she died, her voice disappears into the mists of old age. All we have is Holberg's picture of an old woman flitting about his city in old-fashioned clothes. We can read in the list of her final possessions that she had a few books, among them Ambrosius Lobwasser's book of paraphrased psalms that got many a Lutheran into trouble because of their supposed infection with Calvinism. A short list, probably because of her losses in the fire, it includes, among others, the work of John Gerhard, *Schola Pietatis*, Wudriani's German *Scholæ Crucis*, and an Italian book.

As we can see from Holberg's memoir, she remained a curiosity in Bergen until her end. By the time she died in 1716, times had changed and her work was considered, as Holberg had noted, old-fashioned and out of joint with the times. Her next biographer, H. J. Birch, also a man of the Enlightenment, in his 1793 book *Portraits of Women*, noted that she was "well known in her own time."[61] He concluded the brief entry on her by noting that her success was likely caused by the fact that there were so few writers in Danish.

---

60. Engelbretsdatter, "Te Deum nos Laudamus," in Valkner, p. 389.

61. H. J. Birch, *Billedgallerie for Fruentimmer, indeholdende Livnetsbeskrivelse over berømete og lærde dansk, norske og udenlandske Fruentimmere* (Copenhagen: S. Poulsens Forlag, 1793), p. 128.

> While in her own time, when rhyme was taken for poetry, and the most learned men wrote but little in Danish, which is why anyone who wrote in his native tongue was taken up with great approval since at the time people did not yet have the taste for anything better.[62]

This condescending note is much in the spirit of Holberg. Most every age has great difficulty with the works of the previous age.

Hymns

Her first book, *The Soul's Song Offering (Siælens Sang-Offer),* which she continued revising and adding to until 1699, included in its last appearance seventy hymns and poems intended to be used in church, in the assembly, and for home devotions through the church year. A major section contains "pericope" hymns that fit with the texts for each festival Sunday in the Lutheran church year, along with songs for morning and evening, with others for traditional occasions in the Christian life such as preparing to receive the Lord's Supper, after receiving it, or facing death and burial, although no hymn about baptism. Like all hymnals at the time, the tune for each hymn was suggested under the title.[63] Many were, as she noted at the end of her first collection, well-known "Church melodies, but the other twenty-five were to be sung with new melodies that went with each text."[64]

Her hymns follow the typical Lutheran homiletical rhetorical conventions of invention and application common in her day. Laila Akslesen, in her book *Norwegian Baroque: Dorothe Engelbretsdatter and Petter Dass in the Rhetorical Tradition (Norsk Barokk, Dorothe Engelbretsdatter og Petter Dass i retorisk tradisjon),* argues that as a pastor's daughter and wife during the period of Lutheran orthodoxy, Engelbretsdatter had absorbed the rhetorical form of a Lutheran sermon of the Baroque era, which she used in most of her hymns. Her regular attendance at church services would have given her the form implicitly even if she did not explicitly study it. Furthermore, even if she had no expectation of an audience for

---

62. Birch, p. 128.

63. Musicians commend Engelbretsdatter for the fine tunes she picked for her hymns.

64. Akslesen, *Norsk Barokk,* p. 189.

her proclamation other than those in her home, as a Lutheran pastor's wife and daughter, she understood the home altar to be an important place for preaching.

From the introduction to her book *The Soul's Offering*, we can see that she understands the work of a hymn writer to be that of a preacher. In it, in a prose prayer addressed to Jesus that he will open her lips so that she can "proclaim his praise," she speaks in the words of Psalm 95, the traditional morning psalm from the Matins service. The word that she uses, however, for what the English King James Bible has translated as "show forth" is, in Norwegian, *forkynde* or "preach." After this long prayer, in which she prays to Jesus that he will help her to proclaim his praise as he helped Miriam, Deborah, Hannah, and other holy women "to praise you with song,"[65] she addresses the reader in a poem, "To the Reader" ("Til Læseren"), a typical literary apology for her work that argues from Scripture and theology that God has given everyone a gift, whether large or small, like the talents in Jesus' parable, and even if they are women, they are to use it.

> I too have got a little talent,
> From all the gifts of grace.
> For me, though, it is good and worthy,
> Why should I bury it?
> O! No! for I will praise his mercy,
> With my own tongue will I sing out
> As he has taught me, like birds who carol
> In their creator's praise,
> Why should my mouth be silent?[66]

We read here how she defends herself by using warrants for her writing from Scripture typical of almost every woman who has tried to take her place in the pantheon of Christian preachers. God would want what he has given her to be used, she notes; in fact, God must be expecting her to use her gift, like those in the parable of the talents, saying she would not be like the one who buried his talent. "Why should my mouth be silent?" she asks.

---

65. Engelbretsdatter, "Jesu Christo/Guds og Mariæ Søn den store/Fredsens Første og Evige Konning," in Valkner, p. 21.

66. Engelbretsdatter, "Til Læseren," *Siælens Sang-Offer,* in Valkner, p. 23.

In back of this argument are generations of discussions as to whether or not women could have the same vocations as men, in this case, hymn writing, and whether they were created as equals to Adam. Whenever Christian women have struggled to be included in church work, they go to the theology of creation and the doctrine of vocation. Why would God have given me this gift if he had not intended for me to use it, they ask. Engelbretsdatter does not claim that her talent is greater than anyone else's, only that her "little talent" deserves expression. Thus she must do what she is called to do by the gift God has given her. As birds, created to sing, must sing, so must she. It is in the creator's design. Although there is modesty in her claim — hers is a "little" talent — she does not back off from the necessity of fulfilling her calling. Lutheran theologians would find it difficult to argue against her Lutheran theology of vocation, especially since Luther had clearly established the notion that women should teach the faith, if not in public, at home.

Her main warrant, however, is the many women in Scripture who have also used their talents to praise God. She has received inspiration from a variety of them for her own work, among them the Canaanite woman, Anna the prophetess, Elizabeth, the woman with an issue of blood, Lydia, Tabitha, and Mary Magdalene, a list drawn exclusively from the New Testament. Surprisingly, she does not include Mary the Mother of Jesus. As God has inspired them, he will inspire her. Later she will include famous women from the Old Testament and take as her name Bergen's Deborah, but her initial warrants for writing these hymns, her soul's offering to God, are all New Testament women. She concludes with the request that her readers not think of her as a woman, but judge her kindly and overlook her faults.

> For if the rhymes are not so fine
> As you would really want them,
> Then simply let them stand alone.
> Still God receives his glory.
> So do not marvel and exclaim
> That womenfolk, so needy,
> Will also want to go along
> To where his praise is ringing,
> I wish you to walk along with me
> Together in our gladness

Till we with joy in heav'n
Will sing our alleluias.[67]

After this address to the reader, really a defense of women's poesy, the collection begins with "A Spiritual Song" ("En Aandelig Sang") "Strax Jonas kom til Ninive." In it and succeeding hymns we can see (1) her use of the Lutheran Baroque homiletical invention processes and outlines, (2) her application of the Baroque conventions of meditation, (3) and her very strong debt to the devotional work of Johann Arndt, *True Christianity*.[68] All three forces are at work in this first hymn in the collection.

1. When Jonah came to Nineveh
   And spoke about God's anger,
   The people all fell to their knees
   And learned to pray for mercy
   And fled unto God's mercy seat
   And in their ashes they sat down;
   With prayers and tears they fasted;
   They feared the might and power of God,
   And rent the gaudy clothes of sin
   And dressed themselves in sackcloth.

2. When Nathan told a parable
   About King David's ruin,
   His rue and sorrow filled with woe,
   It moved his heart to weeping.
   When God once looked at Peter's face,
   It moved his heart to bitter tears
   And right away repented.
   But I, a disobedient Bride,
   So often hear my Lord's commands
   And still I stumble on them.

3. Now I who often grieve my Lord
   To terr'ble fits of anger

---

67. Engelbretsdatter, "Til Læseren," in Valkner, p. 25.
68. Johan Arndt, *True Christianity*, trans Peter Erb, Classics of Western Spirituality (Mahwah, N.J.: Paulist Press, 1978).

Will now just like a Ninevite
Again for grace be praying.
With David I will now repent
And fall before the Savior's feet,
Like Peter weep in sorrow
And leave the scornful company
That sits beside me fraud'lently
With evil in their being.

4. I am with Manasseh prepared
To bow my heart to Jesus.
Now sin cuts deeply through my heart;
I fall onto the pavement
And with Maria I'm prepared
To cast myself before Christ's feet
Like a repentant sinner
And wet his feet with my salt tears
And dry them with my haughty hair
That I know he will favor.

5. And so just like the Prodigal
Who turned to see his father,
I go to Jesus with my prayers
To say I am a sinner;
Just like the needy publican
I'll pound my breast in great regret
And yearn for your great mercy;
And like the thief I'll cry to you,
O Jesus Lord, remember me,
And take me home to heaven.

6. For when one sinner does convert,
The angels break out singing,
And Jesus who is mild and good
Is filled with grace inviting.
He went to find the only one
The little lamb that had been lost
And left the nine and ninety

Who trusted in themselves alone
   And were not ready to repent;
   His word can never save them.

7. I do not think it is a shame
   Acknowledging my evil
   To flee to Christ, God's precious Lamb
   With penitence to find him.
   If I could not depend on grace,
   I'd fall to pieces suddenly,
   And die in pain and sorrow.
   Now that I've sent my heart to him
   With tears upspringing from my faith,
   The world may want to question.

8. If Satan prosecutes me now,
   My Savior will defend me;
   The law may press down hard on me,
   My Lord will always clear me.
   The world will always bear a grudge,
   Cause pain and trouble in my heart
   But death will never move me,
   Should hell then open up its mouth
   And swallow me into the ground,
   God's power can overcome it.

9. O Jesse's branch, O David's root,
   O heaven's highest regent,
   The whole world worships at your feet
   and all of God's creation.
   I bow before your mercy's door,
   With hope and bowed head I now come,
   I know you'll not despise me.
   Take me to yourself with love;
   My eyes brim up with pain and tears,
   O my heart's dear ransacker!

Engelbretsdatter is preaching both to herself and others who will be singing and hearing the hymn. As Laila Akslesen noted, Engelbretsdatter had learned as a pastor's daughter and wife the typical form of the Lutheran sermon in the Baroque era which included: (1) Scripture paraphrase, (2) explication, (3) the theological understanding, (4) consequences, and (5) an application and exhortation of some kind. First, the preacher would have to examine the literal text and in some way retell or paraphrase it for the congregation who, despite their biblical knowledge, though perhaps superior to ours, still needed to hear the story again. This hymn, however, is not on one Scripture lesson; it is more of a theme sermon on the topic of *Poenitentze*, repentance or contrition, one of the great themes of the Baroque era, and the Reformation. Luther's Ninety-Five Theses began with the fundamental importance of repentance: "When our Lord and Master Jesus Christ said, 'Repent,' he willed the entire life of believers to be one of repentance." Given her theme, Engelbretsdatter had to find biblical texts that would clearly illustrate repentance, in this case, Bible stories that she could retell to her congregation.

Her first stanza begins with one of the great stories of repentance in the Bible: the people of Nineveh hearing Jonah's sermon urging them to repent. After his name in the first line of the hymn, Jonah disappears. What we are told about is the response to the sermon: the people's repentance, as the people "fell to their knees," "learned to pray for mercy," "fled unto God's mercy seat," "sat down" in ashes, wept, prayed, and fasted, and "rent the gaudy clothes of sin/And dressed themselves in sackcloth." Her retelling of the story, or paraphrase of it — which cuts short some of the details in the text, such as the king's response to Jonah's words — gives the people singing/hearing the hymn a picture of something that happened long ago, rather like Nathan's parable used to convict David. The Ninevite response as she marks it here spells out the process of repentance, a paradigm so to speak, which she will explicate and amplify through the rest of the hymn.

Stanza two adds two more great penitents, David and Peter, both of whom had sinned and, as her audience knows, are brought to repentance by sermons: David when he hears Nathan's parable and Peter when he hears the cock crow, which in Engelbretsdatter's hymn is the voice of God, or in Lutheran terms, a sermon. Like the Ninevites, they too repent in tears. Still, these are stories from a long time ago. She needs to interpret them and apply them to her situation, which she does at the end of stanza two: She is a "disobedient bride" who "stumbles" on the law of God, or his commands. This is the first move in application: rather like supplying the minor premise in a syllogism, the major premise of which is that "God forgives all sinners." Her minor premise "I am a sinner — a disobedient bride" gives her access to God's forgiveness. This is the logical move — or metaphorical move — that every Christian sermon must make in some way or another.

It is important to notice that she does not immediately fall to her knees in repentance — for the rest of the second stanza she is unrepentant, like those whom Paul describes in 1 Corinthians 1:23 who find the gospel to be a stumbling block. In stanza three, however, she resolves to follow the example of the Ninevites, David, and Peter by turning from the "scornful company" she is in, like those in Psalm 1 who "are seated in the seat of the scornful." She now determines to repent like Manasseh, the traitor son of Hezekiah, who, as her audience also knew, repented after being led back to Babylon as a slave with a hook in his nose. For Engelbretsdatter he is an emblem of the slavery of sin from which he is freed by his repentance. In comparing herself to these great sinners, she is also preparing to show how the mercies God granted to them will also be given to her. Now her rhetoric changes as she moves from telling us about these old stories, to doing things *like* what the characters in the stories did. The focus changes from the biblical story, to her acting *like* those in the story. Thus she falls *like* Mary Magdalene "before Christ's feet/Like a repentant sinner/to wet his feet with my salt tears/and dry them with my haughty hair/That I know he will favor." She has learned from Mary how to approach Christ. As Christ has reached out to Mary, so he will reach out to Engelbretsdatter, or anyone singing the hymn. This is the beginning of what the Baroque sermon form would call "interpretation" or application *(applicatio)*.

She further amplifies this theme with more examples *(exempla)*. Amplification, rhetorically speaking, is the preferred trope of the Baroque era with its love of decoration, contrast, and repetition. Not surprisingly, she chooses to amplify her theme with the central text for repentance in the New Testament, the story of the lost coin, lost sheep, and Prodigal son in Luke 15. "Like the Prodigal, who turned to see his father," she will go to Jesus with her prayers. Every singer in her congregation will hear the voice of the Prodigal in the far country putting down the husks he is eating in the pig yard come to himself and say, "I will get up and go to my father, and I will say to him, 'Father, I have sinned against heaven, and before you; I am no longer worthy to be called your son'" (Luke 15:18-19). Once again she is not simply talking about the Prodigal but saying that she will do as he did. In another example, she turns to the parable of the Pharisee and the publican and once again notes that she will do as the publican did: "I'll pound my breast in great regret," or *like* the thief on the cross cry out, "O Jesus, Lord, remember me/And take me home to heaven." In all of these *exampla* she is finding warrants for her argument that Christ will receive her as he did these others.

After her paraphrase and interpretation or application of these stories to her own life in which she has learned, and is now teaching, what must be done, she concludes with the thief on the cross. This is central to Lutheran preaching — pointing to the cross, especially this image of the thief crying out to Jesus, as she suggests her readers should. Then she returns to Luke 15 to find further reassurance that Christ will give her grace, as did the shepherd who went to look for the lost sheep, leaving behind the ninety and nine. This turning to Christ, she knows, will bring joy to the angels in heaven, a reference to the woman searching for the coin as well as the shepherd who has found his sheep. Thus, in stanza six she can argue theologically that he will, as the Lamb of God, take her in. Here she makes reference again to the cross and Christ's sacrifice on the cross. She has given her heart to Christ and now awaits the verdict. There is a curious turn in the direction of this stanza that does not quite fit with the previous penitential imagery — instead of going to Christ in bitter sorrow over one's sins, she now pictures Christ seeking the lost, a more orthodox Lutheran image than the carefully drawn out pictures of the "process" of repentance, which to some Lutheran minds looks like a return to medieval "penitence" and an overmuch dwelling on our penitential actions.

She now addresses herself and her audience to the question of what will happen. In stanza eight she takes the focus off the penitent and changes the images of repentance to the images of a courtroom where Satan is prosecuting her and all sinners, a picture of what theologians would call "forensic justification." Christ is her lawyer and will clear her of the sentence she so readily deserves. Despite the sentence, which Christ takes upon himself, she can triumph over the world, the flesh, and the devil because "God's power can overcome it." This language sounds very much like Luther's in "A Mighty Fortress": "Though hordes of devils fill the land/All threatening to devour us,/We tremble not, unmoved we stand;/They cannot overpower us." Her confidence that nothing can overpower Christ rings through this stanza. Her final stanza shows how this good news makes it possible for her and the congregation to sing directly to Jesus, worshiping him with awe and joy, their "heart's ransacker." The Norwegian word *randsager* has slightly less of the sense of plunder than we have in English — the old Norse means to search a house for stolen goods. It is the word used in the Norwegian version of Psalm 139 for search — "Search my heart."

She concludes with this ecstatic love for the one who knows her best, and we hear her awe and joy in the love relationship between the soul and Christ as she stands before him in tears, with confidence that he will take her in. She has moved herself and the singer from Nineveh to the courts of heaven, where she is now waiting before the Lord, who knows her heart. She has used Scripture and applied it to those who are hearing her sermon; they now know what to do and what to expect from the Lord — all in all, a successful sermon. Those for whom she was writing this hymn would recognize it as a traditional Lutheran sermon and be edified by it. A slightly uncertain note even at the last, probably not a little influenced by her interest in the penitential piety of the day, shows that she is still waiting for the Lord's ultimate verdict, not yet in the heavenly courts.

To see it as a Baroque sermon with a Lutheran bent may be enough, but there are some themes in the hymn that such an analysis does not quite pick up. The mass of devotional books with their instructions on how to read Scripture for edification streaming out of England and Europe can also be shown to have influence here. The method of meditation set down by St. Ignatius and the practice of meditation he recommended had made a powerful impact on the devotional works of the time: (1) a deep engagement with the actual scene in the gospels (memory); (2) a searching to understand what it meant in the terms of a larger theological theme (mind); (3) a revelry that overwhelmed the affections and moved one to devotion (will — affections).[69]

It is possible to find these motives in Engelbretsdatter's hymn as well. Once again, because she is preaching on a theme rather than a text, she does not so much paraphrase Scripture as *remember* several significant lessons on repentance in it. Engelbretsdatter's memory has engaged her deeply with many such passages from the Bible — as noted above: Jonah, Nineveh, David, Peter, Psalm 1, Manasseh, Mary Magdalene, the Prodigal, the publican, the thief on the cross. At the point of the words from the thief on the cross, "Jesus, remember me," she turns to *understanding* what

---

69. Louis L. Martz, *The Poetry of Meditation: A Study in Religious Literature of the Seventeenth Century*, rev. ed. (New Haven: Yale University Press, 1962), pp. 34-35.

these texts mean. By this method, her recollection of Luke 15 and her increased understanding that there is rejoicing in heaven over the one that is found make more sense. She is trying to fit her memories into the theological theme of penitence and recalls the Prodigal, the biblical *emblem* for forgiveness. While, as we noted above, most of her previous examples are of those who have been under conviction of sin, this stanza turns from the sinner going to Jesus, to Jesus going to find the sinner. This gives her a deeper understanding of what Christ will do for her. The next three stanzas, six to eight, help assure her that Christ is for her and that these stories, now interpreted theologically, have to do with her as well as the ancients. Here the turning point is in stanza seven, "If I could not depend on grace/ I'd go to pieces suddenly." With that she waits in tears for the verdict. While waiting, she professes her faith in her Lord, which by stanza nine turns into a change in the will, or affections, as per Ignatius's third step, a rapturous hymn of "revelry that overwhelms the affections" and moves "the soul to devotion":

> O Jesse's branch, O David's root,
> O heaven's highest regent,
> The whole world worships at your feet
> with all of God's creation.

Although the bride image, also an important part of Baroque devotional literature, does not seem to be the major image in this hymn, it underlies it from the second stanza to the end when Christ the lover searches *(randsager)* and knows the heart.

As we have noted, one very important source for Engelbretsdatter was Johan Arndt's book *True Christianity,* (1610). Engelbretsdatter's hymns, according to Akslesen, can be understood best when seen in the light of Arndt's works. Paging through his works one can see how significantly he influenced her. We can easily see her use of his work especially in his description of the four stages of true repentance in his Book II, Chapter x: (1) awareness of one's unworthiness, (2) self-abnegation, (3) turning to the cross, and (4) mystical union with Christ. Comparing her hymn with Arndt's, we can see a very close correspondence with his language. He uses many of the same Scriptural references in his work on penitence that Engelbretsdatter uses in her hymn. First, Arndt writes, one must account oneself unworthy of all the mercies of God. While Arndt does not mention

Nineveh, he does refer to the psalmist's language, "I have eaten ashes like bread." Any close reader of the Bible on hearing the word "ashes" would have remembered Nineveh and its repentance in sackcloth and ashes. Not surprisingly, her first stanza focuses on the image of the sackcloth and ashes as she found it in the narrative in Arndt. The picture of sackcloth and ashes would also have given her the idea as she read Arndt of other scenes in Scripture where there were "sackcloth and ashes," such as David's bitter repentance after his transgression with Bathsheba and Uriah. Although Peter did not tear his clothes or sit in ashes, his bitter repentance also appears in Engelbretsdatter's head, as she looks for illustrations of penitents in the host of other biblical stories she has used.

Second, Arndt says, one must hate oneself. Although difficult for us to understand, the Baroque period lived on the theme of self-abnegation. Lancelot Andrewes (1555-1626), one of the leaders of the committee that translated the Bible into the King James Version, is said to have spent nearly five hours every day in penitential prayers considering his terrible sins:

> For me, O Lord, sinning and not repenting, and so utterly unworthy, it were more becoming to lie prostrate before Thee and with weeping and groaning to ask pardon for my sins, than with polluted mouth to praise Thee.[70]

We see the same kind of language when Engelbretsdatter describes herself as a "disobedient Bride," like David and Peter, and like the publican, beating her breast in sorrow for her sins. These emotions, and the acknowledgement of their complete distance from God and his holiness, have the paradoxical effect of giving the sinner more to praise God for, since he has stooped so low. For these people, the abnegation of the soul and its distance from God lead them to realize the grandeur of God's love for us, as Wendy Olmsted argues in an article on Augustine's rhetoric.[71] Arndt says much the same when he notes that "The person who is most wretched in his heart is

---

70. As found in Adam Nicholson, *God's Secretaries: The Making of the King James Bible* (San Francisco: Harper Collins, 2003), p. 32.

71. Wendy Olmsted, "Invention, Emotion, Conversion in St. Augustine," *Rhetorical Invention and Religious Inquiry: New Perspectives*, ed. Walter Jost and Wendy Olmsted (New Haven: Yale University Press, 2000), p. 82.

most beloved of God," in the heading of his Book I, Chapter xix. The more worthless one feels before God, he argues, the more "glorious" we are in God's sight.[72] It is easy to see why the orthodox Lutheran would become uneasy before this focus on the penitential actions of the sinner, which can become fascinating to us as we look at ourselves rather than Christ. Even the word *Poenitenze* at the head of the hymn could worry the orthodox because of its focus on the actions of the sinner. The word, while close to repentance, is penitence. And it must be admitted that Engelbretsdatter's focus is as much on the actions of the penitent, as the action of Christ.

Third, Arndt says, one must take up his or her cross and go to the Savior, which Engelbretsdatter does in the fifth stanza, where she refers to the thief on the cross as he turns to Jesus to say, "Remember me." Not surprisingly, Arndt uses the Prodigal Son as his emblem for the one who turns from his sin and goes to his Father as does Engelbretsdatter in stanza five.

> And so just like the Prodigal
> Who turned to see his father,
> I go to Jesus with my prayers
> To say I am a sinner.

She can go to the Savior for many reasons, knowing that he gave himself to look for her. This turning is once again directly from the notion of conversion, *metanoia*. All of the penitents in this hymn follow this same pattern and turn to the Lord.

Fourth, according to Arndt, the repentant sinner is united with God in a mystical union. Engelbretsdatter is united with God when she confesses that Jesus will not despise her tears and will take her unto himself, as a lover might. It is obvious from just this brief look that Engelbretsdatter read Arndt closely and used him as a source for many of her hymns. While she does not rhapsodize on the wedding imagery as much as Arndt, Engelbretsdatter uses it frequently and with conviction as do her successors, Berthe Canutte Aarflot and Lina Sandell.

To some of her contemporaries the language of this hymn and others of her hymns felt too personal to be used in a hymnal, perhaps because her use of herself as a "disobedient bride" made it distasteful for men, even if they might have been able to understand it as a metaphor for their soul, as

---

72. Arndt, *True Christianity*, Book I, Chapter xix, trans. Peter Erb, p. 99.

Bernard had, along with Brorson and other Pietist hymn writers in the next generation. There were those who never accepted Engelbretsdatter's work because it seemed too personal for them, and too "tasteless," maybe too feminine. It was an effective charge. To account for her fame, critics pointed to her social connections with greater poets such as Dass and Kingo,[73] not her own poetry. Engelbretsdatter is not the first to use the collective *I*, so she should not be singled out for doing so. Luther spoke from his own point of view, with an *I*, in "Dear Christians, One and All Rejoice" ("Nun Freut Euch"). Many people singing these hymns can find such language acceptable and appropriate to their own situation. It speaks for them in words they themselves could not invent but find appropriate for their own experience of the faith. When Engelbretsdatter concludes this hymn with a prayer to Jesus, the branch of Jesse, she gives the singers language with which to pray for these gifts and comforts them with a prayer on their behalf which now is their own language. There is one major drawback with her use of the collective *I*. One could wonder whether men would sing lines in which the hymn referred to the singer of the hymn as a "disobedient Bride," or *Synderinde* ("female sinner") or *Tienerinde* ("female servant")[74] ("Ansee din Tienerinde"). This happens with some frequency in her hymns, but there is no getting around it in the Norwegian language. If one is speaking from a personal point of view, no matter how anonymous, the feminine ending is inevitable, unless she is trying to disguise her identity. As noted above, it may be the reason these hymns were considered too "personal" even in her time. Later hymnal editors like Pontoppidan or Landstad changed these endings so that the more "universal" masculine endings are used.

Engelbretsdatter recommended that the hymn be sung to an old church tune, "That Blessed Day" ("Den signede Dag"), which would give a kind of palimpsest effect as they sang this hymn about God's grace, hearing echoes of the many other hymns also sung to that tune. The aural theme of the *contrafecta* (the feeling one gets when singing a new text to an old tune) intensifies their sense of the bounteous grace of God, which they would hear underneath the old tune and text as they sang the new words.

---

73. N. M. Petersen called her a "woman rhymer" *(Rimerinde)*. "Her Bible songs are without inspiration, and her occasional verses, which should be enlivening or somewhat satirical, are tasteless." *Bidrag til den danske Literaturs Historie*, III, 1855-56, p. 590, as found in Skaar, pp. 586-87.

74. See, for example, her hymn, "Som Hiorten mødig skriger," in Valkner, pp. 31-34.

In addition to being a typical Lutheran sermon, rhetorically, the association with the old tune would add to the experience of the new hymn. She is using old familiar tunes, old stories, old conventions and associations to communicate very intensely with her audience and move them, the object of any preacher.

Pericope Hymns

After several hymns on topics in the Christian life, Engelbretsdatter turns her attention to what she called "pericope" hymns for the festivals of the church year, beginning with a Christmas hymn, "On Earth Peace and Gladness" ("Paa Jorden Fred og Glæde"). "A Hymn for the New Year," once an important part of the Lutheran church year, gives us a glimpse into the old pieties. The remaining festivals are few, but common to the Lutheran church year prior to the nineteenth century — Holy Week, Easter, Ascension, Pentecost.

Her hymn on Pentecost, which I have translated in full, also follows the paradigm of the Lutheran Baroque sermon: the announcement of a theme, followed by a close paraphrase of the Ascension and Pentecost lessons in John 21, and Acts 1 and 2, a theological interpretation of the story in stanza 9, and then a brief reflection on its consequences to the singers, concluding with an application in her own life.

1. Welcome! O blessed Pentecost,
   A blessing for the entire world.
   You gladden every Christian soul
   That cherishes Immanuel.
      Hallelujah!

2. Now our Victorious one so dear
   A winner's victory crown you bear
   So we must celebrate with joy
   And sing the honor of our Lord.
      Hallelujah!

3. For when he bid this world farewell
   Preparing to ascend to heav'n.

He told his own disciples then
What great things would come to them.
    Hallelujah!

4. "I go to yours and to my God,
So I can send with grace to you
My Holy Spirit, by power divine
To give your dry hearts juice to drink."
    Hallelujah!

5. Now ten days later as he said,
The Holy Spirit joyful, mild,
Came down to his disciples' house
Just like a rushing roaring wind.
    Hallelujah!

6. Like fiery tongues of fire they saw
The Spirit settle on th'Apostles' heads,
It made them all so smart and wise
They spoke all languages of earth.
    Hallelujah!

7. So they proclaimed God's mighty deeds
And in his teachings strong became,
The story of our God's own Son
Was spread through many foreign lands.
    Hallelujah!

8. And some were right away made new
Who had not known the Christ before.
When they believed, they were baptized,
And leaped with joyful hearts and minds.
    Hallelujah!

9. Lord, with your mighty power divine
You set all things in your control,
O send me now your Spirit's power,

Unloose my tongue so I can sing.
   Hallelujah!

10. Let faith and hope with charity
Remain in me until the end,
   So that my heart is free of sin
   So he may build his temple there.
      Hallelujah!

11. My dove, with God's own olive leaf
Make me glad with your own gifts
And go to God with prayer for me;
I know that he is merciful.
   Hallelujah!

12. O! Jesus, be my faithful friend,
When earthly joys come to their end,
And give me heav'nly comfort now
Instead of fading worldly lusts.
   Hallelujah!

13. When death's dark shade and bitterness
Will press from me my cold hard sweat,
Strive with your servant here below
So I can break away from here.
   Hallelujah!

14. You are my treasure, heav'n's share,
My noble gem and jewel rare;
Be now my cane and wandering stave
Until I'm settled in my grave.
   Hallelujah![75]

Here we see her homiletical methods once again at work. Beginning with a theme urging us to rejoice, she then explains why we should rejoice, in

---

75. Engelbretsdatter, "Om den Hellig Aands Udsendelse," in Valkner, p. 95. "Velkommen salig Pintze Dag."

carefully remembered and paraphrased versions of the Pentecost story, beginning with the Ascension, followed by the great commission from both John 21 and Acts 1 and 2. She does not move to *explicatio* until deep into the hymn, stanza nine, where she begins to explicate why this was important for her and the singers of the hymn. There she begins to apply it to herself and her understanding, as per the Baroque mode of devotion, even as she uses the *applicatio* of the Lutheran sermon to apply the text to herself and those singing the text.

> O send me now your Spirit's power,
> Unloose my tongue so I can sing.
> Hallelujah!

As in her previous hymns she is arguing, as the Psalmist does, that if it happened in the past, so should it happen to her, as Luther had it in his explanation to the third petition of the Lord's Prayer, "The kingdom of God comes indeed of itself, but we pray in this petition, that it will also come among us." The image she uses of Christ coming to dwell in the temple of her heart begins a vivid picture of the dialogue that is true prayer. She asks that Faith, Hope, and Charity should triumph in her heart, even as she knows sin is ever before her. Even as her prayer arises, however, she wants the dove to descend to her as it did to Jesus in his baptism. Once again we can find the influence of Johann Arndt. The image of the dove from the story of Noah, and, now also, as the Holy Spirit who appeared at Jesus' baptism, is a commonplace for these devotional writers, but it is worth noting that Arndt included in his *Paradise Garden* prayer at Pentecost both the dove and olive leaf.[76] Without doubt, she had read Arndt's prayer; it may well be the source of the image in this hymn, but it is also a typical treatment of the dove in Christian thinking. As a good theologian, she knows that it is the Spirit who intercedes for her and gives her communion with the Father and Son; thus her prayer that the dove will go to the Father and intercede for her and establish communion with him. Then she expands on the joy there will be with Jesus in heaven; once again, it will be a mystical reunion with her bridegroom. The rhetoric of this hymn follows the basic form of her first

---

76. Johan Arndt, *True Christianity: A Treatise on Sincere Repentance, True Faith, the Holy Walk of the True Christian, etc.*, 1605-1609, trans. Anton W. Boehm (Philadelphia: The United Lutheran Publication House, 1868), pp. 197-98.

Dorothe Engelbretsdatter

hymn: paraphrase, then *explicatio, applicatio,* followed by prayer and praise. This is her last hymn for the high festivals of the church.

Evening and Morning Hymns

Finally, she provides hymns for the time of day, a common subject for Lutheran hymns and usually based on Luther's morning and evening prayers in the Small Catechism. A morning and evening hymn conclude this first version of her *Soul's Offering*. One of her most well-known hymns, the evening hymn "Daylight Fades and Dies Away" ("Dagen viger og gaar bort"), participates fully in that tradition.[77]

> XXV
> **Evening Hymn**
> **Daylight Fades and Dies Away**
> *(Dagen viger og gaar bort)*
>
> 1. Daylight fades and dies away,
>   Twilight deepens, skies turn grey.
>   Valleys lose the yellow sun.
>   Darkest night has now begun.
>
> 2. Slowly time, which seems to pass
>   Quickly, empties out our glass.
>   Death is ever at our heels,
>   Endless night before us wheels.
>
> 3. I grow older every day
>   Dusk reminds me on my way.
>   As I take my wand'ring stave
>   Nearer to my narrow grave.
>
> 4. Now the sun has slipped away,
>   Dusk takes over every place,

---

[77]. Lewis Bayly, *The Practice of Piety: Directing a Christian How to Walke, That He May Please God* (London, 1656), p. 188.

So all things will change and shift
Till we make our final trip.

5. O dear soul, do not forget
   To confess your sin and guilt.
   You are Adam's sinful heir
   Caught in webs that make you err.

6. You cannot be quit of day
   Without falling on your way.
   Rise and pray to God above
   Who abides in heav'n with love.

7. Pray for grace, repent your sin,
   Open up your eyes and weep,
   Do not let him get away
   Till he blesses you today.

8. Jesus, come, my soul's rare jewel,
   Take up lodging in my heart;
   See, I have prepared a place
   In my heart where you may rest.

9. Let your holy angel watch
   As I soundly take my rest
   That my body dull with sleep
   Will be safe from Satan's troops.

10. So my body, sack of worms,
    Will not waken with a shriek,
    Keep my husband, children, kin,
    Safe in your protective hand.

11. Be your congregation's help;
    Keep your servants of the word
    Safe so they as shepherds may
    Feed their sheep in peaceful ways.

12. Keep our king and royal house,
    Be our monarch's sword and shield,
    Let him rest himself in you,
    Give him what he needs from you.

13. That through him, and through his line,
    Streams of grace come flowing down.
    So that in the royal blood
    They give comfort through its flood.

14. May he live for many years
    Till he, filled with earth, may leave;
    Give him here all joy and peace,
    Then eternal blessedness.

15. Those who are his counselors
    Lead them in their daily deeds,
    That they truly, every one,
    Counsel what is right and meet.

16. Calm the sick, their hearts of woe,
    Those afflicted by our foe,
    Comfort all the fatherless,
    Hear the lonely widow's voice.

17. Just before my senses doze
    And before I slumber off,
    I will go into my room of rest
    Where I'll stand and think a bit.

18. It is true that one day soon
    I will sleep the long night through
    And be counted with the dead
    Sleeping in the death's dark bed.

19. All the glory I will have
    Is four planks where I'll be laid,
    Winding sheet, and little more;
    I own not a feather more.

20. Worldly things I now give up,
    Soon I'll drink a joyful cup;
    When God lets the trumpet sound,
    I will then with him be found.[78]

The hymn uses a common stanza form for daily prayers: *aabb* (7.7.7.7.), which follows not only the poetic form of a typical Lutheran evening hymn, but also includes the list of concerns conventional for this kind of piety. Beginning with an observation of the position of the sun, it uses images that go as far back into Christian hymnody as the Psalms and the early office hymns of Ambrose: The fading daylight, while lovely and peaceful, reminds us of the passing of time, and that we are growing older and closer to death. Thoughts of death force her to think of her soul, always addressed as feminine, to think of her original sin, inherited from Adam. Because of her sin, she enjoins her soul to "Rise and with prayer go up to your Father in heaven." The first thing to do is repent: "Pray for grace, and repent, open the flood of your eyes, and ask him to bless you." Then she addresses Jesus directly: "Now my Jesus, the treasure of my soul, come take lodging here this night; see that I have a resting place prepared in my heart for you." Here we see the two-way movement of the relationship: the soul rising to the Father in heaven, but also praying that Jesus will come into her heart and take up lodging, on the basis of Jesus' promise in John 14:23, that he and his Father will come to make their home with those who love him. Furthermore, she is not the one preparing the heart so that it is worthy of Christ; he must. Then, as in Luther's evening prayer, she invokes the Holy Angels to come and watch over her so her sleep-heavy body will not be hurt by Satan's troops. We see also the Lutheran concern for the neighbor/family in her concern for her family: "So that my poor sack of worms is not awakened in terror, keep watch over my husband, children, and relatives." Although her prayers for the safety of her family are conventional in the rhetoric of the evening prayer — Johan Arndt in his *Paradise Garden* evening prayer[79] prays to be free of the terrors of the night — Engelbretsdatter makes it a bit more vivid, and motherly, with her picture of awakening in terrified concern for her family.

---

78. Engelbretsdatter, "Dagen Viger og Gaar Bort," in Valkner, pp. 184-87.

79. Johan Arndt, "A Thanksgiving for the Sending of the Holy Ghost," *The Garden of Paradise: or Holy Prayers and Exercises,* 1612, tr. Anton Wilhelm Boehm (London: J. Downy, 1716), p. 201.

DAYLIGHT FADES AND DIES AWAY
(Dagen viger og gaar bort)

Dorothe Engelbretsdatter 1678
Bohemian Brethren 1566, Danish variant

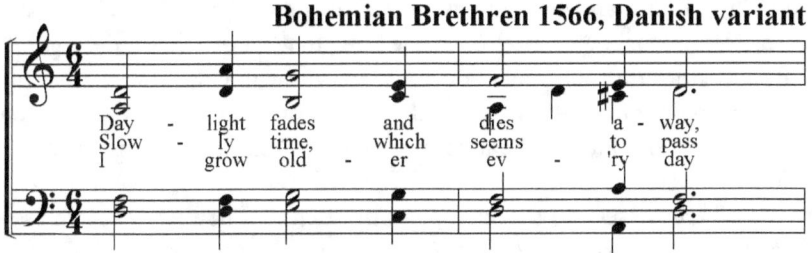

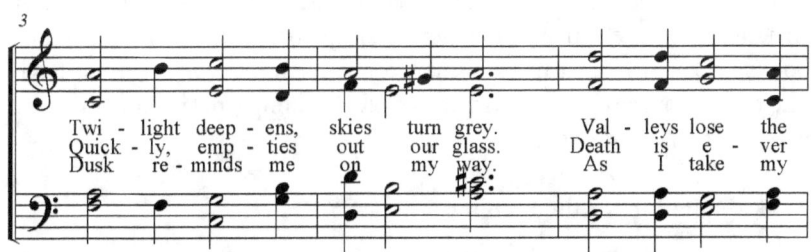

Figure 5 "Daylight Fades and Dies Away."

Another typical motif for Lutheran evening prayers is the concern for the congregation's defenders, its pastors, "the servants of the Word protect, so they as shepherds can feed the sheep in peace." Then she turns to the kingdom on the left, as Lutherans refer to the civil realm, praying for the king's house and the king as the protector of the country. Then she turns to pray for the counselors to the king, that their advice will be good. After her prayer for the king's house and the government, whom Lutherans are told to pray for in Luther's Small Catechism, she turns to the sick, the fatherless, and widows. "Be a comfort to the fatherless/and listen to the widow's voice."

Where we see the Baroque piety most clearly, however, is in the sobering, if not terrifying, reflections on getting ready for bed. "Before I slumber, I will in my resting room stand and think a bit about this all." What she thinks about is, of course, death, following almost exactly the instructions for such meditation before sleep that were in the devotional books of the day. One can see similar concerns in the work of Lewis Bayly, one of her sources, whose instructions for evening prayers are consistent with Engelbretsdatter's:

> Meditation for the Evening
>
> ... Sit down a while before thou goest to bed, and consider with thyself what memorable thing thou hast seen, heard, or read that day, more than sawest, heardest, or knewest before.
>
> Read a chapter in the same order as was prescribed in the morning; and when thou hast done, kneel down on both thy knees at the bedside, or some other convenient place in thy chamber, and lifting up thy heart, thine eyes, and hands to thy Heavenly Father, in the name and mediation of his holy Son Jesus, pray to him, if thou have the gift of prayer.[80]

He then gives the conventional form of the evening prayer, which we can see that Engelbretsdatter has followed almost exactly.

> (1) Confessing thy sins. . . . (2) Craving most earnestly, for Christ's sake, pardon and forgiveness for them. (3) Requesting the assistance of

---

80. Bayly, p. 188.

his Holy Spirit for amendment of life. (4) Giving thanks for benefits received, especially for thy preservation that day. (5) Praying for rest and protection that night. (6) Remembering the state of the church, the queen, the royal posterity, our ministers and magistrates, and our brethren visited or persecuted. (7) Lastly, commending thyself and all thine to his gracious custody.

As a help to the future sleeper, he gives an exhaustive list of what to meditate upon as one is "putting off thy clothes": (1) The coming day when you will be stripped of all your clothes in death; (2) When you see your bed, let it remind you of your grave, which is now the bed of Christ; and (3) The bed clothes are to remind you of the mold of earth, the sheets, of your winding sheet, the flap of the bed curtain, of your death.[81]

The last stanzas in Engelbretsdatter's hymn vividly pick up these instructions. Her bed reminds her of "death's dark bed." Her casket or bier will be nothing but "four planks," her "winding sheet" almost her only possession. When she is laid there, she will wait for the trumpet to sound, when she will be raised to eternal joy. Engelbretsdatter's hymn helps people pray their daily prayers. For the Baroque mind, these images are commonplace and necessary for Christian meditation.

She concludes her collection of hymns in Jesus' name, with a short poem of praise to God.

> Now in Jesus' name, here ends my book of songs,
> O praised be our God, O many thousand times;
> I trust he will not despise the offering I bear him,
> He cannot get anything more than he has given me,
> Small birds lay only tiny eggs as becomes them;
> Even if these poems are good, God's power I make famous,
> All glory be to him, he is the only one to be praised,
> So I close all things in a simple Woman's way.[82]

Almost as though she has tacked them on, she adds a few long poems called "Sighs" *(Suk),* for both morning and evening, which were conventional devotional poems like those of her friend Thomas Kingo, who had

---

81. Bayly, p. 188.
82. Engelbretsdatter, "Nu da i Jesu Naffn . . . ," in Valkner, p. 188.

just completed a collection of hymns and poems for home devotions, which included hymns for the time of day as well, with very similar poems called "Sighs." She adds a poem "Longing for Eternal Life" ("Længsel effter det Evige Liff"). In it she expresses her longing for an ending, "O that I soon will be done with this deadly suit [of clothes]," she begins. Weary of her time in the vale of tears, and eager for the mansions of joy, she longs for the time when she can enter into her resting place and sleep away all her tears:

> Receive your bride, my soul's dear friend,
> Crown her, honorable poet, the inherited queen of paradise,
> So I will travel from the earth,
> My last wish are these words,
> God give me a blessed ending,
> Let my soul be turned over to you.[83]

This is the ending of her first collection published in 1678. To it she continued to add poems and hymns, revisions of earlier hymns, and more treatments of old themes such as the Prodigal Son. Of some interest is her revision of the first poem, "To the Reader," which has many of the same images and lines in it, but now she includes figures from the Old Testament as well: Jacob, Judith, and especially Deborah, the judge over Israel, called in the Bible, a "mother in Israel."

Akslesen suggests that Petter Dass, an old-fashioned Lutheran preacher, stands outside the movement of the text and proclaims it to his people, while Engelbretsdatter puts herself in the hymn and becomes the one who is suffering shame and pangs of conscience and proclaims from the inside. Dass addresses, as a pastor, the concerns of sinners. He is concerned for those in his congregation with tortured consciences, not as one himself wracked with sorrow. Those who sing a hymn by Engelbretsdatter, however, will use her words, for example, to speak of their own preparation for the sacrament and learn also what is at stake in the sacrament for them.[84] Does she do this because as a woman she lacks the confidence to preach? Is it a womanly thing not to attack the congregation without attacking oneself? One does not find in Engelbretsdatter much of the shrinking violet; her attacks on her critics are rich with courage and colorful language.

---

83. Engelbretsdatter, "O at jeg snart maa bliffe qvit," in Valkner, p. 198.
84. Akslesen, *Norsk Barokk,* pp. 148-49.

Does this show her lack of theological and homiletical training? Deborah Tanner's scholarship on *Difference Theory* adapted into homiletics contends that men "report" as preachers and women try to gather "rapport." That Dass and Engelbretsdatter fit so conveniently into the theory is tantalizing.

Engelbretsdatter's first book is the most enduring because it is most public, intended for people to use in church and in the home. She has written these hymns to be sung in church, or at family devotions, as she clearly noted in her farewell poem to the world. From the first, as we have noted, she understood herself to be a proclaimer of the Word, if not in church, at least at home in the daily round of devotions and hymn singing. She often preaches to the assembly of believers in her hymns, but more often she gives them language, words, and phrases and concepts with which to understand how the gospel applies to them.

Offering of Tears

Because her next book, *Tear Offering (Taare-offer)*, does not contain hymns, but poems written to help people in their private devotion, I will not discuss it except to note it was written in her year of mourning ("Sørgeåret") after her husband's death in 1683. It focuses on Mary Magdalene as the ideal Christian repentant. For the most part, these are long, complicated, somewhat tedious poems in difficult rhyme and metrical schemes that cannot be analyzed fruitfully without full English translations, which are not available. Suffice it to say, they serve as a vehicle for her great grief over not only the death of her beloved husband, but also her children.

Baroque Poetry and Orthodox Lutheran Piety

Kristen Valkner, the editor of Engelbretsdatter's works, says that she has to be understood as one who used the patterns of Baroque poetry within the bounds of orthodox Lutheran piety.[85] Having thoroughly absorbed the Lutheran notion that a hymn should preach, Engelbretsdatter wrote hymns from within Lutheran orthodoxy, but like many hymn writers at the end of the period of orthodoxy, such as Paul Gerhardt, she points to

---

85. Valkner, "Forord," p. 307.

Figure 6 Dorothe's house in the Old City in Bergen today.

the coming of the Pietist movement in her work. Her obvious affection for the works of Johann Arndt, an important source for Lutheran Pietism, and Lewis Bayly, the English Puritan, gives her work accents different from the orthodox poetry of her compatriots Kingo and Dass. As we have seen, Johan Arndt's popular *True Christianity (Bücher vom wahren Christentum)* (1610) and his *Little Garden of Paradise Full of Christian Virtues (Paradiesgärtlein voller christlicher Tugenden)* (1606-1609)[86] clearly inspired many of the images and themes in her hymns.[87]

86. The first of the four books came out in 1605; after many requests from correspondents, he completed the next three, so it is hard to set a precise date.
87. Laila Akslesen, *Femfaldig festbarokk: Norske perikopedikt til kyrkjelege høgtider* (Sofiemyr, 2002), p. 14.

We can see also how closely Engelbretsdatter followed the spiritual movements of Europe in her use of Lewis Bayly (d. 1631) whose *Practice of Piety* rivaled John Bunyan's *Pilgrim's Progress* in popularity throughout Europe and America.[88] Bayly's book had been translated into Danish by Mette Giøe (d. 1666) in 1646 and, because of its popularity, went through several printings in the Kingdom of Denmark and Norway. According to Carl Trueman, Bayly's book, with its practical theological and pastoral advice on the Christian life, combined the grand themes of Christian theology with advice on how to live a daily life of faith. It, and many books like it, filled a void left after the Reformation. Trueman suggests that the spiritual movements during the period after the Reformation arose because people needed something to replace the old medieval spiritual disciplines. These new works placed an increasing emphasis on the duty each layperson had to work out his or her own salvation in fear and trembling; thus the high demand for new devotional works which poured from the pens of concerned pastors and spiritual leaders in Europe.[89] Engelbretsdatter became one of those who provided such spiritual works for people hungry for spiritual food.

Engelbretsdatter's Legacy

Today, partly because of the great fire of 1702, we have little evidence of Dorothe's life except in Bergen's Old City outdoor museum where there is a house, now a private home, in which she lived. The people of Bergen also erected a monument to her and Petter Dass in the churchyard of the cathedral. The side facing the street had a small engraving of Dass and the opposite side one of Dorothe. Not long ago, in an effort to give her more pride of place, the pillar was turned so that her name and face can be seen more easily by those walking by. Her hymns, moreover, became beloved in the memory of many, especially in the western parts of Norway. Johannes Gulbranson in an essay, "How Green Was My Childhood Valley," on his life in a Norwegian parsonage, remembers, as a young boy in the late nineteenth century, coming to Austevoll in Hordaland and hearing people

---

88. Akslesen, *Femfaldig*, p. 15.

89. Carl Trueman, "Lewis Bayly and Richard Baxter," in *The Pietist Theologians*, ed. Carter Lindberg (Malden, Mass.: Blackwell Publishing, 2005), pp. 53-54.

singing a hymn as they bore a coffin to the graveyard. It was a hymn he did not recognize and could not find in any hymnal he knew. The older people told him it was a hymn by Dorothe Engelbretsdatter, but unfortunately Gulbranson does not mention which one.[90]

Her books lay on the bookshelves of many Norwegians through the next century and became dear to many Norwegians throughout the following centuries. The Danish hymn writer Hans Adolf Brorson must have known her work, since his friend Erick Pontoppidan had included several of her hymns in his 1740 *Hymnal*, but, except for his choosing tunes from her book for his own texts, we do not know how closely he read her hymns. We do know that she was alive in the memory of Berthe Canutte Aarflot, probably her most significant successor, who used many of Engelbretsdatter's motifs and images.

As a woman close to the oral language of the people, she knew their language and found an audience among the common people, especially the women.[91] On the other hand, she never lost the consciousness of her position in society that came with her birth into the clergy class and her marriage to a pastor. The coming together of the two cultures in her poetry is perhaps one reason that her poetry became popular; she could speak both languages well. Still, while her work is held in high esteem by Norwegian scholars and those who are proud that a woman held such a high place in Norwegian letters, her actual work is not widely known to ordinary Norwegians.

We have here a unique Lutheran voice that still can speak above many of the stereotypes of the day. A product of the Baroque sensibilities of her age, she had every reason to have a dark view of this world. One can commend her hymns and spiritual poems for their richness and help for her readers in their devotions through a rigorous intellectual exercise, which Louis L. Martz says had as its aim the "right ordering of memory, understanding, and will so as to accomplish a successful experience of religious devotion."[92] This form of devotion, while it had enormous influence on the Christian imagination in its time, soon declined in the next era

---

90. Johannes Gulbranson, "Grønn var min barndoms dal," *Prestegårdsliv: Minner fra norske prestegårder*, 3d ed., ed. Elisabeth Christie (Oslo: Gyldendal, 1968), p. 14.

91. Andreas Gotlieb Rudelbach, *Om Psalme-Literaturen* (Copenhagen: Iversen, 1856), p. 341.

92. Martz, *The Poetry of Meditation*, p. 10.

when people as distinguished as Dr. Johnson reacted against it, blustering in his *Life of Waller* that "Contemplation cannot be poetical, Omnipotence cannot be exalted, Infinity cannot be amplified, and Perfection cannot be improved."[93] This change in fashion, as much as anything, has kept her out of currency as a hymn writer today.

Dorothe Engelbretsdatter has attracted the interest of current Scandinavian feminists because she was the first great woman writer in Norway, and a very impressive first at that. They like her because she was the first woman poet but find her piety, to say nothing of her baroque poetic style, difficult to swallow. Critics will search through her work for evidence of oppression, of which there is a good plenty, but that search misses her gift as a poet. Her piety, on the other hand, repels even modern Christians, who cannot understand her self-abnegation and bridal mysticism. In order to fully receive her work, we must see all of those parts to her work.

The genius of Dorothe Engelbretsdatter's work may be precisely because she was a woman who knew the worlds of both men and women, and whose language and work spoke to both worlds. High-born poets, clergy, and nobility greeted her with high praise and poetic encomia that impress us with their true admiration. On the other hand, the people walking with the coffin in Austevoll, who knew her hymns by heart, paid the most enduring tribute to her.

Dorothe Engelbretsdatter's Works in Later Hymnals

There is a brief bit of history to tell about Engelbretsdatter's survival in the memory of the Norwegian church. Erick Pontoppidan (1698-1764), who became Bishop of Bergen in 1748, knew about her before he arrived, since he had already chosen two of her hymns for his 1740 *New Hymnal*, now known as Pontoppidan's *Hymnal*: "Daylight Fades and Flies Away" ("Dagen viger og gaar bort") and "When I Behold My Mistakes" ("Naar jeg mine feil vil skue"). While these are not her most typical hymns, they could be sung by a congregation, after a couple of revisions, which change her reference to herself as a woman, to more "generic" language. For example, Pontoppidan changed her tenth stanza

---

93. Samuel Johnson, "Life of Waller," *Lives of the English Poets* (London, 1781), pp. 173-74.

Keep my husband, children, kin,
Safe in your protective hand.

Keep my friends and all my kin
Safe in your protective hand.

None of her hymns were included in the later Dano-Norwegian hymnal of 1788, edited by Guldberg, Høegh, and Boye, nor in the *Evangelical Christian Hymnal* of 1798-99. She was not included in an official Danish or Norwegian hymnal until Magnus Brostrup Landstad, Norway's first hymnbook compiler, chose to include four of her hymns in his hymnal of 1869. Landstad wrote that "She had not previously found entry into our church hymnals, but she has in any case found entrance into the homes and hearts among our people, which is remarkable, and gives her the right to be sung now in church."[94] Landstad, by his assignment, and also by his own nationalistic predilections, was eager to include the work of Norwegian hymn writers such as Dass and Engelbretsdatter because there were so few other Norwegian hymn writers of any stature besides them. By including Engelbretsdatter's hymns, also revised so they were no longer in a woman's voice, and somewhat modernized, Landstad kept true to the nationalism of the time in Norway while showing the problem associated with her work: too old-fashioned and less universal because it was in a woman's voice. The other great compiler of a Norwegian hymnal at that time, Andreas Hauge, son of the great revivalist Hans Nielsen Hauge, also included four of her hymns, similarly revised.

Pastor Ulrik Vilhelm Koren, of Washington Prairie, Iowa, the compiler of the Norwegian Synod's hymnal, *Synodens Salmebog* (1874), included her hymn "Daylight Fades and Dies Away" ("Dagen viger og gaar bort"). Koren had grown up in Bergen and had no doubt heard of her work and seen her home in the city. The men, however, who worked to put the Norwegian hymnic tradition into English had no apparent interest in including her work, since they failed to translate any of her hymns. It is only with the revision of the *Lutheran Hymnary* (1996) by a small Norwegian Lutheran church in America, the Evangelical Lutheran Synod, based in Mankato, Minnesota, that she appears for the first time in an English-

---

94. Landstad, *Om Salmebogen: En Redgjørelse* (Christiania: Jacob Dybwad, 1862), p. 55.

language Lutheran hymnal in a translation that includes only seven of the original sixteen stanzas of her "When Earth with All Its Joys Defeats Me" ("Om verden med sin Glæde sviger"). In Norway and Norwegian hymnals, interest in her has grown, but her work is confined to two hymns, "Dagen Viger" and "Om Verden," both edited to include fewer than half of the original stanzas. The revisions in themselves show the issues the contemporary church has with her work, removing what moderns might regard as sick self-understandings and too much talk of heaven, especially the image of the reunion of the soul with its Bridegroom. The little we have of her is from edited versions by nineteenth-century hymnbook compilers now "improved" upon by their twentieth-century editors.

But she has not utterly disappeared. Recently, when a contemporary Danish organist, Jesper Topp, was looking for a way to memorialize his friend Peter Møller, another organist who had died an untimely death, he chose to begin and end his compact disk recording with two versions of Engelbretsdatter's hymn "Daylight Fades."[95] It should not surprise us that only Engelbretsdatter's poetry, in all its baroque sensibilities, seemed to go deep enough to express the grief that Topp felt. Dorothe Engelbretsdatter continues to speak to people whose lives are deeply tinged with loss and sorrow.

---

95. Janne Solvang and Jesper Topp, *Dagen Viger: In Memoriam Peter Møller and Jesper Madsen* (Classico 429), October 1, 2003.

CHAPTER 2

Birgitte Hertz Boye (1742-1824)
Falling Star

Until recently, for nearly two hundred years, every Christmas, Easter, and Pentecost, usually before the Gospel reading for the day, Norwegian and Norwegian American congregations would stand to sing a "festival" hymn *(høytidsvers)*. For Christmas it would be "Rejoice, Rejoice, This Happy Morn" ("Os er i Dag en Frelser fød"), for Easter, "He Is Arisen, Glorious Word" ("Han er opstanden, store Bud"), and for Pentecost "O Light of God's Most Wondrous Love" ("O! Lue fra Guds-Kierlighed").[1] Written by the Danish hymn writer Birgitte Cathrine Boye (1742-1824), these hymns became so closely knit to the three major church festivals in the minds of the people that long after the old liturgy had changed, pastors who knew

---

1. This one hymn appears in the *Lutheran Hymnary* (1912) in a translation by George T. Rygh.

> O Light of God's most wondrous love,
> Who dost our darkness brighten,
> Shed on Thy Church from heaven above,
> Our eye of faith enlighten!
> As in Thy light we gather here,
> Show us that Christ's own promise clear
> Is Yea and Amen ever,
> O risen and ascended Lord,
> We wait fulfillment of Thy word:
> O bless us with Thy favor.

little of the origin of the tradition continued it.[2] The tradition of linking specific hymns to every Sunday and lesson of the church year had begun with Kingo's hymnal of 1699, and it continued through every Dano-Norwegian hymnal long into the twentieth century.

Boye's hymns became the solemn hymns for these festival Sundays after the 1783 publication of the Dano-Norwegian *Hymnal or a Collection of Old and New Hymns to God's Glory and the Edification of His Congregation (Psalmbog eller en Samling af gamle og nye Psalmer, til Guds Ære og hans Menigheds Opbyggelse)*, approved by the Danish court in 1778, and otherwise known as the Guldberg Hymnal. In many ways, it was Boye's hymnal. She had worked on the editorial committee and contributed over one hundred forty original hymns and translations. Little remarked on today, when hymnbook editors try to rediscover hymns by women, Boye's work ranks among the first major contributions by a woman to a Lutheran hymnal, perhaps the most significant work by a woman on a Lutheran hymnal until the American Lutheran Harriet Krauth Spaeth's (1845-1925) editing of the 1872 version of *Church Book with Music*. As fast as Boye's star rose, however, it also plummeted. A mere twenty years later, the next Danish hymnal of 1798, *The Evangelical Christian Hymnal (Evangelisk Kristelig Psalmebog)* contained only twenty-eight of her hymns. Magnus Brostrup Landstad (1802-1880), the first compiler of a Norwegian hymnal, included nineteen of her hymns in his 1869 hymnal, which preserved her fame among Norwegians; in Denmark, however, only one hymn by Boye survives today. The current Norwegian hymnal (1985) contains the three festival hymns named above, plus her translation of a hymn by Johan J. Rambach (1693-1735), "Ich bin in Christum eingesenkt" ("Jeg er frelst og dyrekjøbt"). The *Lutheran Book of Worship* retained Boye's Christmas and Easter verses, but they were dropped in the current hymnal of the ELCA, *Evangelical Lutheran Worship* (2007).

The question remains: How was it that a woman from a relatively low station in eighteenth-century Denmark could have assumed such an important place in the ritual life and piety of both Danes and Norwegians and then be almost completely forgotten, and only remembered, if at all, for her pompous language and what contemporary Danes regard as her laughable style? The story gives us an interesting glimpse into the making

---

2. My own father, Pastor Harald Grindal, followed this custom until the end of his ministry in 1989.

Figure 1 A portrait of Birgitte Hertz Boye, National Portrait Gallery, Royal Library, Copenhagen.

of hymnals, the life and times of the Enlightenment in Denmark, and how that era is viewed in later Lutheran history, especially as regards women and hymnody.

Her Life

Birgitte Cathrine Jensen Hertz Boye was born March 7, 1742, in Gentofte, today a prosperous suburb northwest of Copenhagen. Her father, Jens Johansen (1711-1772?), was a bailiff, or steward, at Jægersborg, the king's hunting park north of Copenhagen, along the eastern coast of Denmark, where he would later become the royal hunting constable. Her mother was Dorothea Henriksdatter (1712-1772?). The few sources we have tell us that her parents raised Birgitte to be a devout woman, "sow[ing] a seed of godliness in her heart which was to be her comfort in her later sorrows in life."[3] While we cannot tell, because we are not told, what kind of practices her parents used to instill the faith in the young girl, we can infer from her first biographer, her contemporary, Hans Jørgen Birch, that she was instructed in Bishop Erick Pontoppidan's (1698-1764) *Truth unto Godliness: A simple and where possible short, though sufficient, Explanation of the blessed Martin Luther's Small Catechism containing all that which those who would be blessed have need to know and do (Sandhed til Gudfrytgtihed)*. Pontoppidan's *Explanation (Forklaring)*, as it came to be known, had been authorized in 1738 by King Christian VI (1730-1746) to be used for the instruction of all confirmands throughout the Twin Kingdoms of Denmark and Norway.[4] Pontoppidan, a beloved pastor, scholar, Bishop of Bergen, and chancellor of the University of Copenhagen, was a major force in the Dano-Norwegian church of the eighteenth century. Pontoppidan's *Explanation* would have most likely been the text used to instruct the young Birgitte in the Christian faith. Pontoppian had also completed a hymnal in

---

3. Hans Jørgen Birch, *Billedgallerie for Fruentimmer, indeholdende levnetsbeskrivelser over berømte og lærde danske, norske og udenlandske Fruentimmere*, vol. 1 (Copenhagen: S. Poulsens Forlag, 1793), p. 202.

4. Erick Pontoppidan, *Sandhed til Gudfrygtighed Udi En eenfoldig og efter Muelighed kort, dog tilstrekkelig Forklaring Over Sal. Doct. Mart. Luthers Liden Catechismo, Indeholdende alt det, som den, der vil blive salig, har behov, at vide og giøre paa Kongel. Allernaadigste Befaling. Til almindelig Brug* (Copenhagen: Kongelig Weysenhuses Forlag, Risel, 1737).

1740, *The New Hymnal (Den Nye forordnede Psalme-Bog)*, which was revised and published in 1742, *Selections from the New Revised Hymnal (Udtog af den Nye forordnede Psalme-Bog)*, the year of Birgitte's birth. Using Kingo's hymnal as its core, Pontoppidan included eighty-seven hymns, twenty-four of them original, by Hans Adolf Brorson (1694-1764), the major poet of pietism in Denmark.

The great Danish hymns by Kingo, Brorson, and Sthen, along with Scripture and the Small Catechism were most likely the resources Birgitte's parents used as they taught her the faith. The decade of Birgitte's birth was known as the period of "State Pietism" or "Official Pietism" because it was the policy of the state to urge pietism and its practices on the people. Both King Christian VI and his wife, Queen Sophie Magdalene, worked to advance this movement as it swept north from Halle, Germany. The movement, born in 1675 with the publication of the pamphlet *Pia Desideria (Pious Desires)* by Philip Jakob Spener (1635-1705), a pastor in Frankfurt, Germany, recommended the reform of the church through small groups (conventicles) gathering for prayer, Bible study, and fellowship. The great leader of the expansion of the movement was August Hermann Francke (1663-1727), the head of the Halle school and institute, founded in 1694. He had established an orphanage, printing press, mission school, university, and library from which his disciples went forth to Europe, America, Greenland, and India, to preach the gospel. Even the bigamist Danish King Frederick IV (1699-1730) supported the movement. In 1705 he had worked together with Francke and the University of Halle to send Bartholomaeus Ziegenbalg (1682-1719) and Heinrich Plüttschau (1678-1747) as missionaries to Tranquebar, thus winning the moniker, the Mission King.

Pietism's most effective evangelizer, after the seminarians who attended Halle University, was the hymnal compiled by Johan Anastasius Freylinghausen (1670-1739), the *Geistreiches Gesangbuch* (1704, 1715, and 1741), whose new hymns and melodies changed hymnody in all the Lutheran countries. One of the chief exponents of Freylinghausen in the Danish and Norwegian kingdoms was Hans Adolf Brorson, the gifted poet and hymn writer from Jutland. He had started translating the hymns in the Freylinghausen hymnal into Danish while he was the third Danish pastor at the Christ Church of Tønder, in Jutland, a few miles north of the current German border. The senior pastor at the church, Johann Schrader (1684-1737), who ministered to the German speakers there, had compiled his own hymnal, *The Tønder Songbook (Das Tønderische Gesangbuch)*, in 1731 for use with the German speakers in the congregation.[5] Since he had studied in Halle, the hymnal was filled with hymns from the Freylinghausen hymnal.

In 1732, after several years of working with Schrader, Brorson published a small collection of his own Danish hymns and some translations from Freylinghausen, among them his most popular Christmas hymns, such as "Thy Little Ones, Dear Lord, Are We," for use among the Danish speakers, *Troens Rare Klenodie (The Rare Treasury of Faith)*. This small volume grew to be a full-blown collection of hymns, published in 1739, many of them translations of the German hymns in the Freylinghausen hymnal. It contained not only hymns for the church year, especially Christmas hymns, but also hymns according to the Order of Salvation *(ordo salutis)*, hymns that taught and preached according to the various steps in the Christian life: *vocatio, illuminatio, conversio, regeneratio, justificatio,* and *renovatio.*

Pious King Christian VI, who instituted compulsory confirmation instruction for all children in the two kingdoms in 1736 and passed a series of laws intended to keep Sunday holy, liked Brorson's hymns. After hearing Brorson preach at the court, the king appointed him Bishop of Ribe in 1741, which effectively ended Brorson's poetic endeavors until his final illness, when, unbeknownst to his friends and family, he wrote a large collection of hymns published the year after his death, called *Svane Sang,* or *Swan Songs,* which included some of his most beloved hymns, "Behold a Host" ("Den store hvide Flok"), "I See Thee Standing, Lamb of God" ("Jeg seer dig, Du Guds Lam"), and "O How Lovely You Are" ("Hvad est du dog skiøn"). Birgitte, as a "God-fearing" young woman, was surrounded by these works throughout her early life.

From the one picture of her that we have today, as an older woman, we can surmise that Birgitte was probably a beautiful and desirable young woman. Birch (1750-1795), who probably knew her, wrote that she had several suitors already by the time she was thirteen when she chose Herman Michelsen Hertz (c. 1735-1775), a royal hunter, to be her husband. She did not marry, however, until she was nineteen, six years after her engagement, on September 23, 1763. During her engagement, while she was still at home, we can assume that Birgitte received an education that prepared her to be a

---

5. Its full name was *Vollständiges Gesangbuch in einer Sammlung alter und neuer Geistreichen Lieder, der Gemeinde Gottes zu Tondern zur Beförderung der Andacht bey dem öffentlichen Gottes-Dienst und besondern Hauss-Ubung gewidmet.*

good housewife and something of a lady. We know that she was required by law to learn to read and to know Pontoppidan's *Explanation of Luther's Catechism*. Whatever else her education included, we can only guess, based on the conventions of the day. Birch, in his 1793 collection of biographies of famous ladies in the Twin Kingdoms, *Women (Fruentimmer)*, described the kind of education he thought it was proper for young girls to receive in order to be fine ladies and managers of the household in the upper classes of the two countries.[6] Although it was written some thirty years after Birgitte's marriage, Birch's curriculum does not represent a major change in what young women might be expected to be taught at home, except for styles and modes of thinking. Dorothe Engelbretsdatter, a century before, had probably received an education similar to what Birch recommended.

While Birch noted that most important for a young lady's education was that she be shaped to have a character that knew true honor, gratitude, and love as the greatest virtues, still, in the very same paragraph of this high-toned set of requirements, he urged that young women receive instruction in both German and French, perhaps so they would be able to read moral works in those languages.[7] He did not mention they should learn English, although he did recommend that young ladies read the long epistolary novel *Clarissa* (1747) by English author Samuel Richardson (1689-1761) because it taught young women much about the world, especially its depravity. Birch suggested the novel revealed this depravity in a way that did not endanger the character of its young women readers.[8] By the time she turned fourteen, Birch recommended, a young woman could be taught how to cook, bake, preserve foods, and everything else that is appropriate for her to learn about keeping house. Along with that, she should become competent in the typically female accomplishments of sewing, knitting, tatting (the making of lace), embroidery, and other skills with the needle. Besides that, she should be able to play the clavier in order to spend her leisure hours profitably. Performing popular dramas would also help the young woman learn about the ways of the world, and, like the clavier, provide amusement for others. This is a very short list of the exhaustive recommendations Birch makes for the education of a young woman in his preface. We can assume Birgitte took the six years of her engagement to

6. Birch, p. 202.
7. Birch, p. v.
8. Birch, p. vi.

learn many of these skills, which she apparently put to good use through the rest of her life.

When she married Hertz, the young couple moved to Ørslev, just north of Vordingborg, a small and lovely village some seventy-five miles south of Copenhagen, on the southeastern coast of Zealand, where he had been named steward of the forest. This was an area where many manor houses had been built, so the young couple would have had many acquaintances from the court and other people of condition who also knew the language of Europe. It was a sophisticated community in which Birgitte and her husband, as an official of the crown, moved easily. Despite the fact that over the next five years Birgitte had four children, she managed, with the help of servants, and very likely a governess and tutor, to educate the young children, especially the boys, in the house. Birch, however, notes with admiration that she still found the time to read and study, especially German, French, and English. We have good evidence that she could read the greatest poets of the day in their original tongues. She and her husband lived a life common to the gentry of the time, enjoying literature, music, and putting on small plays in their parlors for the entertainment and edification of the family and neighbors.[9] She probably knew some German since, at the time, German was the language of the elites in Copenhagen, especially the court. Anders Malling (1896-1981), author of the most authoritative work on Danish hymnody in the twentieth century, wrote in his biographical entry on Birgitte, that her studies were her "secret" as she would take the dictionaries and grammars of these languages from their hiding places and study them on her own.[10] For reasons we are not privy to, she set herself to the task of learning all three languages well enough to be able to read and translate the best poetry of the time into Danish. We can read in these reports that the young woman had obviously developed somewhere a great thirst for knowledge, especially for literature.

Although we can assume that Birgitte's early influences, religiously speaking, were shaped by Pietism, by the time of her adolescence, as a reader with an obviously lively curiosity, she would have picked up the texts and ideas of the Enlightenment that were swirling around Europe,

---

9. For this insight I am indebted to John R. Christiansen, Professor Emeritus of History of Luther College.

10. Anders Malling, *Dansk Salme Historie*, vol. 6, *Digterne A-K* (Copenhaven: J. H. Schultz Forlag, 1971), p. 76.

and even Denmark, at the time. Ludvig Holberg (1684-1754), the first great dramatist of the Twin Kingdoms, and the Dano-Norwegian *philosophe* who had studied in England, Italy, France, Germany, and Holland, lived and taught in Copenhagen until his death. Thought by some to be second only to Voltaire in his learning and writing in Europe, his life spanned both the time of Official State Pietism and the beginnings of the Enlightenment in Denmark. Just when Pietism in Denmark had reached its apex, King Christian VI died in 1746. With the accession of his son, Frederick V (1746-1766), things changed markedly: the theaters which had been closed, to Holberg's great joy, were now reopened, and the old piety began to fade as the influence of the Enlightenment, and the popular and genial new king, gained hegemony. Erick Pontoppidan, whose earlier works had been the stuff of official state church Pietism, wrote in 1757 in his book of pastoral care that "in my youth most believed everything that the pastor said, but now people hardly believe what God has said, indeed, people question whether God has spoken to people other than through the light of nature, or sound reason."[11] H. Blom Svendsen in his work on Norwegian hymnody said that when Brorson and Pontoppidan were laid in their graves, in 1764, it was as if another time with new spiritual convictions stood beside their coffins. A new spirit, like a cold wind, had swept over the land like a tidal wave.[12]

One of the chief exponents of the Enlightenment in Denmark was Johann Friedrich Struensee (1737-1772), the German doctor from Slesvig to whom the next king, Christian VII (1749-1808), took a liking during his Grand Tour of Europe. Christian VII, who had a dissolute and wild youth, suffered from schizophrenia, caused, some think, by his brutal rearing. The shrewd doctor soon learned how to soothe the young king's troubled mind.[13] When he was only seventeen, shortly after his accession to the throne in 1766, Christian VII had been forced to marry the even younger Caroline Mathilda (1751-1775), sister of King George II of England, with whom he had one child, who later became Frederick VI. While accompanying the young king on the grand tour (1767-1768), where he met other

---

11. Erick Pontoppidan, *Collegium pastorale practicum*, 1757, pp. 42-43.

12. H. Blom Svendsen, *Norsk Salmesang: Arven fra gammel tid*, vol. I, *Bibliotheca Norvegiæ Sacræ* VIII (Bergen: Lunde & Co., 1935), p. 240.

13. For a fictional treatment of this relationship read the novel by Swedish author Per Olof Enquist, *The Royal Physician's Visit* (New York: Washington Square Press, 2002).

European royalty and advocates of the Enlightenment, Struensee was urged by some of the *philosophes* to bring the Enlightenment to Denmark. Struensee used every opportunity, as close advisor to the mad king, to urge the reform of Danish law and life, in an attempt to advance the Age of Enlightenment in Denmark.

When he became regent of Denmark in 1770, Struensee used his newly acquired powers to effect many reforms. A brilliant man with apparently little political sense, he took over the Danish court, appointing himself to be the State Cabinet Minister who could issue orders that the King, lost in his own world, only needed to sign, which he did because he loved and trusted Struensee. Very quickly Struensee began issuing cabinet orders that transformed Danish society and government. He built a civil service organization based on qualifications, reduced the influence of large landowners, created freedom of the press, abolished torture while prisoners were in jail, and tried to improve the situation for serfs, among many other reforms. All agree he did these things too quickly, without much awareness of the danger he was in, especially after he began an affair with the Queen, lonely and abandoned by her mad husband. After the Queen bore their child, in January of 1772, Struensee, hated by many in the court, suffered a palace coup led by the Dowager Queen Juliane Marie; Crown Prince Frederik, son of Caroline Mathilde; and the theologian and professor of rhetoric, Ove Høegh-Guldberg (1731-1808), who was to become the Cabinet Secretary and virtual head of the new government. Struensee and his colleague Enevold Brandt were pronounced guilty of *lese-majesty* (violating the dignity of the king,) and poor King Christian VII was forced to sign Struensee's death sentence, brutal even by the standards of the day, and then watch while Struensee had his right hand cut off, then his head, after which his body was cut into pieces and put on wheels and crushed. Guldberg then began to rule the kingdom. This cruel series of events, grisly as they were, however, worked to the advantage of Birgitte, who would benefit from the patronage of Guldberg.

A year later, in 1773, Guldberg began the process of getting approval to prepare a new official hymnal for the kingdom, one whose language would not be as old-fashioned as Kingo's, now almost one hundred years old, and not as Pietistic as Pontoppidan's *Hymnal* (1740). The movement toward a new, more enlightened hymnal had been building from the 1750s. Not long after the establishment of the Belletristic Society *(Selskabet for de skiønne Videnskabers Forfremmelse)* in 1751, it began agitating for a revision of the old hymnal by searching for a poet who could write "sacred poesy." Fashions had changed, even musically. No longer was the old-fashioned lute or "harp" of Brorson or Kingo considered worthy for sacred poetry. What was needed was the shepherd's flute, a more contemporary and pastoral instrument, popular in the eighteenth century. These ideas were now the rage in Copenhagen, coming as they did from Germany and the movement to create a German high style for German poetry being advanced by the work of Friedrich Gottlieb Klopstock (1724-1793), who tried to purify German poetry for German ears. To do this he "modified the classic models [of poetry] by using free rhythms, grand abstract subjects, with a heavy influence from the Lutheran psalm [hymn]."[14] Klopstock had come to be an influential figure in Danish letters because in 1751, Count Johan Hartvig Ernst Bernstorff (1712-1772), an old friend of Klopstock, and at the time Foreign Minister, recommended that King Frederick V invite Klopstock to come to Copenhagen, with an annuity of four hundred talers, where he could finish his epic *Messias*. Klopstock accepted the offer. On his way to Copenhagen, at a stop in Hamburg, he met Margareta (Meta) Möller (the "Cidli" of his odes), an enthusiastic admirer of his poetry. They married in 1754. After she died, only four years after their marriage, a grief-stricken Klopstock published her work, *A Legacy of Works by Margareta Klopstock (Hinterlassene Werke von Margareta Klopstock)* (1759), in which she revealed, in not very great poetry, her sensitivity and deep piety. Without a doubt, the young Birgitte, studying languages and literature in Vordingborg, knew of this poetry by a woman and of Klopstock's work as well.

After the death of his wife, a blow to his spirit, Klopstock produced less and less. Although he remained in Copenhagen as a literary force, his work turned more and more to ideas about how to create a truly Germanic literature that used the ancient myths of Nordic mythology much as the ancient Greeks and Romans had used their myths to create a great literature. He still continued to live and work at Copenhagen and, with Heinrich Wilhelm von Gerstenberg, turned his attention to northern mythology. His greatest legacy, however, was his grand epic, *The Messiah (Messias)* (1748-1773), the literary rage of Birgitte's adolescence, so one should not be surprised that she adopted his forms and styles as she took up her pen to

---

14. Stephen F. Fogle, "Ode," *Princeton Encylopedia of Poetry and Poetics,* ed. Alex Preminger, Frank J. Warnke, and O. B. Hardison Jr. (Princeton: Princeton University Press, 1972), p. 586.

Figure 2 Friedrich Klopstock, whose poetry inspired a young Birgitte.

write contemporary hymnody for the day, even though by the time she was writing her first hymns, Klopstock's chief exponent in Denmark, Bernstorff (1712-1772), had lost his job to Struensee.

In December of 1761, an article appeared in one of the weekly journals of Copenhagen, *The Patriotic Spectator (Den patriotiske Tilskuer)*, on the improvement of church song. Revising the old hymns would help make religion "more reputable and agreeable to the people," which would create more propriety and joy in the official gatherings of the church.[15] Seven years later, Peder Olrog (1741-1788), a leading writer of the day, wrote a similar article, "Treatise on What Hymnody Needs" ("Afhandling om Psalmernes Fornødenhed"), in which he complained about the laughable language in the old hymns. He recommended the ideas about hymnody that Klopstock had developed and had found in German hymns by writers such as Christian Furchtegott Gellert (1715-1769), Extraordinary Professor of Philosophy at Leipzig. Gellert, teacher to both Goethe and Lessing, stood at the turning point between Pietism and the Enlightenment, and his hymns, while deeply pious, have, largely, been considered, like Birgitte's, too didactic and intellectual to suit any taste but that of their own generation and the interests of those compiling the Guldberg hymnal. They fit the taste and sense of the day. Only one of his hymns survives in the *Lutheran Book of Worship*, "Jesus Lives! The Victory's Won!"

With the collapse of Pietism, Danish church leaders had reason to be anxious about the state of the church. Its rapid decline, evidenced by a drop in attendance at church, made church leaders eager to remedy the situation with something that might appeal to the modern intellectuals and the spirit of their age. Not surprisingly, they turned to the worship and hymnody of the day. Not only were the hymns to be updated and changed to fit with contemporary thought, but preaching also needed to use language that fit the spirit of the day, with its high styled, rhetorical figures and vivid illustrations. Eloquence became the mark of a great preacher, whether it was the gospel or not. Not surprisingly, many thought the worship services needed to be updated and modernized as well, to fit with the spirit of the age. Something needed to be done. Christian Bastholm (1740-1819), a Danish pastor, published a famous book on the subject in 1785, only a bit more than a year after the Guldberg hymnal finally appeared, *Proposal for an Improved Plan for Public Worship (Forsøg til en forbedred*

---

15. Svendsen, p. 241.

Plan i den udvortes Gudstieneste). Among his proposals were to shorten the service by not singing so many hymns and not to include all of the elements of the traditional Lutheran service. This was to meet with great opposition from the orthodox contingent of the Dano-Norwegian church, chief among them Johan Nordahl Brun (1745-1816), Bishop of Bergen, who wrote a fiery reply to the very idea of changing the services to meet with current taste.

In the midst of this cultural uproar, the decline of attendance in church, and the conviction and execution of Struensee, Guldberg, now the state and home secretary, himself a theologian, began making plans for a new hymnal. The learned Belletristic Society issued an invitation asking whoever had the "call and desire" to contribute to the writing of "sacred poetry" to send in at least ten trial hymns written to known melodies. Some of Denmark's most famous poets of the day, including Peder Olrog and Jakob Johan Lund (1725-1798), known for his translations of classical poetry, biblical texts, and later, hymn texts, entered the contest, but Birgitte, a virtual unknown, especially in regards to her poetic gifts, took the prize. She had sent in twenty original hymns, the first ten meditations on Psalm 104, and the last ten on Jesus, focused most closely on Luke 9, especially the transfiguration, which the Enlightenment mind liked, but she also did treat other scenes in Jesus' life. All but one would be included in the Guldberg hymnal. Clearly written from the point of view of the new intellectual movements in Europe, these hymns were also in the more elevated and pompous style of the day. Her themes were typical Enlightenment themes: Creation, especially the new cosmology, and Jesus as a peerless example of the Christian life. For her the God of the Old Testament was to be known as the Creator whose great power and wisdom could be read clearly in nature. Malling suggests that her hymns on creation and the creator, which sound something like the hymns of Joseph Addison in English, are more affected by the Enlightenment than were the hymns on New Testament themes, such as Jesus' life and work, where the early imprint of the Pietist works of Brorson and Pontoppidan would have remained.[16]

It is difficult, if not impossible, to convey in English the high, elevated, pompous style and diction Boye used in her hymns. We can, however, see from her subject matter how she attempted to fit her hymnody with the Co-

---

16. Malling, p. 76.

pernican revolution and be "modern." The language and content of one of her most famous hymns, however, make modern Danes laugh.

1. Prodigious earth! A crowded dwelling.
   What holds you as you turn around?
   You tumble around, but tumble calmly,
   With your innumerable kin,
   Can anyone with any ease
   Find out how much you weigh?[17]

This new voice and these early hymns struck Guldberg and others as just the thing for the day, sounding as they did like a new voice in the hymnody of Denmark. They were attractive to her patron, Guldberg, for their pathetic — descriptive — style of the day, something like that of the minor English poet John Wolcot (1738-1819). This example from Wolcot's ode to the English painter Turner may illustrate the style as well as anything.

To Turner

The bard maketh a bow to the genius of Mr. Turner, and expresseth wonder at the absence of his landscapes:

Turner, whatever strikes thy mind
Is painted well, and well design'd;
Thy rural scenes our plaudit must obtain.
   Though Nature (and where lies the harm?)
   Has given thee not a giant *form*,
The dame has plac'd the giant in thy *brain*.

Say, why are not thy landscapes here —
Landscapes where truth and taste appear;
That prove thy pencil's power, and grasp of mind?
   Who nobly canst exalt thine head,
   Who, like Eclipse, canst take the lead,
And leave with ease their rivals far behind.

---

17. "Uhyre Jord! Opfyldte Boelig," Guldberg's Hymnal, no. 62.

This high style had been very popular in English poetry at about the same time as Birgitte was learning to read English. Many of the English poets she had studied had written odes. John Milton (1608-1674) wrote his ode "On the Morning of Christ's Nativity," and John Dryden (1631-1700) showed, with his ode "Alexander's Feast," that it was possible to write successfully in this form and style in imitation of their classical originators like Pindar. Birgitte would have learned as she was reading English literature that such style was to be admired.

In contrast to her psalms, Hertz's Jesus hymns, however, sound more conventionally orthodox or Pietistic, although like her mentor Klopstock, she appears to be more attracted to the glory of Christ, as her favorite scenes in Jesus' life tend to be those from the Epiphany season, Christ's transfiguration, and the Ascension. The themes of the cosmic Christ, shining with light, and his connections to God's creation and heavenly kingdom, are brightest in her work. This was also in line with Klopstock's ideas about the high style. In his long epic, *The Messiah*, he stressed more of Christ's divinity than his humanity.[18] The following rough translation of one of her Transfiguration hymns gives a sense of her involvement with the new thinking of the Enlightenment:

1. While divinity's gleaming plays
   Upon the mountain top,
   Like heaven's representatives
   They woke up,
   The highest three
   Of God's apostle's flock
   Who later would be witnesses
   In Gethsemane.[19]

One can hear in this hymn layers of the past, especially as she picks up themes of the penitential piety of both Dorothe Engelbretsdatter and Hans Adolf Brorson. Like them she puts herself at the Transfiguration and identifies with Peter, who wants to remain on the mountain. How Jesus treated the one with whom she identified would be the way he would treat her for

---

18. Just Bing, "Klopstock og den Klopstockske Kreds i Danmark," *For Kirke og Kultur*, ed. Christopher Bruun and Thorvald Klaveness, vol. iv (Christiania: 1897), p. 591.

19. "Mens Guddoms Straale Spiller," *Guldberg*, no. 137.

her similar sin. This causes her to pray, as they did, that God would overlook her failures as he had those of the disciples in order to be her comfort.

> 7. While eternity's Father
> has witnessed to his Son
> Whom the witnesses abandoned
> In the shadows of prayer.
> When in my wretched breast
> The highest thoughts arise
> O, may I gladly find
> What God for me desires.
>
> 8. O spokesman! My comforter!
> Who between the night and day
> In life's evening speaks,
> Speak of God's kindness!
> My heart's penetrator,
> Speak when my deaf ears
> Can no more hear
> In my ice cold bed.[20]

All ten of these hymns on the life of Jesus were to make it into Guldberg's hymnal some five years later.

Winning the prize for these texts encouraged the young woman to continue her work. Difficulties, however, began to overwhelm the family. Her husband's job as manager of the forest was imperiled by Struensee's decision to turn over some public lands to private ownership. Showing her pluck, the young woman went to Copenhagen to appeal to the new prime minister, Ove Høegh-Guldberg, for economic support, especially for the education of her two sons, Christian Hertz (1765-1810) and Jens Michael Hertz (1766-1825), who without their father's support would have been cast into extreme poverty with no chance for an education. Guldberg took pity on her and got the crown prince, Frederik, to finance the schooling of her two sons. While making the appeal on behalf of her sons to Guldberg, Birgitte showed him her translation of the English poet Edward Young's (1683-1765) paraphrase of the Book of Job, done in 1719. That she chose

20. *Guldberg*, no. 137.

Young shows her awareness of the literary scene and English literature, the language with which she was least familiar. Young had been a celebrity in Europe for his *Night Thoughts, or The Complaint, and the Consolation; or, Night Thoughts* (1742-1745), which the English poet and painter William Blake illustrated. Although Young contributed some few quotable maxims to the English language, this work in heroic couplets is of dubious worth.

Not long after this, Birgitte's husband died in 1775 of dropsy, what we today would call edema, a symptom of another disease, probably heart or kidney failure. This left her penniless and helpless before her husband's creditors. Birgitte's pluck came to her rescue as she continued to work on her hymnody, receiving sponsorship from Guldberg, who continued to support her with help from the crown prince and the Queen Dowager. Guldberg saw that Birgitte would be a worthy colleague in the work on the new hymnal he and Bishop Ludvig Harboe (1709-1783) were preparing in secret. Harboe, Bishop of Zealand, where Copenhagen is situated, was a competent administrator whom the Danish authorities highly valued. He had helped to bring order to the Icelandic church and had served as Bishop of Trondheim from 1746 until 1748, when he was called back to Copenhagen as assistant to Bishop Peder Hersleb, one of the last of the Pietist leaders of the Danish church. Appointed Bishop of Zealand in 1757, he named his son-in-law, Nicolai Endinger Balle (1744-1816), as his assistant. Born in Jutland, Harboe had studied in Hamburg, and later Rostock, Wittenberg, and Jena, where he became a learned student of church history, especially the Danish church. As a student in Germany, he had also imbibed deeply in the spirit of the age. Malling says that Guldberg had the political power, and Harboe the theological intelligence and authority, so that when they got the king to appoint them as the secret hymnal committee, they were able to work alone, with only the help of a young theological student as secretary, along with Birgitte Hertz, whose work became, for them, the new exciting voice in their hymnal.[21]

In order to proceed, Guldberg had gotten an order from the king's cabinet to the effect that a new hymnal be prepared. The order was signed by Guldberg and probably written by him after consultation with Bishop Harboe. Their first task was to examine the hymnals of Kingo, Brorson, and Pontoppidan to find hymns still suitable for use in the contemporary church, discard those that were unusable, and revise others that with a few

---

21. Malling, pp. 78-79.

corrections could be retained if they were needed for the official edification of the church. The order directed, "The spirit and expressions of the Holy Scriptures shall be the rule by which you alone have to judge the worth of a hymn."[22] Further, the order noted that it was preferred that the hymns of praise be in the spirit of the psalms of King David. The hymnal was to follow the church year, although the court could retain Pontoppidan's hymnal for its own private use, in which the hymns were placed according to the order of salvation *(ordo salutis)*. The decree especially found fault with Kingo's hymns for being "altogether too old fashioned, too long, with too much ignoble diction."[23]

In closing their petition, they asked that they be able to do their work in secret so that no one in the kingdom would know they were doing it. Their request was granted, so Birgitte, Harboe, and their assistant worked privately to accomplish the work they had been given by the royal decree. After about five years of work, they had a manuscript ready to receive Royal approval, which was given on February 2, 1778, for use in both the kingdoms as soon as enough copies of it had been printed. The printing, however, went slowly; even though it was to have been delivered by Advent 1781, it did not arrive until Advent 1783. While they were awaiting the publication, there must have been some talk about it, at least in the city, for there is record of a performance at the Christianborg palace during Lent of 1781 of a motet on one of Birgitte's hymns, "Mænd fra Udødeligheds Land" ("Men from the Land of Immortality"), composed by Johan Anton Peter Poul Darbés (1750-1815), one of Denmark's most accomplished violinists at the time, first chair in the Chapel orchestra, and later considered a professor of music, but not known for his moral character or abilities as a composer.[24] While this hymn had been among the twenty that Boye had sent in to the Society some years before, and may have been known before it appeared in the final hymnal, the record clearly indicates that the audience knew it would be in the new hymnal. The performance of the motet in the palace may have been in the spirit of what we would call "building an audience" for the new hymnal.

22. Svendsen, p. 242.
23. Svendsen, p. 243.
24 *Dansk biografisk leksikon*, ed. Sv. Cedergreen Bech (Copenhagen: Gyldendal, 1979-84), vol. 3, p. 588.

> Men from the land of immortality,
> See the time has come!
> Inside the holiest, you can
> Now each sinner enter.
> The curtain has been torn in two;
> Redemption's festival can now be held
> Within the bare sanctuary.

The text dealt with the Crucifixion. The beginning lines, especially, come directly from Enlightenment thought. The word "immortality" is not from the typical word hoard of the Baroque era with its concentration on sin and eternity. The line, however, is arresting in both Danish and English, and the crowd observing Holy Week in the palace would have felt quite modern and up-to-the-minute.

When the Guldberg hymnal finally did appear some two years later, how did it compare with previous hymnals? The editors had kept one hundred and thirty-two hymns from Kingo's hymnal and one hundred and forty-three came from Pontoppidan, many of which they had revised to bring up to modern standards and taste. They were most pleased, however, to report that the new hymnal contained one hundred and forty-six hymns by Birgitte Hertz, now Boye, who one month before the book had been delivered to the king, married Hans Boye, the comptroller of the malt mill in Copenhagen, who later became clerk of customs. Her hymns, Guldberg stated, showed that

> God had given a poor woodsman's widow from Vordingborg, Birgitte Catherine Hertz, now recently married to Boye, a peculiar gift for sacred poesy, for which she had the fortunate wit to bring to this work. While most of these are her own, either on religion's great truths, or David's psalms or others from other parts of the scripture, some were free translations from Gellert's spiritual songs.[25]

Guldberg obviously had high hopes for her work as a poet. She was the poet, he thought, who could appeal to the educated Danes' taste and bring them back to church, as many hoped the liturgical revisions of Bastholm would do. Guldberg hoped that when the rough, old-fashioned hymns

---

25. Malling, p. 77.

from Kingo would have overstayed their welcome, her hymns would still be sung.[26]

Tastes, however, continued to change markedly, so by the time the book appeared, people began to feel it was already too dated and pompous. By 1790, N. E. Balle, Harboe's son-in-law, who had helped with the previous hymnal, assembled a group of poets and scholars to begin working on the next hymnal, *The Evangelical Christian Hymnal* (1798), by Scandinavian standards a very short time between hymnals. Boye's work would be among its first casualties. As the work on that project sped along, it occurred to members of the committee that they had not solicited Birgitte's advice for their project. In a meeting in January 1791, after much of the work had begun for the new hymnal, the committee agreed to write a letter to Birgitte Boye, inviting her to contribute to the new hymnal, a rather tardy invitation when one considers how much she had been involved with the former hymnal. Balle, however, had been unwilling to ask her to help precisely because of those contributions, according to the record of their meeting from February 20, 1791. He had apparently disliked what she had done or had developed some prejudice against her from working with her and his father-in-law Harboe on the previous hymnal. Thus, it is not surprising to hear that at the March 13, 1791, meeting of the commission, Bishop Balle reported to the group that he had received a letter from Birgitte Boye in which she, understandably, excused herself from taking part in the work of the new hymnal.[27]

After her work on the hymnal, and probably her clear understanding that she would not be asked to continue such work, Birgitte turned her writing efforts to other secular literary pursuits. It is important to note that Birgitte was not the only woman of her generation to write poetry or drama. Anna Catharina von Passows (1731-1757), one of Holberg's favorite actresses, began writing plays that brought the French bourgeois play to Denmark; in 1757 her five-act play, *Marianne, or A Free Choice (Marianne: Det frie Val, Et Original Lyst-Spil ude Fem Optoge)* was printed. The play deals with the rights of a woman to choose her own husband, a common topic among enlightened women at this time. Charlotte Dorothea Biehl (1731-1788) wrote seven comedies from 1764 to 1771. While they were writ-

---

26. Svendsen, p. 145.
27. Fredrik Nielsen, *Bidrag til den evangelisk-Kristeligt Psalmebogs Historie* (Copenhagen: Karl Schønbergs Forlag, 1895), pp. 48-49.

ing plays that went out of style almost as soon as Birgitte's hymns did, Birgitte, now living in Copenhagen, also began writing plays. In 1780, she wrote a two-act pastoral, *Melicertes,* in the high pompous style of Klopstock and his school, which was performed for the Queen Dowager's birthday. In it she praised the Queen for her part in the coup against Struensee, connecting her with ancient Nordic myths and history. One year later, she wrote her best-known drama, *Gorm, the Old: A Heroic Play in Three Acts (Gorm den Gamle. Et heroisk Skuespil i tre Handlinger),* a heroic tragedy, on Nordic themes, printed by the Belletristic Society in 1784 and performed at the Royal Theater on the King's birthday that year. Once again, she praised the current royals for their heroic legacies in the ancient past. In 1795 she wrote another play, *Sigrid or Regnald's Death (Sigrid eller Regnalds Død).* This received some attention, perhaps because she used Saxo Grammaticus, the medieval Danish historian of the thirteenth century, as her source, for which she was commended. It was performed on the King's birthday in that year. In using the myths and legends of Scandinavia for her sources, she showed herself to be in tune with Klopstock's ideas about furthering the ancient myths of the North as the source for Scandinavian literature. This was an idea her successors, Oehlenschläger, Grundtvig, and even Ibsen and Strindberg, would continue in their works, much to the acclaim of the Nordic peoples. Although Birgitte did not originate this move, she certainly helped maintain its place in the hearts of those who would become Pan-Scandinavians a generation later. For example, the great celebrations of the male chorus movements, which included the young men of all the Nordic countries, featured pompous pageants of Norse mythology, which would have reduced today's youth to tears of laughter as famous actresses paraded about in Wagnerian costumes proclaiming the superiority of Odin and Freya.[28]

Birgitte did not, however, completely abandon her hymn writing. Between 1781 and 1785, she published three volumes of her paraphrases of the Psalter, from Psalms 1-89, *David's Psalms in a Free Translation (Davids Psalmer i en fri Oversættelse),* and she continued to write occasional poems for the royal house. These paraphrases had almost no impact on the life of Danish or Norwegian hymnody. Her final work was a poem on the terrible fires that destroyed Copenhagen in 1794 and 1795, in which she once again

---

28. See my unpublished article on Vilhelm Koren's participation in the 1845 festival in Copenhagen, "The Week Vilhelm Koren Fell Silent."

Figure 3 Trinitas Church, Copenhagen, Laurids de Thurah, 1748.

praised the crown prince as the people's comfort and help. "He heard the sigh of the poor, assumed his duties, and called upon a flock that had lost everything and, like a friend, housed them and fed them for a long time."[29] After the turn of the century, we hear very little from her. Mai, in her article on the women dramatists in Denmark, says that after these poems, Birgitte was content to be still, to watch how the next generation took up the Nordic themes and to give her vocation over to her children, who did not bring her only glory.[30] We do know that her two sons brought her a mixture of grief and pride. The elder, Christian, devoted to drink and other debaucheries, took sixteen years to finish his exams, during which time he became deacon at Roskilde Church, where his wife, Malling reports, being less debauched, had to fulfill her husband's calling. Jens Mi-

29. Anne-Marie Mai, "Blandt Nordens guder, danske borgere og royale heltinder," I Gud's navn: 1000-1800, Nordisk kvindelitteraturhistorie I (Copenhagen: Rosinante, 1993), p. 463.

30. Mai, p. 463.

chael, on the other hand, who had also fallen into the same debauchery, did better, leaving Copenhagen and its temptations to be a teacher in a home. Ordained some years later, and after some time as a pastor, he was called to Roskilde to be dean and then was named Bishop in Ribe in 1819. Birgitte lived to see her two sons grow old, as well as to witness their failures and successes. On October 17, 1824, she died, and was buried from Trinity (Trinitas) Church in Copenhagen in the Assistens graveyard, where there is no stone commemorating her.

As early as 1793, Birch, her first biographer, noted that she had a

> pure poetic spirit, good taste, a solemn and deep temperament in her poetry. But not all of her hymns should have been included in the new hymnal. So many of them were not written for public worship, but for private devotions, for lovers of high thought, and those who could follow the poet's flight, when many of her songs were closer to the high swing of an ode than to the simple tone of a hymn writer. At the same time, she has won for herself a remarkable name among Denmark's poets, and a great number of her hymns will always be sung with applause and spiritual uplift, and that will earn her an immortal place in the Danish church.[31]

It is interesting to hear Birch, a contemporary, comment on Birgitte's character. We can take it as a comment from one who knew her, since Copenhagen was a fairly small town; he obviously felt warmly toward her and her accomplishments as a wife, mother, and housewife. In her, and in Charlotte Dorothea Biehl (1731-1788), Birch saw that it was possible to be effective both at home and in one's writing. He hints that if they could have worked exclusively on their poetry, they might have done even more, even though with what they had already done, they had "won for themselves immortality for their deeds, their knowledge, and their efforts, which had better prepared them for their eternal joys and rewards."[32] One can also see that he shared the opinion of his day, similar to that of Balle and others, that Boye's style was too pompous and inappropriate for official worship. Mai, however, concludes that Boye's talents were greater than her reputation.

31. Birch, pp. 222-23.
32. Birch, pp. 223-24.

Boye's Work

Boye's work, simply for its volume and official reception, is astonishing and needs closer study. In addition to the twenty hymns she wrote for the contest, nineteen of which were included in the Guldberg Hymnal, another one hundred twenty-four of her hymns appeared there also. Six of her hymns were for high festivals such as Christmas, Easter, and Ascension, plus her single-stanza hymns to be sung as responses to the Gospel for the day, on Christmas, Easter, Ascension, and Pentecost. Then, in the time-honored Kingo tradition of supplying hymns that fit well with the texts of the day, she wrote seven hymns to fit the Bible passages for the morning service, thirteen on the texts chosen for the evening service, eleven for other biblical passages, seven for occasions in the life of the court, confirmation of princes and princesses, and travel. She also wrote six single-stanza hymns for other occasions, eighteen for Christ's passion, which resemble in style the passion hymns of Rist, Kingo, or Hallgrímur Pétursson, the Icelandic hymn writer, twenty-eight psalm paraphrases, fifteen paraphrases of German hymns by Gellert, ten more from various sources, and thirty-two from her own hand, Birch notes. However, some of them are translations of other German hymns, most notably, one by Johan J. Rambach (1693-1735), "I Am Saved and Dearly Bought" ("Jeg er frelst og dyrekjøbt"), which today appears in the Norwegian hymnal.

Very few of Boye's hymns have been translated into English, probably because translating her pompous style and diction is not very productive. Most of Boye's hymns have long since been discarded by any of the traditions that should have cared to cherish her legacy; thus, it is not necessary to do an analysis of her hymns, beyond what I have already done, except for one. Among the hymns by Boye included in the Guldberg hymnal is a hymn to be used for the ceremony known as the "churching" of a woman after she had given birth. Because it must be one of the only hymns on this subject written by a woman who gave birth to four children, at just about the time that the custom was waning, it gives us an interesting glimpse into a tradition long since vanished, as well as a glimpse into what a woman of her time thought of such a rite.

In northern Europe, the ceremony involved bringing a woman to the church door some weeks after the birth of her child. She would stand outside in the entry until the appropriate time in the service when the priest would come to the door, sprinkle her with holy water, and lead her, as she held on to his stole, into the church, where she would go forward, accompanied by her friends and the young girls in the community, to give thanks, and especially in Norway, give an offering to the priest. It was fairly universal in the Christian church until the eighteenth century, but rare after that, although the ceremony has been retained in the *Book of Common Prayer*.[33] When most people hear about the custom today, their usual response is one of amazement that women should be considered ritually "unclean" after giving birth.

Scholars are quick to point out the difference between the popular and the theological understandings of these words, but no matter how hard they have tried, the folk have tended to interpret the ceremony as "cleansing" or "purifying" the woman so she can come into contact with people again.[34] The origins of this lie deep within human culture. Nothing is more fundamental than the birth of a child, for the child, the mother and father, and the entire family. The notion that women were ritually "unclean" after giving birth has most likely to do with the shedding of blood during the birth and the resultant need to be "purified" in order to reenter society. "Purified" is not really the right word, although it is used even to describe Mary's purification in Luke 2:22, but it continued to be the word throughout the history of this rite.

---

33. *The Book of Common Prayer* (American, 1979), Version 1.0, 13 December 1993, p. 440.

> As soon as convenient after the birth of a child, or after receiving a child by adoption, the parents, with other members of the family, should come to the church to be welcomed by the congregation and to give thanks to Almighty God. It is desirable that this take place at a Sunday service. In the Eucharist it may follow the Prayers of the People preceding the Offertory. At Morning or Evening Prayer it may take place before the close of the Office.
>
> When desired, a briefer form of this service may be used, especially in the hospital or at home; in which case the Celebrant may begin with the Act of Thanksgiving, or with the prayer "O God, you have taught us." A passage from Scripture may first be read. Either Luke 2:41-51, or Luke 18:15-17, is appropriate.
>
> During the prayers, some parents may wish to express thanks in their own words.
>
> At the proper time, the Celebrant invites the parents and other members of the family to present themselves before the Altar.

34. David Cressy, "Purification, Thanksgiving, and the Churching of Women in Post-Reformation England," *Past and Present* 141 (1993): 106-46.

Western Christianity traces it back to Leviticus 12, which gives elaborate instructions for the reintegration of the mother into society. If the mother has borne a male, her period of uncleanness lasts seven days, and the boy baby is circumcised on the eighth day. After forty days, the baby is to be taken to the tabernacle, or temple, to be presented, a different rite from the circumcision, or naming ceremony. In the tradition, the mother is to remain away from holy places until after the passage of forty days. It is after Mary's purification, or forty days, that she and Joseph bring the baby Jesus to the temple to make their offering.

If the child is a daughter, the period of purification is twice as long. Mary Douglas, in her book on *Leviticus as Literature*, defends the practice as a time of rest for the mother, so that she can recover from the birth.[35] She is not being despised, according to Douglas; rather, this is a liminal time in which the mother is being given time for herself, away from her work of caring for the family and away from sexual relations with her husband. Medieval English tradition says that the husband had to care for the baby during this time, calling it the "gander" month. Why the girl causes a lying in twice as long as the boy is something of a mystery, according to Douglas, except for the fear that a girl could have been born menstruating, which would make the mother twice as ritually unclean. In any case, it gave the mother much needed respite. In addition, it was a festive time for the mother in which she looked forward to returning to the tabernacle, temple, or later, church, with her offering, after which she would be reintegrated into society with prayers, greetings, and celebrations by her friends, her pastor, and community. It was an official recognition that she had fulfilled her vocation as a mother and passed through the waters of death with the help of God.

Folklore began to develop around the notion that an "unchurched" woman was heathen. Maxims grew up to the effect that the grass under the foot of a woman who had not yet been "churched" would not grow, or that if a woman died in childbirth, she could not be buried in holy ground. Both Catholics, and later Protestants, tried to focus the ritual as one of thanksgiving for the woman's safe deliverance, but unsuccessfully. The rite looked to the people rather like another baptism and could easily have been interpreted to be a rite of cleansing that re-christened the woman.

---

35. Mary Douglas, *Leviticus as Literature* (Oxford: Oxford University Press, 1999), pp. 180-82.

Since the ceremony involved keeping the woman outside the church until the priest had met her and sprinkled holy water on her and said some prayers, the impression that this was indeed another baptism, or a "churching" of her in the same sense that baptism changed a baby from a heathen to a Christian, persisted, especially in the medieval church where virginity was prized over marriage.

Very quickly after the Reformation and Luther's growing understanding of the sanctity of marriage as a blessed vocation for both man and woman, the theologians and hymn writers did their best to change the understanding of the practice. Luther had very clearly noted, in his treatise on marriage in 1522, that a woman should consent to fulfill the desires of her body, within marriage, and see the giving of birth as part of the vocation God had given her, even if it should result in death. Speaking directly to the issue of "churching" he wrote:

> The Pope has also commanded that after their confinement, they should stand outside the church door as though they were unclean. They dared not enter the church or go among people. But that is wrong. Because the uncleanness that was reckoned unto women by the Law is not natural, but an imposed uncleanness that is not effective without the Law, it should not be imposed by anyone.[36]

Peder Palladius (1503-1560), the first evangelical Danish bishop of Sjælland, addressed this same issue in his *Visitation Book (Visitatsbog)* written in 1553 after his first visitations around his diocese. In it he reports on what he found in the parishes and gives advice on everything from the windows in the churches to the way in which the cantors should be paid. When he comes to the issue of the churching of women, he addressed the new mother with his typically robust evangelical theology.

> But my dear honest woman, you are not a heathen woman when you are in childbed, you do not have anything to fear from the devil, if you are a Christian woman and baptized in the name of the Father, Son,

---

36. Martin Luther, "Paa Barnens og Moderens Marie renselsis dag" found in Ann Helene Bolstad Skjelbred, *Uren og Hedning: Barselkvinnen i norsk folketradisjon* (Oslo: Universitetsforlag, 1972) p. 59.

and Holy Spirit. You have no need of a candle, water, or hat to take away the evil or drive the devil away.[37]

Two hundred years later, in 1757, Erick Pontoppidan, in his own book of pastoral theology, *Collegium Pastorale Practicum*, noted that the practice of "officially" welcoming the new mother into the church in order to thank God for her safe delivery and offer the pastor a gift, while an ancient practice in the churches, was falling out of use, to the financial loss of the pastor. The issue was the rather extravagant parade into the church especially from the wealthy with their gifts. Referred to in the liturgical texts as the *innledelsen* or "leading in," the focus of the ceremony was on the new mother, dressed to the hilt, meeting the pastor at the door, who then led her company of women and girls, in their new dresses, from her place outside the church. Oftentimes, it was thought to be simply too cold for her to wait there, until the ceremony began, given her weakened state of health at the time. Another objection to it was the time it could take from the service. One solution to that was to have the "leading in" ceremony before the service began. Who should lead the new mother into the church? The friends of the new mother or the pastor?[38] Pontoppidan suggested that some pastors, out of their own financial need, looked "between their fingers" in order to continue the practice among the upper classes and those who had the wherewithal to give a generous offering. The loss of income, apparently, was enough so that the pastors complained about their new penury. In 1748, by royal decree, the church was advised that it could continue the custom in parishes where it still was a living tradition, but only in private. Then, in 1756, the practice of the parades was shut down, no matter what position the woman had in society. However, Pontoppidan noted, the proper way to follow the custom was to mention the mother's name from the pulpit and give thanks for her safe passing through, as she gave the pastor her gift.[39] Pontoppidan thought even that reformed practice would disappear, as it did, but not until later in the twentieth century: hymnal edi-

---

37. Peder Palladius, Sjællands Første evangeliske Biskop, *Visitatsbog*, ed. A. C. L. Heiberg (Copenhagen: Den Danske Literaturs Fremme, 1867), pp. 134-35.

38. Helge Fæhn, *Ritualspørsmalet i Norge 1785-1813: En liturgisk og kirkehistorisk undersøkelse med særlig henblikk paa geistlighetens stilling til tidens reformplaner* (Oslo: Land og Kirke, 1956), p. 259, note 44.

39. Pontoppidan, pp. 299-300.

tors continued to include such a hymn until the twentieth century. Surprisingly, it is included in the Lutheran Free Church's 1906 version of Landstad's hymnal![40]

Boye, by the time she became involved with the editing of the Guldberg hymnal, had given birth to four children. She thus knew something about the actual situation of the mother reentering the church and society after her lying-in period. Since one of the assignments she and Harboe had was to help fill in missing or inadequate sections of Kingo and Pontoppidan's hymnal, she may have felt that the hymns there were too old-fashioned and inappropriate. Kingo recommended his hymn for Mary's purification day, Candlemas, "How Goes It, Then, O Pure Virgin" ("Hvor gaaer det dog, O rene jomfru!), the second stanza of which began, "I am unclean from top to toe." The hymn had been the only one designated for such an event in Kingo's hymnal. Pontoppidan used Kingo's hymn as well, plus another hymn for the ceremony that was only marginally better: "How Surely Blessed Is the Man" ("Ret Salig forvist er den Mand"), which spends most of its time praising the man for the birth of the child. It is not until the third stanza that it even addressed the mother's situation in the words of Psalm 128:

> So also blessed in your pious wife,
> Whom God himself gave you here,
> Who like a fruitful vine branch
> Gives birth with honor;
> She is an ornament in your house,
> As the sun's clear light
> Ornaments the lovely heavens.

Thought to be by a fairly unknown hymn writer, Rasmus Hansen Lollik, the hymn focuses more on the husband than the mother, praising him for his children and giving advice on how to raise them. Since one of these hymns was probably used at her own "churching," no doubt Boye had some feelings about their focus and maybe even theology.

We can read in Boye's hymn "Be Filled with Holy Gladness" ("Bliv fuld av hellig Glæde") that she knew something about the customs of

---

40. Magnus Brostrup Landstad, *Kirkesalmebog: udforandret efter den norske Udgave med Tillæg* (Minneapolis: Frikirkens Boghandel, 1906), no. 585.

churching of woman from Luther and Palladius, and, most likely, Pontoppidan, who had clearly marked the decline of the ceremony that was occurring in the kingdoms. Her hymn, however, still contains directions for the ceremony as well as the proper evangelical theology for the event, but it is markedly different from Kingo.

1. Be filled with holy gladness
   O blessed one, come forth
   And prayerfully go meet him,
   Who made you out of earth.
   Sing goodness' praise abroad:
   Let ev'ry gift rise upward
   To heaven's sturdy kingdom
   With praises to your God.

2. For you whom pain hast driven
   To heavy cries of woe,
   You hast been blest most richly,
   As you with faith and trust
   Have met your troubling trials
   With God and loving fam'ly
   And bravely gone to battle
   Against death's bitter wiles!

3. Though you will soon forget it:
   The pain of facing death,
   When happy voices shouted
   "A child, a child is born!
   Who gladly will be giv'n
   The legacy of heaven,
   A hope without comparing."
   You will forget the pain!

4. See! God has given children
   As fruit, a loan for life,
   And what a joy receiving
   A worthy little child!
   I shout: "My grave is free;

It does not hold my body.
And you are here, Lord Jesus,
With those you gave to me.

5. Sing! Praise and strength and glory
   Through all eternity
   Belong to God in heaven
   Who saw me pained and weak.
   O God! By grace so new:
   My lips sing out your praises,
   A happy sigh that struggles
   To rise up unto you!

6. To you! — I scarce can say it —
   To you, O risen Christ,
   My soul, with all its powers,
   Still lifts itself to you;
   Still sings my Lord and God,
   The Alpha and Omega.
   He was the strength I trusted,
   My all! Hallelujah!

We can hear in the language of the hymn that the writer has experienced the pain and joy of child-bed. Throughout it, the first three stanzas of which are in the character of a sermon or exhortation to the new mother, we can hear Boye not only preaching the gospel, but also giving some rather sage advice to the new mother. The first stanza is like a stage direction for the leading-in ceremony and the reasons for it: thanksgiving, not the offering. The second stanza is almost a poetic paraphrase of Luther's and Palladius' advice, including the reference to God's curse of Eve, that in pain and sorrow she would bring forth children, but that as a believer, she should bravely do battle against death. The third stanza is more in the character of a baby shower, where experienced mothers speak to the expectant one, assuring her that although the pain will be severe, it will be soon forgotten: "You will forget the pain." We can hear that the speaker knows whereof she speaks: referring to the moment when the mother hears the shout of joy that a baby has been born, and that she has given birth, and now knows the joy of having provided a successor to the family

Figure 4 "Be Filled with Holy Gladness."

line, although in this case, while it is true that she is speaking of the fact that the new baby's heritage is of the kingdom, not of the family, she does imply the family heritage as well.

Before embarking on the dangers of child-bed, women traditionally went for confession and communion, after serious self-examination, because giving birth presented young women with the clear possibility of death. While these little "liturgies" have not been recorded, they are part of the Christian tradition, and we can read of them in diaries of women who, just before their labor, go to Scripture and the catechism to find strength and assurance of their salvation before this very dangerous passage in their lives. Boye urges the new mother to rejoice that she has "cheated the grave and brought forth a son." (We know that Boye had four children, and that two of them were sons. That does not necessarily mean the other two were daughters, although we can assume so.) One wonders whether the poetic form caused her to use "son" or whether she thought a son was better than a daughter, since it would be difficult to substitute the word for "daughter" in the metrical line she is using.

She makes a slight reference, in stanza five, to Mary's song and her praise to the Lord who had regarded the low estate of her handmaiden. Boye tells the new mother to sing to God "who saw you pained and weak." (Poetic paraphrases of the Magnificat are suggested as alternatives to the suggested hymn by Lollik in both Pontoppidan and Kingo and succeeding hymnals.) By the end of stanzas five and six, one hears the writer of the hymn speaking from the inside of the woman's utter weariness and her complete dependence on God for strength. The poetry of the last stanza is almost rhapsodic in its weariness and thanksgiving, just at the edge of reasonable grammar, with its passionate repetitions and wonder, "To you, I scarce can say it, to you." It sounds more autobiographical than hymns written by men on the subject. Despite the pompous heightened style of Boye, her voice clearly comes through in this hymn in a way that is unexpected and not usual for the time.

Although we cannot be sure that it was Boye who felt the need to write a more appropriate hymn for the churching of women and insisted on doing so, or whether the men on the committee told her to write one of her own for such an occasion, we hear a pronounced change in the tone and theology of her hymn from the older hymns. That the old hymns by Kingo or Lollik were excised does not necessarily mean that Boye wanted them out, but something happened. While we cannot be sure she was the one who kept the Kingo and Pontoppidan hymns out of Guldberg, the difference between her hymn and the others shows that the meaning of this event had changed, and obviously both men agreed that the old hymns should be abandoned and hers substituted for it. However, on her original manuscript in the Landsarchiv in Copenhagen, one can read the strong hand, probably of Bishop Harboe, changing her delicate poetry to something more theological in the fifth stanza of the hymn.[41] While she had addressed Jesus, her comforter, as "Opstaanden Du" or "arisen you," Harboe had changed it to "O store Gud" or "O Great God" and then edited the next rhyming line to "ud" ("out") rather than "nu" ("now"), which misses some of the immediacy of the passionate cry in the hymn, especially the notion of Christ's resurrection and victory over death, something the woman who had just lived through childbirth may well have clung to in her hour of pain and in her rejoicing over her survival.

Although revisions are standard fare for hymnal editors — rare are the editors who resist the blue pencil — this does show in microcosm what would happen to her and her hymns in the very next few years. Both in the Swedish hymnal edited by Johan Olof Wallin in 1819, and also in Landstad's of 1869, the hymn intended for the churching of women was not Boye's but one by the Swede Franz Michael Franzén (1772-1847): "God, My God, Who Wills That the Child and Wife Be Saved" ("Gud, min Gud, som wille än Mig åt barn och maka frälsa!"), which appears under the rubric, "For a housewife who is going to be churched." Landstad changed the text to "To your house with thanksgiving" ("Til dit hus med Takkesang"). That Landstad dropped Boye's hymn and substituted one of his translations is of some interest. Perhaps he thought her style was too pompous, as he had noted in his comments on her work, or more likely, a bit too passionate and too much from the woman's point of view. Apparently he thought that his version of Franzén's was better. It did keep the thanksgiving piece of the rite central, as did hers. Why he did not include Kingo's hymn is not clear, because he did say that he could not explain why so many dearly beloved hymns of Luther and Kingo were kept out of Guldberg, among them Kingo's hymn about Mary's purification, but he said nothing about why in his book *On the Hymnal: An Account (Om Salmebogen: en Redegjørelse)*, only that he missed the "dear" hymn of Kingo "from top to

---

41. Sjællands Landsarkiv, Sjællands Stifts Bispearkiv, VII. Diverse Dokumenter. K. Litteraria. Madame Birgitte Cathrine Boyes Psalmer.

toe."⁴² That he would note the loss of the hymn by Kingo, but not include it, and leave out both Boye's and Lollik's and substitute his own may simply indicate that he thought his was better and that there was no need for more than one hymn for a custom that was dying away.

The ceremony and hymns for it did not survive past the original Landstad hymnal, greatly revised in 1937. In Norway Boye's work lived much longer than in Denmark because Landstad decided to include eighteen of her hymns in his hymnal, saying that there were bits of gold in her work, and that despite her stiff and pompous poetry, she had planted many fine flowers in the garden of the church. "She should not disappear without any footprints wherever there is a historic selection of hymnody."⁴³

Mainly Forgotten Works

The age in which Birgitte lived and wrote has not been highly valued among Lutheran church historians of late. The Enlightenment, with its abandonment of Pietism and preference for reason over faith, has always been represented by the generations that followed as a dark and dead time when pastors preached on good farming practices because Jesus was born in a manger. By these interpretations, only with the revival of Hauge did the church survive the dead period of Enlightenment and Rationalism. Not much has been written on the spiritual virtues of the Enlightenment in the Dano-Norwegian church, probably because it is not as interesting as the following awakening that erupted and transformed the churches again. Although Birgitte's Jesus hymns are in line with the work of Dorothe Engelbretsdatter and Brorson, they were quickly excised for reasons that are not completely clear without resort to some accusations of sexism. Her work suffers on all these accounts. Does her pompous style hide a heart that is not alive with faith? Not really. Except for those who loved the Guldberg hymnal and came to know her work well until Landstad, Boye's decline was not so much her fault as the fault of the times that were changing and a hymnal committee that had its obvious prejudices against her, chiefly against her style. That may be an easy excuse. She certainly was

42. Magnus Brostrup Landstad, *Om Salmebogen: en Redegjørelse* (Kristiania: Dybwad, 1862), p. 24.

43. Landstad, *Om Salmebogen*, p. 63.

gifted enough to have been able, herself, to change her style and even revise her own hymns to fit the current age.

Times and traditions can change on a dime. Such change is almost cataclysmic. In the small world of Danish hymnody, it is difficult to say why, although her contemporary Birch must be echoing a commonly held view that her poetry was old-fashioned almost immediately after its publication. Balle and his colleagues on the committee to create a new hymnal, the *Evangelical Christian Hymnal*, did not like her work. Ironically, however, their own hymnal created conflicts, especially in Norway, where the book was roundly criticized, in the words of the great Danish figure, Grundtvig, for being neither "evangelical nor Christian." Its revisions were even more rationalistic than those in Guldberg, making the old hymns, as H. Blom Svendsen, the Norwegian scholar, noted, rather like looking at the old, colorful medieval paintings in the old churches through the whitewash of the Reformation. Balle and his colleagues may have rejected Boye's hymns for their style, rather bombastic and rotund, as over against the plain elegant style they had come to prefer. We should not forget, however, that her taking in of Norse mythology from Klopstock and others paved a way for Grundtvig, among others, and the Golden Age in Denmark, themselves true romantics, who were quite able to engage in bombast and a grand, if not laughable, style.

Leif Ludwig Albertsen, in an article on the two hundredth anniversary of the Guldberg hymnal, defends her work against many of her critics, especially Malling, whom he accuses of sexism in his judgment that Boye's work was filled with "girlish fantasy," even though most of her work was written during the fourth decade of life. He points especially to her hymn on the churching of women as being one they should have examined if they were going to dwell on her "girlishness" or "femininity." Furthermore, he opposes Malling's judgment that her high style "harmonized poorly with the gospel." What the gospel is and how it "harmonizes with a contemporary congregation should not be too quickly decided," Albertsen concluded. After his close analysis of the only hymn still included in the Danish hymnal today, a paraphrase of Psalm 139, he concludes that the revisions have changed it so much from its original poetry that the text is really not Boye's. Finally, he notes that "Boye's work is not without its radiance or interest."[44] We do see the radiance of the light and sun in much of

---

44. Leif Ludwig Albertsen, "Forsvar for Digteren Birgitte Boye: i Anledning af 200-

her now-forgotten poetry. Those who followed her did not like her work for many reasons, not all of them rational.

When Birgitte Boye was buried from Trinitas Church in 1824, she left remarkably little behind her. Only one picture of her is found in the extensive archive of Danish portraits. We are not even sure where she is buried. In a small country that treasures its culture with statues and portraits of many of its leaders, and extensive entries on even minor officials in biographical reference works, this is a curious omission. That her star plummeted from the pantheon of Danish greats is very clear, but why is not quite possible to fathom. We cannot, however, know what work will live and speak to ages and ages hence, as Guldberg had hoped Boye's would. For many reasons, we should know and admire the work of Boye more than we have. For all our amusement at her style, we at least owe her some honor and respect. Perhaps it is possible to argue that, in fact, her star did not plummet completely. Although she is not remembered very well by modern Danes, generations upon generations of Dano-Norwegians and now Norwegian-American Lutherans have stood to sing her solemn verses in response to the three great festivals of the faith. Given the thousands of hymns in existence, having at least two of your hymns sung regularly in Lutheran churches for over two hundred years is no small thing for "a poor woodsman's widow," as Birch called her, "from Vordingborg . . . with a peculiar gift for sacred poesy, which she had the fortunate wit to bring to this work."[45]

Året for Guldbergs Salmebog," *Hymnologiske Meddelelser* (Copenhagen: Salmehistorisk Selskab, 1978), pp. 28-29.

45. Malling, p. 77.

CHAPTER 3

Berthe Canutte Aarflot (1795-1859)
Bride of Christ

In a eulogy for Berthe Canutte Aarflot, Bjørnstjerne Bjørnson (1832-1910), the most popular nationalistic writer in nineteenth-century Norway, noted her significance as one of the more famous of the women raised up by the Haugean revival in Norway.

> When one comes unannounced to a farm in the north on a Sunday, one hears people [in the house] singing a hymn which is not known from church, but that seems to fit the people and the place and gives a better welcome than any words. Afterward, during a conversation, one will look at the books that are lying on the table, and find a title like this: *The Fruits of Faith, a Collection of Spiritual Song in Two Parts* by Berte Kanutte Siversdatter Aarflot.[1]

Aarflot was one of what came to be known as the "regiment" or "host" of women leaders that rose up in the generation following the early-nineteenth-century Hauge revival in Norway. Her life and ministry give us insight into Hauge's movement and its effect upon Norwegians of his day, especially the young women who felt called into a ministry of preaching and who were able to answer that call because of Hauge's work. We can read in Berthe's autobiography, *Selvbiografi*, a description of her journey to a living faith and how she began to write her hymns, songs, poems, and

---

1. Bjørnstjerne Bjørnson, *Aftenbladet* 1859, nr. 218 (/12).

Figure 1 Berthe Canutte Aarflot

edifying letters.[2] One of her hymns, written as she thought she lay dying, namely, "In Jesus' Name I Now Prepare to Take My Last Journey" ("I Jesu navn eg no til siste ferd meg reiser"), still survives in the current Norwegian canon of hymns, along with another Lenten hymn by her, included in the latest *Syng for Herren* hymnal (1993): "O Lamb, I See Thee Filled with Wounds" ("O Lam, jeg ser dig fuld af Saar"). Her popularity has faded over the years through the ordinary and expected winnowing of hymn texts, as well as her unfashionable piety and dependence on the work of Thomas Kingo, Hans Adolf Brorson, and Dorothe Engelbretsdatter, which gives her work a feeling of being derivative. Still, her accomplishments are signal and deserve attention, if only to give a better reading of the women in the Haugean revival of which she was a vital part. How was it that women felt empowered to take leadership in this movement, and what were Berthe's particular contributions to the hymnody of the Lutheran tradition as it developed in Norway? To understand her better we need to briefly examine the life and legacy of Hans Nielsen Hauge.

Hans Nielsen Hauge

When Hans Nielsen Hauge (1771-1824), the son of a peasant living in the Tune parish near Fredrikstad in the southeastern section of Norway closest to Sweden, had a spiritual experience in 1796, a revival began that changed the face of Norway, both spiritually and economically. The movement had its genesis when Hauge, a young teenager, began suffering typical adolescent spiritual Anfecktung about the time of his confirmation, when he began to ask questions about God, the truth, and his own beliefs. The young Hauge had been raised by devout parents who made sure that he learned the three major components of the Norwegian Lutheran's upbringing: Scripture, hymns, and Luther's *Small Catechism* alongside Erick Pontoppidan's *Explanation to Martin Luther's Catechism*. His pastor, Gerhard Seeberg (1734-1813), an odd and brutal man, had enough sense to realize that the young man had gifts for the ministry and told him so.

2. Berte Kanutte Sivertsdatter Aarflot, *Selvbiografi, indeholdende optegnelser om hendes aandelige livs udvikling, tilligemed sognepræst Wraamanns tale ved hendes grav, samt nogle mindesange,* n.d.

Figure 2
Norwegian lay evangelist Hans Nielsen Hauge.

Like many gifted young people with a bright future before them, Hauge was restless and plagued by anxiety and depression as he struggled to find his way, asking, "What does God require of me?" The Pietists would call his anxiety one of being "under conviction of sin" driven by his clear sense that he could not keep the First Commandment.[3] He did not doubt that God existed; he doubted that God wanted to save *him,* a sinner. After almost drowning in the Glomma River near his home when he was thirteen, Hauge feared that he "had not loved God as I should have."[4] Like Martin Luther before him, Hauge felt burdened by the righteousness of

---

3. Joseph Shaw, *Pulpit Under the Sky: A Life of Hans Nielsen Hauge* (Minneapolis: Augsburg Publishing House, 1955), p. 18.

4. Shaw, p. 18.

God. True to the *order of salvation*, which Hauge knew well, his near-drowning was his call from God because it made him aware of his own need for salvation. He could not find what the Pietists have called "assurance" of his salvation. They would have understood this to be his call *(vocatio)*, the second stage in the "order of salvation" *(ordo salutis)*.

As a somewhat odd and troubled teenager, Hauge worked hard on the farm of his father, and like many farm boys, he became an all-around handyman. In addition, he also learned from his mother and sisters how to embroider, knit, crochet, and weave, domestic arts he probably practiced in the long winter evenings as the family sat around the fire in their home. In his early twenties, Hauge moved for a short time to Fredrikstad, the nearby town. After he had spent some time in the city, his parents, worried about his situation, came to take him home to the farm so that he could regain his spiritual and mental balance. On April 5, 1796, while Hauge was plowing one of his father's fields, he had his famous experience. It happened while he was singing the second stanza of a well-known hymn translated by Bishop Peder Jacobsen Hygom (1692-1764), a leader of the Pietist movement in southern Jutland, Denmark, "Jesus, for Thee and Thy Blessed Communion" ("Jesu, din søte forening å smake"):

> Strengthen my soul's inner chamber with power
> That I may see Thy good Spirit prevail;
> Each word and thought must to Thy prison tower,
> Lead me and lure me, my own steps will fail;
> All that I am and possess I surrender,
> If Thou alone wilt abide in my soul,
> Evil surrounds me, be Thou my Defender,
> Nothing can harm me when Thou dost control.[5]

As he was singing, suddenly, he felt a bolt from heaven, almost like the apostle Paul had experienced on the road to Damascus, which threw him to the ground. From the experience, Hauge gained an assurance of his salvation and the power to begin a ministry that changed Norway completely.

---

5. Thought to be a translation of the German hymn "Jesu-Sophia! Ich such und verlange," which has been attributed to the German pastor Johann Ludwig Conrad Allendorf (1693-1773). Carl Døving translated the Danish poem into English in 1911 and it appeared in *The Concordia Hymnal*, no. 315 (1932).

My heart was so uplifted to God that I don't know nor can express what took place in my soul. As soon as my understanding returned, I regretted that I hadn't served the loving and all-gracious God; now I felt that no worldly thing was of importance. It was a glory which no tongue can explain; my soul felt something supernatural, divine, and blessed. . . . I had a completely transformed mind, a sorrow over all sins, a burning desire that others should share the same grace, a particular desire to read the Scriptures, especially Jesus' own teachings, as well as new light to understand them and the teachings of godly men; toward the one goal: that Christ has come to be our Savior, that we should be born again by His spirit, be converted, and be sanctified more and more in godliness to serve the triune God alone in order to improve and prepare our souls for the eternal blessedness.[6]

In this description of the experience, we can see the pattern of spiritual experience and thought so fundamental to Pietists: the order of salvation *(ordo salutis)*, or the steps through which one went on the way to assurance of salvation. Salvation began with the awareness of, and terror at, the majesty of God, which made the sinner painfully aware of his or her unrighteousness. We see it in Hauge whose terror led to his call *(vocatio)*, which very clearly showed itself in his anxiety, then his illumination *(illuminatio)*, when he was thrown to the ground by a "glory no tongue can explain," followed by his "transformed mind, a sorrow over all sins, a burning desire that others should share the same grace," in other words, being born again *(regeneratio)*, and finally, his conversion *(conversio)*, which helped him to change directions: "that Christ has come to be our Savior, that we should be born again, be converted," which was to be followed by sanctification, or the fruits of faith, or "be sanctified more and more in godliness to serve the triune God alone." Hauge's experience, as he described it here, fits the order of salvation precisely.

After recovering his sensibilities, which took some days, the young man, whose education consisted only of what we might call grammar school, sat down and wrote a book on the terrible conditions of the world, the church, and its pastors at the time, including his own pastor, Seeberg. The book was entitled *A Meditation on the Folly of the World (Verdens Daar-*

---

6. Hans Nielsen Hauge, *Om Religiøse Følelser og deres Værd* (Christiansand, 1840), pp. 33-34, quoted in Shaw, p. 23.

lighed). After its publication, Hauge started peddling it, walking throughout Norway with it, talking to others he met along the way about Jesus. Soon, his work had raised up in many a living faith in Christ. His compelling witness came, not only from what he said, but also from who he was and how he appeared. One of his contemporaries described him as a man with a "powerful and erect figure with clear, open features, with a manly voice and most of all a clear, simple, and gripping proclamation of the catechism's truths, which everyone could understand."[7] As he walked over mountains, fields, and forests and sailed the fjords of Norway on his mission, young people began following along with him, talking to him and singing favorite hymns. Later he wrote in his *Religious Feelings and Their Worth*, "When I traveled, and in my work, I found my heart revived by singing."[8] As he went and conversed with others about their spiritual condition, he knit mittens, silk gloves, and stockings and did other handiwork, which his followers prized.

Hauge's ministry was like the proverbial spark to dry tinder. At that time, the religious situation in Norway and Denmark was what the Pietists called "dead." The Enlightenment had had deleterious effects on the personal spiritual lives of the average person, not because the farmers were Enlightenment people, but because of its effects on the clergy, who no longer could recommend the old ways of the first Pietist revival. In addition to the poor spiritual conditions of the day, Norway had begun suffering from the consequences of the Napoleonic Wars raging to the south. For a poor country, the last years of the eighteenth century were a terrible time of economic and natural disasters, especially the years 1800-1801, when a cold summer prevented the crops from maturing and people starved. On his travels, Hauge observed the dire poverty of his people. As a clever farmer and shrewd businessperson with an entrepreneurial genius rare to Norway at the time, Hauge saw these privations and began to think of how to relieve the suffering of his countrymen as a way to fulfill his calling to "serve God and his neighbor."

His success, however, threatened not only the old mercantilist interests of the elite in the kingdom, but also the state church, which had passed the Conventicle Law of 1746 forbidding laypeople to meet together for prayer and Bible study when there were no state church pastors present. This law, passed by Christian VI who came to fear the Moravian move-

---

7. Anders Hauge, *Hans Nielsen Hauge I* (Christiania, 1924), p. 25.
8. H. N. Hauge, *Om Religiøse Følelser og deres Værd*, p. 29.

ment in Denmark, which he had once championed, was now used against Hauge, whom the authorities threw into jail on several occasions for preaching illegally, as well as for breaking the vagrancy laws of the day, both forbidden in the Conventicle Act, which stated very clearly (paragraph 16) that it was unlawful for "men or women alone or in company, to travel about and conduct meetings." Hauge, however, who carried a copy of the law around with him, would point to the previous paragraph, "Those who demonstrate genuine concern for their own and others' edification should not be mocked or persecuted."

After his personal appearances and letters, his capacity to organize a movement strengthened the revival. Like Moses' father-in-law Jethro, he saw that in order for his movement to prosper, he needed to appoint lieutenants who could do the work. Thus, he encouraged the laity, both men and women, to be leaders in the movement, to preach and pray, to write letters and hymns, and to travel around with the gospel as he himself did. Many laypeople rose to the occasion and began their own work of evangelizing Norway. Among them were numerous women whom Hauge had called into leadership from the beginning of his ministry. As early as 1798, after a revival meeting in Elverum, Norway, he met three young women whom he asked to be his colleagues in the work: Their *modus operandi* became the same as his: walking from farm to farm, finding work with the family and, in the evenings, leading meetings where they would sing hymns and songs, pray, read God's word, and converse *(samtale)* with the people.[9] These are the first women preachers known to have emerged from the Haugian awakening. The first woman to achieve notice for her preaching was Sara Ousten from Vingelen in Tolga, Hedmark, a county northeast of Oslo. When her ministry began to awaken criticism, several of Hauge's friends asked him on what grounds he could ask women to preach. Hauge's answer, according to the tradition, was two questions and a command: "(1) Do you believe that she is a serious and humble Christian with as much Christian knowledge and experience as is necessary to lead others?" When they answered "yes," he would ask the second question, "(2) Is she capable in her earthly calling?" When the answer was that she had gifts high above all others, he answered, "Then you can let her speak unhindered!"[10]

---

9. Olav Golf, *Den Haugianske Kvinnebevegelse* (Oslo: Webergs Boktrykkeri, 1998), p. 17.

10. Golf, p. 17.

With the number of women in his movement increasing, this question became a constant one. Hauge wrote several times on the ability of women to fulfill the calling of preacher and leader in the movement, first in his *Simple Teaching and Powerful Strength (Eenfoldige Lære og Afmægtiges Styrke)* (1798) and also in his next book, *Christian Doctrine (Den Christelige Lære)* (1799). That the Conventicle Act had very strongly proscribed the ministry of women and their increasing prominence in his movement meant that he heard its language many times: "Women should not imagine that they have a call to teach or preach." This sentence gave his opponents reason to criticize him. Even those who were a part of the movement as it matured found themselves in opposition to the leadership of women. Scholars have wondered whether he had retracted his first openness to women after his release from prison, but others argue that he had not. Recent scholarly opinion holds that he continued to argue for their ministry until his death, although it is possible to read both conclusions into his later statements, made after he was released from prison in 1814 and retired to his home, a man whose health and vigor had been broken.[11]

In his first work on the issue he used Scripture to interpret Scripture and set Paul's proscription against women speaking in church (1 Cor. 14:34) next to Joel's prophecy about the latter days, which he believed had come: "Your sons and daughters will prophesy" (Joel 2:28). At first, this silenced his critics, who could not argue against his use of Scripture to interpret Scripture. It is not surprising that the many young women who heard him and came to understand his encouragement of their gifts for ministry flocked to his movement. Because it was a youth movement that attracted young women, Hauge shrewdly picked both young men and women to lead the revival. By 1802, he had named five women and twenty-eight men who could function as "elders" despite their youth. One of Norway's historians of the Hauge movement, Hallvard Gunleikson Heggtveit (1850-1924), in his history of the Norwegian church in the nineteenth century, gives a careful accounting of the sixty-two laypeople called to preach by Hauge in the first decade of that century.[12] Sixteen of them were women. In his 1800 book on *The Basis for the Doctrines of Christianity (Christendommens*

---

11. For a short account of this see Golf, pp. 36-39.
12. H. G. Heggtveit, *Den norske Kirke i den nittende Aarhundred: Et Bidrag til dens Historie*, vol. 2 (Christiania: Cammermeyers, 1912-1920).

Lærdoms Grunde) Hauge included poems and other works by women. In his pamphlet on *Religious Feelings and Their Worth (Om Religiøse Følelser og deres Værd),* which came out three years after his release from prison in 1814, he named with respect the work of seven women and eleven men. In a small pamphlet from 1818, *Life in Death,* Hauge eulogized fifteen of his supporters, eight of whom were women.

In 1804, Hauge was thrown into prison for his longest sentence for breaking the Conventicle Law and was confined to a bleak cell in the Oslo jail, where he languished for nearly ten years, except for a short reprieve when the government needed his services to build a salt mill necessary for the existence of the country. A vigorous man of the outdoors, his confinement ruined his health almost immediately. Already by his first month in prison, the bad diet and poor light had caused him to lose most of his teeth.[13] He felt attacked by Satan and almost lost his mind and his faith, but as he waited for the church and state to handle his case, he began reading and continued writing. His reading, especially of Luther, helped him moderate some of his less nuanced theology. Meanwhile, the case dragged on and on, in an agonizing legal and bureaucratic set of arcane processes that seemed never to end, partly because the government was otherwise occupied with matters of famine, war, and the blockades.

Although Hauge had not married before his imprisonment, after he was released from jail, he married Andrea Nyhus on January 27, 1815, a woman he had met on one of his first journeys north. She, however, died on December 19, 1815, after giving birth to their son, Andreas, who was to become a well-known pastor in the Norwegian church. After another year, on January 22, 1817, he married Ingeborg Marie Olsdatter, a woman who had worked as a servant in Eiker. She and Hauge moved to a large farm, Bredtveit, near Oslo, which became a new center for the revival. With his broken health, he had to depend on her to provide hospitality for their many visitors, although very soon, even in his much-reduced condition, he had acquired enough wealth to be one of Norway's richer men, whose name and gifts were sought for public projects such as the new university in Christiania. Before Hauge died in 1824, he left a *Last Will and Testament* urging his friends to remain faithful to the Scripture, the Augsburg Con-

---

13. Dag Kullerud, *Hans Nielsen Hauge: Mannen som vekket Norge* (Oslo: Forum Aschehoug, 1996), p. 286.

fession, and the Catechism and not to leave the state church. In it he gives advice on how to choose leaders, teachers, and preachers.

Hauge's movement helped both men and women to reform their personal lives so that they could work for the kingdom as well as clean up their own societies. Women, who suffered the most when men did not fulfill their responsibilities because of liquor or sheer inability, must have found Hauge's call to leadership irresistible. He was an evangelist and social reformer who knew Scripture, the hymnal, and his catechism better than almost anyone in his time. It is easy to see why the Dano-Norwegian establishment felt threatened; he changed the entire spiritual landscape of their country. His persecution is one of the most unattractive episodes in Norway's history. Karen Larsen in her well-regarded *History of Norway* wrote that

> The measures taken against him and his followers were efforts to maintain time-honored authority and privilege rather than religious persecution. The business enterprises sometimes ran counter to old special rights to which the burghers still clung, while the lay preaching interfered with what was considered the monopoly of the clergy.[14]

Hauge's influence in Norway cannot be overestimated. Dag Kullerud argues in his book, *Hans Nielsen Hauge: The Man Who Awakened Norway* that Hauge was the first modern Norwegian, whose Protestant ethic changed it economically as well as spiritually. When Hauge went into prison in 1804, Norway was an old-fashioned, backward country. When he was released, ten years later, he found a different country, one that had changed into a modern capitalistic state with a different feeling about the church. Many regard him as the one who finally Christianized Norway by teaching the faith from one end of Norway to the other. Many of the emigrants who left by the thousands for America went forth with faith in God and the confidence that by hard work they could build a Norway in America, as they called it, which they did, establishing colleges, seminaries, hospitals, orphanages, old people's homes, and missions that reached around the world, so much so that finally the new American church and culture rivaled that of the old country for its wealth and missionary expansion. His con-

---

14. Karen Larsen, *A History of Norway* (Princeton: Princeton University Press, 1948), p. 359.

cern that he and his followers "love both God and their neighbors" resulted in the remarkable success of his movement both here and in Norway.

Although Hauge had many well-known and effective women disciples of whom we know through anecdotal histories of the movement, Berthe Canutte has lived on in her own writings. Her work gives us a helpful glimpse into a world long gone. Although we are not certain she met Hauge on his many trips through her area, and she was still a young girl when he held meetings near where she lived, her unique work and witness proceed directly out of Hauge's ministry and teaching, which her mother probably knew quite well.[15] We can read in her own spiritual biography a story very like Hauge's story, one that gives us a glimpse into a typical conversion experience of a Pietist, from the point of view of a woman, an experience that was shared among Scandinavian Lutherans until the middle of the last century and the reemergence of baptismal universalism similar to that of the state churches in the old country.

Berthe Canutte

Berthe Canutte Sivertsdatter, or B. C., as she signed her name, was born on January 3, 1795, in Ørsta, but grew up in the Volda parish in Sunnmøre, Norway, amid the lovely fjords and mountains, about halfway between Bergen and Trondheim. Her father, Sivert Knudsen, and mother, Gunhild Rasmusdatter, raised her in the faith as it had been passed on to them through their parents. Sivert was an Enlightenment man. His first vocation was as a schoolteacher in the small village, a job he filled until 1798, when he was appointed *lensmand,* a county official, making it possible for him to share his learning with a wider group. He started a school in the area where the young could continue their studies, and founded a society for the improvement of Volda parish. As a typical man of the Enlightenment, he dabbled enough in science to build a small pharmacy where people could receive medicines as well as advice on their medical problems. His collection of five hundred books, quite large for the time, became the basis for the lending library he later established in the parish. In addition, his work

---

15. Bernt Støylen, *Berte Kanutte Aarflot: To Livsskildringer, forfattede af Præsten Bernt Støylen og Klokker G. H. Heggtveit tilligemed en Samling af hidtil utrykte Breve og Sange fra Forfatterindens Haand* (Volden: Udgivet af Knud Aarflot, 1894), p. 18.

as an enlightened farmer always interested in the latest agricultural science made him aware of the most current methods in farming. His interests extended to natural history, especially learning about the flora and fauna of his region. After a time, he became the publisher of a local paper, *Norsk Landboeblad (Paper for the Norwegian Farmer)*, in which he could communicate his knowledge about sundry things of value to the community. The publishing house that he built in Volda, was the first established in the countryside of Norway, and only the fourth or fifth in the entire country.[16] His accomplishments became widely known, so much so that he received two gold medals and a silver cross from the king. As a man of his age, he saw the need to teach those around him. Berthe, like the other women we have met thus far, was most likely one of her father's more eager students. Whether or not Hauge ever visited Berthe's home on one of his many trips through Sunnmøre, we cannot be sure, although we have proof that he visited the region at least five times in his travels. Stoylen supposes that Hauge's frequent appearances there awakened many in the area, and that the family, especially Berthe's mother, was an avid reader of the material that Hauge recommended for spiritual edification.

Berthe's mother, Gunhild, also an accomplished woman, had interests that were more spiritual. It was she who made sure that her children knew their Scripture, hymnody, and Luther's *Small Catechism* as put forward in Pontoppidan's *Explanation*, all of which the Norwegians valued as the center of the Christian faith, calling the collection *Children's Teaching (Børnelærdom)*. Already by the time she was twelve, Berthe, whose mother "was eager to remind us and advise us against all evil and therefore recommend to us that which was good and edifying," suffered a spiritual crisis, or *Anfektelse*, like Hauge's.[17] From her mother's instruction and her own reading in Scripture, Berthe had heard that "the devil shoots evil thoughts into our heads like glowing arrows."[18] Soon, she wrote, she experienced the truth of that statement. It was evening and the family had just finished eve-

---

16. Email from Andreas Aarflot to the author, July 25, 2007. Aarflot, retired bishop of Oslo and professor at Menighetsfakultet, is one of the foremost scholars of the Haugean movement. See his *Tro og Lydighet*, 1969 translated into English by Joseph M. Shaw, *Hans Nielsen Hauge: His Life and Message* (Augsburg, 1979).

17. A. F. W. Prytz, "Berte Kanutte Aarflot," *Et Treklover fra Norges Kirke: Livsbilledera f Gjertrud Egede, Berte Kanutte Aarflot og Henriette Gislesen* (Christiania: Norske Luthersiftelse, 1884), p. 26.

18. Prytz, p. 26.

ning prayers, at which they had sung a hymn by Luther's colleague Johann Agricola (ca. 1484-1566), "I Cry to Thee, O Jesus Christ" ("Ich ruf zu dir, Herr Jesus Christ," "Jeg raaber til dig, Herre Krist"), traditionally sung for family devotions on Thursday evening, according to Kingo's hymnal.[19] When they got to the second line in the last stanza, "I am lying here in spiritual strife, The Devil makes me fearful, and uses all his strength and wit, To take me as his prisoner," she felt as if the devil had "rammed his arrow through me so unexpectedly, like an evil shot, wounding my soul and heart so that I was at once filled with terror, anxiety, and unrest: my entire soul was like a rolling and restless sea."[20]

She wanted to be free of this sense that made her feel doomed. She feared that the Lord, with good reason, would cast her away into eternal suffering, thoughts from which she could not free herself. Her only hope was that her Father in heaven would transform her will. After retiring with her twin sisters, who immediately fell asleep, she began to weep until her pillow was soaked with tears. She wanted to stay in bed for the next day because of her weakness, she wrote, or maybe to escape, to run away, to beg for her bread, and be completely isolated.[21] This "heavy" situation, she noted, was not surprising for a person who felt abandoned by both God and the people around her. Among her family and acquaintants she could find no one in whom she could confide her terrible situation. Not even her mother could help her, she decided after trying to tell her about her experience. In such situations, she concluded, only God through his word could give comfort, but now even this "source of comfort" was dead to her. The Scripture, which had once given her comfort and joy, now pierced her soul, and wounded her, whenever she read or heard it. Everything in it seemed to condemn her; in fact, it seemed *especially* written to condemn her.

Later, on reflection, she noted that even though her Father in heaven knew she was suffering, she still had to bear these feelings as a heavy cross, one from which she desired to be set free. "For a long time, I had to hold out in this darkness and the turbulence of the *Anfektelse's* buffets and storms

---

19. This hymn by Luther's dearly beloved student and then his bitter enemy for his Antinomiansm was Jacob Philipp Spener's favorite hymn and sung at his funeral. It obviously appealed to the Pietist mind since it moved both Spener and Berthe.

20. Prytz, p. 26.

21. Prytz, p. 26.

until the Lord's time of help arrived." This is a classic example of God's call ("vocatio"), the first stage in the order of salvation. She knew how this worked from her own experience, but also she knew how to describe these categories from being steeped in the hymnody of Hans Adolf Brorson (1694-1764), whose hymnal, *Rare Treasury of Faith (Troens Rare Klenodie)*, had taught her the order of salvation, since Brorson had arranged his hymnal according to the order. Berthe's experience follows almost exactly the process Brorson describes. The experience of terror caused by the righteousness or holiness of God makes her think immediately of the state of her soul. After much unrest and terror, finally, she wrote, "he who knows our going out and our coming in from temptation, and what we can tolerate, finally let the sun of grace break out in me, and drove away the dark, black shadows that for so long had occupied my soul."[22] The moment of illumination *(illuminatio)* comes to her in a flash of light, or in her language, "the sun of grace." Suddenly, into her darkness came the words of a hymn from the book *Singing Pastime (Syngende Tidsfordriv)*: "No One Lives Who Does Not Sin ("Ingen lever, som ei synder"),

> No one lives who does not sin;
> I confess to my inner being, my courageous tears
> Hurry me to God for help and comfort.[23]

These few lines, she wrote, "gave my weary heart some comfort and some hope that the Lord would not condemn me for eternity."[24] The words also helped her to trust in God, although weakly, until one evening she found an old hymnal by Pastor Ivar Brinch (1665-1728) of Copenhagen, *A Christian's Pillar of Thought (En kristens Tanketøile)*. In it she found the hymn "Lord, O Lord, My God and Father, Graceful, Patient, Kind, and Mild" ("Herre, ak Herre, min Gud og min Fader, Naadig, barmhjertig, taalmodig, og mild"). As soon as she began to sing the hymn, she recalled, it was as if the Holy Spirit "opened my closed and locked heart, so that the word had a special power and effect, and I felt such a sweet and new sensation in my soul that through my lifetime I would never forget it."[25] These few lines

---

22. Prytz, p. 28.
23. Prytz, p. 28.
24. Prytz, p. 29.
25. Prytz, p. 29.

freed her and her heart began to be fed. Very shortly she began to be refreshed and her life made fruitful. "I do not know," she wrote later,

> whether a prisoner who has unexpectedly received a pardon and his freedom, could have walked out of prison as gladly as I felt now. Now the *Anfechtung's* storm was stilled and instead of my former anxiety, God's peace, which passes human understanding, triumphed and came into my heart, and then I knew that God's spirit was soaking my heart. O wonderful love and grace, whereby my soul lost itself in wonder and praise, and thanksgiving, when I think about and examine the boundless goodness and mercy shown to me, that you, my sweet soul friend and heavenly bridegroom, would in my childhood give me such a powerful visitation of grace in my heart and already let me feel a powerful foretaste of your redeeming love for me.[26]

This account is a classic description of the second and third stages in the order of salvation: Illumination and Regeneration. Like Luther and Hauge before her, and many others in the same tradition, the holiness of God and his demands were the beginning of the problem for the young soul. How can I love God and keep the first commandment? Like Hauge, she knew that it was not in her own will to love God; God had to change her will. As Joseph Shaw in his book on Hauge noted, there are those "rare" souls who understand the awful claim of the first commandment and know they cannot keep it without God's help.[27] She knew that until the Lord worked in her will, her spiritual strivings were hopeless. Illumination and Regeneration could not occur without God's help. Brorson, whose hymns had laid down in her mind the order of salvation's shape, describes the illumination as letting the soul's sun shine through the darkness and blindness of the sinner. Brorson's original hymn on this subject, "Break through My Heart's Desires to Relieve Them" ("Bryd frem mit hiertes trang at lindre"), describes the soul as being blind, deaf, and lame. "You see that we are walking in blindness, with no sense for the situation of our souls. O let the light of your grace rise also in my heart, so that I can see the way I am tending, the path I am walking, and its ending." Not surprisingly, this language is almost identical to Berthe's as she realizes, or *sees*, the

26. Prytz, p. 30.
27. Shaw, p. 19.

darkness she has been wandering in — what she has seen was so terrible she wanted to escape somehow from where she was going.

Her Regeneration *(regeneratio)* brings her the knowledge that she is now walking in the light. With this she has moved into another reality, and her past condition can be described from the future. Brorson's great hymn on the New Birth, or Regeneration, "God's Regenerated New Living Souls ("Guds igjenfødde, nye, levende siele!"), portrays this change in vivid poetry:

> 3. Evil by nature, and dead in transgression,
>   Cold as a statue, and hard as a stone,
>   This was our state when thou, moved by compassion,
>   Choose in thy wisdom to call us thine own.
>   Led by thy Spirit, and called by thy favor,
>   Heard we the life-giving voice of our Savior.

After this rebirth, she, like Brorson, is taken into a living, intimate relationship with the Lord.

> 6. When we realize what the Father thought
>   When he began to drag us out,
>   When he poured out life to us
>   And bejeweled our soul as the Savior's Bride,
>   That he loved us, the evil and hurt,
>   Then we must shed tears of love.

This begins the next stage, the mystical union, which is a frequently recurring image for Berthe as she describes herself as a bride whose bridegroom has come into her heart to dwell. In order to understand the rich meaning of this image, and its Scriptural sources in the Song of Solomon and Matthew 25, describing the wise virgins who await their bridegroom, one needs to understand a bit about the anthropological theology of Lutherans, going back to Matthias Flacius (1520-1575), who developed the notion that the fall so destroyed the image of God in us, that it was replaced by the image of Satan. In other words, original sin was no longer an accident but a substance in us. Regeneration involved a change that replaced the devil's image with God's once again so Christ could dwell within the heart. Although Flacius's idea was roundly rejected by the writers of the *Book of Concord* for denying the good of creation, it survived in Dano-

Norwegian piety, partly because the Dano-Norwegian church did not adopt the *Book of Concord* and Erick Pontoppidan used Flacius's notion in his catechism so young Norwegian Lutherans believed that the image of Satan lived in their hearts until they were regenerated.

We can see in Brorson's hymn that the soul, which had been stinking refuse, as he says in this hymn, cannot be joined to Christ until it has been completely reclothed in his righteousness. We cannot be saved until we are completely re-created in Jesus' image, and God has planted in us a "heavenly sense" or his image. In other words, our old self has to die, so the new one can be born. These stages are not a matter of knowledge or feelings for Brorson or Berthe; they both knew a living faith could not be born in them without a true conversion *(conversio)*, the fourth stage of the process, which meant a giving up of one's own will to the will of God. Conversion had to begin in the heart of God's own character and righteousness. The surrender of the will was fundamental. Conversion, like the other stages, was not caused by feelings or understanding; it was God who made it possible for the soul to turn around, as a favorite illustration of conversion in Scripture showed: the weeping woman washing Jesus' feet in Luke 7. Conversion, *metanoia*, could not be effected until the regenerated soul gave itself totally up to God's will. This struggle is a battle to the death, as Luther argued in his magisterial *Bondage of the Will*. The notion of turning around involved, for Brorson and the others, a terrible struggle to die to one's will, the hardest death, Luther had said. For the Pietists, however, their stress was not only the constant and daily dying and rising, but how the birth of new life made it possible for them to take their first step toward God, only by the power of God, and grow in his mercies. God is always the actor for Brorson and Berthe, but the sinner has to take a step, after being empowered by God. "Jesus, yes my one Jesus, He alone can and will move these stuck feet that I am so bound by; it is they, my soul, that you must, one by one, move a little at a time."[28]

While the Pietists understood, theologically, that the order of salvation was not a list of prescriptive steps that one must follow in order to be saved, practically, in their concern to teach holy living, they found it much more difficult to keep the notion of steps from looking prescriptive. They knew the terrible struggle of the will comes as a result of the call. God's Word works in their hearts for some time, until a moment of illumination, often described very clearly as light. For Berthe, it is "the Sun of righteous-

---

28. Hans Adolf Brorson, *Rare Treasury of Faith*, pp. 352-53.

ness that breaks upon her like the day." After that comes her regeneration — she is utterly changed, God's image is renewed in her heart, she is a new person finally, converted, or turned around. Pontoppidan's *Explanation* had given them the chart for the experience:

223. What is regeneration, or the new birth?

> That gracious act of God's Spirit by which he makes his abode in our hearts, renews in us God's image, and thus creates a new man of God.
>
> What change takes place in us when we are born again?
>
> We obtain a new heart, or a new spiritual life, that is:
> In the understanding, a new spiritual light;
> In the conscience, true peace and joy; and
> In the will, a holy desire, power, and longing.

After regeneration and conversion the "fruits of faith" naturally follow. It is of interest that Aarflot used *Fruits of Faith* as the title of her first book of hymns, all of which drive toward conversion so that spiritual fruit will grow. Both Hauge and Aarflot understood the fruits of faith to be the result of sanctification — a process that took a lifetime, or as Pontoppidan's *Explanation* made clear in one of the key sentences in his work, "What is sanctification? That gracious act of God's Spirit by which He daily more and more renews the believer after the image of God."[29] Once again, we see Pontoppidan's stress on the importance of the "image of God" being renewed in us, fundamental to this view of the Christian life.

In 1810, when she was sixteen, Berthe was confirmed. Her pastor, Jørgen Peter Meldal, during the rigorous catechization required before the youth could be confirmed, asked her the question from Pontoppidan, "What is it to examine yourself?" After she had given the appropriate answer from the text, he noted, "Yes, you have answered well. Our Lord help you to live according to these words." These words, she said, went straight to her heart, she said, and she prayed that she could keep them.

On her confirmation day, she took seriously the "dear promise" that she would make, and wept many tears, feeling the "warm" desire to live in

---

29. Pontoppidan, *Norsk-engelsk udgave af H. U. Sverdrups Forklaring* (Minneapolis: Augsburg, 1933), p. 117 (Answer 229).

Preaching from Home

Figure 3 Typical catechization scene in a Norwegian church by Adolph Tiedemand, Norway's greatest painter of peasant life.

the faith she had promised to take as her own. Her pastor's comment shows us a typical Pietist pastor at work, using these tender moments with the teenager to drive for some kind of conviction, if not conversion. As she grew into maturity, she wrote, she loved God so much that sometimes she hoped that she could die and go to be with Christ more quickly. As she was thinking these thoughts, common to many young people, she began writing a stanza of a hymn, which focused on the soul's marriage to Christ.

> My bridal dress is lovely, fine,
> My bridegroom is God's only Son,

Who sits above in heaven.
In heaven is the wedding hall
Where God's angels shall lead me;
I go from the tears of today
To heaven's joy and gladness.[30]

These songs, which she began writing while she was still a rather precocious newly confirmed teenager, show her to be much taken up with her own sinfulness, her lack of righteousness, her joy in God's undeserved love, and the glories of the heavenly home, themes well known to Arndt and his followers with their stress on the unworthiness of the soul, and the mystical union with the Savior.

Bishop Bernt Støylen notes in his short biography of her that Berthe grew up with many hymnbooks and Lutheran spiritual classics popular at the time: Arndt's *True Christianity,* Scriver's *Treasury of the Soul,* and Müller, with several books of Luther's sermons. Among the hymnbooks were Kingo's hymnal, Brorson's *Rare Treasury of Faith,* Petter Dass's catechism hymns and Bible songs, as well as Dorothe Engelbretsdatter's *Soul's Offering of Song,* among others.[31]

When she was twenty-two, Berthe married Amund Knudsen Aarflot, from the same farm as she. Their marriage was blessed with seven children, three sons and four daughters. The new vocation of wife and mother brought her new experiences and difficulties as well. The dependence of children on their mother surprised her, she wrote, as she had been very naïve when she married. Most of all, the duties of the household and the heavy labor on the farm, plus her children, left her little time to hear and read God's Word. She began to feel as though she had fallen away from it. "I lost the good stirrings and strong effects of grace, which I often felt in my youth, so that the spiritual life which the Lord had poured out to me in my baptismal covenant, seemed to fall into a deadly slumber."[32] This is also a very typical testimony of a Pietist. Talk of falling away

---

30. Aarflot, *Selvbiografi,* p. 11.

31. Bernt Støylen, *Berte Kanutte Aarflot: To Livsskildringer, forfattede af Præsten Bernt Støylen og Klokker G. H. Heggtveit tilligemed en Samling af hidtil utrykte Breve og Sange fra Forfatterindens Haand* (Volden: Udgivet af Knud Aarflot, 1894), p. 12.

32. Berthe Kanutte Aarflot, *Troens Frugt: En samling af aandelige Sanger i tvende Dele med tre Tillæg* (Bergen: Beyer og Beyer, 1871, 9th edition), p. 9.

from one's baptismal covenant and one's vows at confirmation is standard language in these accounts.

For Berthe, her falling away into a spiritual sleep lasted until she was twenty-seven years old, about 1823, when she and her husband received a visit from Amund Knudsen Brække, a well-known lay preacher also empowered by Hauge's ministry, whose words brought her back to a closer relationship with God. Brække was one of two followers of Hauge whose work in the Sunnmøre area resulted in a strong awakening among the people in the early 1820s, about the time he visited Berthe.[33] Berthe later believed he had been sent by the gracious Savior to awaken her. Brække stayed overnight with them, along with two other guests they were entertaining in their home that evening. Like all evangelists on the prowl for backsliders and the unsaved, he would not let the moment pass, she wrote, without speaking with the other two guests about the "one thing needful" as he laid out for them God's counsel for salvation and blessedness. While he was speaking, Berthe, occupied with her kitchen duties, listened as "much as I could." Berthe came under conviction, especially when Brække remarked that "no one is so good that they do not need conversion, and no one can be so hard of heart that he cannot receive grace in a true conversion."[34] These words, she reported, through the power of the Holy Spirit, were meant for her. She then realized that her civil righteousness, something she probably felt quite good about, could not stand before God on the last day, because he could see the evil in her heart. These words, she noted, were the means by which she was reawakened and re-converted. That night she prayed, after going to bed, asking her Heavenly Father to tell her whether or not she had wandered away from him, and if she had wandered away without knowing it, that he would call her back.

> And my prayer was heard, indeed, it was not long before a new light broke in my soul, and the Lord taught me to understand my own deeply sinful nature, and when I tried myself before God's command in its spiritual understanding, then it was easy for me to see that it was not as good with my soul as I had thought and believed.[35]

33. Støylen, pp. 19-20.
34. Aarflot, *Troens Frugt*, p. 10.
35. Aarflot, *Troens Frugt*, p. 10.

Not long after this she discovered that Pontoppidan's *Explanation*, Question 672, "How is it that one falls out of one's baptismal covenant?" had explained it was possible to do so. After reading it, she realized there was no way she could hide under "the fig leaf" of her own making, but had to receive her Savior's righteousness through faith, as Luther had discovered after struggling with the same issue three hundred years before. With that she found comfort in two old hymns in the hymnal of her day, "A Poor Sinner, I Must Go with a Highly Troubled Heart" ("Jeg arme Synder træde maa/Med høit bedrøvet Hjerte") by Johann Heerman,[36] and "Lord Jesus Christ, Kind, Mild, and Good, the Fountain of All Grace" ("Herre Jesu Krist, from, mild, og god, Du Kilde til al Naade," "Herr Jhesu Christ, du höchsten gut") by Bartholomæus Ringwaldt (1532-1600).

What she learned from this experience, she said, was that she could not stand before God clothed in her own righteousness. The Lord would have to tear off her old clothes so that he could dress her in the blood of his righteousness. "We are, however, unable to understand this truth, and would rather come on our own terms, than receive the free gift of grace that our Savior offers us," she wrote. With this she found comfort in one of Paul Gerhardt's hymns, "O Lord, How Shall I Greet Thee," with its references to the maidens in Matthew 25 waiting. "Despair not, he is near you,/ There, standing at the door,/Who best can help and cheer you/And bids you weep no more" (LBW 23). With that, her feet had been planted on the rock that could not be moved. Scripture was newly opened up to her; in addition, she began looking deeply into the traditional Lutheran sources of spiritual edification, especially the works recommended by the Pietists, Johan Arndt's *True Christianity* and Christian Scriver's *The Soul's Treasury*, along with what A. F. W. Prytz, her first biographer, called the "great treasury of our spiritual lives, which we Lutherans, especially, have in our many glorious hymns."[37]

This new experience gave her increased zeal for her spiritual work. She and her husband, who did not experience conversion until later, opened their home to visitors who came seeking a spiritual counselor, or *sjæleven*, soul friend, or *sjælesørger*, spiritual caregiver. Because of her large family and duties on the farm, she found it difficult to travel around the area to preach as many women in Hauge's following did, but her collection

---

36. Johann Heerman, "Ich armer Sünder komm zu dir," *Devoti musica cordis*, 1630.
37. Prytz, p. 46.

of hymns for the church year and her prayers and hymns to be used for daily devotions through the week, along with many spiritual letters, came to be highly prized by the awakened Christians in Norway at the time.

M. J. Wefring, a contemporary of Berthe Canutte, wrote in his memoirs that he had visited her farm in the fall of 1834 because he knew her "religious songs, which had spoken to me in a very profound way."[38] When he arrived he found the couple threshing their grain, but after some moments, Berthe left the work and invited him in for the evening. He never forgot the experience, he said. She was a very gifted woman, he could tell. "She was not very talkative, but when she spoke of spiritual things, one got a living sense that the word lived in her heart. Her speech and sociability bore the stamp of her humility and peacefulness."[39]

Berthe Canutte continued her writing and works until 1846 when she became seriously ill. As she lay in what she supposed was her final illness, she dictated a long spiritual song, which she thought would be her "Swan Song," something in the spirit of Brorson's last hymns, which were also called "Swan Songs." The song is entitled "My Days on Earth toward Night Are Turning" ("Min Levedag hen mod sin Aften skrider"). She, however, recovered enough to continue her vocation as a hymn writer and soul-caregiver, publishing several new works after that, including revised editions of her previous works. Not long before she died, however, it was clear to her friends, Prytz writes, that she longed to go home to be with the Lord. Some time before she died, however, she may have suffered what we might call Alzheimer's Disease today. As he puts it: "Her sensibilities were more and more turned inward, and the tearful glances of her eyes showed that her spirit dwelt more and more in the coming eternal glory."[40] On October 29, 1859, after a short battle with a cold, she had a stroke, which left her unconscious for a few days before she died.

Aarflot's Works

Aarflot began writing her poetry and spiritual songs about the time of her confirmation, when young girls often begin writing. She did not immedi-

---

38. M. J. Wefring, *Minder fra mit Reiseliv* (Christiania, 1897), p. 17.
39. Wefring, *Minder*, 1897, p. 17.
40. Prytz, p. 64.

ately tell her father or family about her work because she thought of it as private. When she showed her hymns to her father as he lay dying, however, he agreed they should be published. As with many precocious young women, her father's approval and encouragement made a difference to Aarflot. Although she was not born into the clergy, her enlightened father cared about her intellectual development and encouraged her.

We have seen in her own spiritual biography that the hymns of the Lutheran tradition, especially the penitential ones, were fundamental to her own spiritual growth and development. They taught her the poetic conventions and themes she would use even as they had taught her about the faith. We can hear in her work the strong influence of the hymns of Thomas Hansen Kingo (1634-1703), Hans Adolf Brorson (1694-1764), and Dorothe Engelbretsdatter (1634-1716), as well as Brorson's translations of German hymns by Paul Gerhardt (1607-1676) and Johann Heerman (1585-1647), to name a few. This would be natural to a young girl raised on the Kingo and Pontoppidan hymnals available to her at the time. While she may have grown up using the Guldberg hymnal with its Enlightenment revisions and new hymns, it had enough of the older hymns by the first generation of Pietists for her to care for them more than she did the Enlightenment hymns of Birgitte Boye. One feels in her hymns, as in many of the hymns of the nineteenth-century revivals, that the Enlightenment had never happened. That is not strange. For the awakened of Berthe's day, the Enlightenment had been a dead time when people thought they could "sleep themselves into heaven," a common expression among the people of the revivals.

Aarflot's hymns and songs, many of which she described as "occasional verse" *(Leilighedsdikt)*, that is, poems and songs written for a specific audience and specific occasion, became significant to the second generation of the Haugean revival, especially in the northwestern region of Norway, as Bjørnson noted. One wonders whether they were especially successful in that region because they were written out of her place and piety, because their references are so local or specific. They do give us a vivid picture of the life that she was leading at the time. They clearly spoke to those in her area who came to love and use her hymns.

The Fruits of Faith: A Collection of Spiritual Songs (Troens Frugt: en Samling af aandelige Sange)

Her first work, *The Fruits of Faith: A Collection of Spiritual Songs (Troens Frugt: en Samling af aandelige Sange)*, came out after her reawakening and was reprinted in nine editions, the last of which was in 1874. Its title, taken from Galatians 5:22-23, was a concern of the Pietists who understood sanctification as a fruit of the Spirit, accompanied by various gifts of the Spirit. She would have seen it most richly described in Brorson's *Rare Treasury of Faith*, with its several hymns on the various Fruits of the Spirit, such as patience. Aarflot understood these topics very well, but it is of interest to note that these hymns are not so much about the fruits of faith, or Christian virtues, as about being saved so that these fruits can come to life.

This collection is divided into two parts, the first containing fifteen hymns and songs, the second, thirty-one songs. For the most part it is a selection of hymns calling people to look to the condition of their souls and their certain death, and then to take measures so that they can meet the Lord at their death. As she noted in the preface and subtitle of the book, she intended it for "unconverted people" so that they would hurry to find salvation and not miss the day of grace, but by God's word and Spirit come to the knowledge of salvation.[41] Almost all of the fifteen songs in the first section are calls to attend to the matters of one's soul and "wake up," one of the most frequently used images in this section of the book. Most of the hymns use the rhetoric of a sermon addressed to those who are hearing the singer. As sermons, they do not paraphrase Scripture but preach it, although in these hymns she is not preaching on a particular Scripture lesson but on a common topic for sermons to these Pietists: awakening and conversion. She ranges freely through Scripture for proofs. Like any preacher, she has her favorite sources in Scripture: Images of awakening from Ephesians 5:14 ("awaken, O sleeper"); the wedding images of Matthew 25, with its parable of the wise and foolish virgins; Revelation 3:20, Jesus standing at the door and knocking; and the Song of Solomon with its rich imagery of the bride. Such images inform these hymns as do the hymns of the medieval mystics on these same themes. Each of these images has to do with the return of Christ and the last judgment, as well as the riches of the relationship with Christ, the Bridegroom.

---

41. Aarflot, *Troens Frugt*, p. 20.

Because many of the hymns or songs usually include fifteen to twenty stanzas, it is difficult to give the English reader a good idea of her hymnal, but one of her briefer hymns, "Now It Is Time to Hasten and Hurry" ("Nu er det fornødent at haste og ile"), can give us a feeling for the style she used.

Berthe Canutte Aarflot
Nu er det fornødent at haste og ile
(Tune: *I Kristne! Som gjerne vil*)

1. O now is the time to be hasting and hurrying,
   For Death is approaching us, daily it nears.
   So wake up, o sleeper in certainty resting,
   Remember that life is a long weary journey.
   The days disappear and cannot be recovered,
   Each moment and minute is passing so quickly
   And death with its judgments is quickly approaching.

2. Come, let us awaken and kneel down in earnest
   And pray to the Lord for our immortal souls,
   For we would be ready when death comes to take us;
   So come, bid farewell to the things of this world.
   So no one will ask us if we have been righteous
   But only how eagerly we have been longing
   To see the redemption upon the horizon.

3. For honor and wealth will not help you nor save you
   When all of the joys of this world disappear.
   For only those found with the Savior will triumph
   If we can be found in the wounds of our Lord.
   Oh, soul, let us rise up and dwell here no longer
   And seek from the world and its joys to be riven
   So we can be one with him, body and spirit.

4. Why are we so eager to flee and to wander
   Away from the strength of our crucified Lord?
   For all that we have is like dung and like refuse
   When he will give grace and pure peace to our hearts.

> O think it not greedy to taste of his mercy.
> God gave it with love so that we could be ransomed
> And given his gifts while we praise him in heaven.
>
> 5. So let us now lovingly wake up each other
> And run to receive this great treasure of life.
> So that on his coming we will not be fearful
> But run with great joy to receive him again,
> Our lamps trimmed and burning and ready to meet him,
> Repeating with Paul that our life is a treasure
> And gladly receiving the grace of our Savior.[42]

This text is a sermon addressed to the singer and those who hear the hymn, including an address to herself in the "we," a familiar kind of hymnic address to the listener that is considered the typical rhetoric of women preachers, as noted in the work of Engelbretsdatter. We know from the hymn's first words that the sermon is about preparing for one's death: hasting and hurrying so we can be ready for the judgment that is coming upon us faster and faster. She preaches the law by describing two ways in which "we" try to save ourselves: our own worldly strength and our own wealth. Neither of these will help, however, at the end. The only hope is our bridegroom, for whom we must be ready, like the wise virgins in the parable. Aarflot is not only preaching the law and gospel in the hymn, which is as natural to her as breathing, but within that form she is also describing the process of conversion, which must begin with an awakening.

The first stanza calls the hearer to wake up because time is passing and death is approaching. The second, third, and fourth stanzas exhort us to awaken and to see what we are doing: trying to find safety and salvation in wealth, worldly goods, or deeds. One awakens to the light when one can *see*, illumination, and then *see* that there is no hope outside of Christ. The only solution is "The redemption at hand" or "wounds and bloody sores," which give comfort that the world cannot give, because our own works are like "dung" next to the taste of grace. This image of dung is an oddly gustatory image, revolting our sense of smell and taste, but a more familiar odor to this farm-wife than we know today. That she follows the "dung" with the "taste" of grace shows that she has used the same sensorium for the image

---

42. Aarflot, "Nu er det fornødent at haste og ile," *Troens Frugt*, p. 3.

of sin and grace. What we have been feeding on without grace is dung. Her contrast of the gustatory pleasures of grace with the disgust of sin, or dung, makes grace sensually attractive and something to be desired.

The final stanza, with its exhortation that we should wake each other up and run to receive the Lord as the five wise maidens did, paints a joyful picture of the conversion, or the turning, rebirth, and the mystical union with the bridegroom. The story of the waiting maidens is a stock trope of the Pietists because it illustrates the significance of time, which is the major image of this text and which makes awakening and sleeping so important to our spiritual lives. Finally, the hymn puts us in the place of the people in Scripture, another common move in Lutheran hymns, from Luther to Dorothe Engelbretsdatter. What happens to the characters in Scripture will also happen to us if we continue in their way, both good and bad. This move is especially true of orthodox Lutheran hymnody such as Johann Heerman's "Ah! Holy Jesus," in which the hymn writer concludes, to his horror, that he, not others, was in fact the one who crucified Jesus.

Aarflot would stay on the topic of conversion to the exclusion of others in this collection. One gathers from her preface that her own experience as a fallen and sleepy Christian had created some urgency on her part to communicate to others that they also need to be awakened, even those who are not yet ready to greet their Lord. The last stanza offers a concrete image of the priesthood of all believers that gives us a glimpse into the notion of the lay movement from which she and other Christians in Norway had sprung. For her and her fellow believers it was the vocation of every Christian to wake the sleeper from the sleep of death and keep alert for the sake of each other's souls.

Only two hymns in this first collection might seem, topically, outside the theme of awakening: two for morning and evening family devotions. They, however, fit into her theme of the urgency of time. In the Lutheran devotional tradition, family devotions were occasions for considering the meaning of time, which is always sweeping us onward toward our end, with the rising and setting of the sun. Evening, as we prepare for sleep, is a kind of mini-death. More importantly, we should be prepared in case we die in our sleep. In the second stanza of Aarflot's hymn "By Grace's Short Time" ("Af Naadens korte Tid") one hears an echo of Dorothe Engelbretsdatter: "O dear soul, think now, before you go to sleep,/Focus first on the judgment of the Lord,/before you take off your clothes." These instructions to the soul before sleep echo the themes Engelbretsdatter used in her evening prayer, that the bed should remind us of our coffin, the sheets our winding sheets, our nakedness, a forewarning of death, something to remember as we undress. Aarflot's morning song encourages us to face the day and work but never forgets that as our bodies awaken, we should also make sure that our hearts, senses, and mouth awaken as well in order to be watchful against our final end.

The second section of *Troens Frugt* continued in the same vein, calling for the conversion of others, but now she adds her own struggles with the Christian life. As the small paragraph introducing it reads, "Mostly about God's Guidance of the author, his unwearying work of grace and call to conversion together with some of her inner strife and work."[43] While these continue to preach conversion to the readers, hymns in this section address the Christian journey or pilgrimage, natural concerns of her personal struggles, and the relationship between the Christian and Christ. Aarflot uses the very common images Pietists used to describe their intimate relationship with the Lord — Bride and Bridegroom; God, or Jesus, as friend — "Your Friendship, O God" ("Ditt Venskab, o min Gud"); and the longing of the Christian to be at "home" with the Savior, another theme of the pilgrim. The theme of "longing" to be released from this world for the next is profound in the language of this movement. The word appears many times in many of Aarflot's hymns, especially in this section of "O You, My Longing and My Pleasure" ("Du min Længsel og Behag"):

> You, my longing and my joy,
> Come and take me soon to you!
> See, I long so utterly
> To be taken home to you.[44]

Longing implies that one is not quite happy in one's place and wants very much to be removed to a better place. Jesus, the one longed for, is always dear, or sweet, the bread of life, our brother, the spring, or source, of life. Life in this world is a journey through the valley of the shadow of death, a journey that each Christian must make, longing for the heavenly home.

---

43. Aarflot, *Troens Frugt*, p. 46.
44. Aarflot, "Du min Længsel og Behag," *Troens Frugt*, p. 95.

Inger Selander in her analysis of the songs of the Swedish revival of the nineteenth century notes that for the Pietist the image of a pilgrim reveals the "eschatological bias of the revival."[45] One wanted to leave this world behind, to be with Jesus.

In this section of the book, Aarflot includes hymns for two high festival of the church year: Christmas and New Year's Day. Once again, these occasions have to do with the time of the year or Christian calendar, but this does not mean she preaches on any other text except "prepare," especially in the New Year's Day hymn. Like the preacher who preaches the same sermon no matter what the text, Aarflot can use any occasion or text to remind us that the time is fleeing and we must look to our spiritual condition before it is too late. No better day could be used for such reflection than New Year's Day. Aarflot's New Year's hymn, "See, How Time Flies" ("Se Tiden, hvor den rinder"), is a sober accounting of the dire situation of the soul.

> See, how the sands are running,
> And softly fall away.
> A year has now departed
> Reminding me to see
> The Day of Grace is coming
> And soon will reach its end.
> Think back, dear soul, consider
> How things are with your soul.[46]

This hymn also used the time-honored tradition from as far back as the Psalms of addressing the soul as some other part of the human psyche. Although the genre is still a sermon, now she is preaching to her soul. The soul must see to this so that "we" (the self and the soul) can "struggle against sin while we are in the world, so that we will receive our reward at the end of our journey."[47] These thirty-one songs in the second section are mostly for general use and are intended to be proclaimed like any sermon, by a preacher or a singer, who addresses them to those listening.

---

45. Inger Selander, *O Hur Saligt at få Vandra: Motiv och symboler i den frikykliga sangen* (Stockholm: Gummessons, 1980), p. 312.
46. Aarflot, "Se Tiden, hvor den rinder," *Troens Frugt*, p. 80.
47. Aarflot, *Troens Frugt*, p. 80.

The First Supplement to Troens Frugt

The first supplement to her work, which was probably published during in the 1820s, continues in the same vein with the themes of pilgrimage, the sweetness of the Savior, the boundlessness of grace, and her own sinfulness. These thirty songs include one evening hymn and one Lenten hymn, still known in Norway today, "O Lamb, I See Thee" ("O Lam, jeg ser deg"). Other hymns include one burial song, one before receiving the sacrament, and one for confirmation, a hymn praying that the one being confirmed will be blessed, "O Thou, Worthy Holy Spirit" ("O du værdig Helligaand").

Internal evidence shows that Aarflot probably wrote the confirmation hymn for the child of a friend who was being confirmed, rather than for her own child, as she was still probably a bit too young to have children of confirmation age. We can see in stanza five the standard practice and theology of confirmation as a serious moment for soul-searching and conversion.

> O, you, my young friends so dear,
> Who renew your baptism's pact,
> And you promise to renounce them,
> All your sinful works and ways,
> Such a high and holy promise,
> Do not store it or forget it,
> What your lips will swear to follow
> Print it also in your heart.[48]

One hears in this sermon the clear suggestion that for many the confirmation rite was a mere ritual, which she hopes it will not be for the person she is addressing. Watch, she says, since the "Lord is now standing at the door of your heart and knocking, so use this holy time to decide" (Rev. 3:20). The importance of catechization and confirmation to this tradition cannot be overestimated. Since 1737 and the requirement of universal confirmation instruction and catechization, with the publication of Pontoppidan's *Truth unto Godliness*, or *Explanation to Martin Luther's Small Catechism*, everyone had to learn these answers by heart. Pietist pastors used the occasion to push the youth to come to the "assurance" of salvation. It became a tender,

---

48. Aarflot, "O du værdig Helligaand," *Troens Frugt*, p. 126.

fearful time for the teenager, especially when the pastor cared deeply about the soul. Whatever its terrors, confirmation did raise the level of understanding of the faith in Denmark and Norway, requiring as it did the skills of reading, thinking, and memorizing. We see it in Aarflot's ability to work well with theological and spiritual questions. Like all spiritual requirements, however, it was easy to make confirmation a routine and a half-hearted exercise, which Aarflot warns against in the hymns: "Not just saying these things with your mouth."

The Second Supplement to Troens Frugt

The hymns in the second supplement are addressed even more directly to very specific occasions and people. It begins with a note from the author saying that she has included fifteen pieces, "some new and some formerly published songs." The themes are the same: death comes suddenly, prepare, prepare. These songs, she goes on to say, were written in connection with the departure of some friends by death, which, she hopes, will teach the reader that neither youth, health, nor strength can stand up against death.

> Happily, therefore, those who know Jesus' grace daily die to themselves and the world and seek to get for their souls the appropriate wedding dress, namely, Christ's righteousness; for those who do not have that, have nothing to protect themselves from shame, but must stand with their own dress before God and all the angels.[49]

These hymns give us a fairly clear glimpse into Aarflot's own life and the experiences common to the people of her time. We see how sudden death is, how she grieves the loss of friends in the full bloom of their adulthood, the frequent drownings in the sea, death in childbirth, and the death of young children.

Her first hymn in this section was written in 1822, after the death of some friends at sea. Here again we see the strongly evangelical flavor of her theology. She knows that the rhetoric of a good funeral sermon should be to address the grieving and say very little about the dead, since it is too late

---

49. Aarflot, *Troens Frugt*, p. 134.

for them. This is in obedience to Jesus' comment to "Let the dead bury the dead" (Luke 9:60), which meant to those thinking about funeral sermons that they should forget about eulogizing the dead or sending them straight to heaven but should speak to the congregation, as they are the ones who are most ready to hear the gospel.

One homiletical ploy and fairly effective literary convention Aarflot begins to use to good effect in these hymns is preaching to the living in the voice of the one who has died, frequently a child. She has the deceased sing to the parents and other bereaved to comfort them and tell them not to grieve, for they are now in heaven. These sermons preached by the dead were likely very powerful to the bereaved. Aarflot's first such hymn, from the point of view of a friend who had died, is the easiest to translate since the dead one, in this case, seems to speak more briefly than the living!

1. Come, friends, and stand beside my gravestone,
   Where I am hidden in the dust.
   Let my example be your warning
   To think about your coming death.
   And take to heart each one of you
   And use the time that you have left.

2. Our days are quickly disappearing
   Which you must rightly realize.
   Too many think their days are many
   Then suddenly are in their graves.
   O take this time of grace today
   To kill your sin with your own might.

3. O do not grieve for me, my loved ones,
   Be joyful in the will of God.
   Think only that we are but pilgrims,
   Our dwelling place, it is not here.
   Farewell, go forth, review your life,
   Do not forget your final strife![50]

---

50. Aarflot, "Kom, Venner, hid til Graven træder!" *Troens Frugt*, p. 139.

In the spirit of Hebrews 12, we hear the dead cheering us on in our journey, exhorting us to be ready, because there is little time left. The one in the casket is "hidden in the dust," waiting for God's judgment. There is no joyful, sensuous picture of heaven or the meeting with the Savior, only a bleak picture of the grave, which hints ever so slightly that Aarflot was not sure about the ultimate destination of the dead. Even if the dead one says, "Do not be grieved for me," it is not clear what the will of God was toward the deceased. The Pietists tended to be very careful about this. It was for God to give the final verdict. We also see the growing belief in the nineteenth century that the soul goes immediately to heaven. The two options in Scripture about the dead — either waiting to be called from the dust on the final day or "today you will be with me in Paradise," from Jesus' answer to the thief on the cross (Luke 23:43) — can both be found in Aarflot's hymns. She tends to speak more frequently of the soul already being in heaven as the Bride.

More affecting than this hymn, however, is the hymn from the point of view of a dead child. The child singing to her parents from beyond the grave, saying she is all right, and furthermore, praying that they will also become Christians so they will be with her someday, must have been extremely effective as a sermon. The dying child is certainly among the most common Victorian themes. Aarflot uses this convention in very persuasive ways in her hymn "Parents Who Are Grieving Me" ("Forældre, som begræder mig"), which she calls "A Spiritual Song, in connection with a child's death, written as the child's words."

"Parents who are grieving me, I now live in heaven, where joy cannot be disturbed. Oh, how I would like to awaken you to the one thing needful, to serve your God." The thirteenth stanza concludes with the wish of the child that while she is standing before the throne as a bride they will also be there. This typically nineteenth-century convention may have been considered acceptable because Hans Christian Andersen had used it in his affecting song, "The Dying Child" ("Den Døende Barn") in 1827, some years before Aarflot's book was published. An almost unbearably sentimental song from the point of view of a dead child, it was included in religious song books of the Dano-Norwegian tradition in America as well. "Mother I Am Tired and Will Sleep" ("Moder, jeg er træt, nu vil jeg sove") ends with the child being taken up into heaven by the angels, who kiss the child in the last stanza.[51]

---

51. Printed in "Kjøbenhavnsposten," udg. af A. P. Liunge, 25. 9. 1827, Nr. 77, 309.

Figure 4 "Come, Friends" ("Kom, venner, hit til Graven træder").

We can see what events in her own life engage Aarflot in each collection. This one appears to be mostly written in the 1820s and 1830s, when she and her friends are giving birth and facing childbirth. One of her most moving, and beautiful, is the hymn "Like the Rose Standing in Its Fullest Bloom" ("Som Rosen, der i Blomstring staar"), which she precedes with the words, "My feelings, put down in verse, on the report of the woman Gjertrud Johannesdatter Sætre's death, when she, in the full strength of her years, received notice from death and with a difficult childbed ended her days on January 1826." Aarflot says these are her own feelings, and even at this remove we can feel her loss, as well as that of the husband and the community. The second stanza describes how the friend had married on the good counsel of her friends and then had given birth in pain and sorrow. The third stanza describes the death:

> In loveliest of life's new spring,
> The notice of her journey came,
> To leave the world behind her.
> The pain of childbirth tortured her,
> She calmly waited death to call.
> Her days were short, not many,
> Before she had to leave us.[52]

The next stanza describes her becoming pale in the arms of death and explains the hidden wisdom of God in this tragedy, even though his ways and thoughts are not ours. The fourth stanza addresses the husband and comforts him for the loss of both his wife and child after he has had to drink the bitter chalice of unwanted divorce. The next seven stanzas continue, but now in a more general way, to comfort the community for the loss, in the sure and certain hope of the resurrection and that one day we will meet in heaven. One hears in this Aarflot's concern for the husband as she urges the community to comfort him so that one day he will be united with her in heaven where all this sorrow will be forgotten. Aarflot's own loss shows through, I think, in her overwhelming concern to comfort the community and the husband. The usual sermon about being ready is somewhat muted by this loss, so she dwells more fully on those in this life and the comfort they will need, rather than preaching on the need to be prepared.

It is also possible to read Aarflot's motherly heart in many of these hymns, especially the hymn for her daughter, Berte Canutte Amundsdatter Aarflot, who died after only seventeen weeks of life. Aarflot wrote two hymns for her. The second hymn, Aarflot noted, she had written as a conversation with her daughter's soul, now in heaven. "For some time," she wrote, "I felt as though I was with her in spirit. The first evening after her burial I felt my senses taken up to heaven with great power. Lord, give me the grace to fight the good fight, be my Savior until my death, so that I can be gathered together with her and other of God's children and be filled with looking at his face for all eternity."[53]

The song, more like a poem, begins with a very personal expression:

---

52. Aarflot, "Som Rosen, der i Blomstring staar," *Troens Frugt*, p. 137.
53. Aarflot, *Troens Frugt*, p. 146.

A few lines at your leaving must be written,
My thoughts rise up with right to you in heaven,
O blessed soul, who from the battlefield
Have now received your legacy of Jesus' grace.[54]

It was a comfort, she wrote, to think of her daughter in her bridal dress before God's throne where she would be united with her bridegroom. The thought of this scene made Aarflot pray that one day she would be united with her. "God, make it possible that I can also come to be with her by your grace."[55] The image of being dressed in the righteousness of Christ is one she used in daily life, as well as in her hymns. In a kind tribute to his mother, in his preface to the Støylen book, Knut Aarflot recounts his mother's concern after giving him his Christmas bath that he not only be clean on the outside, but also pray that his soul be clean on the inside, "made clean in Christ's righteousness, pure and white clothing, the only thing that can bring you to stand before God."[56]

The Third Supplement of Troens Frugt

The third supplement continues these same themes, but now we can read that Aarflot is getting older, entering her middle years. These hymns focus on the stages of life one goes through as one's children are old enough to marry and one's siblings begin to die. The collection includes songs for those facing other trials or life stages: one to comfort those who lost everything in a fire, a greeting to those getting married, especially to her own daughter, Gurine Marie Aarflot.

One deeply felt hymn in this section tells about her friend who died suddenly in a windstorm that blew down the building she had fled to for security. The hymn was

---

54. Aarflot, "Faa Linjer till Affsked vil jeg da nu fremsætte," *Troens Frugt*, p. 145.
55. Aarflot, *Troens Frugt*, p. 145.
56. Knut B. Aarflot, "Forod af Udgiveren," *Berte Kanutte Aarflot: To Livsskildringer, forfattede af Præsten Bernt Støylen og Klokker G. H. Heggtveit tilligemed en Samling af hidtil utrykte Breve og Sange fra Forfatterindens Haand* (Volden: Udgivet af Knud Aarflot, 1894), p. v.

> Written in connection with the sudden and untimely death of Mrs. Rasmine Larsdatter Digernæs (living on Fidske in Vanelven), in the month of March 1854 in very unusually hard weather which was at the time raging. She was crushed when a building, in which she found herself, either fell or was blown down by the wind. This teaches us how uncertain the times are, that we know neither the time, the place, the day, nor the hour when death will come, and those who are happy are always ready and prepared for it because of their faith in the Savior.[57]

This song sounds with true grief, but here she uses the occasion to return to her major theme of preparation.

1. Do not forget that you are dying,
   Come learn of this example here!
   For here you can see very clearly
   How soon it can come near to you;
   We do not know the day or hour
   So learn to know it from this song.

2. A woman at the peak of lifetime,
   The best years of a fruitful life,
   Whose blossom fell before the reaper
   While in its finest dress it stood,
   Just like the fiercest windy blast
   That brought her to a sudden death

3. The Lord sent in a terrible wind storm
   The notice of her death to her;
   It said her days on earth were over,
   She had no time for betterment.
   That morning she was well and strong
   But she lay dead when darkness fell.

4. She could not bid her friends or neighbors
   A warm or loving last farewell.
   Nor could a prayer sound from her body

---

57. Aarflot, "Nogle Vers," *Troens Frugt*, pp. 176-77.

With grace to comfort her poor soul.
God, stand beside us with your grace,
And keep us from a sudden death.

5. O God, who gives both joy and sorrow,
   Who pours out on us weal and woe,
   In your mysterious counsel's wisdom
   You send us also joy and tears.
   O teach us to receive it all
   And know it serves to do your will.

6. Come, strengthen us, in days of trial,
   And give us patience to endure
   And not forsake you in our suff'ring,
   But rather put our hope in you,
   So when you lay on us our cross
   That you will help us bear it well.

7. Your will is for the best, we trust you,
   Though it is hard for flesh and blood;
   Our hearts are bound to you securely,
   For when the world opposes us,
   Then you will snatch us, soul and mind,
   From all the world into your heart.

8. Although we do not know the hour
   When Jesus Christ will take us home,
   How blessed is the one who knows him
   And who in truth to him is bound.
   With joy he bids the world farewell
   And gladly goes to wear his crown.

9. So then we with our hearts are yearning
   To taste the sweetness of God's grace.
   All else is worth but very little
   Compared to heav'n's great reward.
   For what is all our pain and woe
   Compared to heav'n's eternal joy.

10. For all earth's glory now is fading
    Like dew before the morning sun.
    Our days and years will soon be ending,
    Next to eternity they're short.
    Best therefore are the ones who chose
    To take from him the better part.

11. O let us not neglect to seek him
    Before the final day of grace.
    And not to dream away the present
    In this world's dark and sinful day.
    For when the final moment comes
    We cannot buy another hour.

12. O Jesus, give to us your mercy,
    So we may rightly come to see
    That we can flee the final judgment;
    Redeemed by Jesus' side we'll stand
    Forever through eternity,
    To sing our praise to you, dear Lord.

The hymn begins, like many a good revival sermon, by setting out the occasion, on which she dwells for the first four stanzas — a narrative account of this sudden death. After the narrative, Aarflot turns to God in prayer for the next four stanzas, accepting that God gives both "weal and woe." By stanza eleven she has turned to address the congregation in an exhortation to be ready. The hymn ends with a prayer to Jesus that we will be ready when he returns. Here Aarflot's thoughts turn more quickly to evangelism than they do in the hymn about her friend who had died in childbed. In all of these hymns, however, and in most preaching of this tradition, Death is the most powerful evangelist. Its sudden appearance, the fact that we know neither the day nor hour, concentrates the mind. Aarflot always understood the homiletical urgency of getting people to realize they were going to die.

As we have seen, Aarflot's hymns focus on the Scriptural lessons having to do with converting before it is too late. She did not flinch from the Scriptural notion that God brings both weal and woe (Isa. 45:7) or kills and makes alive (Deut. 32:39). God will make "all things work together for good to those who love God" (Rom. 8:28). The hymn above, once again, uses such Scripture to help "explain" why God would allow such things to happen. Her first two stanzas point to the particular occasion of the woman's death in the windstorm. After the first stanzas, the hymn would fit any sudden death, something that the people in Aarflot's time faced much more frequently than we can even imagine today. It is not surprising her hymns were popular in the western Norwegian farmsteads of the middle decades of the nineteenth century. People needed these words and knew the particular situation out of which they were written. They expressed in poetry the feelings the grieving needed to express when they did meet such difficult moments in life.

The Soul's Morning and Evening Offering Containing Prayers, Sighs, and Songs for Every Day in the Week Along with Songs for the Four Seasons (Sjælens Morgen= Og Aftenoffer)

In 1846, Aarflot released her book *The Soul's Morning and Evening Offering*, the title of which brings one directly back to the titles of Dorothe Engelbretsdatter's *The Soul's Song-Offering (Siælens Sang-Offer)* or her last book, *Tear Offering ("Taare-Offer")*. Aarflot's book follows the form of Kingo's second book published in 1681, *Andelige Siunge-Kors, Anden Part*. Like Kingo's book, Aarflot's consists of twenty sections, each with two hymns and one poem, or "Hjerte-Suk" ("Heart Sigh"), intended for daily devotions. Her scheme shows how aware she was of her tradition with its Sigh *(Suk)*, a prayer appropriate to the time of day, and the day of the week, then a hymn, which is in some ways a versification of the prayer. Aarflot is heir to the hymns and devotional materials developed over the years for family altars in Lutheran homes.

Her hymns, prayers, and poems responded to such devotional needs. For Sunday morning, for example, she begins her poem on the day, "Help, O Jesus, to begin/The day of rest in your dear name." The prayer refers to the daylight of the first day of the week, comparing it to the living light of the word, which she hopes will have free entrance into our heart so that it can do its work. Sunday also reminds her of eternity. Her song prays that God will bless his "living Word, which will be proclaimed on earth so that it will bear fruit. Let them in your vineyard stand so the pure seed of the word can be sown." Typically, she does not pray that she can worship God, but that her heart will be ready to receive the word. Each morning and evening of the day has its special sigh, prayer, and song. After these daily devotions, she adds four hymns for the seasons and concludes with "Heart Sigh," a song in which she bids farewell to the earth and notes, in the second stanza, that her passport has been written in the blood of Jesus so that she can greet death with a smile, a frequent wish for the Pietists. With that, she concludes the book, which she had expected to be her last. Not long after it came out, she had an illness that she thought was her final one, but she was spared and continued to write more songs, as well as prayers and edifying letters to her many followers, which she also published.

The Soul's Spiritual Festival of Joy

Her next work, *The Soul's Spiritual Festival of Joy* (1853), included prayers and songs for the year's festival times, with a supplement of some hymns with reminders of how to know about the soul's condition before going to the Lord's Table. It followed essentially the same form as the previous book, only this time the hymns and poems were focused on the church year. She noted in her preface that she decided to write it because "a dear friend and brother" had pleaded with her to provide a similar resource for the high festivals of the church year. She did so with pleasure, she said, in the hope that she could provide a resource that would help those who had "fallen from the confirmation's promise." She prayed that God would use her words to feed the thousands, as he had used the five loaves and two fish.

With that she provides a prayer for each day, along with a short rhymed prayer, followed by a prose prayer, and then a hymn. The festivals she included are the traditional festivals of Lutherans from the Reformation: Christmas Eve, Christmas, Second Christmas Day, Holy Thursday, Good Friday, Easter, Second day Easter, a Penitential Day, the Ascension, Pentecost, and Second Pentecost Day. She has included festivals a bit strange to us today, but in Europe Second-Day Christmas (the day after Christmas) is a holiday, as are Second Easter and Second Pentecost days. Because of the unique organization of Kingo's hymnal into hymns for each Sunday morning and evening Scripture reading, a practice which continued through Landstad's hymnal of 1869 until 1985, Norwegian Christians knew the church year very well and understood which hymns and Scripture lessons belonged together for the festivals and ordinary Sundays of the year.

Aarflot concludes the book with a prayer in preparation for receiving the Lord's Supper. She approaches the altar with little of the penitential piety of Engelbretsdatter and no sense of being unworthy to receive the sacrament, which came in the next generation of Norwegian piety. Aarflot's theology of the Lord's Supper focuses on the communicant's hunger for grace. That becomes clear in this hymn when she preaches to those who, like the lame and blind, were hungry for grace, "Naadehungrig," as the appropriate way to approach the altar. One goes to the altar, she says in her poem, because one needs to receive the righteousness of Christ for which the soul must be thankful. "So thank you, Immanuel, for this meal of heaven,/Have thanks that you have fed my poor soul." The table was also for her a place for the union of the soul with Christ, as the bride of Christ, a theme frequently used by Engelbretsdatter and, as we will see, Lina Sandell.

Religious Letters

Her next book, *Religious Letters, for the Support and Edification with the Strengthening of Faith, Hope, and Love, with the Addition of Occasional Songs together with Morning and Evening Prayers with Appropriate Songs,* was to be her last. These letters, addressed to various family members — sisters, brothers, fathers, mothers, friends, sons, daughters — reveal almost nothing about Aarflot's daily life or about the recipients of her letters. They are more in the spirit of the letters of the apostles, concerned to teach the receivers about the faith and encourage them in it. Writing letters to one's followers became one of Hauge's most effective techniques for nurturing his followers and building up the community. In the same way, one does not read Aarflot's letters to learn pedestrian things about the writer, her activities, her feelings about the receiver of the letter, or anything particular about the receiver. They are purely spiritual in nature, what the Pietists could call "edifying literature" — and they were used much as the letters of the apostles were used, read over and over again to the small groups of believers around the area to which they were sent, and, finally, receiving the attention and gravity of being included in the canon of Scripture. Aarflot's letters — like Hauge's — would be read in the small groups of believers to whom they were sent, and became another way for her to preach. They are repetitively biblical, something like riffs on the Scripture, with generous quotations from well-known and popular hymns of the past. Aarflot frequently uses the hymns of Brorson as proof texts, along with Scripture.

In her preface to this collection, she expressed her surprise that she had been persuaded to publish these letters, which she had intended to be private and to never really see the "light of day."[58] She begs the reader to take what seemed godly "as from the Lord," and what did not as her own "simple work clad in simple clothes, for I have written the feelings of my heart in a very uncrafted and simple manner."[59] Because God had called her out of darkness into light, she felt duty-bound to share this gospel with all her readers so they could also be converted and come to faith, so that they could be advised in their own journey through the "Order of Salvation which God in his word had written."[60]

One of her letters to a "Beloved Sister" contains many of the themes we find in her hymns, poems, songs, and letters: The need to be clad in the righteousness of Christ, the bridal relationship, the images of Matthew 25 of the wise and foolish virgins, and the glories of heaven, because the time is short.

> Beloved Sister!
>
> I finally have time to send you some lines, for it is not certain that more time will be found for us to speak in person with each other. Since we are both suffering a dilapidated vessel: a weak body, so I am often reminded in my spirit that the end cannot be far away, and should there be some time left, it is nothing to count on in the face of the long eternity, toward which we go daily. Therefore I will lovingly counsel you, sister, in addition to myself, indeed, every person who will take it to heart, that it should always be our greatest concern to make sure our souls are clad in the bridal dress, namely Jesus' righteousness, with which we alone can stand before God, and that we could be found righteous when the voice of the bridegroom will be

---

58. Berthe Kanutte Aarflot, *Religiøse Breve til Opmuntring og Opbyggelse samt Bestrykesle i Tro, Haab og Kjærlighed med et Anhang af Leilighetssange samt en Morgen og Aftenbøn med hosføiede Sange* (Bergen: F. Beyer and J. D. Beyer, 1874), p. v.
59. *Breve*, p. v.
60. *Breve*, p. vii.

heard, so we can follow him into eternity, where there are beautiful rooms at God's right hand, and where we shall be satisfied by looking at God's face. Many people have the wish and desire for heaven, indeed, they have hope that with their death and at the end of their days they will be able to take part in the blessedness of heaven; but if they personally have not learned to know in themselves and do not have ground for that hope in God's Word and Spirit, it is only vain working of the imagination and the person has built on sand, whereby then, if not before, at their end they will find themselves deceived. Experience teaches us that it is very common for people to believe and comfort themselves in Christ without any previous change in their hearts or conversion or new birth, which always has a divine affliction with it, as Pontoppidan clearly says in his *Explanation* that the faith, which believes in Christ, must be awakened in our sinful tearful feelings; otherwise we are of those who are well and whose health shows they have no need of a physician, Matthew 9:12. What can be more needful after such words from God's Word than that we need to examine ourselves so we will not deceive ourselves in this most important matter; has the Holy Spirit made it clear in our hearts, that we, like the prodigal son, have given up our heavenly inheritance, and because of that feel an inner sorrow and affliction, then the Lord has already begun the work of conversion in our souls, and then we must be awakened, so that we do not still the voice of conscience within us with our own made-up comfort, which can be more than a strike, for example, since our case is not so dangerous, because our sins have not been of the very worst. Should such thoughts come to us, then you should know, dear friends, that they are of Satan's lively temper and our own traitorous heart, for truly, we are each of us the unworthy servant who owes ten thousand talents and has nothing with which to pay, so we must well confess as it stands in the hymn "Our Virtues and Good Works" ("Vor Dyd og gode Gjerninger").[61]

No, let us not crave grace or blessedness as a kind of wage for our works or neither for our suffering or for our own worthiness; for even if we have not had one happy day from the cradle to the grave, all of our suffering will not take away one of our sins; let us therefore pray God that he by his grace will drive down all the false pillars, on which

---

61. This hymn is not in any of the major hymnals Aarflot knew.

all our sins will build their hope of salvation, so we can come to feel our spiritual nakedness and in the poverty of spirit turn us only and alone to the crucified Savior and pray that he will heartily give us forgiveness of our sins, and that he with his daily sanctification himself will cleanse our hearts and work faith and love in us. Indeed, give us the power to go forward in a daily renewal until the end, so that the day of our death can be for us a day of redemption, and we, saved from sin and sorrow, can praise God through all eternity. Amen![62]

This almost breathless sermon, with hardly any breaks for sentences or paragraphs, follows the typical Lutheran sermon form of Law and Gospel, and assumes the order of salvation, references to well-known hymns, to Pontoppidan and, of course, the Holy Bible, as proof texts for her arguments. She does not need to persuade anyone of the truth of these quotations; they contain in themselves the authority of Jesus' apodictic sayings: simply quoting them gives her their original authority. There is only the slightest personal note at the beginning, in reference to her weakness, but these are fairly common complaints among women of the time. The spiritual letter was a well-known convention, and "the children of light" used it as a major tool of evangelism, so much so that they hardly knew how to write anything else.

Aarflot's letters show how she uses these conventions to comfort the thousands of people who read them. While they are not original or particularly compelling to contemporary readers, as, for example, the letters of a good diarist would be, they give us a glimpse of a time and a piety that Lutherans are heir to but may no longer understand or value. One does note she writes a few more letters to her "dear sons," urging them to remain faithful, than to her daughters, but one reads them in vain for particular references to their lives, something we would find in abundance if she had written them today.

We can see in Aarflot's life and letters that the Haugean movement, besides being a youth movement, was also a literary movement. Hauge's followers, "the children of light," began writing, as he did, almost immediately after their conversion. Letters were probably the more popular genre, since it took poetic skill to write hymns and songs. Life stories, or spiritual

---

62. Tr. Gracia Grindal. In the typically intimate, familial language of the Pietists, she addresses the recipient as "sister."

autobiographies, were also produced by many of these Haugeans, who had learned from the Moravians that a life history *(Lefnadshistorie)* was a testimony, a way of telling others of the gracious work of God in one's life at the same time it gave the writer a chance to take spiritual stock of his or her own progress in the Fruits of Faith. These were testimonies of one's life of faith, and it was natural for these people to want to write their autobiographies for their own edification and others.

Eva Hættner Aurelius, in an important book on Swedish autobiographies by women, *Inför lagen: kvinneliga svenska självbiografier från Agneta Horn til Fredrika Bremer,* connects many of the Pietistic women's biographies with the Moravian movement and its recommendation that Christians write an autobiography. Although the Haugean movement took exception to Moravianism, the spirit of the Moravians, as well as the earlier Puritans, was still strong among the Haugeans. They were also well aware of the *Confessions* of Augustine and Rousseau, as well as the writings of people like Madame Guyon, among thousands of others. It was easy for the women in Hauge's movement to take up the pen and write their autobiographies for the edification of other Christians.

Aurelius does allow that many of these are filled with religious clichés and not very interesting to read.[62] At the same time that the production of these works was massive, they have not attracted much scholarship, no doubt because the works are so predictable and oddly impersonal. Devotional literature, while produced by publishing houses even today, rarely achieves the rank of a classic, except for a few highly valued works, such as those by Johan Arndt, Christian Scriver, John Bunyan, Kierkegaard, or Oswald Chambers, to name a few. They do not record much about daily life, only their own inner lives. Still, if one wants to map the heart of this second wave of the Pietistic revival, there is no better place than in these dusty archives, in pamphlets whose pages are brittle, yellowed, and falling into crumbs on the library shelves of old Lutheran institutions. These antique devotional records have been left in our libraries for the most part because they spoke deeply to many in their own time. They are admittedly secondary texts, repetitive and derivative, with little original in them. As we look at this material anew, it is important for us to know how much they lived on the writings of Arndt, Spener, Scriver, Francke, Müller, Brinchman, the old

---

62. Eva Hættner Aurelius, *Inför lagen: kvinneliga svenska självbiografier från Agneta Horn til Fredrika Bremer* (Lund: Lund University, 1996), pp. 272-73.

hymn writers of the Lutheran tradition, and the English dissenter, John Bunyan, so we can see how united they were in their thought and belief, how lively and unitary the tradition actually was.

Her contemporaries knew Aarflot to be preacher of the gospel, so much so that even as she was buried, her pastor called her a preacher. On November 13, 1859, as her pastor, H. N. Wraamann, stood beside her grave in the church yard at Volda with many grieving friends and family, he noted that her entire life was a "serious sermon." After praising Bertha Aarflot for being a wife, mother, and friend, he spoke to those who had come to faith "through her writings, because in them they have found a help in the time of the awakening, a guide in their search after comfort and peace, and a strengthening of their strife with the world, the devil, and their own flesh."[63]

---

63. Aarflot, *Selvbiografi*, p. 35.

CHAPTER 4

Lina Sandell (1832-1903)
Young Preacher of Grace

In the summer of 2002, heirs of the Swedish Augustana Lutheran Church met in Lindsborg, Kansas, for one of their triennial reunions. During their celebration, they sang songs from a newly printed book of songs that included four hymns by Lina Sandell, the Swedish pastor's daughter whose songs and hymns had played a major part in their first songbooks of the nineteenth century. In a collection of five hundred songs, called *Hemlandssånger (Songs of the Homeland)*, published in 1892 by the Augustana Synod, over one hundred of the songs had been written by Lina Sandell. By 1925, when the synod published its English hymnal, however, only three songs attributed to Sandell survived: "Children of the Heavenly Father," "Strait Is the Gate," and "Jerusalem." Still, today in both Scandinavia and America Sandell's hymns are some of the most beloved of all songs in their hymnals.

Although Lina Sandell never traveled to America and had little recorded contact with the Swedish emigrants of the nineteenth century, they brought scores of her hymns with them. Her influence on the spiritual life of Lutherans in America was as great as any other Lutheran hymn writer, excepting Martin Luther and perhaps Paul Gerhardt. Her best-known hymn, "Children of the Heavenly Father," is a favorite anthem of several Lutheran college choirs, especially choirs of the American colleges rooted in the Scandinavian Augustana Synod (1860-1870). Many Lutherans were baptized to this hymn, have sung it through various trials, and were buried to it. It is one hymn many Scandinavian-Americans can still sing by heart. However, few know the story of the woman who wrote it or her place in

Preaching from Home

Figure 1
Lina Sandell.

the life and times of the Lutheran church in Sweden and America. Of all the women studied here, Sandell's life and work had the most influence, and her work has lasted the longest.¹

Early Years

Like many Scandinavian women writers of the nineteenth century, Lina was a pastor's daughter. Her father, Pastor Jonas Sandell (1789-1858), whose parents died when he was very young, was adopted in 1791 by his

---

1. Four books tell the story of Lina Sandell in Swedish or Norwegian: Anne Nilsson, *Flickan i Trädet* (1986); Ann Marie Riiber, *Lina Sandell* (1954); Sigrid Storckenfeldt, *Lina Berg, född Sandell* (1906); and Oscar Lövgren, *Lina Sandell* (1965). What follows is derived from them. My contribution to the scholarship on Lina Sandell will not be found in the biography — although it will give non-Swedish readers more than they could find in English. My main interest in writing this chapter is what I discuss in the final section: how her hymns and songs fared in America over the past century and a half.

father's sister and brother-in-law, a pious man. By the time Jonas Sandell was five years old he could not only read, but also write, copying out long passages of Johan Arndt's *True Christianity* with the dream of becoming a pastor. At the university, however, like many of his contemporaries, he began to lose his childhood faith under the pressures of the rationalism regnant at the time. After his foster father died in 1806, the youth had to fend for himself. He secured a position as a tutor in the home of a rich family on a country estate. Before long, he later recounted, he fell into worldly amusements, such as cards, drinking, dancing, and hunting, all despised by the Pietists for their frivolity and tendency to lure the young away from the faith. In 1809, Sandell began teaching at a private school in Lund with the famous Swedish poet Esaias Tegnér (1782-1846), who introduced him to writers such as Snorre Sturlasson, Voltaire, Schiller, and Goethe. According to his own descriptions, he did not feel a very strong call to the ministry when he arrived at the theological school for study. He began to long for his home and the life he had lived there. To overcome his homesickness, he participated in the student choruses that were such a prominent part of student life at the time and found refuge in the botanical gardens at the university where Carl von Linné (Linnaeus) (1707-1778), the father of taxonomy, had studied for a short time.[2] He, like Sandell, was from the province of Småland, in south central Sweden.

Although he was ordained in 1813, Sandell chose to continue his studies for a master's degree, which he received in 1817. While in Lund, he came into contact with Henrik Schartau (1757-1825) and Peter Lorenz Sellergren (1768-1843), two of the most influential spiritual leaders of the day. Schartau's powerful preaching, catechetical practices, and confessional theology, however, did not appeal to the young Sandell. He began a long correspondence with Sellergren, a popular spiritual mentor to many young pastors in the south of Sweden at the time. Sellergren had experienced a powerful conversion while a young pastor after he had disgraced himself with a drunken appearance at a morning service and baptism. Young Sandell, in a period of spiritual distress, called upon Sellergren for

---

2. Linné's influence on the pastors of his time had been enormous. He had taught that pastors should have a solid botanical grounding in their education, partly so they could see the handiwork of God in their daily lives. While his influence had declined by the time Sandell began university, the tradition of Linné's homiletical school, as it was called, was still alive.

help. Sandell soon realized that he "could no longer resist the spiritual wisdom that spoke through this man [Sellergren] and cast himself down before the Savior's feet and prayed for mercy."[3] Sandell began studying the Bible more closely, and reading the works of Jacob Phillip Spener whose *Pia desideria* began the Pietist movement, August Hermann Francke, the founder of the University of Halle, and Erick Pontoppidan, the Danish bishop and scholar whose *Mirror of Faith*, an almost mystical work in the tradition of Johan Arndt's *True Christianity*, was highly regarded by the Swedish Pietists of the day.

The woman to whom Jonas Sandell was engaged, Fredrica Engstrand, herself the daughter of a pastor, was somewhat taken aback by her fiancé's conversion and wondered whether or not she should break the engagement, but, as Sandell wrote in his journal,

> When I assured her that I had only the most honorable intentions and would keep them, she gave the truth room in her heart and gave up the reading of novels and took to prayers and began to use the Scriptures I frequently sent her. Her conversion did not happen immediately and was not as complete as mine.[4]

They married in 1818, a year after his graduation. Sandell began serving as vicar in a small congregation in his father-in-law's parish in Växjö. Sandell started a secret Christian club for the gymnasium students, which violated the Conventicle law still in force. Out of this group arose many leaders of the Rosenius revivals in Sweden, among them Peter Wieselgren, later to become Dean of Gothenberg. While Sandell served in Vaxjo, Esaias Tegnér, whom Sandell had known in Lund, became bishop of the diocese. Tegnér, at the time, was one of Sweden's most distinguished poets with an international reputation.[5] Although Tegnér was no Pietist and tended toward the deism of his youth, he felt kindly toward the young Sandell, overlooking his illegal evangelical work with the boys at the school, and appointed him chaplain in the cathedral, where he would often come to hear Sandell's preaching. Although Sandell did well in this position, he longed

---

3. Anne Marie Riiber, *Lina Sandell* (Oslo: Lutherstiftelsen, 1954), p. 15.
4. Riiber, p. 15.
5. Henry Wadsworth Longfellow translated his "Children of the Lord's Supper" ("Nattvardsbarnen").

to return to the countryside where he and his wife had grown up. On September 23, 1829, Sandell was named pastor in Fröderyd, a small village in the middle of Småland where there were many "hungry souls waiting to be fed," Sandell later wrote in his diary. He began his ministry there in the spring of 1831.

On October 3, 1832, Carolina Wilhelmina was born and was known as Lina from the beginning. She was named for an infant brother, Carl Wilhelm, who had died just before the move to Fröderyd and whose body had been taken in a little casket in the wagon with them to be buried in the graveyard in their new home church. She had three older siblings, Christina, Charlotte, and Nils Johan. Later she would acquire a younger sister, Mathilda. The young children flourished in Fröderyd. They enjoyed their environment, close to the plants and animals around them, in the middle of a forest with many lakes nearby. From the first, however, Lina loved being with her father as he worked. She even was given a little desk near him where she could read and write. This was a classic scene for a young woman of her time who would become a writer. Mentored by her father, she was preparing to preach, as he did, but in another venue.

Early on, her father saw that she loved the flowers in the area and wanted to know about them. In addition, he noted that although she was the weakest and least attractive of the children, she was the brightest and most spiritually apt. When she was old enough, he began to teach her languages and speak with her about spiritual things. "I think God has given her to me for company in my old age, to please me by reading aloud when my eye-sight begins to fade," he wrote.[6]

Very early, Lina began keeping a diary that reveals a spiritually precocious and poetically gifted young girl. As soon as she learned how to write, she wrote poetry expressing her delight in nature and her love for God. When she was twelve, she was bedridden with a serious illness. While her parents were at church one Sunday, she read the text for the day, the story of the healing of Jairus' daughter, who was also twelve at the time. As she lay in bed thinking of the text, she realized that Jesus could also heal her, so, with the help of a serving girl, she got up, dressed, and found the strength to greet her parents in the doorway when they returned from church. Some months later, she began keeping a journal entitled *Childhood Attempts by Carolina Sandell, 1845 (Barndoms försök af Carolina*

---

6. Lunds Universitet Bibliotek, Jonas Sandell Collection, vol. 5, 18/1, 1847.

Sandell, 1845). In it, we can find her poetry, as well as reflections wise beyond her years on such issues as illness and suffering, such as "The Body's Disease and Health." Along with that, we see her love for nature. One of her biographers notes that Lina had a "high heaven" above her, for she wrote so often of the stars, the moon, and rainbows, in addition to poems about the woods, the lakes, waterfalls, flowers, and birds in her region.[7] She had clearly inherited her love of nature from her father who, like many pastors of the day, left behind a considerable collection of plant, insect, and mineral samples from the area, which was exhibited at the Jönköping city museum after his death.

Young Lina was, like many future writers, a passionate and precocious reader as well. When she was thirteen years old, she was already reading, in French, a novel by Eugène Sue, *Les mystères de Paris*, which she wrote about in her diary: "After reading such an extensive book, which holds so much, but which contains so many dreadful and horrible events, one feels a certain emptiness in the soul."[8] In the fall of 1847, while she was learning German from her father, she began translating poems by Goethe, Schiller, and others. She loved the romances of the Swedish feminist Fredricka Bremer, books by Walter Scott (which she read in English), Madame de Staël, Alexandre Dumas, and Goethe's *Faust*, about which she wrote in her diary, "One is moved to terror and pity by the poor misled Margaretha, as well as loathing toward the terrible Mephistopheles. Madame Staël v. Holsteins has the opinion in her [book] *D'Allemagne* [*The Germans*]: *Faust* is neither a tragedy nor novel."[9] Here we see the young student working with a wide sense of the Western literary conversation. Lina already knows that the reading of novels by young women was regarded with suspicion and writes in her diary *On Reading:* "A woman must learn everything about music, painting, dancing, etc., she must learn about cooking, and housekeeping, and be made known and praised for that, but to read [novels], that she should not do."[10]

The young Lina also enjoyed the visits of many who came to visit with her father. Bishop Esaias Tegnér was a frequent guest, as was Dr. Peter

---

7. Lunds Sandell Collection, vol. 5, p. 35.
8. Anne Nilsson, *Flickan i trädet: En bok om Lina Sandell* (Stockholm: LTs förlag, 1986), p. 128.
9. Nilsson, p. 131.
10. Nilsson, p. 132.

Fjellstedt, the biblical scholar whose commentary on the Bible was widely used by the Pietists in Norway and Sweden, who had also taught at the mission school in Syria for fifteen years. Peter Wieselgren, Sandell's old student from gymnasium days in Växjö, also visited. Fjellstedt's school had a profound influence on the pastors of the time, and especially those pastors who immigrated to America. Lina learned from her father's catechetical instruction to read, not only the Bible, but also the traditional Lutheran spiritual classics: Martin Luther, Christian Scriver,[11] Johan Jakob Rambach,[12] Johan Arndt, and other Swedish writers not so well known today, most prominently, Anders Nohrborg.[13] Like most Pietists, she and her father regarded confirmation as a serious time in which she would receive assurance of salvation. After her confirmation, she wrote an ecstatic letter to her sister exclaiming about her first communion.

> Oh, my sister, today I have celebrated my wedding day with him whom my soul holds so dear. I am now bound to my heavenly bridegroom's heart with unbreakable bands and I cry out with joy at my endless blessedness: He is mine and I am his![14]

---

11. Christian Scriver (1629-1693) was one of the first Pietists, a friend and colleague of Spener. At Spener's advice Scriver took the call to Quendlinburg as court chaplain for Anna Dorothea, Duchess of Saxony. His writings are mostly collections of his sermons. The most famous is *Seelenschatz*.

12. Rambach (1693-1735) is an important link between the Pietism of Halle, where he studied with August Hermann Francke, and the Enlightenment. Francke's successor at Halle, he did not fear using the scientific method of the time and learned much from the theologian Christian Wolff. His works were mostly in the practical arts — homiletics, catechetics, and devotional literature. His most famous work was *Erbauliches Handbüchlein für Kinder*. He also published collections of his hymns, one of which survives in the *Lutheran Book of Worship*, "Baptized into Your Name Most Holy."

13. Anders Nohrborg (1725-1767) served as a pastor of the Finnish congregation in Stockholm from 1754 to 1765. After his death, his brother published a collection of his sermons, *The Order of Salvation for Fallen Mankind*. In it Nohrborg carefully described the stages of spiritual conversion. The book went through twenty editions. It was this work that gave Nohrborg his reputation among Swedish Pietists at the time. Ernest E. Ryden, in his article on Nohrborg in the *Lutheran Cyclopaedia*, suggests that he is a clear intellectual father to Schartau.

14. Sigrid Storckenfeldt, *Lina Berg, född Sandell "L. S.": Lefnadsteckning Huvudsakligen hämtad ur hennes egna bref och anteckningar* (Stockholm: Evangeliska Fosterlands-Stiftelsens Förlags-Expedition, 1906), p. 18.

A short time later, Lina Sandell wrote her most famous hymn, "Children of the Heavenly Father" ("Tryggare kan ingen vara").

Her exterior life continued quietly in the small village for several years, with a brief trip to her sister Charlotte and brother-in-law, Knut Almqvist, in nearby Jönköping. During this time, she was growing in her skill as diarist, poet, and hymnwriter. When she was twenty-one, in 1853, she traveled to Stockholm for the first time. The young woman drank in all that she saw: King Oscar I and his family on promenade and the palace where she would later be a frequent guest.[15] Back home, she continued her study, spending evenings as many pastors' families did at the time: doing fine hand-work while listening to someone read works by Goethe, Schiller, Walter Scott, and Dickens, in their original languages. That same year (1853) she published, anonymously, a book, *Spiritual Dewdrops (Andeliga Daggdroppar),* and in 1856, *Spiritual Spring Blossoms (Andeliga Vårblommor).* It was in the former that her hymn "Children of the Heavenly Father" first appeared.

On May 7, 1856, the Evangeliska Fosterlandsstiftelsen (EFS, The National Evangelical Missionary Society) was launched and became one of the most powerful spiritual forces in Scandinavia.[16] Carl Olof Rosenius (1816-1868) was a major force in the movement promulgated by the company. In 1857, the editor of *Budbäraren,* Evangeliska Fosterlandsstiftelsen's monthly paper, Bernhard Wadström, received a small packet of hymns from Thor Hartvig Odencrants (1817-1886), one of the friends and supporters of the Rosenius revival. He attributed the hymns to a "pastor's daughter in Småland." When Wadström found out who had written these fine songs, he wanted to attribute them to Lina, but Lina preferred that the hymns be published anonymously. This he did in the February 1857 issue of the magazine, when he published her song on Luke 19:44, "Det gifs en tid för andra tider" ("There Is a Time before All Others"). For a while, Odencrants served as intermediary, sending Wadström articles Lina had translated from English religious magazines. On December 5, 1857, Odencrants wrote Wadstrom a letter in which he included some more of Lina's work:

---

15. The king and his family were very much affected by the Pietist revival of the day. The general in *Babette's Feast* does well at a Swedish court because he has learned the language of the movement from his time with the pastor in the story.

16. See Sverre Norborg, *C. O. Rosenius — Nordens evangelist* (Oslo: Lunde Forlag, 1975), pp. 56-58, for an accounting of the phenomenal success of Rosenius' publications through this press.

> This one I have gone through at her own request and corrected a bit here and there so it holds its voice consistently with the original which she at the request of James Lumsden has translated. The verse, "Allt i allom Kristus," belongs to and ought to be printed together with the story, "Tom's Story." If these should be printed in their own special volume, which I think they should be, Lina Sandell wishes to see some samples. The other article which treats the subject of prayer, L.S. has translated from an English manuscript which a friend in England has loaned her and which she must return. This short article I have not had time to review. Read through it before it is printed because it needs it.[17]

Shortly after the first appearance of her work, Lina's songs began to appear one after another. Among them are some of her very best, and, ultimately, most popular: "Herre, fördölj ej ditt ansikte för mig" ("Lord, Hide Not Thy Face from Me"), "Tusen, tusen stjärnor glimma" ("Thousand, Thousand Stars Are Gleaming"), and "Lefver du det nye lifvet?" ("Are You Living the New Life?").

Odencrants knew, from the stir these new poems were receiving, that they needed to steward her gifts as a writer. He wrote Wadström, advising him

> to write quickly to her and ask her to sing praise to the Lord. She needs to attend to the great gift the Lord has given her and let its rich streams flow out to the congregation. It is even more urgent for I do not believe that she has very long to live, as weak and fragile as she is.[18]

Although Lina's health was always an issue, she did not succumb as early as other members of her family. In the summer of 1853, Lina's sister Charlotte lost a very young child and soon contracted tuberculosis, which ultimately proved to be fatal. In 1857, her sister Mathilda lost her first child, and not long after that Mathilda's husband, Per August Peterson, died. The next year, 1858, however, would be the worst for Lina.

In the summer of 1858, Jonas Sandell received an invitation from his old student and friend, Peter Wieselgren, now Dean of the Gothenberg Cathedral, to come for a visit. Sandell accepted the invitation with some trep-

---

17. Riiber, p. 71.
18. Riiber, p. 71.

idation. Such a journey was not usual for him — it would involve taking the canal route from Lake Vättern in Jönköping across Lake Vänern and then a river canal to Gothenburg on the west coast of Sweden. Although he asked his wife to accompany him, she refused, and Lina, whom he called his secretary, went instead. Sandell addressed his congregation with a farewell address that seemed almost prescient about his demise. The evening of July 27, 1858, he and Lina boarded the boat in Jönköping. Before retiring, Lina read Psalm 77 for her devotions, and later it is said that she had remarked on how wonderful it was to read, "Thy way is in the sea, and thy path in the great waters, and thy footsteps are not known."[19] The next morning, on deck, as her father reached out to take her hand, a large wave swept him into the lake. All she could see of him was his white hair bobbing in the water. Then he disappeared. Reports are that she became catatonic with horror. It was only after she heard the words of the psalm again that she was able to collect herself. She got off at the next stop and went home immediately with the terrible news. This new sorrow sent her into Scripture in order to find the loving God who she believed had somehow been in the middle of this. In her diary and letters, she continued her struggle with herself and God throughout the ordeal of recovering his body, the funeral, and the aftermath of his death. A year later, on September 1, 1859, she wrote,

> O, Jesus, my bridegroom of blood, I cast myself with all my burdens on you. I have nothing, nothing to give you, not one gift to bring you. I need to receive grace for grace, to buy without money. Give me what you see that I need, give me a greater faith and love. Especially look to my situation now, you see that I am so uncertain and doubtful in many things. I am not very loving with those I am together with. O Jesus, I am so hungry, feed me with your rich gifts. I am so unclean, wash me in your blood. Open my eyes so that I may see clearly what you have done for me.[20]

Not long after her father's death, Lina returned to Jönköping to care for her sister, Charlotte Almqvist, as she gave birth. On her way there, she wrote in her journal, "Help me to do the work you have set before me.

---

19. Riiber, p. 61.
20. Storckenfeldt, pp. 49-50.

Keep me awake and sober. Restrain my idolatrous heart."[21] While with her sister, Lina became acquainted with Aurore Storckenfeldt, a woman who was to become a lifelong friend. Storckenfeldt, a well-known woman with a great appreciation for both secular and Christian literature, had started a school in the city. Every two weeks the school held mission meetings where Lina encountered the missionary zeal that was to mark much of the rest of her life. Her greatest mission hymn comes from this period: "Thy Kingdom come, O Lord, our God, Thy kingdom come here on earth./Send out your witnesses with salvation's word" ("Tilkomme ditt rike, o Herre, vår Gud"). She also became better acquainted with her patron, Odencrants. A layman, he led Bible studies using Fjellstedt's commentary, alongside sermons by Johan Henrik Thomander (1798-1865), the bishop in Lund, and the writings of Rosenius, the leader of the revival. Odencrants also had great interest in missions and kept in close contact with mission societies in England, France, Spain, Finland, Norway, and Italy. In addition to his concern for missions, Odencrants took a fatherly interest in Lina and her work that continued until his death. Her frequent letters to him, housed now in the University of Lund archives, are a rich source for her life story. She was just beginning the richest period of her song-writing career. With a good audience like Odencrants, to whom she nearly always sent her work, she produced hundreds of songs. She could hardly keep up with the outpouring of song that overwhelmed her at this time. Songs came to her as she walked the street and heard ordinary people use the language, in the middle of the night, when she could not sleep for the songs that flowed from her pen. Because this happened so frequently she set a writing board beside her bed so she could record them as they came to her, word for word.

In 1860, Lina had to return to Fröderyd to nurse her mother through her final days, a task she dreaded, partly because the new pastor in her hometown was not evangelical and the congregation had come to blows over his spiritual emphasis. As she went home, she wrote, "O, dear Jesus, you see what now makes me unhappy. Strengthen my weak faith, let everything go well!"[22] After her mother's death, Lina wrote that she believed her mother had found peace and had rested in the promises of the Lord. She noted in a letter,

21. Storckenfeldt, p. 50.
22. Riiber, p. 70.

> Every time the Lord takes one of our dear ones away, it is like the view becomes wider. We stand there rightfully lonesome and abandoned, but then our invisible home becomes, instantly, so much more realistic. And that is important. We know that we are poor, but are eternally richer in the Lord himself![23]

The night before her mother died, in October 1860, Lina met Oscar Ahnfelt (1813-1882) who came to Fröderyd for the first time. Ahnfelt, known as the evangelical troubadour of Sweden, traveled the Nordic countries singing spiritual songs accompanying himself on a ten-string guitar. In addition to his own lyrics, he set both Rosenius' and Sandell's texts to tunes that made them immediately popular throughout the country. With Ahnfelt now a personal acquaintance, Lina had the musician she needed. From this first meeting, until his death, he pestered her for texts every time he was with her. "I have no peace," she wrote once, "Ahnfelt is here." She knew, however, that Ahnfelt had sung her songs into the hearts of the Swedish people. In 1861, when he was ready to publish the seventh volume of his *Andeliga sånger (Spiritual Songs)*, more than half of the verses came from Lina, whether original or as translations.

Alone in the World

Lina was now alone in the world, and her inheritance was not enough to support her. Most women in her situation would have moved in with a brother or sister and helped to care for the children, but Lina had greater ambitions. Her work of translating, writing, and editing had already become her vocation. Wadström, the editor of *Budbäraren*, asked her to come and work in the publishing house. The possibility of a job overwhelmed her. She worried that Wadström "had overvalued my gifts and expects more from me than I am capable of." While she considered the offer to work for them, she and her brother-in-law, Pastor Knut Almqvist, attended a pan-Scandinavian pastors' conference in Oslo.[24] Despite her sea-

---

23. Riiber, p. 70.

24. Almqvist generally supported the revival, but he had written a letter warning against the antinomianism of Ahnfelt. Rosenius had been charged with antinomianism as well and had found it necessary to defend himself against the charge.

sickness on the way from Gothenburg, she found the entire trip to be an experience she would never forget. As they disembarked, a group on board sang the pilgrim song, Bernard Severin Ingemann's "Through the Night of Doubt and Sorrow." Answering back was a mass of people on the shore singing Grundtvig's "O Day Full of Grace," which she noted was a "gripping moment" for her. That evening she attended a festival in honor of Josephine, the Queen Mother of the Kingdom of Sweden and Norway. The next morning, after a communion service at the cathedral, the conference moved down Karl Johan Street, the main street of Oslo, to the university where the venerated pastor Wilhelm Andreas Wexels (1797-1866), chaplain of the Oslo cathedral, opened the festivities with prayer. Although she admired Wexels for his popular mission hymn, "O Happy Day When We Shall Stand," she thought he was far too great an admirer of Grundtvig: "He gave Grundtvig all the praise instead of giving God the glory." Then she witnessed first-hand the Danes and Norwegians at their favorite indoor sport, fierce theological debate, this time a debate between the Grundtvigians and Haugians. "What Grundtvig was or was not, seemed to be a really fundamental question to the Danes and Norwegians, but the Swedes soon wearied of the strife," she wrote. The third day of the conference, they heard a lecture by Dr. Christian Andreas Herman Kalkar (1803-1886), the reason they had come to the conference. Kalkar, a Jewish convert, was well-regarded as a historian of mission throughout Scandinavia. He spoke on the three ages of mission and thrilled Lina, who wrote, "O, if I could only reproduce the wonderfully large diagram he rolled out."[25] Theological conflict interested her but little throughout her life. What she loved was Bible study and Christian history.

In September 1861, Lina, who had finally agreed to take the call, came to Stockholm for a few weeks to arrange for her work. On July 22, 1861, Odencrants had written to Wadström, "She wishes to begin with translations, small things, not too big pieces." She needs, he continued, "a good salary," for her gifts are many and will do much for the publishing house. Not only would she like to contribute her own materials to the house, but she would also translate and edit articles as needed.[26]

When Lina came to Stockholm to take up her work at the publishing house, the Conventicle law forbidding the gathering of lay people for reli-

25. Storckenfeldt, pp. 75-76.
26. Riiber, p. 78.

Figure 2 Lina as a young woman, EFS Archives, Stockholm.

gious meetings had been repealed for two years, and activities for laymen had greatly increased. Laymen were preaching and proclaiming God's word in mission houses, private homes, and at other gatherings. Colporteurs, laypeople who did evangelism through tracts, needed printed materials to take with them as they traveled the highways and byways of Sweden. Many important Swedes at the time came to a living faith through the revival, among them singer Jenny Lind (1820-1887) and the king's sister, Princess Eugenia (1830-1889), two of Sweden's most famous women at the time.

Although the churchly establishment took a dim view of these meetings because they threatened the unity of the church and its authority, breaking the connection between the pastor and his congregation by turning the spiritual life of the people toward the meetinghouse, the revival had a profound effect on many people throughout Sweden.[27] Rosenius, one of the main forces in the revival, had also grown up in a parsonage and had planned to be a pastor, but spiritual conditions at the university were such that he could not finish the course of studies he had begun. He went to Stockholm where the English Methodist preacher, George Scott, gave him spiritual counsel. Scott had come to Stockholm to minister to the English population there, but his influence quickly spread to the Swedes. Scott had collected money for his mission to Sweden in both England and America, on behalf of the American and Foreign Mission Society; since his talks had presented the Swedish church in an unflattering light, he was not allowed back into Sweden. This meant that Rosenius, his chief disciple, had to take over at the age of twenty-six. Rosenius acquitted himself well. He wrote and edited the paper *The Pietist (Pietisten)*, writing devotions on the biblical books of Romans and John, which were later collected and published. Lina had read this paper from the time she was a young girl, as had thousands of others in Sweden. In 1855, it is said, it had almost twice as many subscribers as the most popular newspaper in Sweden, *Aftonbladet*.

When she came to Stockholm, about September 15, 1861, a friend found her a place at a girls' boarding house run by a Mrs. Hammarstedt. "I have my own pleasant room," she wrote, "four stories up, with the most beautiful view. I can see the palace and five churches from the win-

---

27. Sven Gustafsson, *Nyevangelismens kyrkokritik (Bibliotheca theologicae practicae)*, ed. Ake Andrén and Sven Kjöllerström (Lund: Gleerup, 1962), p. 22.

dow."²⁸ Almost as soon as she arrived in Stockholm, she was invited to the Rosenius' home for dinner. "It was wonderful to be invited into his home. He received me with a fatherly spirit. O, how he exudes love and confidence! I have even heard him preach in Bethlehem Church; just as he writes, good and glorious."²⁹ Quickly getting started, by November 1861 Lina was working very hard editing the new songbook *The Pilgrim's Harp (Pilgrimsharpan)*, plus a translation of a German history of missions. Her immediate concern was the production of a history of the journeys of St. Paul, and then a series of stories about Christian heroes. The publisher was thinking of beginning a paper called *The City Missionary (Stadtmissionären)*, but Lina needed to prepare other songs for *Budbäraren*, their main journal. It was pressing work for her amid the theological debates of the day. "O that we could only see everything in the light of eternity, then we would sing and speak completely otherwise," she sighed in a letter dated November 8, 1861.³⁰

Lina's work brought her into close contact with Rosenius and his wife. She was a frequent guest in their home and spoke warmly of her times with them, but her involvement in the publishing house also brought her into contact with the theological conflicts of the day. It surprised her that in Stockholm one had to be more careful of what one thought.

> Because of my position at the Evangeliska Fosterlands-Stiftelsen, I have come to be in the middle of the storm between two different emphases, and that has cost a lot of struggle... which proves the point of Luther that the law lives in our hearts every day, but the gospel is a special guest.³¹

In August of that year, when the new songbook *Pilgrimsharpan* appeared, it was such a success that the publishers had to plan another edition of it. Her work editing the book took the entire winter. It contained many of her hymns. Over all, it sold nearly sixty thousand copies and became the basis for *SionsToner*, the songbook that the Evangeliska Fosterlandsstiftelsen

---

28. Storckenfeldt, p. 79, from a letter written from Brunkebergs Hotel on September 17, 1861.
29. Storckenfeldt, p. 79.
30. Storckenfeldt, p. 81.
31. Storckenfeldt, p. 83.

Figure 3 Sandell's sponsor, Carl Olof Rosenius.

published later, and which was really Lina Sandell's book. Over one hundred and fifty of her hymns were included in it and the book became a favorite in Sweden over the generations. (By 1949, almost six hundred seventy thousand copies had been sold.) Very quickly into the revival, Ahnfelt, Rosenius, and Sandell had created an impressive body of evangelical songs that rivaled the number of American gospel songs of the same era. "No one," said Rosenius, "can sing of the free gift of grace like Lina Sandell." During the time that she was editing the book, she was living with her sister, Mathilda, and brother-in-law, Per August Peterson, in Hökaberg. There she renewed her acquaintance with Luther's commentary on Galatians, which she had read with her father and Rosenius. "How indescribably precious and dear. When the Lord works, even what I have read before is made new in an altogether special way."[32]

In 1863, she had to spend considerable time caring for her two sisters,

---

32. Storckenfeldt, pp. 85-86.

who were ill with tuberculosis. As soon as Charlotte died, the other one, Christina, now the pastor's wife in Fröderyd, became ill.

> My dear sister is very ill and it looks as if she will go under with the same disease as my other sister. My heart has always been particularly attached to this sister, and we have been united more than the other siblings, but maybe this is a bond which the Lord in his great zeal must break apart.[33]

Once again, she regarded these losses as necessary for her to keep her trust only in God.

During the next four years, Lina continued to produce materials at an impressive rate. She wrote some of her best-known songs at this time, along with the usual work associated with being an editor. As her vocation flourished, she faced a new, and surprisingly troubling, question in her life. A wealthy businessman, Carl Oscar Berg, had asked her to marry him. They shared a common interest in mission, evangelism, and temperance, all part of Rosenius' movement. He was seven years younger than she was. She had settled into being something of an old maid, married to her work and Jesus. The thought of marriage panicked her, and the letters sent back and forth to her friends, mentors, and family are filled with her questions as to what she should do. The proposal changed the vision she had of herself. Her very successful life as an author and editor was not an ordinary one for a woman in those days. One could imagine that for a woman who had achieved this much on her own such a proposal might cause panic. Would she have to leave her work, which she loved, and exchange it for housewifery? Whatever the reason, her letters and journals tremble with fear and indecision. "Earthly happiness has never interested me," she wrote. On January 19, 1866, she noted, "A bitter morning. I have wept much this morning. Who knows how God will lead in all this?"[34]

Even by the fall of 1866, she had not decided. While she continued to consider the proposal, she went with her brother-in-law, Almqvist, on a trip that was originally intended to take them to Germany, Switzerland, and France. For whatever reason, they turned back in Hamburg, after visit-

---

33. Storckenfeldt, pp. 90-91.
34. Storckenfeldt, p. 110, Lina Sandell's diary, January 19, 1866.

ing several museums with their host, Johann Hinrich Wichern (1808-1881), known as the "Father of Inner Missions." A pioneer in establishing the German Sunday School movement, he had begun a mission to juvenile boys in Horn, a suburb of Hamburg, known as the Rauhe Haus.[35] Here they made further contacts with missions other than their own, in particular, Sister Roerdick, the leader of the Bethesda Deaconess home, but after a short time, they returned to Sweden. On their way home, they stopped in Copenhagen, where Lina went to see an opera, something she had always wanted to do. She does not record which opera it was, but she writes,

> I have many times wanted to see a performance of this kind, but of course, I couldn't attend in Stockholm since I hadn't wanted to trouble the consciences of others. During the performance, I had the most unpleasant feeling. Simply that it was theater troubled me, at the same time I felt the inner need to thank God for the grace to live in a kingdom of reality and truth.[36]

Lina's severe piety did not allow much room for frivolity, and the stage was a special worry for Pietists, partly because it was based on illusion, not truth. The theater, with its representation of life, not always edifying, troubled her, a not uncommon attitude for those influenced by Spener and the Pietist movement.

On her way home to Stockholm from Copenhagen, Lina stopped off to visit friends and family in Jönköping. While there, she wrote her mentor, Pastor Wadström, on October 23, 1866, concerning the proposal from Berg. "I have regarded Oscar in a way that I do not think is the way a woman loves a man. It has made me happy to think that I can do his soul some good," but she wondered whether his love for her would "drive him away from the Lord." She admitted that his "friendship and kindness toward me when I was sick, upset, lonesome, have many times made me glad and edified me, and I have taken it as God's gift and thanked God for it." She worried that Oscar held her in too high regard and had "almost made

---

35. Wichern is most famous in Germany for his espousing of the conservative side in the political struggles of his day. He is best remembered for his rousing speech at the Kirchentag in Wittenberg in 1848 in which he argued that "love not less than faith is the church's indispensable mark."

36. Riiber, pp. 109-10.

an idol of her."[37] Her letter goes on for pages with such wildly contradictory emotions. For the next few months, she was not clear as to what her decision would be, until Odencrants intervened in a letter. According to Riiber, Lina's letters to him had so many sentences cut out that they were gibberish for those who might want to read them.[38] It is apparent that she felt his letter had accused her of "playing" with God's will for her life. This struck hard. She asked forgiveness for her response, but noted that it was difficult for her to hear such.[39]

Berg, ever the patient suitor, visited her in February 1867, but before he did so, he stopped to visit with Odencrants to discuss what he should do. Finally, Odencrants wrote: "I, therefore, in the name of the Lord, give Lina the counsel to take Berg as her husband. I at the same time ask Lina to rest in this as a final request and no longer think of this case anymore as troubling to her conscience."[40] With this, Lina decided that she should indeed marry Berg. On May 21, 1867, they were married at her sister's home in Småland. She was almost 35 and he was 28. Along with her brother and sisters, Rosenius and his wife attended. Everyone must have been both surprised and relieved.

Marriage and Family

The newly married couple set up housekeeping in Stockholm. Berg, whose wealth made it possible for them to live comfortably, had found a home that was far beyond what she had known back in Fröderyd. Now she was living in a gentleman's home in the middle of Stockholm. Almost immediately, Lina began to describe her marriage as part of God's will. She wrote a letter to Odencrants describing her feelings. She was thankful to God, she wrote, for he had shown her in many new ways the truth that "he gives far more than what we think or understand we should pray for."[41]

For their wedding trip, they traveled to Finland where Berg had some business affairs to attend to. While there, they met Professor Zacharias Topelius (1818-1898), a Finnish patriot, and one of the poets of nineteenth-

37. Lina Sandell to Wadström, October 23, 1866, in Riiber, p. 111.
38. Riiber, p. 115.
39. Riiber, p. 115.
40. Riiber, p. 115.
41. Riiber, p. 118.

century nationalistic Finnish literature. When they met, Topelius was working on a Finnish version of the Wallin hymnal. At this time in his life, he was experiencing something of a religious awakening, and found the writings and work of Rosenius to be helpful. In the summer of 1868, he and his wife visited the Bergs at their summer cabin, Fjällstugan, in the Stockholm Archipelago, where they exchanged insights into the writing of hymns and the editing of hymnals.

Shortly after Lina's marriage, her friend Rosenius became mortally ill. By this time, she and Oscar had been frequent guests in the Rosenius home, and they had come to be close friends and colleagues. His declining health through the last part of 1867 had been a sorrow to her. In a letter written some weeks before his death in February 1868, she described a typical meeting in Rosenius' home:

> We went there about 8:30 because he seems to be stronger in the morning than in the afternoon. A good number of friends had come together that morning. Flowers filled the room along with other small gifts that witnessed to the love and care they had for him. After coffee Lindberg read Psalm 103 and gave a short exposition of it. R. spoke after that for over an hour on the ending of the psalm. It was like heaven on earth. Among other things that R. said, "We must never abandon the belief that sinners must live each day by grace, until it has been decided in heaven that there will be nothing else on earth." He spoke incredibly beautifully about God's fatherly love for us, of which he is a living example here on earth.[42]

When he died, Lina wrote to a friend that the death struggle was hard and long, but many of his friends surrounded his bed, singing and praying for him, while one of the brothers read aloud thanks and praise. Some nine months after Rosenius' death, on October 4, 1868, Lina gave birth to a dead baby girl. All the references to this event in Lina's letters and journals have been carefully clipped out by Lina or later archivists. Anna Nilsson, Sandell's most recent biographer and one who has a more modern interest in sexual matters than the pious biographers preceding her, is the only one to note this event, which was found in the St. Clara parish record of births.[43] Why Lina

42. Storckenfeldt, p. 128.
43. Nilsson, p. 158.

chose to suppress this event we do not know. We do know that she was quite ill the next few months and needed to return to Hökaberg, her sister's home, to recover her strength.

Meanwhile, her work was continuing at full speed. *Korsblomman*, the almanac she had prepared for every year, seemed a burden to her at this time. Writing to a friend in January 1868, she had called it her "child of pain, that poor *Korsblomman* which has caused me much woe, although God has his hand in this as well."[44]

During this time, because of trips to her home province to recover her health, she became good friends with Gunnar Wennerbeg's wife, who came to Lina for spiritual counsel.[45] By this time, in her very short period as homemaker, Lina and Oscar had established their home as a hospitality center for those interested in the Swedish revival. She and her husband warmly received guests from the Scottish Free Church, which had been supporting the revival, from the Moravians in Germany, the Waldensians in Italy, missionaries from China, Persians, and native Africans. With Oscar's wealth, she was able to keep at least one, sometimes three, servants who helped with the tasks which would have overwhelmed Lina; according to her friends, she had neither the health nor the skill for housekeeping.

About this same time, Lina and Oscar received a call to serve in the mission field in Massaua, Ethiopia, where Oscar could set up an export business between Sweden and Ethiopia, while establishing a refuge for Swedish missionaries in East Africa, especially those sent out by Evangeliska Fosterlandsstiftelsen. The couple struggled with their call. Lina had read about the great need of the mission ever since it had started. The missionaries had suffered in establishing the mission, and the Swedes had just heard that two of their pioneer missionaries, Kjellberg and Elfblad, sent out in 1865, had been brutally murdered. The entire organization and Swedish supporters of mission became intent on working even harder to bring the message of Christ to Ethiopia after this tragedy.

---

44. Storckenfeldt, p. 127, letter by Lina Sandell, January, 1868.

45. Wennerberg, one of the most popular composers of songs in Sweden at the time, was leader of the Ecclesiastical Department of the church. It was also during these years that he was putting together a collection of *David's Psalms (Davids psalmer)* for solo and choirs, which became a fundamental part of the repertoire of the Scandinavian male choruses of the day. His version of Psalm 139 survives in LBW 311.

After much prayer and conversation, Lina decided that it would not be good for Oscar to give up his successful business, which made it possible for them to do good. Nor would it be wise for her to leave her established career and place in the publishing house. The delicate state of her health she took as a welcome sign from God preventing her from going. To help her with her daily tasks, her niece, Hanna Peterson, the oldest daughter of Mathilda, moved in with her. Not only was Lina's health quite precarious, but she also felt she was needed in her work. By now, Lina was breaking new paths in the production of edifying literature for children, following the example of the Sunday School Unions in the Anglo-Saxon countries. Sigrid Storckenfeldt, the daughter of Lina's old friend, Aurore, suggests that Lina Sandell was the main force behind the development of Christian literature for children in Sweden at that time. Storckenfeldt writes,"If she did not translate the piece herself, a great many of them were published at her initiative."[46]

Along with her spiritual songs and *Korsblomman*, she found the energy to prepare a *Library of Christian Biographies*, a 576-page book with illustrations on the great heroes and heroines of the faith. She delighted the young with books like *Jessica's First Prayer (Jessicas första bön)*. One of her colleagues, Pastor Lundborg, had returned from Scotland with the idea of establishing Sweden's first illustrated children's magazine, *The Child's Times (Barnens Tidning)*. Not long after his death, in 1871, Lina took over as editor, a work she continued until 1901, shortly before her own death.

A much-abbreviated list of her works for children includes a series of Sunday school short stories with such titles as: "From Our Savior's Life on Earth," "Noah's Ark," "Our Friends among The Animals," "Summer Days in the Woods," "Jesus' Childhood," and poems "Christmas Bells" and "Morning and Evening Stars." These she did while continuing to edit the monthly version of *The Child's Times* and *Korsblomman*, as she also supported her husband in his many projects. In the midst of all this creative work, in 1873, after her sister died, she took over as foster mother to her many nieces and nephews.

Also during this time, Paul Peter Waldenström, Rosenius' successor as editor of *The Pietist*, began in 1868 to preach his covenant theology of the redemption: that Christ died for us to show his love for us, not to satisfy an angry God. Waldenström did not believe that Christ's righteous-

---

46. Storckenfeldt, p. 214.

ness was imputed to sinners as St. Paul had written in Romans. True righteousness, he taught, comes from the believer when he or she is made a new creature in Christ. Waldenström was a charismatic man, known for his eloquence and warmth, but his teaching created much strife in the movement; this resulted in the formation of a new group called the Mission Friends, which in America became the Swedish Covenant Church. While these were the formal grounds for the disagreement, Mark Granquist, historian of the Augustana Synod, opines that the real issues were ultimately around biblical authority, and what would become Biblicism.[47] When the conflict broke out, Lina was distressed. Despite her lack of interest in theology and its conflicts, she was nevertheless involved. "O," she wrote, "if we could only let everything go and hold more to the Lord." One can imagine that with her deep biblical sense of sin and the Moravian emphasis on the blood of the Lamb, alongside her own unworthiness, she would not be able to go against St. Paul's teaching about righteousness.

> One night as I lay in bed during my last illness, I was so weak that I thought I would die, it came clear to me that I would be lost if I could not come in the dear name of Jesus on account of his merit and be clad in his righteousness. Without him, I wouldn't dare to live, but in and with him was everything done for me and God was made my dear father. The notion hasn't left me since. I do not speak of it, but I wonder why all of our dear friends who will now barely mention Jesus' name because they are afraid to lower the Father, could come to know this in such a serious moment. The Lord help us to get through this dangerous world. O, how narrow the way![48]

During the same time, Lina's family needed her help and concern, despite the many demands of her work. Her sister's oldest child, Anna, who was married, contracted tuberculosis and asked that her Aunt Lina be with her in her final days, which Lina did without regard to her own health. The work and grief, however, depleted her energy enough so that she could not leave her home throughout the winter. In the summer, she and Hanna took a long-awaited trip to England where they stayed for four months. There she worked on Sunday School materials, most likely look-

---

47. Mark Granquist, email to author, November 11, 2008.
48. Riiber, pp. 131-32.

ing up the leaders of the Sunday School movement there, but neither her letters nor diary is reported to have mentioned anything about the trip except that they had traveled to England primarily by land in order to spare Lina seasickness. When they returned from England, Oscar and she established another magazine for children called *The Children's Friend (Barnens vän)* for Sunday School children. Over the next twenty years, until 1901, Lina edited this magazine, which had forty thousand subscribers during many of those years.

Her close relationship to her nieces and nephews helped give her a good sense for what children needed to know about the faith. She thought of them as her own children. "My children, my little girls," she would call them affectionately. She was especially close to Hanna, Natanael, and Maria, who lived with her for some time. "Hanna is dearest to me," she wrote once,

> she plays the piano so beautifully, and translates for me and spreads comfort and sunshine wherever she is. Maria is also a fine and industrious little lady, she plays well and gives music and language lessons, and when Natanael comes home from Uppsala, where he is studying, it is as if the sun dawns in the house.[49]

As a writer, teacher, and aunt, she wanted these children to know Jesus Christ personally. She and Oscar took the example of a British woman, Mrs. Trotter, who taught people how to establish small reading circles and Bible studies for the young. Every Friday afternoon they sponsored a gathering for the young they knew, asking them to invite other youngsters of their acquaintance to their home for food and Bible study.

After her brother-in-law Almqvist died, Lina remained close to Augusta, his second wife and an old friend of Lina's. She regarded the children of Augusta and Almqvist as her own. She and Augusta maintained a vigorous and warm correspondence for the rest of their lives. A pastor's widow at the time did not receive much of a pension, so Lina's gifts, as well as the translating jobs she farmed out to Augusta, were very welcome. Augusta would send her baskets of fresh baked goodies with knitting or other sewn gifts, and Lina would return the baskets filled with similar gifts which she had hired a seamstress to do since she had neither time nor in-

---

49. Riiber, p. 133.

terest in sewing. Every time they received a basket from Lina, they would receive little verses and poems written to the children especially, warm-hearted and witty pieces that included the names of the children rhymed with other words in the verses, such as, "God's peace, my little Esther dear,/ May God forever keep you near."[50] Her warm-hearted care for them came from her heart, not from any sense of duty, and they knew it.

Lina's husband, Oscar Berg, had long dreamed of opening a seaman's mission in Stockholm but could not get the Evangeliska Fosterlandsstiftelsen to agree to such an undertaking, despite the fact that he was a member of the board. Finally, at his own expense, he bought the old Jewish synagogue on the German wharf in the old city of Stockholm and remodeled it so that it would be a place for people to meet. Along with a reading room and a library, there was a large meeting room where people could hear edifying speeches. Berg spoke frequently on the subject of temperance, one of his most burning issues. Berg attracted support from many for his work, among them one thousand crowns from King Oscar II, and many in the military who particularly felt the need for his reform in their midst. In 1875, he began publishing a paper called *The Worker's Friend (Arbetarens vän)* modeled on *The British Workman,* which opposed the liquor traffic. Soon he was elected the director of the Swedish Sobriety Society. This position took many hours of time for organization and travel. A good administrator, Berg found his talents were much needed by the organization after the death of Wieselgren, who had been the leader of the movement. For him to launch a magazine and yet continue his other work worried Lina, who wrote Odencrants: "Now and then I think that Oscar has been so sick this summer because of that paper. It sounds strange, but uncle will understand what I mean. I can't speak so openly with others here, but do not forget to pray for us, and especially for the work and the dangers which are associated with it."[51]

His efforts earned him both scorn and veneration. The Södre Theater in Stockholm made him an object of ridicule, but in 1879 he was made a knight of the North Star for his work to improve the society. The work continued to pile up. Lina thought it was altogether too much for both of them, now especially that Berg took over the publication of *Morgenbladet,* another paper for which he began a printing press. "He is so busy he comes

---

50. "Älskade lilla Ester!" Riiber, p. 138, tr. Gracia Grindal.
51. Riiber, p. 143.

home around eleven or twelve o'clock at night. The Lord help us!" she wrote to Augusta.[52]

In 1875 Sweden suffered a financial panic, and Lina worried about whether Oscar could ride it out. Even though the revival flourished, and she had much to be thankful for, she found it difficult to sleep. "I awaken often with Gustaf Adolf's war cry, 'Help me, Lord, to fight today — to glorify your name!'"[53]

At about this same time, they moved to a larger apartment that gave them a view of the harbor. Their new opportunities and challenges stretched their resources of both time and money. It was not unusual to see Lina at her desk at four in the morning, editing, translating, writing, studying the Bible, praying. Together, they supported each other's work and found joy in their shared purposes.

The Swedish court at the time viewed their work favorably, especially Princess Eugenie, the daughter of King Oscar I and sister of the reigning king, Oscar II. In 1869, shortly after Lina's marriage, Princess Eugenie invited Lina to join her sewing circle. Soon, the two became good friends. Princess Eugenie supported Lina's work, especially her songwriting, and Lina offered the princess a close spiritual friendship they both valued. The princess was a gifted artist — a fine singer, composer, painter, and sculptor, whose works were highly regarded in her day.[54] She would send Lina gifts of paintings and sculptures, among other things, along with warm letters. Plagued with chronic bronchitis, the princess could not take part in many official activities in the winter, but she worked hard to further the ministry of the gospel, working to build up Fjellstedt's School in Uppsala. She held frequent bazaars to raise money for the city mission, the deaconesses, and even two organizations in Norway — one for the memory of Hauge, and another that was called the Luther Seminar. The princess had a home, "Fridhem," in Gotland, where she spent her summers. In the summer of 1881, she invited Lina and her husband to visit her there. Both the women

---

52. Riiber, p. 144.
53. Riiber, p. 145.
54. Even today the popular hymn "My Heart Is Longing to Praise My Savior" is attributed to Princess Eugenie in the *Lutheran Book of Worship,* and many a pious talk by pastors who knew her story would point to this hymn as a view into the heart of "the suffering Princess," as she was frequently called. The song, however, was first written by Fredrick Engelke and recast into another hymn by Lars Oftedal, the brother of Sven Oftedal, one of the founding fathers of Augsburg College.

needed refreshment and rest in the sunshine and sea air. One summer morning, Lina wrote from Fridhem to her sister: "I am writing this to you from the second floor room where I have the most glorious view of the sea with Högklint on one side and the forest on the other. It is early in the morning before any in the house have thought to rouse themselves."[55] Every letter to Lina from the princess concludes with a greeting to Lina's dear husband, Oscar, who was no stranger to the palace either. Princess Eugenie's brother, King Oscar II, regarded him highly and invited him there for Christmas celebrations, as he had been appointed by the court to be the general consul for Romania. Riiber notes that these activities must have strained Lina's fragile health as well, since these activities took her from her work, but she remained a close and true friend of the princess until Eugenie's death in 1888.

Collected Works and Final Years

When Lina celebrated her fiftieth birthday, she had good reason to celebrate. She had accomplished more than most women of her time. To mark the event, she collected and published her songs — by this time over seventeen hundred of them. Gathering these songs together was a major task. To do the work, she went to the summer villa of a friend, Consul Olson, while Oscar went to London in connection with the seaman's mission. Here she had time to reflect and read as well. Because the villa was on an island in the Öresund, the water between Sweden and Denmark, she received an invitation to visit the Danish crown prince and princess at Charlottenlund. She was glad to meet the niece of Princess Eugenie, as well as King Carl XV's daughter, Louise, whom Lina praised for her warm personal Christian faith.[56]

The three volumes of the collection, printed in 1882, 1885, and 1892, contained more than 656 songs. They did not include, by any means, all of her songs, but the best part of them, including many of her translations from German, English, Danish, and Norwegian. She began the collection with a text characteristic of her work:

55. Riiber, p. 159.
56. She became the mother of King Haakon VII, the first modern King of Norway, 1905.

> O, may the song of Jesus ring out
> Beautifully over valley and mountain,
> Like a refrain of the song
> That comes from the wedding of the Lamb![57]

The themes of her many hymns are widely representative of the Christian tradition. Although her work is most clearly influenced by the Moravian tradition, she had become an expert hymnologist in her own right, and included translation of hymns by Grundtvig, Kingo, American Gospel song writers, and many others from hymn-writers whose emphases were not her own.

In 1886, she and Oscar traveled once more to Norway, visiting Trondheim, meeting Bishop Niels Laache (1831-1892), who had translated Rosenius into Norwegian, and who Lina thought resembled Rosenius in his preaching.[58] From Trondheim, they traveled to Oslo, where they had friends and acquaintances they were glad to meet again.

In 1887 her dearly beloved "uncle" Odencrants died. She and Oscar moved from their home in the central city to their summer home. She was beginning to feel her powers fade. Although she was still capable of a great deal of work, she needed more rest. Oscar had also been stretched. His many irons in the fire continued to worry Lina since he did not have the power to say no, she wrote to one of her friends. Finally, they faced an economic catastrophe. One of Berg's sisters went bankrupt, and he lost thousands of crowns supporting her. Lina wrote, "Soon we await a catastrophe here also. But we cannot do anything more than we have done."[59] As things began unraveling for Berg, Lina's brother, Nils Johan Sandell, died. Lina had called that winter a hard winter, but it was nothing compared to what the fall would bring. Berg's publishing house, Aksjeboktrykkeriet, went bankrupt, as did Berg. The bankruptcy attracted a lot of attention and questions; the legality of his business practices began to be whispered about. He was accused and convicted of abusing the trust of his investors by using illegal bookkeeping practices and had to spend some time in jail. Only a few loyal

---

57. "O, må Jesus-sången klinga."

58. Bishop Laache was widely admired among Norwegians for his devotional book, which many have said combined the strong Haugian teachings moderated by the Rosenian emphasis that he acquired in translating Rosenius.

59. Riiber, p. 185.

friends stuck by them. Berg admitted that it was not possible for him to say he was not guilty, for some things had happened that he was not entirely able to control but for which he was responsible. For Lina this was the bitterest experience of her entire life. In her declining years, when they should have been able to retire comfortably, they were now forced to move to another, smaller apartment. Oscar quit giving speeches and devoted himself to his business which, once again, began to flourish, and he was able to pay back those who had suffered because of the bankruptcy.

Lina's strength began to fail toward the end of the 1890s. She continued writing and editing, but she could not do the great amount of work she had done before. In 1899, she contracted a severe case of influenza, from which she never fully recovered. In 1901, she was no longer able to do her work and began to slip away. When Swedish Americans heard of her suffering, letters poured in to Evangeliska Fosterlandsstiftelsen from emigrants who wanted to tell her how her songs had helped them as they settled the new land. She could not appreciate them for long. Gradually she lost her grip on reality and finally lost her power of speech, but those who tended her reported that she seemed to be at peace. The last sensible words she spoke were from a hymn she had written, "Nu all sorg jag kastar, som min själ belastar Jesus, uppå dig" ("Now all sorrow I cast, all that my soul is burdened with, Jesus, onto you"). She died July 27, 1903, in Stockholm. She was buried at the Solna church cemetery in Stockholm, and her old friend, Pastor Wadström, presided. He used the text of Psalm 13:6, "I will sing to the Lord because he has dealt bountifully with me." Beside her coffin stood thousands of people who sang, as a final farewell to her, the song she had written so many years before, "Children of the Heavenly Father."

Sandell's Hymns

The corpus of Lina Sandell's work is massive. Oscar Lövgren, her most reliable biographer, suggests she wrote over two thousand songs.[60] In his *Psalm och Sång Lexicon* (1964), Lövgren notes that some one hundred fifty of her songs are still in use around the world. One reason for their popularity is that Sandell's hymnody comes from the deepest understanding of Scripture as it meets the joys and sorrows of life. Scripture was her lan-

---

60. Oscar Lövgren, *Lina Sandell: Hennes liv och sångdiktning* (Stockholm, 1965).

guage; it supplied the phrases she used to describe her life, especially when she experienced suffering. From her father she had also learned how to preach Scripture so that it came alive in the minds of her listeners. Although many of her hymns are prayers, her most famous ones are in the form of a sermon, addressing the hearers with Scriptural notions and images they can understand.

Combining Scripture with images from daily life helped make her hymnody accessible to the simplest child, as all good sermons should be. Her hymns and other writings brim with references to the natural world she loved in Småland. This is true of her most popular hymn, "Children of the Heavenly Father." In it, she refers to the natural world around her, the birds in the trees, and the stars in the heavens. Using the comparative adjective with which the Swedish text begins, *Tryggare kan ingen vara* — more secure can no one be — she vividly describes the birds and stars in heaven as being less secure than the children of God. Like Jesus in his parables referring to the simple things of earth with the confidence that they can speak of heavenly things, Sandell uses what she sees around her to speak of what she cannot see. As she describes the stars and birds, we are led to believe she can see the heavenly courts as clearly as the stars.

These images are probably as responsible for the success of the hymn as its tender picture of the father. Also appealing is the image of children, tenderly referred to in Swedish as "the little flock of children" (*lilla barnaskara*) for whom the Father has tender regard. He hovers over them and holds them in his fatherly arms, translated successfully as "safely in his bosom." He is a friend before all other friends *(Han, vår vän för andra vänner)* who knows all of his children's needs. Thus his children should praise him, Jacob's God, for he will protect them; in fact, his will is so powerful that even his enemies fall to earth before him. Whatever happens for good or ill, he is steadfast: "Though he giveth or he taketh, God his children ne'er forsaketh" is a typical confession of Sandell, stated in the language of Scripture. Typical for Sandell, whose language is drenched with Scripture, this is a poetic version of Job 1:21, "The Lord gave and the Lord hath taken away, blessed be the name of the Lord." In either case, the Father wills good for his children. This intimate picture of the Father's care and concern for his children, one might be able to show, depicts not only Sandell's warm and intimate relationship with God but with her own earthly father as well. For Lina Sandell, God the Father was as gentle and nurturing as her own father.

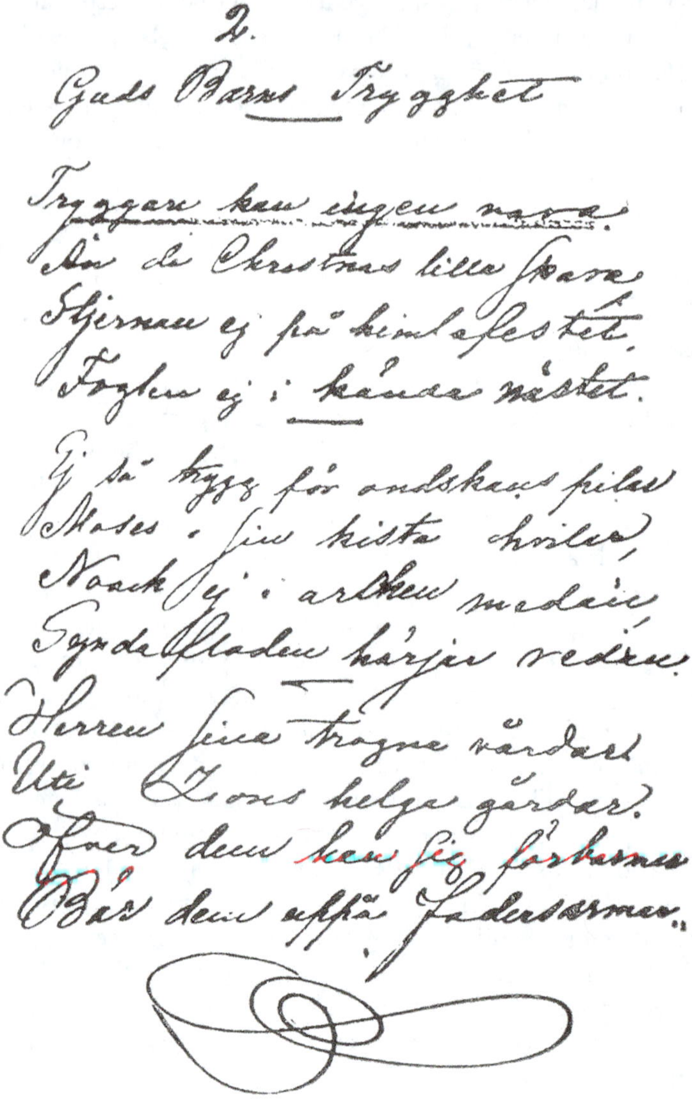

2.

Guds Barns Trygghet

Tryggare kan ingen vara
Än de Christnas lilla skara,
Stjernan ej på himlafästet,
Fogeln ej i kända nästet.

Ej så trygg för ondskans pilar
Moses i sin kista hvilar,
Noach ej i arken medan
Syndafloden härjar redan.

Herren sina trogna vårdar
Uti Zions helga gårdar;
Öfver dem han sig förbarmar,
Bär dem uppå Fadersarmar.

Figure 4 "Children of the Heavenly Father" written in Sandell's hand.

Inger Selander, in her book *O hur saligt att få vandra*, notes that one of the most popular themes of the hymns of this movement is the family.[61] God is the Father, and we are children, brothers and sisters, safe in God's arms, not only in heaven, but also in this world. Further, Selander argues that this Father is a personal and intimate figure. Sandell's hymns revel in her intimate relationship with God the Father and the Son: "O Tender, Gracious Father" ("Du ömma fadershjärta"), "The Father's Arms Are Open to Receive Us" ("Se, öppen står Guds fadersfamn"), and "One Can Never Count All of God's Mercies" ("Jag kan icke räkna dem alla").

Intimate images for Jesus also abound in her hymns. He is a brother, friend, and bridegroom. One of her more popular hymns, "Is It True That Jesus Is My Brother?" ("Är det sant att Jesus är min Broder?"), takes Romans 8 and makes it a much more intimate picture of the relationship than St. Paul's "joint heirs." The rhetoric of this hymn is once again that of a sermon. Here she preaches both Romans 8 and Martin Luther's notion of the *fröhliche wechsel*, the joyful exchange, making it more accessible to the ordinary person, beginning with a rhetorical question that engages the hearers so they listen for the answer:

> Is it true that Jesus is my brother?
> Is it true his bounty is my own?
> Then, be gone, my tears and pain and suff'ring;
> I am free, my fearfulness is gone!
>
> Oh, how wonderful to know Christ loved me
> When he died for me upon the cross.
> So much grace for this poor sinner given
> From my Lord who did not count the cost.
>
> Jesus said, "My Father is your Father,"
> Jesus said, "My God will be your God!"
> Oh, my soul, rejoice with songs of gladness;
> We are one with Christ, sing praise and laud.
>
> We are heirs with Christ and all his riches,
> Heirs of grace, and heirs of God's own might.

---

61. Inger Selander, *O hur saligt att få vandra: Motiv och symboler i den frikyrkliga sången* (Stockholm: Gummessons, 1980), p. 140.

Open, Lord, my eyes to see your treasure,
See it streaming from the throne of light![62]

Not surprisingly, her hymns show the influence of the Moravian Nicolas von Zinzendorf, who in his own hymnody developed these same themes. Lina Sandell came from a long line of Scandinavian women whose intellectual and religious formation had been influenced by the Moravians. In fact, it is almost impossible to understand the rise of women's writings in Scandinavia without understanding Zinzendorf's appeal to women. His expectation that women could function as priests and leaders in the community attracted women to his movement. Furthermore, as Eva Hættner Aurelius argues in her book, *Inför lagen*, Zinzendorf's notion that faith was best expressed through the arts, especially hymnody, appealed to women, especially those of artistic temperament.[63] The images of Jesus as bridegroom, friend, brother, and so on attracted them because they focused on relationships, not theology. The marriage of the Lamb, represented in the agape feast created by Zinzendorf, was the highest moment of the faith, the end of our journey home to partake of the marriage feast.

Sandell also learned from Zinzendorf to use mother-images for God. "Day by Day" ("Blott en dag") first appeared in *Korsblomman* around 1865 in connection with a story she had translated from an unknown English magazine about the pendulum of a clock who wearied of his constant work. The pendulum, speaking to the face of the clock, complained about how tiresome it was to go back and forth millions of times every day, but the face of the clock reminded the pendulum that it had to go only one more time, and it would always have a moment before it had to beat again. This comforted the pendulum and it continued. Because she had gotten the story from an English magazine, she used the English biblical language, not the Swedish, as her source for the hymn, Deuteronomy 33:25b, "As thy day is, so shall thy strength be." When it was originally published in *Korsblomman* in 1865, Sandell had used mother-language for God — "He who bears for me a mother's heart." Later editors changed it to "father's heart." Her uses of these maternal images were not innovations: mother-language for God was

---

62. "Är det sant at Jesus är min broder," tr. Gracia Grindal.
63. Eva Hættner Aurelius, *Inför lagen: Kvinnliga svensk självbiografier från Agneta Horn till Fredrika Bremer* (Lund: Lund University Press, 1996), p. 243. "Man kan utan tvekan säga att Zinzendorf vände sig till konstens språk och speciella kunskapsförmedling."

common to Moravian hymnody. Zinzendorf spoke of God as having motherly characteristics, especially a motherly heart. He wrote a "Sophia Song," a close paraphrase of Psalm 131, which Sandell translated in 1860. In 1846, when she was 14, she had already written a verse about fleeing to God as a "child would to its mother's breast to rest."[64] In 1848, she read a biography of Zinzendorf by Christian Gottlieb Frohberger (1742-1827) in which she encountered these same images.[65] As early as 1858, during her sorrow over her father's death, she wrote in her diary, "I had never before thought so much of the lovely picture of a mother's heart." In 1863, she wrote a song about Jesus in which she called him "Father, mother, home, and future." When the hymn was printed in *SionsToner* in 1889, this stanza was omitted. In 1872, years after Sandell had written "Day by Day," she translated a sermon by the German pietist pastor, Friedrich Wilhem Krummacher (1789-1864), "God's Motherly Heart."[66] Although this language was certainly a part of the piety of the Moravians and of the time, it was not long before editors began to censure it and change it to father-language.

The same holds true for the children's evening hymn that she wrote about the same time, "Thy Holy Wings, O Savior, Spread Gently over Me." Her biblical sources are Psalm 91:4, Deuteronomy 34, and Matthew 23:37, where Jesus cries out "How often would I have gathered your children together as a hen gathers her brood under her wings, and you would not!" The first version of the song as it appeared in her home town of Fröderyd was known as the "hen song": "Spread warm mother's wings so lovely over them and the entire circle of siblings in every Christian home."[67] Originally she had used the term "henmother" but it had been changed to "Father's" heart; "mother's wings" was changed to "father's hand." This prayer, in its revised version, became the Swedish children's evening prayer. The picture of Jesus as a mother bird, however, is still very strong, regardless of what the editors have done to it.

Ragnar Värmon, in "God as a Mother in Lina Sandell" ("Gud såsom

---

64. Nilsson, p. 150.

65. Christian Gottlieb Frohberger, *Grefve Nicolaus Ludvig af Zinzendorf's Lefverne och Karakter* (Gothenborg: Lars Wahlström, 1801).

66. Krummacher, a favorite of the Prussian Crown Prince, eventually became Court Preacher in Berlin. Friedrich Engels called him "the most bigoted preacher" of the "Zion of obscurants" in his "Briefe aus dem Wuppertal," *Werke* (Berlin, 1961), I, p. 419ff.

67. Ragnar Värmon, "Gud såsom en moder hos Lina Sandell," *Kyrkohistorisk Årsskrift* (Uppsala, 1982) pp. 149-57.

en moder hos Lina Sandell"), has compiled an impressive list of the hymns and poems by Sandell in which she used the image of "mother's wings" or "mother's heart" but which were edited out of subsequent publications.[68] The image of God as mother, while not a dominant one, was natural to her. She was not trying to find a new image for God, but she is expressing herself in what she feels to be deeply biblical truths, consistent with the sentimental and romantic view of motherhood in her time. Along with her most respected biographer, Oscar Lövgren, we could well regret that a hymn he considered one of her better hymns, "Nu vill jag sjunga om modersvingen" ("Now I Will Sing of the Mother's Wings"), did not become popular.[69]

The image of the mother's wings persists even in her mission hymns, a theme Lutherans in America have not included in their small selection of hymns. As we have seen, Sandell's concern for world missions was intense from the first so it is not surprising to find she has written many hymns on the subject. Her most highly regarded mission hymn was written on the news of the martyrdom of Swedish missionaries in Ethiopia, "Tillkomme ditt rike" ("Your Kingdom Come").

1. Your kingdom, come quickly, our Father and God,
   Your kingdom, come quickly, among us,
   Send out all your witnesses, here and abroad
   To call and invite every nation
   To hear of your glorious salvation.

2. You promise the desert will bloom like a rose,
   The wilderness grow like a lily.
   We hopefully wait for your will to be done,
   But more, your majestic appearing,
   Your time, O Lord Jesus, is nearing.

3. Lord, bless those who witness for you in your name,
   And carry your Gospel before them;
   Your mercy will be like a harbor for them

---

68. Värmon, pp. 149-157.
69. Johan Rinman, *Lina Sandell ("L.S."): hennes samtid och vår; ett hundraårs minne* (Stockholm: Evangeliska fosterlandstift, 1932), p. 77.

When o'er them you tenderly hover,
Embracing their cares like a mother.

4. For you are their strength, you have clothed them with pow'r,
And given them courage to serve you,
To go forth in hope sowing seeds that will flow'r,
To patiently wait for the harvest
Which you in your mercy will give us.

5. O water the seed of the martyrs who die,
Proclaiming your grace and your glory,
To further your kingdom, most peaceful and high.
O teach us to know from your meekness
We're strongest when we are the weakest.

6. We cast all our troubles upon you,
Lord, You promised that you would not leave us;
O show us the way in your pure holy Word,
We go in your name, Lord, be with us.
We thank you and praise you for all things![70]

She also wrote several hymns in which she struggles with her doubts and fears more directly than in her most famous hymns. Best known of those is "Herre, fördölj ej ditt ansikte för mig" ("Lord, Hide Not Your Face from Me"). Written before her father's death, it expresses her hope for the Lord's speedy return. Although many would like to place it as a response to her father's death, it appeared some time before he died. It reveals her longing, even in her relative youth, for an ending to this world's sorrows: "Will you not come soon? Will you not come soon?"[71]

One of her later hymns, still popular in Sweden, expresses her thanksgiving and joy in the mercies of God: "Jag kan icke räkna dem alla" ("I'll Never Count All of God's Mercies"). It is also an address to the singer, in the form of a sermon. It was written after she saw a drawing of a little boy trying unsuccessfully to do his sums, saying "I can't reckon them all."

70. "Tillkomme ditt rike," tr. Gracia Grindal, 2002.
71. This was set to the Finnish folk tune "Fjärran han dröjer," which Americans know as the tune for "Lost in the Night," which has a similar text.

She immediately heard, "I can't reckon them, all of God's mercies." This text shines with thanksgiving from the heart of Sandell's piety.

> The numberless gifts of God's mercies,
> My tongue cannot fathom nor tell.
> Like dew that appears in the morning
> They come to us shining and full.
>
> Like all of the stars in the heavens,
> God's mercies can never be told.
> They shine through the darkness of midnight,
> Their beauties can never grow old.
>
> I'll never count all of God's mercies,
> But, O I can give God my praise!
> For all of that love, my thanksgiving
> And love to the end of my days.[72]

These hymns breathe her intimate relationship with God, and give us, even in translation, words to use when we need to express our own sorrows, doubts, fears, and pure joy in the love of God.

Sandell's Swedish Songs in America

The story of Sandell's influence among Lutherans in America has not been told. Very little scholarship exists in English, and what little there is, is tinged with filio-piety. The story of her disappearance and reappearance in the Lutheran church hymnals of America gives us glimpses into a part of Lutheran history in America that is not well understood today.

When Swedish immigrants began to pour into this country in the late 1840s, they were already affected by the Rosenius revival sweeping Sweden. With their newly enlivened faith, they brought the spiritual songs of the revival with them, many of them dating back to the eighteenth century, when spiritual songs began sweeping Sweden. The first songbook had been *Moses and the Lamb*, published in 1717, by George Lybecker. This book came al-

---

72. Tr. Gracia Grindal, 1983.

most directly out of Halle and the Freylinghausen *Geistreiches Gesangbuch* of 1704 and 1715. Lybecker's book included new translations of Paul Gerhardt's hymns, many Jesus hymns by St. Bernard and other medieval mystics, along with mystics of the late seventeenth century.

Lybecker's book was an important source of spiritual songs for the immigrant pastors, as were several other songbooks, especially one by Anders Karl Rutström, a Moravian pastor in Stockholm. His collection of songs, *Sions nya sånger (New Songs of Zion)*, published in 1778, concentrated on the mystical bride theology, with special attention to the blood and wounds of Christ; it became the most popular example of Moravian song in Sweden. It shaped Swedish pietism for the next generations; Sandell, like the young pastors who came to America in the 1840s and 1850s, knew it well. They cherished these songbooks more than their hymnals.[73] The first songbook mentioned in the histories of the nineteenth-century Swedish immigration to America is that published in 1826 by Peder Håkansson Syréen (1776-1838), *Christelig Sång-Bok till bruk wid enskild husandakt (Christian Songbook for Use with Private Home Devotions)*. Lars Paul Esbjörn (1808-1870), the first Swedish pastor to arrive, used a song from Syréen's book as the band of Swedish emigrants approached New York harbor in their ship in 1849. This songbook had an immediate connection with the Sandell family: Syréen had admonished Peder Sellergren, Jonas Sandell's mentor, to live a more careful Christian life. His songbook included many songs from the Lybecker collection, as well as the later Moravian collections.

The most popular songbook among the emigrants, however, was a collection of songs, *Andeliga Sånger (Spiritual Songs)*, by Oscar Ahnfelt, first published in 1850, the year after Esbjörn's arrival. Most of the early Scandinavian Augustana pastors knew his work, and some of them knew him personally. Tufve Nilsson Hasselquist (1816-1891), the patriarch of the Swedish Augustana Synod, had met Ahnfelt when he was pastor in Önnestad, about ten miles northwest of Kristianstad on the southeastern coast of Sweden. Eric Norelius (1833-1916), the founder of Gustavus Adolphus College, suggests in his biography of Hasselquist that he was nei-

---

73. The Thomander and Wieselgren version of Wallin was strongly recommended by the immigrant pastors who thought Wallin was too rationalistic. Wieselgren, as previously noted, was close to many of the pastors in the Rosenius movement. Jonas Sandell was his mentor, and he died on his way to visit Wieselgren.

ther a supporter nor detractor of Ahnfelt.[74] In America, however, Hasselquist vigorously promoted Ahnfelt's songs in his ministry, publishing them and using them in his morning services. In 1856 he published a collection of fifty of Ahnfelt's songs, *Femtio andeliga sånger (Fifty Spiritual Songs)*, the first book of songs published by Swedes in America. In 1860, Hasselquist began printing selections from Ahnfelt's songs in his monthly paper, *Det rätta hemlandet*. These came to be called *Hemlandssånger*. These songs were published every month, with psalmodikon settings, on the front page of every issue of *Det rätta hemlandet* from 1860 to 1863, until all of the two hundred forty tunes were published.[75]

Hasselquist's closest colleague, the chair of the board at Augustana Seminary and his colleague in publishing *Hemlandssånger*, Erland Carlsson (1822-1893), shared Hasselquist's enthusiasm for these songs. Carlsson had grown up in Småland, in Älghult, some forty miles from Kalmar on the southeast coast of Sweden. When he was a boy, his widowed mother had the rule that before they could eat breakfast, they had to recite Luther's Small Catechism and sing songs and hymns, especially those from *Moses and the Lamb's Songs (Mose och lamsens wisor)* and *Songs of Zion (Sions sånger)*. In 1838, when he was 16, he also sought advice and counsel from Sellergren.[76] The young man studied for the ministry, distinguishing himself as a good student and living in Lenhovda where, some years later, Lina Sandell's sister and brother-in-law would live and which Sandell frequently visited.

After some trouble from his bishop for contravening the Conventicle Law, in 1853 Carlsson received a call to America, which he accepted immediately, and organized a small party to sail to Chicago. From the time of his arrival, Carlsson kept in close contact with his friends at home in Sweden, especially Peter Wieselgren. This contact, plus others, kept him intimately aware of the work of the Evangeliska Fosterlandsstiftelsen (EFS), its publications, and its activities in Sweden. On a visit to Sweden in 1873, he attended the annual meeting of the EFS, where he almost surely met Lina

---

74. Eric Norelius, *T. N. Hasselquist: Lefnadsteckning* (Rock Island, Ill.: Lutheran Augustana Book Concern, n.d.), p. 19.

75. A psalmodikon was a single-stringed instrument fretted like a dulcimer but played with a bow.

76. Emory Lindquist, *Shepherd of an Immigrant People: The Story of Erland Carlsson* (Rock Island, Ill.: The Augustana Historical Society, 1978), p. 5.

Sandell. The collection of *Hemlandssånger* that Carlsson and Hasselquist published in *Det rätta hemlandet* contained forty-seven songs attributed to Ahnfelt's *Andeliga sånger (Spiritual Songs)*, forty-four to Lina Sandell, twenty-five to *Moses and the Lamb's Songs (Mose och lamsens wisor)*, twenty to Syréen's Songs, and eight to English sources.[77] Sandell's work comprises almost twenty percent of the collection, a phenomenal number, considering that she had began working at Evangeliska Fosterlandsstiftelsen only that year and had published only two small collections of her songs before 1860.

The first exposure of Americans to the songs of Lina Sandell came in 1850, when Jenny Lind took a triumphant tour of America, sponsored by P. T. Barnum. A devout Christian, she promoted the work of Ahnfelt and Sandell, singing their songs at her concerts and other gatherings. On her travels, she generously supported many Christian efforts and established a scholarship to be used for Scandinavian theological students at Capitol University.

By 1860, the Scandinavian Augustana Synod, made up of Danes, Norwegians, and Swedes, established their organization and school in Paxton, Illinois. They were vigorous promoters of these new songs of the Swedish revival, whether they were Swedish or Norwegian. As more Norwegians began arriving, tensions developed between them and the Swedes. August Weenaas, the Norwegian professor, began agitating for the two major traditions to separate, which they did in 1869 when the Danes and Norwegians went off to establish the Marshall Academy, later to become Augsburg Seminary, in 1869, and the Norwegian-Danish Augustana Synod, which ultimately became Augustana College in Sioux Falls. Because they had parted amicably, the spiritual song tradition from *Hemlandssånger (Songs of the Homeland)* continued to flourish in both communities. Two early graduates among the Norwegians, the two pastors of Trinity Congregation in Minneapolis, Ole Paulson (1832-1907) and M. Falk Gjertsen (1847-1913), were tireless proponents of the Swedish spiritual song. Paulson, for some years a colporteur for the Scandinavian Augustana Synod, and a musician of some accomplishment, is known to have taken his psalmodikon on trips throughout Southeastern Minnesota, singing and playing Ahnfelt's and Sandell's spiritual songs, along with some of his own.

While the Swedes continued publishing versions of *Hemlandssånger*,

---

77. One should immediately note here, however, that in these counts I have taken the indices at face value and not checked to see that the attributions are correct.

the Norwegians began a decade of vigorous publishing of spiritual songbooks edited by individuals. In 1875, Lars Oftedal, a popular preacher, newspaper man, member of parliament from Stavanger, and brother of the colorful Sven Oftedal, an Augsburg professor, came to Minneapolis to celebrate the dedication of Augsburg's new Main Building. While in Minnesota he introduced his new book of songs, *Basunsrøst og harpetoner (Trumpet Voice and Harp Melodies)*, published in Stavanger. It contained many songs of the Swedish revival; out of one hundred thirty-eight hymns in the collection, two are associated with Sandell: "Har du mod at följe Jesus" ("Have You the Courage to Follow Jesus?") and "Herre, mitt hjärte längtar i stillhet" ("Lord, My Heart in Stillness Longing"). The next year, Augsburg Publishing House published an American version of Oftedal's collection.

A year later, in 1877, M. Falk Gjertsen, the new pastor at Trinity Congregation in Minneapolis, published *Hjemlandssanger (The Songs of the Homeland)*, a Norwegian version of the Swedish *Hemlandssånger*, which introduced many of the songs of the Swedish revival into the Norwegian community in this country. His book included sixty-six songs from the Swedish song tradition, among them twenty-nine by Ahnfelt, twenty-one from *Pilgrimsharpan*, and two by Sandell herself: "Har du mod at följer Jesu," and "Om dagen vid mit arbeide" ("During the Day in My Work"). His work as a compiler of songbooks continued. In 1899 he and Theodore Reimestad, Professor of Music at Augsburg Seminary, produced a book, *Sangbogen*, with a similar collection of hymns from the Swedish revival, as well as the hymns of Brorson. In 1902, however, his involvement in a scandal with a woman in Norway brought his career as a pastor at Trinity to a close, and his work as a writer of hymns and songs had no public.

The Augustana-Sioux Falls branch of this tradition also loved these songs and championed them. One of the major lights in the Norwegian-Danish Augustana Synod, Andreas Wright, a president of the small synod, published a songbook that same year, 1877, called *The Turtle Dove (Turtleduen)*. Wright, a gifted preacher, also served on the committee for the American version of Landstad's hymnal. His book included in its selection of seven Swedish spiritual songs, two by Sandell, but as in the previous collection, none of these was brought forward into English by either the Swedes or Norwegians.

As the century progressed Swedish-Americans suffered the controversy over the atonement, which split them into two different churches. Soon the Mission Friends, which we know now as the Covenant Church, were organized and began a vigorous program of publishing songbooks. Their work also included large selections from Ahnfelt and Sandell, but their community also raised up three great troubadors who were the equal of Ahnfelt in tunes, if not of Sandell's texts: Nils Frykman (1842-1911), Andrew Skoog (1856-1934), and Johannes Alfred Hultman (1861-1942). Together these three created a canon of beloved Swedish-American spiritual songs that made their way into many Swedish songbooks as well. Their songs, along with Sandell's, were popular and well represented in many different Scandinavian evangelical songbooks published at the turn of the last century. Too numerous to catalogue, these songbooks appear in a variety of traditions, produced by publishers that have long since disappeared.

As the Covenant tradition began to organize, it also needed a songbook. The best-known of the songbooks, *Sionsharpan*, was independently published in 1890 for the Mission Friends. Compiled by David Nyvall, Fridolf Risberg, and Nils Frykman, it included a wide selection of songs by the Swedish-American evangelical troubadors. Gustav Peters (1832-1918), one of the early editors of *Hemlandssånger*, argued that the two traditions might just as well have published a common songbook, although a close look at *Sionsharpan* proves Peters to be wrong in his assertion.[78] The 1892 *Hemlandssånger* was as large and comprehensive a book as the Mission Friends' *Sionsharpan*, but it included not nearly so many of the same songs as one might have expected. Of the five hundred songs in the 1892 edition, barely more than one hundred of them are the same as those in the Mission Friends songbook. What is certain is that the Covenant Church fostered the Sandell tradition in a way that Swedish Augustana after 1892 did not. *Sionsharpan* contains six hundred twenty-four hymns and songs, and seventy-eight of them are by or attributed to Lina Sandell. It is hard to see much difference in these selections compared to the selections in the 1892 version of *Hemlandssånger*. Fifty-two of Sandell's hymns are common to both books. Interestingly enough, "Thy Holy Wings" does not appear in *Sionsharpan*.

Swedish Augustana continued to compile editions of *Hemlandssånger* through the 1870s and 1880s until 1888, when the convention of the Augustana Synod voted Nils Forsander chairman of the Hymnal and Songbook Committee. His work soon came to fruition in the 1889 convention,

---

78. G. P., "Hemlandssånger. Några wänliga anmärkinger af en som warit med från början," *Augustana och Missionären* (1889), pp. 436-38.

when the synod authorized the production of a songbook, putting to the side the perplexing question for them of a hymnal, which they kept wanting to produce with the Church of Sweden, but which never got started. In his article describing the piety of the editors of the book, Peters wrote that the Baptists in Sweden had produced *Pilgrimssånger*, making way for the explosion of Anglo-Saxon revival hymns in Sweden. Immigrants from Småland — the majority of the pastors — preferred the songs of the 1721 songbook *Moses and the Lamb's Songs (Mose och lamsens wisor)* along with Syréen's songs. Their preference for these songbooks with strong Moravian influences made them choose the songs of Lina Sandell over others. Thus their various editions of *Hemlandssånger* included an increasing number of Sandell's works. The 1860 and 1872 books, which are virtually identical, contain forty-three hymns by Sandell. Interestingly enough, none of the three hymns we now treasure, "Children of the Heavenly Father," "Day by Day," nor "Thy Holy Wings, O Savior," appeared in these two early collections by Hasselquist, nor in the 1881 edition of the same book, which included thirty-two of Sandell's hymns. They first appear in the 1892 version of *Hemlandssånger*, which became the official songbook of Swedish Augustana.

The publication of the songbook was greeted with enthusiasm. It contained five hundred hymns. Over one hundred seventeen of them were attributed to Lina Sandell. Her hymns and songs shaped the heart of the Augustana Synod as long as the people knew Swedish. Her influence on the piety of Swedish Augustana could be said to have been peerless. No other hymn writer had such an impact on the songs of these people. When English came, however, only a few of her songs would make it across the language barrier. It may be that they were so well known and beloved in Swedish that they could be understood even by the third generation, who would not have liked an English version. One can still come across old Swedish-Americans who can sing these texts in Swedish but who cannot speak much Swedish at all. Why Sandell's hymns seem to have disappeared, however, cannot be easily discerned from the sources. Possibly, other forces at work in the synod, such as the increasing Anglicization of the people, the growing sense that Sandell's hymns were more consistent with the Mission Friends theology than Lutheran, and the failure of the synod to provide good translations of her hymns, caused her hymns to fall by the wayside over the next century, but this is difficult to prove since the argument is one of silence. For whatever reason, her songs virtually disappeared from view over the next decades.

Lina Sandell

The 1890s were a vibrant time in the production of Scandinavian song. Ethnic male choruses that continued the patriotic traditions of the old countries flourished in America, the Lutheran churches sponsored choral unions for their youth, and the college choirs were about to become central to the life of the colleges. The diversity of America's immigrant population attracted the attention of songbook publishers, who were looking for collections of songs that would represent various national traditions. Valborg Hovind Stub, the second wife of Hans Gerhard Stub, herself a fine opera singer, put together a collection, *Songs from the North*, published by the Oliver Ditson Company in 1895.[79] She was a Norwegian opera singer in Leipzig, where her gifts had attracted the attention of musicians such as Franz Liszt. Her book is dedicated to the memory of Jenny Lind, whom Mrs. Stub had probably met in Leipzig. Included as the first song in the collection is one by Ahnfelt and Sandell, "Är det ödsligt och mörkt och kallt" ("Art Thou Weary and Sad and Dark in Thy Troubled Breast?"), a song that, as Stub reports in her introduction and dedication, Lind numbered among her favorites.[80]

As the immigrants' memory of Sweden began to fade and the press of the American scene began to catch the attention of the Swedish Lutheran pastors, the Swedes began singing, in English, the Anglo-Saxon revival hymns that they had first learned in Swedish in *Hemlandssånger*. In the first English hymnal of the Augustana Synod we see what happens as the immigrants begin to try to bring their tradition across the language barrier, not just the ocean. It was not nearly so successful. When the leaders of Augustana realized, in the 1890s, that they needed worthy English translations of these heart-songs, they rose to the challenge, gathering together in the hot summers of Rock Island, Illinois, for long writing workshops, working on producing good English versions of the texts they cherished in Swedish.[81] While they did yeomen's work, they did not succeed in getting much of Sandell into English. Only two songs attributed to Sandell appear in their 1899 Hymnal: "Jerusalem," and

---

79. *Songs from the North: Representative Songs of Norway, Sweden, and Denmark*, ed. Valborg Hovind Stub with English text by Aubertine Woodward Moore (Auber Forestier) (Boston: Oliver Ditson Company, 1895, 1907).

80. *Songs from the North*, p. 1.

81. Ernst William Olson, *Olof Olsson: The Man, His Work, and His Thought* (Rock Island, Ill.: Augustana, 1941), p. 186.

"Jesu, du mit Hjärtas" (which is no longer attributed to her). Neither of these is remembered, even though "Jerusalem" was Sandell's translation of the English song "Jerusalem, My Happy Home." The English text was included in the 1925 *Augustana Hymnal*, the subsequent *Service Book and Hymnal* (1958), and the *Lutheran Book of Worship* (1978). On the other hand, the favorite "Tryggare kan ingen vara" does not appear. Only thirty-three translations in the 1899 book were from *Hemlandssånger*, while another thirty-three were favorite American and English Gospel hymns, which had been translated into Swedish, now reset to their English texts. Thus, the American Gospel songs dear to Swedish Augustana made it into the English hymnals they produced, not only because they were American songs, but also because they were, by now, beloved Swedish songs. "In the Sweet By and By" and "Shall We Gather at the River" were cherished by Swedish-Americans because they knew them first in Swedish.

Among the Norwegian Lutherans in America, Lina Sandell's songs persisted in the first edition of *Concordia: A Collection of Hymns and Spiritual Songs*, published in 1916 by Augsburg Publishing House in Minneapolis. A bilingual English/Norwegian book, the English side contained no hymns by Sandell, but the Norwegian side contained seven of her songs, translated into Norwegian. While there are many translations into English of Norwegian, Danish, and German hymns, the editors seemed content to leave Sandell's songs, including "Children of the Heavenly Father," in the old languages.

One can wonder what was happening to her songs in this period of change. Was "Children of the Heavenly Father" as popular then as now? One searches in vain in the church magazines to find its inclusion at high festivals of the Augustana Church. One can read detailed accounts of funerals of the old saints, and the hymns included, high services of the church institutions, and not find any reference to "Children of the Heavenly Father." It seems obvious that those who can still sing this hymn in Swedish learned it from *Hemlandssånger*, but one finds very little in the literature that gives conclusive proof of this. And why was it translated so late? Was it because it was too well known in Swedish, or because no one could come up with an appropriate English version? The documents where one would usually look for this are silent. Ernst E. Ryden, Augustana's hymnological expert, wrote an article in the *Augustana Quarterly* in 1930 on "Hymnody in the Sunday School." Suggesting that the hymns one teaches the child would last forever, he praised the simple language in such hymns as "Savior, Like a Shepherd Lead Us," "I Am Jesus' Little Lamb," and the first known Christian hymn, "Shepherd of Tender Youth," but he did not mention any by Lina Sandell.[82]

It was not until 1925 with the production of Augustana's new hymnal that "Children of the Heavenly Father" appeared in English, translated by Ernst Wilhelm Olson (1870-1958). It appeared along with "Jerusalem" and "Strait Is the Gate" ("Den port är trång, den väg är small"), which had been included in the Norwegians' first English hymnal, *The Lutheran Hymnary*, 1912. Otto H. Boström, in a review of Augustana's new hymnal, was happy to see both the objective hymns of the Lutheran tradition and a "happy proportion of the personal and that which interprets the faith life of the individual"; at the same time he rejoiced that "the trivial or the sensational or the overly sugary which today is so common in so-called religious song collections, is totally absent."[83] Olson's translation made it possible for Sandell to appear in other English Lutheran hymnals, including *The American Lutheran Hymnal* of 1930, *The Concordia* in 1932, and the *Service Book and Hymnal* in 1958.

"Day by Day" made it into the songbooks for youth that the Swedes and Norwegians published throughout the 1940s and 1950s. *The Junior Hymnal* of the Augustana Synod, published in 1928, and reprinted for twenty years, included "Day by Day."[84] Edited by Ryden and Wendell, it was meant for Sunday school children and fit into the spiritual songbook tradition of Lutherans, which used spiritual songs for informal evening services, Sunday school, Bible camps, and other gatherings and used the hymnal for formal Sunday morning worship. It was from this source that young Augustana youths learned to cherish Sandell's songs, which were now established as the canon of Sandell's work in English. George Fahlund, in an article in the *Lutheran Companion* concerning the new *Junior Hymnal*'s prospects, remarked that it was much anticipated. "It cannot be expected to take the place of the pastor's Church Book, 'Svenska

---

82. E. E. Ryden, "Hymnody in the Sunday School," *Augustana Quarterly* 9 (1930): 352.

83. Otto H. Boström, "The New Hymnal and Liturgical Service," *Lutheran Companion* 34.9 (February 27, 1926): 206.

84. E. E. Ryden and C. A. Wendell, *The Junior Hymnal: Containing Sunday School and Luther League Liturgy and Hymns for the Sunday School and Other Gatherings* (Rock Island, Ill.: Augustana Book Concern, 1928).

Psalmboken,' 'Hemlandssånger,' 'Luther League Hymnals' or any other of the twelve varieties supposed to be necessary for a pastor to bring with him at any or all meetings."[85] From his comment, we can see that *Hemlandssånger* was still used and highly regarded among the Swedish Augustana pastors. "Thy Holy Wings" ("Bred dina vida vingar") appeared first in the Covenant hymnal with a translation by E. E. Ryden.

Carl Manfred and Wilton Bergstrand's *Youth's Favorite Songs* included "Children of the Heavenly Father" and "Day by Day" a generation later.[86] This was republished by the Association of Free Lutheran Churches, an offshoot from the Lutheran Free Church whose early pastors in the Scandinavian Augustana Synod had promoted the songs of Sandell so many years before. They are also included in the Association's updated version of *The Concordia, The Ambassador Hymnal* (1990). John Ylvisaker, the evangelical troubadour of this age (with strong connections to Mt. Carmel and Lutheran Bible Institute through his father, Carl Ylvisaker, the religion teacher at Concordia College in Moorhead, Minnesota), began singing "Thy Holy Wings" in his concerts in the late 1980s, and it soon became a standard. The GIA publication in its *Hymnal Supplement* (1991) included "Thy Holy Wings," now seen as a baptismal song, not an evening hymn, and appropriate for the more liturgical emphases of the day.

"Children of the Heavenly Father" traveled even farther afield from the Lutheran fold when the Billy Graham Crusade came to Scandinavia in the 1950s. Because they have always placed a high premium on using sacred music from the traditions of their audience, they brought the hymn with them, which many of them knew since the Crusade had its home offices in Minneapolis, a center for Swedish life and culture. Cliff Barrows describes in his book *Crusader Hymn Stories* how the chorus learned to pronounce the Swedish for singing in Sweden.[87] The 1989 United Methodist hymnal included both "Children of the Heavenly Father" and "Thy Holy Wings."

The true repository of Sandell in English is the current *Covenant Hymnal* (1996), which contains eleven of Sandell's hymns — the three that

---

85. George A. Fahlund, "The New Sunday School Hymnal," *Lutheran Companion* 34.16 (April 17, 1926): 376.

86. Carl Manfred and Wilton Bergstrand, *Youth's Favorite Songs: Augustana Luther League* (Minneapolis: Augustana Luther League, n.d.).

87. *Crusader Hymn Stories: With Hymn Studies and Personal Stories by Billy Graham and the Crusade Musicians,* ed. Cliff Barrows (Chicago: Hope Publishing Company and Minneapolis: The Billy Graham Evangelistic Association, 1967), p. 115.

Lutherans know: "Children of the Heavenly Father," "Day by Day" and "Thy Holy Wings," and eight others, including "O Tender, Gracious Father" ("Du ömma fadershjärta"), "Great Hills May Tremble" ("Bergen må vika"), and "Hide Not Your Face" ("Herre, fördölj mig").

In 1995, when Augsburg Fortress Publishing House published its songbook *With One Voice,* it included both "Day by Day" and "Thy Holy Wings." The song tradition of Scandinavian Augustana churches and the piety of Lina Sandell had found new loyalists.[88] Pressure from those who had come to love Sandell's songs through the work of John Ylvisaker and the GIA *Supplement* (1989) made it difficult for the compilers of *With One Voice* to refuse their inclusion in their book. Why these two were restored is almost as much a mystery as why they were ever lost, but they are now being sung with as much vigor as they were one hundred fifty years ago when the Swedish pioneers brought them to America in their songbooks from Sweden.

Sandell's Legacy

The early pastors of the Augustana Synod were guided by what Emmet Ecklund calls a mosaic of influences, among them the new evangelism of the Rosenius movement, the biblical methods of Peder Fjellstedt, and the confessional theology of Henrik Schartau.[89] All of these factors were at play in the pastors when they first arrived in America. Like Lina Sandell's father, they had also been students of Fjellstedt's Bible methods and had not been opposed to the Methodism of George Scott as they had learned it from Rosenius. As they worked in their chosen Zion in Illinois, however, their sympathies with the evangelicals around them began to wane. With the outbreak of the theological battle that resulted in the founding of the Evangelical Covenant Church, they began more and more to define themselves as confessional and even liturgical. Hasselquist's efforts to persuade Uddo L.

---

88. The author retranslated "Thy Holy Wings" in 1980 for the baptism of her first god-son. To make it appropriate for a baptism, she changed "Forgive me all my sins" to "O wash me in the waters of Noah's cleansing flood," changing it from an evening prayer to a baptismal song, which it has since become.

89. Emmet E. Ecklund, "The Mosaic of Augustana's Swedish Lutheran Origins," *Aspects of Augustana and Swedish America: Essays in Honor of Dr. Conrad Bergendoff on His 100th Year,* ed. Raymond Jarvi (Augustana Historical Society, 1995), pp. 8-24.

Ullman (1837-1930), Sweden's foremost hymnologist and liturgical scholar at the time, to teach at Augustana Seminary show the gradual change in his understanding of hymnody. Ullman's book on hymnody moved Hasselquist toward Wallin and gave him the idea that Augustana should work with the Church of Sweden to produce a joint hymnal that would be purged of the tinges of rationalism they disliked in Wallin's 1819 hymnal.[90] For a variety of reasons, Hasselquist's dream did not reach fruition. As the Swedish revival movement seemed to be less and less Lutheran, and more and more Covenant, the leaders of Swedish Augustana moved away from this body of hymns and toward a more Lutheran and American treasury of hymns. Still heartily evangelical — their 1925 hymnal includes American Gospel songs that many other Lutheran hymnals shunned, such as "In the Sweet By and By" — they did not seem to promote the work of Sandell until much later, when nostalgia for the old country surged.

It was Lina Sandell's work, ironically, that had prepared the Swedish and Norwegian immigrants for America. Her translations of many of the great American Gospel songs, such as "Nearer My God to Thee," set the American Gospel song into the hearts of her people. These Gospel songs were popular in Sweden, so much so that many thought they were originally Swedish. Joe Hill, the International Workers of the World (I.W.W.) organizer, learned many of these English Gospel songs when he was growing up in Sweden, and parodied them in his songs for the I.W.W. *Little Red Book:* "There'll Be Pie in the Sky By and By" and "Hallelujah, I'm a Bum."[91]

The gifted translator of Sandell's most famous hymn, Ernst Wilhelm Olson, died on October 6, 1958, after a long life of literary work in the church. The obituary in the *Lutheran Companion* noted that he was at the height of his poetic powers when Augustana's 1925 *Hymnal* was being prepared. Twenty-eight of his translations from the Swedish were included in the hymnal, as were three original hymns and a paraphrase of Psalm 121. The obituary does not mention his translation of Sandell's hymn; an edi-

---

90. Uddo Lechard Ullman, *Om den kyrkliga psalmboken: liturgisk-kritisk undersökning med särskild hänsyn till den svenska kyrkans psalmbok av år 1819* (Uppsala: A. Virgin, 1871).

91. "Hallelujah, I'm a Bum" is a parody of the Swedish hymn "Lov, ära och pris dig vår Fader och vän," no. 11 in the current Swedish Hymnal. It is a translation of "We Praise Thee, O God, for the Son of Thy Love" by the English Presbyterian pastor, William Paton Mackay. The melody is by John J. Husband, an English composer who worked in Philadelphia around 1809.

torial in the same issue eulogizing him does mention that translation as one of his works, but it makes as much of his other translations.

Historians of the Augustana tradition have always noted the mosaic of pieties that came with the emigrant Swedes. It is clear, as one looks at not only the Augustana Synod, but also the many other ethnic Lutheran churches, that the pietism of the early emigrants was not as attractive to the second generation of immigrants as they made their ways up and out of the ethnic enclaves into which they were born. One could surmise that they sought to leave behind the log cabin and the simple religion of their elders in order to assimilate. Many have noted that the Swedes, of all immigrants to America, were the most eager to assimilate. As I argued in the *Lutheran Quarterly*, hymnals are an excellent way to see the truth of Hanson's Law: that the third generation wants to remember what the second generation wanted to forget.[92] It is possible to see in the appearance of the large corpus of Sandell's hymns, their disappearance, and then the reappearance of a remnant of her work a perfect example of Hanson's Law.[93] No Lutheran hymnal in America during the first quarter of the twentieth century is more American than that of Swedish Augustana in 1925.

The part of Augustana that allied itself with the Lutheran Bible Institute and the Youth Department, led by Wilton Bergstrand, trained the youth of Swedish Augustana to sing Sandell, among other hymns of the Swedish revival, in their conventions and gatherings.[94] Another, more high-church strain of Augustana began to define itself over against these songs of the Swedish revival as that strain sought to become more American and more Lutheran.[95] The move is almost always toward the tradi-

---

93. Gracia Grindal, "The Swedish Tradition in Hymnals and Songbooks," *Lutheran Quarterly* 5 (1991): 464.

94. Marcus Lee Hanson, "The Problem of the Third Generation Immigrant," *Augustana Historical Society Publication* (1938), 1-27.

95. See Wilton Bergstrand, "Youth Ministry and the Luther League," *The Augustana Heritage: Recollections, Perspectives, and Prospects,* ed. Arland Hultgren and Vance Eckstrom (Chicago: Augustana Heritage Association, 1999), pp. 259-63.

96. The memoirs of Swedish Augustana by contemporary heirs of the tradition frequently praise what Herbert Chilstrom calls its dignified worship, contrasting it to the piety of the pioneers, not unfavorably but with some sense of the difference. See Herbert W. Chilstrom, "What Was/Is Augustana?" *The Augustana Heritage: Recollections, Perspectives and Prospects,* ed. Arland Hultgren and Vance Eckstrom (Chicago: Augustana Heritage Association, 1999), pp. 5-6.

tional Lutheran hymns of the Reformation, both in Germany and Sweden. Furthermore, there is a kind of spiritual version of Hanson's Law when it comes to Pietism: the white heat of the first generation's personal experience of the faith comes down to the second generation as legalism, the empty forms of the first experience. The third generation, looking for some personal experience of the faith, looks back to the first and tries to recapture it, or has a new experience of the faith that takes them elsewhere. In America, that usually means re-conversion to another, more evangelical, faith tradition.

History, however, matters. On the whole, it is the heirs of the Scandinavian Augustana Synod of 1860-1870, both Swedish and Norwegian, who have kept Sandell's legacy alive in America. These groups ultimately broke into two confessions: the Evangelical Covenant and the Evangelical Free Churches, whose roots are also in the Swedish and Norwegian revivals of the nineteenth century and who also treasured Sandell's hymns. Lutheran pietists, who had learned the Swedish spiritual songs in their youth, gathered together with Swedes in parachurch organizations such as the Lutheran Evangelistic Movement, Mt. Carmel Bible Camp, and Lutheran Bible Institute. These communities of faith assured Sandell's three hymns a future. Hanson's Law holds: we should not be surprised that the third generation of the Scandinavian Augustana Synod, whatever remnants there are left of it, loves to sing at least three of Sandell's songs in English. They gave her songs to the American evangelical movement, such as Billy Graham's crusades, which brought them to the world, as did the missionaries from all of these various traditions. For this reason they are no longer the sole possession of Scandinavian Lutherans. This precocious pastor's daughter from Sweden now has a parish that stretches from Sweden, to America, to Africa, China, and wherever there are people who love to sing her hymns.

CHAPTER 5

Britt G. Hallqvist (1914-1997)
A Twinkling in God's Eye

When I met her in Lund, Sweden, at the meeting of the *International Arbeitsgemeinschaft für Hymnologie* (IAH) in August of 1987, Britt Hallqvist already knew who I was: "The American," she said drolly. We talked for a few minutes and then she tottered off, frail but keen of mind, her eyes twinkling with amusement. At the time, I knew little about her, but paging through the new Swedish hymnal, which had just been published the year before, I saw that she figured very prominently in the editing process of revising and updating the hymnal. Not only that, but she had also written many new hymns already prized by the Swedish and Norwegian people, especially those from her joyful collaboration with Norway's most prominent composer of church music at the time, Egil Hovland (1924-). Although she had not been the original architect of the Scandinavian hymn explosion and its push for hymns that expressed the faith in simple, nontheological language, easily available to ordinary people — a movement put forward most forcefully by her fellow Swede, Anders Frostenson (1906-2006) — she became one of the major proponents of the movement as she gradually began to write her own hymns and take her place in the pantheon of Scandinavian hymnody. Her development into a hymn writer of note came later in her life, after she had established herself as one of Sweden's well-regarded writers of children's literature and translator of German, English, and Danish poetry. This work contributed to her increasing mastery of the poetic challenges required for the simple, but profound, hymn texts she began writing at almost the same time.

Figure 1 Britt G. Hallqvist. Photo: Björn Larsson.

Her Life

Britt Gerda Nyman, or Britt G., as she came to be known in her later years, was born on February 14, 1914, in the northeastern Swedish city of Umeå on the Baltic. She was the third child of Wilhelm Nyman (1878-1936) and Dagny Henschen (1885-1960). Her father, a gifted linguist, received his Ph.D. in French in 1907. Brit's mother, Dagny, had earned a degree in languages from Uppsala, where she would later teach. In 1910 she married

Nyman, who had also studied at Uppsala. Together they established a home of high intellectual achievements, as both were well versed in the modern cultures, languages, and literature of Europe. They had begun their married life in Umeå, but moved when Britt was three, to Visby, a town on the western side of the long island of Gottland, in the Baltic, just off the southeastern coast of Sweden, where her father taught French and German. Throughout her life, Britt referred to Gottland as her "childhood isle." By 1926, when Britt was twelve years old, her parents' marriage had failed, and her mother moved with the children to Lund. Her father, whom she felt she never got to know very well, moved away, and died in Stockholm, after a long illness, in 1936.

The move, at one of the most difficult times in a young girl's life, changed many things for Britt G. Now she had to deal with all the turmoil of adolescence as she was adapting to a new home town, a new school, and new friends.[1] Lund, with its cathedral and university, provided her a rich intellectual and cultural environment. There the young teenager took to her studies at the Lindberg Girls' School in the city with enthusiasm.

Her best subjects, not surprisingly, given her family background, were languages and literature. When she began learning Latin, she started translating some of the best-known Latin poetry, exploring its forms as she learned to use them in Swedish. In addition to the ancient *ars poetica*, she began reading modern poetry, especially that of the most well regarded Swedish writers of the day: Karin Boye (1900-1941), Harry Martinson (1904-1978), and Birger Sjöberg (1885-1929), whose new, modernist poetry and songs were creating interest among students at the time. In addition to these worldly songs, there were the hymns and spiritual songs of the Lutheran church. As in any small European country with a Protestant heritage, the tradition of "hymns and spiritual songs" is considered to be part of the literary treasure of Sweden.

Thus, it is not surprising that Britt G., an aspiring writer, although not raised in a particularly religious home, began examining the tradition of Swedish song and hymnody as a source for her own poetry.[2] Her attraction, she wrote, was not the piety, but the poetry, especially its imagery.

---

1. Inge Löfström, *En bok om Britt G: Forfattaren och översättaren Britt G Hallqvist* (Värnamo: SkeabVerbum, 1982), p. 27. Most of the facts of Britt G.'s life in this chapter come from this very helpful book.
2. Britt G. Hallqvist, *Lunds Stifts Julbok*, 1970.

Figure 2 The cathedral in Lund (Creative Common).

"The language of Psalm 90, for example, 'A thousand years in thy sight is as an evening gone' became words to taste, drink, feed on."³ Even the old hymn by the German prosodist and poet, Martin Opitz (1597-1639), "Light of Light, O Morning Star" ("O Liecht geboren aus dem Liecht") with its fifth stanza, "Let the oil in our lamps burn as you judge the whole wide world," reminded her of her childhood, sitting in school in the twilit autumn mornings, with "hundreds of other sleepy, and probably a little giggly, girls, thinking about other things, certainly not foolish virgins — especially not that group of foolish virgins!"⁴ If she did go to church at the time, she said, it was for the sake of the hymns, not much else.

When it came time for her to consider whether she should take the traditional Lutheran confirmation instruction, her free-thinking mother allowed Britt G. to make up her own mind as to whether or not she would go. While her inclination was to refuse such instruction, it interested her that their instructor would be Anders Nygren (1890-1978), at the time professor of theology at the university. Because Nygren had a reputation as a famous teacher, and Britt G. was intellectually curious, she chose to attend the classes with ten of her young friends. Later she noted that these classes were "highly theoretical and not always easy to follow."⁵ When the time came for her to be confirmed, she suffered some anxiety about making her promises to renounce the world, the flesh, and the devil, and renew her baptismal vows. She did not consider herself to have much faith, so, after some angst, normal to an adolescent, she went to Nygren to announce that she would not go forward to make her promises. What he said is not recorded, but he must have known that he had interested her in the faith, and perhaps, wisely, let her be.

All this time she continued writing poetry. Along with her friends she established something of a teenaged literary salon, where they could read each other's work and meet some of their literary idols living and writing in Lund. Britt's mother, whose social group included many well-known poets and artists, had been married for a short time to Ivar Harrie (1899-1973), a well-regarded Swedish poet of his day. It was exciting to the young girls to know these poets, as they wrote their own poetry, most of which, Britt said later, with her typically droll humor, was love poetry, es-

3. Löfström, p. 29.
4. Löfström, p. 29.
5. Löfström, p. 29.

pecially unhappy love. The object of her most passionate poetry was a window cleaner in Lund, she noted, who lived in complete ignorance of the love burning for him in her poetry.[6]

The girls continued their literary salon in the summer, traveling from one summer home to another in the country, in the province of Värmeland, straight north of Lund on the Norwegian border, where their families had homes. Britt spent most of her time with her especially close friend, Kerstin, whose father Hjalmar Holmquist was a professor in church history at the University. After her graduation with very high marks from gymnasium in 1933, Britt began university, where she specialized in literary history, especially Nordic languages and philosophy. Already she was getting notice for her poetry and writing, even as she was studying closely her own Swedish poetic tradition. In 1936, she wrote a paper on the "Images in the Salvation Army's Songbook," beginning her long engagement with the language of Christian hymns and songs. As her reputation increased, she was asked to become one of the editors of the student paper, *Lundagård*, the first woman to be asked. She received other honors during her time at the university and became known as a writer, living something of a bohemian life typical of writers at the time. Among the many opportunities she received was the request from Professor Annie Löfstedt, the editor of *Natur och Kultur (Nature and Culture),* who asked her to translate children's literature from English and German for her anthology of children's literature, *Min Skattkamaren (My Treasury).* It was her first commissioned translating job with pay. Later she reported that she had earned 50 öre for each stanza, maybe a nickel in American money at the time.[7] Other requests such as this started her on her long career of translating and writing poetry.

In May of 1938, she and Sten Hallqvist (1911-1978) were engaged to be married. Sten, a gifted, good-looking theological student, had literary interests as well and was a poet himself. He had grown up on a farm near Vänersborg, a town near the southwestern shore of Lake Vänern, one of the two large lakes in the southern part of Sweden. His confirmation pastor, Yngve Rudberg, who later became his bishop, had a strong influence on Sten's ultimate decision to become a pastor. Another important influence in Sten's Christian life and call to be a pastor was Adolf Kloo (1878-1972), pastor in Vargön, also near Lake Vänern. Sten had announced that

---

6. Löfström, p. 30.
7. Britt G. Hallqvist, *Min text och den andres* (Lund: Sanby Grafiska, 1987), p. 8.

should he become a pastor, he would do his internship with Kloo. In October of 1940, after Sten's ordination in Skara cathedral, and his military service, the young couple began three years of service with Kloo. Kloo had an enormous effect on Britt G. as well. The year before she died, in 1996, in an interview with Lars Westman, she noted that Kloo was truly an admirable Christian: "He could clean a toilet if one needed help," she said.[8] His witness strengthened her faith, even as she thought later about how difficult it was to become a pastor.

Sten was an intellectual pastor who had been strongly influenced in his theology by Anders Nygren, later bishop of Lund; Bo Giertz (1905-1998), writer of the novel *Hammer of God (Steingrunnen)* and Bishop of Gothenberg, an influential theologian and writer; and Yngve Brilioth (1889-1959), Bishop of Växjö from 1938 to 1950 and Archbishop of Uppsala from 1950 until 1958, and a well-regarded writer on liturgy. These theologians gave Swedish theology an international reputation, although Sten disagreed with them significantly on the way the church viewed contemporary society, especially as it was related in modern literature. In a sermon he gave at Sofia Church in Stockholm in 1951, he had argued that the secular writers of the day, while on the periphery of the church, may have expressed the gospel more clearly in their works than these theologians. Both he and Britt worked to open the dialogue between the religious and secular, dogma and poetry, theology and literature. His admiration for literature made him an ideal partner for Britt, whose work he encouraged and appreciated.

Britt's marriage to a man who was to become a pastor caused her friends, to say nothing of her, some surprise and amusement. Not long after her engagement, an announcement appeared in the paper she edited with a caricature of her, noting with astonishment that Britt G. was "going to marry a pastor."[9] The thought of her having to be the hostess at sewing circles and pastors' meetings, baking and preparing meals for many guests, was not her idea of fun. She, however, did well. Later, she would write that "instead of sitting and sewing in young people's societies — something that I was not very good at — I began to write short Bible plays which we performed in the parish house."[10] As her family began to grow, these pro-

---

8. Lars Westman, "Hon gör det himmelska mera mänskligt," *Vi* 10 (1996): 17.
9. Westman, p. 32.
10. Löfström, p. 42.

Figure 3 Caricature of Britt Gerda Nyman-Hallqvist.

ductions were probably the only writing for which she had time. Her biographer, however, notes that her interest in people, the understanding of their problems, her friendliness, humor, and prudence made her a fine addition to the parish and her husband's work.[11]

In 1947, Sten and the family moved to Bredared parish in Alingsås, about halfway between Gothenburg and Jönköping. There he began teaching theology, in addition to his pastoral duties. He did so well that the rector suggested that he study for his teacher's certificate, which he did. After a couple of years, he was called to teach in Lund at a private school, so in 1958, he, Britt, and their four children moved back to her hometown, where she would live until her death. With that, Britt continued her writing, flourishing in the exciting world of the university and cathedral where she had spent her student years.

11. Löfström, p. 42.

Her Career

At the beginning of the new decade, in 1950, Hallqvist made her debut as a writer of children's verse with a book on *The Rapps of Blaasopp (Rappens paa Blåsopp)*. Several of the poems were set to music; and somewhat surprisingly, given her skepticism, many of them turn to biblical themes. We can read in these works Hallqvist's sense for the way families worked and the child's view of the drama of the family, along with her very well-honed sense of the biblical story. Even though these simple and charming books appealed immediately to children, they were not immune to the spirit of the age with its declining interest in the church and the Christian faith. Hallqvist, as both pastor's wife and scholar, had a unique perspective on her work, since she lived in the world of the church and university at the time of enormous change in both worlds. Both worlds, however, preferred complexity to simplicity. Almost as if in answer to the preference for complexity, her 1955 collection of poetry, *Simplified (Förenklat)*, looked for simple, but profound, ways to live with the problems of the Christian faith as it was being debated at the time. The agonies of doubt, widespread among the Christian intelligentsia of the era, interested her, as did the question of language and how one could speak of the Christian faith which needed, according to New Testament scholar Rudolf Bultmann (1884-1976), to be demythologized or at least made consistent with a modern worldview. This collection received high praise from many in Sweden who greeted the publication of the book as containing some of the "most beautiful and gripping Christian poetry that has been published in a long time in Sweden."[12] In later collections she continued such simplicity, which we see in this poem from 1971:

> I went one early morning
> To look at heav'n above,
> And saw it was transparent
> With incandescent love.
> I noticed high archangels,
> In violet and white,
> And near the sweet forget-me-nots
> Sat God in glorious light.

12. Axel Liffner, quoted in Löfstrom, p. 79.

> And some might want to question
> How I could see again
> What I'd not seen before,
> My Maker and my friend.
> He had no crown upon him,
> And none could see his name,
> But he was God, I knew for sure,
> By the children in his arms.

This elegantly simple verse describes concretely, and in the language of nature, what the heavenly beings look like. That she is seeing God, and seeing God's simplicity, is not simple, but with these bright images, she is communicating something very deep, yet in a way that children can see and understand. One can assume that in her writing of these poems, she not only made her reputation as a writer of Christian poetry, but also as one whose complete simplicity in the poetry, with their comic charm, and depth, set her out on a path quite different from what she might have expected as a bohemian student and writer in Lund in the last years of the 1930s.

While she marked the theological debates of the day in her work, Hallqvist went her own way. Her response seems to have been to move toward simplicity, to rediscover the simple things of the faith, found especially in the biblical narrative, rather than trying to develop a complicated theology to solve or explain the problem. In many ways, she was the poet for whom modern theologians was calling, in their agony over the loss of meaning that came with the modern world.

We see her responding to this problem in song by writing verses for children with whom it was necessary to be simple. She demonstrates this skill well in her first collection of songs written with several Dutch composers, *I Will Sing a Song to God (Jag vill sjunga en visa för Gud)*. It contained twenty simple songs which marked the times of the year, the day, and several Christian festivals such as Christmas and Easter. Her song for Christmas, with music by Gerard van Hulst, communicates the style and tone of most of the rest of the small collection.

1. A boy so small and tiny
   Was born in Bethlehem,
   The heavens shone so brightly
   It set the skies aflame.

2. So many long had waited
   Within their darkened rooms
   To see the boy so tiny
   Who made the darkness gleam.

3. He helped both small and grown-ups,
   We know he does again;
   His name is our Lord Jesus,
   He is our closest friend.[13]

This song for children illustrates in its language her conviction that hymns should be bare of theological concepts and simply tell the story — in other words, teach the Bible. One of the features of this sort of hymn, as it developed with her and her contemporaries, is that there is no naming of Christ until the very last two lines, almost as if to draw singers in without having them realize the song is religious, and after describing who the boy was, naming him. Except for the title "Bethlehem," which most singers would be able to associate with Jesus' birth, it is a description of some kind of miraculous birth, as the skies go "aflame." Still the words are very concrete and simple, and even the last two lines are simple: The announcement of Jesus' name and the assertion that Jesus "is our closest friend." There is no word here that a very young child could not understand, and the concept of Jesus as a friend is well within the realm of the child's conceptual categories. *Friend* is a much more accessible notion than *Savior*, and for the young child, is much more understandable. These first songs and hymns show us not only her skill in writing for children, but also point toward the path she would follow throughout her life as she wrote narrative hymns with concrete rather than theological or abstract terminology.

One of her first and most famous hymn texts, from 1955, is the story of Jesus coming to the children. As she did in other hymns, she established the voice in the poem as someone asking the innocent question that is then answered. Someone ignorant of the Bible story might have asked the same question and found in the hymn an answer. The question, however, in this hymn, already gives us a vivid picture of Jesus coming into town, with

---

13. Britt G. Hallqvist, "Pojken, Betlehem," *Jag vill sjunga en visa för Gud: visbok för barn* (Amsterdam: Nederlansche Zondagsschool Vereeniging, and Lund: Håkan Ohlssons Förlag, n.d.), p. 27.

"light shining bright in his hair." The rest of the hymn changes voice, so that the one answering seems to take over.

Who Is It We See on the Highway?
(Vem är det som kommer på vägen?)

1. Who is it we see on the highway
   With light shining bright in his hair?
   Oh, that is our Master, Christ Jesus,
   To him, yes to him, we will fare.

2. The children, they hopped from their jump ropes,
   Their forts made of clay and of straw.
   And all of their mammas came with them,
   To bring him their children so small.

3. But St. James and Peter got angry:
   "Leave Jesus alone, he is tired!
   Your pushing and shouting is noisy,
   The Lord wants to preach, so be quiet!"

4. "No, now's not the time to be preaching
   For I want to care for the young.
   For such is the kingdom of heaven,
   Now I want to bless them, each one!"

5. He took in his arms all the children,
   He hugged them and blessed all who'd come,
   His face shone as bright as the morning
   And gladly the mammas went home.[14]

The children, engaged in the typical rowdy activities of active children — jumping, making forts — are brought by their "mammas" for Jesus to bless them. The idea that James and Peter got angry is probably new to children's hymns. In Hallqvist's hymn, one sees and hears the Bible story from

---

14. Britt G. Hallqvist, *Den Svenska Psalmboken,* hymn 41 (Verbum, 1986), tr. Gracia Grindal, 2005.

the point of view of the children. Her version makes it more dramatic: old people wanting children to be quiet so serious things like preaching can continue undisturbed, something Jesus does not agree to; a God who reaches down to the children, who will never forget this encounter for what it shows about Jesus. It is sentimental in a modern, ironic way, different from nineteenth-century sentimentality. While it was an innovation to use the word "mammas" *(mammorna)*, it may be a little cute for a hymn. In an interview with Lars Westman, in 1996, the year before she died, Hallqvist supposed that her use of "mamma" was perhaps the first time the word had appeared in a Swedish hymn.[15]

It is in her hymns about heaven, however, where Hallqvist revealed her shrewd sense for the theological currents swirling around her that tended to deny the existence of the three-story universe and excised all such images from contemporary hymns and sermons. As a story teller, she made no effort to demythologize the story; in fact, she was one of the few contemporary hymn writers who made heaven appear to be as charming for children as for adults. Influenced by Martin Luther's note to his son Hans detailing what heaven will be like, with its bow and arrows and infinite places to play, Hallqvist used these images in several of her most famous hymns. The first one we have is from 1958:

There by God's Heav'nly Throne
(Inför Guds himlatron)

There by God's heav'nly throne,
We hear the angel's song.
Orchestras tune their strings,
Music plays on and on.

The angel Michel plays
Tunes on his shining horn.
He plays a glad fanfare
In praise of God's new morn.

The angel Gabriel
Tries out a blessed tune

---

15. Westman, p. 15.

On his new violin,
Praising the morning sun.

Pipes and a shepherd's flute
Play with the kettledrums,
Saints without number sing,
Praise to the Lord of love.

There by the heav'nly throne,
I want to play along.
There with my wooden flute,
Playing the new, new song.[16]

Along with Luther's picture of heaven, this poem has features of the *Songs of Innocence* by William Blake, with the shepherd playing on his oaten flute with joy. The concrete simplicity of the images and the tone of uncomplicated joy in the heavenly music of the angels appeal to children. Hallqvist, although quite wise in the issues surrounding theodicy and God's nature, thinks the truth is best understood through images. Furthermore, the hymn is in the voice of a child, one who is telling the singer what heaven looks like and what he or she wants to do in heaven. At first the orchestra is playing, but at the end the child is hoping to play his or her new little wooden flute in the orchestra. There are no theological abstractions in the hymn. Using the spare poetic dictum of the twentieth century, "show, don't tell," she gives us concrete images so we can have the experience of heaven.

Her picture of Zacchaeus in her hymn "Zacchaeus Was a Publican" ("Sackeus var en publican"), also from 1958, has the same appeal to young children, who delight in the story of the "wee little man," probably because the tax collector is small. Once again, Jesus is a "friend," not the great God or Savior of other hymns.

Zacchaeus Was a Publican
(Sackeus var en publican)

1. Zacchaeus was a publican,
   He was the city's richest man.

---

16. Hallqvist, *Den Svenska Psalmboken*, hymn 613, tr. Grindal, 2005.

Britt G. Hallqvist

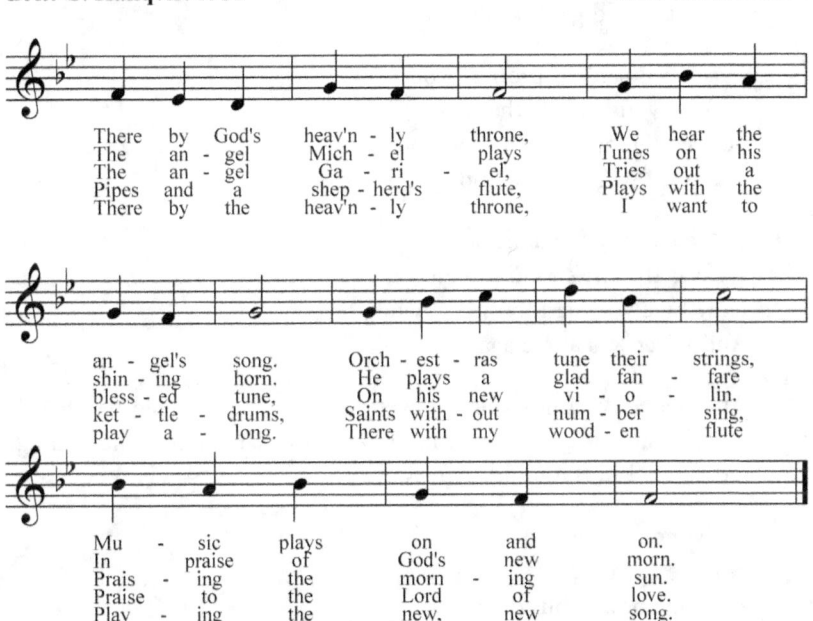

Figure 4 "There by God's Heav'nly Throne."

But he had spent his life alone,
And he was lonesome as a stone.

2. When Jesus came to Jericho,
   He wondered who it was he saw,
   The little man who clambered up
   And watched him from the high tree top.

3. He sat there looking down into
   The teeming multitude below,
   Then Jesus said, "Prepare a feast,
   For I am going to be your guest!"

4. The little man came climbing down
   To welcome him into his home,
   His house was clean, the candles lit,
   So Jesus could gladly enter it.

5. Zacchaeus said, "I promise you,
   I'll give you half of what I own,
   To feed the hungry, and the poor,
   For you I will do that, and more!"

6. Zacchaeus was a publican,
   He was the city's richest man,
   Now finally he had found a friend,
   And never was alone again.[17]

Another very famous text, "Everyone's Rushed" ("Alle har hast"), from 1958, became the basis for a family worship service that she and Egil Hovland created in the middle 1970s.

1. Ev'ryone's rushed,
   No one has time.
   Ev'ryone now is busy.
   No one can see
   I am afraid,
   No one has time to listen!

2. God has some time,
   Eternity!
   And he is softly list'ning.
   He makes me glad
   When I'm afraid
   Even when I have been naughty.

3. Can you hear me?
   Though I was bad,
   Let me be close beside you.
   Please take my hand!

17. Hallqvist, *Den Svenska Psalmboken,* hymn 614, tr. Grindal, 2005.

Please take my hand.
Ev'rything's right
When you're with me.[18]

This hymn, written about the time when women were beginning to leave home in droves to work, speaks to the anxieties of the young child who has been left alone. Hallqvist must have remembered her own childhood when her single mother had to leave her alone while she worked, as well as the complaints of her own children. Once again, God is a friend, a companion, someone who will listen and take the hand of the child. The hymn helps the young child understand also that he or she can tell everything to God, even if one has been naughty or bad. These are among the most famous of the hymns that appeared in the book *Kyrkovisor för Barn* (1960), and their popularity made them prime candidates for inclusion in the coming Swedish hymnal. Her success with these hymns paved the way for a new understanding of hymnody and what belonged in a hymnal for modern people.

The consequences of these ideas about the language of the faith, especially for children, appeared in full bloom, appropriately, at the beginning of the 1960s, in the book *Church Songs for Children* (*Kyrkovisor för Barn*) (1960) which, when it was published, met with great enthusiasm and marked the beginning of the hymn explosion in Scandinavia.[19] Hallqvist had been on the hymnal committee with Frostenson and others who came to be leaders of the "Hymn Explosion" in Scandinavia.[20] Its genius was in providing "Christian songs for children such as gave expression to their joy and security in the Christian faith."[21] It also marked the beginning of Hallqvist's serious reflection on what a hymn for the modern Christian could be and do: why not have some humor in hymns, she wondered; Jesus' parables were outrageous and sometimes funny. Why not get that into hymns, rather than the sentimentality of the past?[22] Frostenson's and Hallqvist's work became foremost in this movement. Seventeen of the

---

18. Hallqvist, *Den Svenska Psalmboken*, hymn 255, tr. Grindal, 2005.

19. See Inger Selander's lecture, "The Swedish Hymn Explosion from a Literary Perspective," given July 31, 2007 in Trondheim, Norway.

20. *Den Svenska Psalmboken: Texter och Melodier samt förslag Till Supplement*, vol. 2 (Stockholm: Statens Offentliga Utredningar, 1974), p. 23.

21. *Den Svenska Psalmboken*, vol. 2, p. 23.

22. Löfström, p. 146.

Figure 5 "Ev'ryone's Rushed."

songs in this early book were by Hallqvist, most of which were narrative hymns, six of them translations. Her most frequent theme in these hymns was the friendship of Jesus and young children.

When she began writing hymns for adults, her ideas come from these same literary and theological convictions. We hear her skepticism but also her use of simple language in this quiet little hymn before Communion, "I Have Come Not That I Trust You" ("Jag kom inte hit för att jag tror") (1966). In it she speaks clearly for herself, but also for the typical modern Swede trying to believe.

1. I have come not that I trust you,
   I have come because I need you now.
   They have said that you are very good,
   I have no one else to help me cope.

2. Gracious God, you now know what I mean.
   Though I do not understand a bit
   Of your festivals; come in a tune
   Or sit by me here and hold my hand.

3. They have said you are a living word,
   More than words I pray for in my need,
   O Lord Jesus, now despite my doubt
   Let me take yourself in wine and bread.[23]

Written in 1966, it spoke to the growing doubt of church people who had problems with both biblical language and theological concepts. The hymnal committee for the 1986 Swedish hymnal, however, would not accept her original last line: "Let me take you, in unbelief, as wine and bread."[24] Its focus on the doubting believer who still wants to come to receive the wine and bread uses the language of the father who pleaded with Christ to heal his son: "Lord, I believe; help thou my unbelief" (Mark 9:24). Hallqvist defended the hymn with this verse, but to no avail. The committee still asked that it be changed.

The hymn raises the typical questions of a twentieth-century Chris-

---

23. Hallqvist, *Den Svenska Psalmboken* (Verbum, 1986), hymn 532, tr. Grindal, 2005.
24. Löfström, p. 177.

tian; its tone is clearly one of a believer who feels that her faith is very weak. The voice in the hymn seems exhausted, lonely, and weary, almost frightened. She has come out of need, not faith, but in some ways this makes her ready to receive more than the confident believer who appears to have no doubts. She has come, not because of her great knowledge of the faith, but because she has heard that God will help, and since she needs help, she has no place else to go: "They have said you are very good." Deep beneath the language of the hymn is the conviction that Jesus will draw all people unto himself. The singer has clearly been drawn to the church and sacrament, even though she does not understand the rites and rituals of the service, but she still is able to ask that God "come in a tune" or simply "come and hold my hand." The last stanza plays with the notion of words and word. If God is a living word, even if she is not interested in hearing more words, she can at least take the bread and wine and receive it, rather than words about Jesus. The raw need that comes through in the hymn is simply and elegantly expressed.

Many of her contemporaries could sing the hymn with her; in fact, she may have expressed more of their doubt than hers. If the hymn writer is to give the congregation words with which to express its faith, or lack thereof, this hymn sounded a completely new idea about what a hymn should do. Modern hymns, she thought, should address the doubts and questions of the people of the day. Modern Christians, she would argue, needed such language in their hymns, no matter how much they might have treasured the hymns of the traditional, old-fashioned faith. She had written the hymn, she said, thinking of confirmands who might have had difficulty in believing the bread and wine is really Christ, probably thinking of her own experience refusing confirmation. For her, "faith was not a finished system that one had completely figured out once and for all."[25]

Another vocation she fulfilled during these busy times was that of writing school textbooks and teaching the young. Given the fact that even Sweden, growing more and more secular throughout the 1960s, still had a state church that received official sanction in the school system, Hallqvist was probably the perfect person to write such textbooks. Writing these textbooks about the Christian faith became a way for her to more fully examine the biblical story and its implications for the young. These books, many of them in rhyme and filled with her droll humor, especially charm-

---

25. Löfström, p. 177.

ing to children, covered a wide variety of subjects, but the most well-received were those that taught Bible stories or used the Bible as the basis for the material, such as a Biblical ABC book, which referred to biblical stories and names to fill out the alphabet:

> Adam came first of all,
> Babel's tower was doomed to fall.[26]

The most important textbook that she wrote was *People and Faith (Människor och tro)* (1966, 1968) in two volumes of four hundred pages for those in the third to sixth year of grammar school, in which Hallqvist told Bible stories to children, frequently in the voice of a child observing the action, for example, of the story of Zacchaeus from the point of view of his fictional daughter, Rebekah, commenting on her "Little Dad."[27] Many of the stories were presented in the form of small dramas, like the ones she had written in her early years in the parsonage when she realized that young children and teenagers, especially, enjoyed playing the parts of the biblical characters in dramatic form.

From 1964 to 1969 she received a yearly stipend from the Swedish Authors' Fund to continue her work. These grants bore much fruit. In 1968, a very productive year for her, Hallqvist wrote *Prayerbook for Children (Bön bok för barn)*. It began with a note in the foreword, "Almost everyone prays. Some pray regularly, others pray only when something particular happens. God listens to every prayer."[28] The prayers deal with many of the issues important to young children in their lives: the death of grandparents, the divorce of their own parents, the fear of the darkness, and so on. He poem "I Have Finished Playing" ("Nu har jag lekt färdigt") speaks directly to the child's fear of the dark and his or her loneliness. The Father in heaven, she assures her reader, is ready to come, as a friend or a father, to comfort and attend to the young child.

> I have finished playing,
> Now I am in bed,
> All my clothes are lying
> Where they have been laid.

---

26. Britt G. Hallqvist, "Bibleskt ABC," *Versboken: Småskolans läse bok* (AB, 1959).
27. Britt G. Hallqvist, *Människor och tro* (1966), p. 119.
28. Hallqvist, *Bön bok för barn*, p. 127.

The room is dark and scary,
And I cannot see,
It is hard to doze off,
Harder still to pray.

Dearest Father, be here
In the dark by me!
While the others slumber
I have only thee.[29]

These new poems and songs created interest in the Swedish population, and Hallqvist was aware that her new work was not only new and different, but that it was replacing older, more traditional hymns that she valued. She proposed writing a prayerbook for adults, which she would call *Shepherdess*, which would be ironic. We can see what it would have been like in a gentle, funny poem that she wrote while in a committee meeting concerning the pros and cons of various musical styles — from Haeffner[30] to the rhythmic chorales to pop songs. Her poem shows the conflict when the old, beloved music of the nineteenth-century Swedish church musician Haeffner is set aside for a new kind of music:

The New Song

"And they sing a new song before the throne. . . . No one could learn that song except the hundred and forty-four thousand who had been redeemed from the earth." Rev. 14:3

The Cantor
Hobbled down to the organist;
He expected to be scolded by the vicar
Who was very musical.
The Lord
Had laid a new song in the vicar's mouth
But the Cantor
Kept to the old one —

---

29. Hallqvist, *Bön bok för barn*, p. 128.
30. Haeffner was the composer who set the Swedish hymnal of 1819 to music.

> For Olivia's sake, he said.
> She would be confused
> If she did not hear Haeffner
> Both here and in heaven.
> But the vicar
> Prayed a quiet prayer
> That God in his grace would give the Cantor some rhythm,
> Although deep inside of him, he doubted it was possible.
> I hope that they will not be standing together in the heavenly Choir![31]

This verse about a common difficulty for writers of new hymns is especially funny in Swedish, but it also shows Hallqvist knew the real difficulties of changing the language of prayer and hymnody. She had to think about these issues as she continued with her own work, which quickly began to displace other more traditional hymns.

In that same year, 1968, she produced many more works, from revisions of previous books to new books of poetry, such as *A Little Mouse Seeks a House (En liten Mus söker Hus)*. The short poem "Post Card," from her collection *Verse on a Journey (Vers på resa)* (1969), shows her at her best:

> We sat on the ferry, on the car deck, in our car, and complained that it was so crammed. Then mama said, "Think of Jonah in the belly of the whale. That was much more crammed."
>
> > In the darkness of the whale's belly,
> > The prophet Jonah sat,
> > Completely doubled over
> > He sighed and then he wept.
> >
> > He blew his nose, and wrote a postcard
> > Telling his old aunts not to fear,
> > "Having a wonderful time," he wrote,
> > "Wish that you were here."[32]

---

31. Hallqvist, quoted in Löfström, p. 136.
32. Britt G. Hallqvist, "Vykort," *Vers på resa* (1969), quoted in Löfström, p. 56.

The language, more simple and direct than it is possible to turn into English, shows not only her skill with verse, but her very keen sense for what children would enjoy as they observed the family drama. Here she shows how the Christian imagination works when parents teach their children to describe their lives in the language and stories of Scripture. Comparing the ship to a whale, and the car deck with the children squeezed into the car to the whale's stomach, took the kind of imagination that helped children deal with their boredom on the ferry. Having the reluctant prophet weeping in the very crowded stomach of the whale but finally pulling himself together enough to write a postcard to his aunts is truly funny, especially since he writes the conventional closing to a postcard, "Wish that you were here." By taking the cliché and using it in a context where it is not appropriate — wishing the aunts were with him in the belly of the whale — she is even funnier. Making this connection took the kind of fey imagination for which Hallqvist became well-known.

In 1970, Lund gave her its cultural stipend so she could continue to devote her time to her work. From that period came one of her most highly regarded poems, "I Went One Early Morning" ("Jag stod en tidig morgon"), from the collection *At The Door of Paradise (Vid Paradisets Port)*, published in 1971.[33]

The first stanza, with its mystical picture of heaven, the archangels, and God "in glorious light," contains no irony or skepticism. Almost as if she realizes that her readers will be wondering how she can be so naïve as to accept these biblical pictures as real, she addresses the question they might have in the second stanza: "And some might want to question/How I could see again." The poem closes with a slight twist. She knows she is looking at God, not by the conventional images of the deity wearing a crown, but by the children in his arms. Her picture of God as a father with children in his arms is also very attractive. She noted several times that she did not pray to Jesus but directly to God the Father. One might wonder whether she was not her longing for her father, whom she did not know well, in her intimate pictures of God as Father. Such a hymn would have been greeted with universal laughter in the demythologizing theological culture of the time in America. As I was beginning to work on the Hymn Text Committee of the *Lutheran Book of Worship* (1978) and trying to find

---

33. Britt G. Hallqvist, "Jag stod en tidig morgon," *Vid Paradisets Port* (Stockholm: Verbum, 1971), p. 228.

new hymn texts that spoke of our modern difficulties with the faith, I saw immediately that such hymns and poems would be rejected out of hand as old-fashioned. Our committee seemed to prefer rhymed modern theology with few images to images as naïve as this.

In September of 1972, Hallqvist and her husband Sven moved to Fanö, an island in the North Sea just west of Esbjerg on the west coast of Denmark, for she had received a grant to live in what was called The Poet's House for a period of about two years. The house, a spacious home some two hundred years old, had been a refuge for Scandinavian writers over the decades. Sten received permission to leave his work and accompany her there, as he was becoming her "right-hand man," both helper and critic of her work. The couple lived there until January 15, 1975. During that time, she completed many original works of her own, as well as translations of operas into Swedish. Her most successful was her collection of poetry, *Nalle's Poetry ("Nalles poesi")*, which she thought was her best book: "None of my books was so much fun to write. The verses rolled out of me."[34] The story is of a small teddy bear who, like Winnie the Pooh, walked frequently on the sandy beaches of the North Sea in Fanö.

> I walked through clay and reeds,
> And stuck a thorn into my paw
> And later on I stubbed my toe,
> Dumb to walk where I would go.[35]

The ease with which the verse tumbled out is apparent, even in translation. It delighted its audience; however, not every critic liked it, thinking the poems were too adult for children and too childish for adults. It, however, proved to be popular, selling thirty thousand copies, a great deal for Sweden at the time. In addition to these successful books of poetry, her translations had begun to establish her as Sweden's premier translator of English, French, and German poetry — everything from children's verse to Shakespeare's *Troilus and Cressida, Coriolanus,* and *Anthony and Cleopatra;* Christopher Fry's (1907-2005) *The Lady's Not for Burning* (1948); and T. S. Eliot's *Cats.* From German, she translated Goethe's *Faust* and several plays by Peter Weiss (1916-1982) — *Marat/Sade, Hölderlin* and *The Searching*

---

34. Liffner, "En Syn," p. 150.
35. Britt G. Hallqvist, "Jag gick i lera och i vass," quoted in Löfström, p. 89.

(*Ermittlung*). Her accomplishments in this field, especially her translation of *Faust*, for which she had won national recognition, proved her to be among the most gifted literary figures of her time, and made it likely that when Swedish musicians were looking for new librettos for their own operas she would be consulted. Her first opera, a children's opera, *The Professor of Fairy Tales (Sagoprofessorn)*, was based on her earlier book by the same name. For the works she had completed during her time in Denmark, she received several literary prizes, among them, the Swedish *Damtidnings Academic* prize in 1973 and two distinguished prizes for translations, one from the Swedish Academy in 1976, and another from the Swedish Authors' Translation Premium in 1977.

She continued turning Bible stories into droll and witty poetry, especially those from the Old Testament: Adam and Eve, Noah's Ark, Abraham and Sarah, the Passover, David's dalliance with Bathsheba, and Job. These stories have always interested writers and dramatists, but there are few poems on the wives of the apostles, whom she treats with understanding and insight into the life of the typical pastor's wife.

> I wonder, said Mrs. Peter,
> When he is coming home
> To fix up his equipment
> And mend his fishing yarn
> And see his children once again;
> But now I hear he's gone once more
> Up to Jerusalem.
>
> For certain, said Mrs. James,
> We all feel rather dumb
> When everyone is asking
> Where are your husband and the Lord,
> They should have stayed at home with us,
> They just as well could preach here,
> Here in Capernaum.[36]

These give clear evidence of Hallqivst's solution to the problem of cliché-ridden materials for children in the church. The old sentimentality and moralistic use of Scripture were no longer effective with children in

---

36. Britt G. Hallqvist, "Jag undrai, sa fra Petrus," quoted in Löfström, p. 142.

the church. She observed, "It is remarkable to note how few narrative gospel hymns there are in the hymnal. In the children's hymnal I believe that the poets who write biblical epics have a calling to deal with hymns that talk about flowers, birds, and sunshine."[37] Clearly, she had struck a new note in Swedish hymnody.

Hymn Explosion

The hymn explosion of the mid-twentieth century came about for many reasons, not simply the need for updated language. Hymn writers from Scandinavia to England, and later, America, weary of the old religious clichés of hymnody, tired rhymes, and old-fashioned translations of the Bible, came to feel that hymns had to be totally different in order to speak to the situation in the modern world. Changes in society erupted during the 1960s, especially during the latter half, when protests against the Vietnam War, the struggle for Civil Rights, and a burning zeal to meet the needs in the third world made everything from the past, especially the hymns, seem irrelevant. At the same time, theologians were moving from their strong emphasis on the Redemption and the Second Article of the Creed to the First Article with its focus on God the Creator. New interest in the Creator also brought a new sense for the environment, plus a new awareness of the social gospel. The need for new hymns, more relevant not just in language but also in topics, seemed especially pressing. If the congregation knew God only as a far-off Creator, then the church needed to provide simple hymns with increasingly simple music in order to communicate the gospel to its people. Thus there was a new emphasis on the hymn as a folk tune, and less interest in the hymn as a piece of art music, with a complicated theological text. Hallqvist articulated this in a piece for the *Statens Offentliga Utredningar* (SOU), published by the organization of the state church that sponsored their work and the new Swedish hymnal.

Hallqvist, like her contemporaries, especially Anders Frostenson, felt that the crisis of language had come about through the increasing secularism and pluralism of the day. Words no longer meant what they had meant, or they meant nothing to people unfamiliar with the Bible. The language of the Bible was no longer a common language. Maybe it was

37. Löfström, p. 147.

time, she mused, to include questions in the liturgy and hymns of the church. It was impossible, she thought, to write hymns in a "timeless" language — it was best to write something that was appropriate to the moment. This did not mean that she felt we should get rid of basic keywords such as redemption, grace, and forgiveness, but she wanted to give them more content by setting them next to contemporary images and ideas. It was possible, she continued, to place a crucifix from the Middle Ages next to a modern altar hanging. In the same way, liturgical language could blend the two ages, but it was always best when the language of worship, from whatever age, was concrete.[38] While these concerns were not original to the Scandinavian churches — there was a similar movement in England, led by Fred Pratt Greene and Fred Kaan — the hymns written by Scandinavians engaged in this movement seem to feature much better poetry and music than those in English, partly because these writers, especially Hallqvist, were better poets and had a more direct connection with their own literary traditions than English or American poets did.

We can see that the hymns Hallqvist wrote for the 1960 children's collection had pointed the way, and their instant popularity helped pave the way for the hymnody that she and Frostenson envisioned. They also met with approval from Swedes beginning to think about a long overdue new hymnal which would finally appear in 1986.

Toward the 1986 Hymnal

In 1976, when the book *Hymns and Songs 76 (Psalmer och visor 76)*, a supplement of Swedish hymns and songs in preparation for a future Swedish hymnal, came out, Hallqvist's eight new hymns and seven translations were second only to Frostenson's seventy-one contributions, twenty-two of which were translations. One of her hymns in this collection speaks to God with a kind of childlike immediacy that included the social concern of the contemporary Scandinavian churches for justice and a concern for God's presence here, his immanence, rather than his heavenly transcendence. We hear the same voice we heard in the first hymn about coming to church out of need, not faith.

---

38. *Statens Offentliga Utredningar* (SOU), 1974, p. 67.

Teach Me to Seek You Sincerely
(Lär mig att bedja)
Britt G. Hallqvist 1970
S.-E. Johanson 1976
SPB 214

1. Teach me to seek you sincerely,
   Not just this evening, but now.
   Help me to keep your commandments,
   Not just this morning, but now.

2. Help me to care for my neighbor,
   Not at a distance, but here.
   Now when they come and disturb me,
   Now when they trouble me here.

3. Help me to trust you, O Father,
   Not up in heaven, but here.
   Here in this world of confusion,
   Help me to worship you here.[39]

The break that Swedish Lutherans were about to make with the past was significant. The church had a tradition of using a hymnal for decades if not a century. Sweden's first great hymnal, by Jesper Svedberg, authorized in 1695, lasted until 1819, when Johan Olof Wallin's book became the new authorized hymnal. The Swedish hymnal of 1937 still bore much resemblance to the Wallin hymnal of 1819. There was clearly a pent-up need for new hymns. This little book of hymns and songs for 1976 became enormously influential as the Swedish church, along with the Norwegian church, began preparing for new hymnals. Under the leadership of Frostenson, the hymn explosion swept the Nordic countries. No less important was the fact that a composer like Egil Hovland, who would become the most prolific composer of hymn melodies for both Norway and Sweden, worked on the hymnal committees of both countries. He had grown up in the prayer-house tradition of Norway and loved the spiritual songs from the Scandinavian

39. Hallqvist, "Lär mig att bedja," *Den Svenska Psalmboken* (Verbum, 1986), hymn 214, tr. Grindal, 2005.

Figure 6 "Teach Me to Seek You Sincerely."

tradition as well as the Anglo-Saxon Gospel songs, which he persuaded the committees they should use in their hymnals.

Hovland's new sound created a revolution in Nordic hymnody. With the new texts of Frostenson, Norway's modern hymn writer Svein Ellingsen, and Hallqvist, Scandinavian hymnody and liturgy began an era of great creativity and innovation. By 1976 Hovland and Hallqvist had prepared a liturgy for children, called *A Family Service (Familie Gudstjeneste)*, which centered on the story of the Prodigal Son. Several hymns from this liturgy became the most famous and beloved of their day, especially "Everyone's Rushed" ("Alle har hast") and "Moonshine and Stars" ("Måne och sol"). This trinitarian *laudamus* was the opening hymn of the service, and since then it has probably become, of all his many hymns, the tune most associated with Egil Hovland. (On his eightieth birthday in October, 2004, he was greeted by his well-wishers all over Norway who sang, from memory, all three stanzas.) This was also one of the first projects Hovland and Hallqvist did together, but it would not be the last. The account of their meeting and collaboration shows the way in which artistic collaborations produce far more than the two would have done by themselves.

Egil Hovland tells the story of their first collaboration in the biography written for his eightieth birthday. It was January 26, 1974. He had just received news that one of his closest friends and collaborators, Olaf Hillestad (1923-1974), had died of the cancer he had been fighting for many years. Hillestad had been a leader in an attempt to connect with the youth movement in the church. As Hovland and his wife Synnøve were absorbing the shock of hearing that Hillestad had died, they got their mail. In the mailbox was a letter from Harald Göransson, one of the leaders of the Swedish church's liturgical commission. Hovland at the time was working as a consultant with the Swedish commission, composing music for its work and attending the meetings and retreats. He had just finished a setting of the Sunday service for them, so he was used to getting such letters. In the letter, however, Göransson had included Hallqvist's text "Måne och Sol."

1. Sun, Moon and stars, water and Wind,
   God has made all, heaven and earth.
   All that there is, O God Creator, we thank you!
   Refrain/O God, we give you thanks
   And we will praise your name!
   O God, we sing in praise of your name!

Figure 7 Hallqvist's collaborator, Egil Hovland.

2. Jesus, God's Son, gave his own life
   So that we may live and live today,
   And he is here, Here with us now,
   O God, our Savior, we thank you!
   Refrain/

3. Spirit of God, living and warm,
   And holy and strong, speak now of God;
   Keep us secure, Day after day,
   O God, Sustainer, we thank you![40]
   Refrain/

As Hovland read the simple text in the room where there were pictures of his children's choir from his church in Glemmen, he said, "It was as if the children in the pictures took wings and were swirling around the room where I was."[41] Suddenly, he took a page of blank music staves and held it up in the air, and it was as "if the children became notes on the staves." In twenty seconds, he reports, he wrote the refrain, followed by the melody for the stanzas. "The entire song was done between three or four minutes."[42] The song became immediately popular, its reception was almost like an earthquake, he reported, that had come from his grief and his thanksgiving for the text. Quickly, it became the theme song of family worship services throughout Norway, Sweden, and Finland. It also helped him understand how to write music for such simple texts and occasions. It was a life-changing event for both Hovland and Hallqvist, as well as for their respective churches, because they saw the possibilities for a new kind of hymn for families and children emerging in this work.

They still had not met, even though they had collaborated on several hymns. It was not until two years later, after they had been working together via mail, in the summer of 1976, while Hovland was at a retreat center near Karlstadt, Sweden, in Ransäter, that they actually met in person. Hovland had been spending part of his summers there, as composer-in-residence with directors and leaders of children's choirs. They would give

40. Britt G. Hallqvist, "Måne och Sol," *Måne och Sol: 1965-1985: 95 melodier til salmer og kirkeviser met satser for orgel/klavér* (Oslo: Norsk Musiforlag A/S, 1985), p. 62.
41. Geir Harald Johannessen, *Egil Hovland: Englene danser på tangentene* (Oslo: Lunde forlag, 1999), p. 115.
42. Johannessen, p. 115.

him texts and during the next few hours Hovland would compose tunes for them. Several of the texts he had received were by Hallqvist. One day, as he was eating in the cafeteria, the door opened, and Britt G. and Sten stepped in. She asked which one of them was the Norwegian composer-in-residence. As they shook hands before those in the room, they were met with shouts and applause. Many in the group knew that this was a historic moment in the life of hymnody in the Scandinavian tradition. Over the next twenty years they were to become fast friends, traveling up or down the west coast of Sweden from Frederikstad in Norway to Lund in Sweden, an overnight journey they took by train many times. As Inger Selander said once in conversation with me, they had the same kind of child-like sensibilities, and their work together was like child's play for them.

The 1986 Swedish Hymnal

In 1982, the Swedish hymnal committee began working officially on the new hymnal. Anders Frostenson, the leading hymn writer on the committee, and Britt G. Hallqvist, his most accomplished colleague, were now old colleagues in the work of preparing a hymnal. They were both valued not only for their wisdom concerning the old hymns, but also as revisers and contributors in their own right. Now hymns were pouring out of Hallqvist, most of which spoke with a clear and simple voice. Several emerged from the summers at Ransäter, as did the following hymn, which has become a popular hymn for Holy Week in Scandinavia.

> He Walked the Tearful Highway
> ("Han gick den svåra vägen")
> Britt G. Hallqvist 1975
> Egil Hovland 1975
> SPB 442
>
> 1. He walked the tearful highway
>   Up to Jerusalem.
>   He went with his disciples
>   Who would betray him very soon,
>   He did it all for them.
>   He did it all for them.

2. He walked the tearful highway,
   Up to Jerusalem.
   He would be cruelly tortured
   And made to wear a crown of thorns,
   He suffered there for them,
   He did it all for them.

3. He walked the tearful highway,
   He bore his heavy cross,
   He cried, My God forgive them,
   He suffered, died on Golgotha,
   He did it all for us,
   For everyone and us.[43]

This is a much more somber hymn than we are used to from her, but it captures the tone of Holy Week. Its voice is still very quiet and concrete. The passion narrative in the first two stanzas recounts what Christ did back then and how all that he did was for "them." In the last stanza, she applies the story not just to "them," but also to us. The hymn is a brief but poignant Lutheran sermon that puts us directly in the passion narrative. Once again, there is no mention of Jesus' name, although with the images and places, it is impossible to miss who it is. The disciples, the betrayal, the crown of thorns, the heavy cross, the last words on the cross, all point clearly to Jesus. The last two lines carry a punch as they proclaim that all this was done for us; it was not just back there in the misty past. Here we see her accessing the Lutheran tradition of Lenten sermons and hymns as she uses the story to proclaim the gospel to her audience.

The next year, in 1976, Hovland and Hallqvist wrote another hymn for All Saints' Day and funerals, "They Will Walk through the Gates of the City" ("De Skall Gå till den heliga Staden").

1. They will walk through the gates of the city
   And be gathered together again.
   They will walk toward the portals of heaven,
   To an unknown world where there is no pain,
   Refrain/They'll be singing, singing, yes, singing,
   A new, jubilant song!

43. Hallqvist, "Han gick den svåra vägen," *Måne och sol: 1965-1985* p. 76, tr. Grindal.

2. They'll remember the green fields of summer
   And the flowers of spring-time once more.
   They'll forget all the sorrow and suff'ring
   Of an ancient life in a vanished world.
   Refrain/

3. They will meet with their friends and their family
   Whom they lost to the earth long ago.
   They will play with the saints and the angels
   In God's paradise, They will dance for joy.
   Refrain/

4. They will meet with the Lord of Creation,
   They will gaze at his wonderful face
   And be changed by the light that is shining
   From the throne of God and the sun of grace.
   Refrain/[44]

Influenced by the language of Martin Luther in a letter he wrote to his son John, "Henschen," about what heaven will be like with its "beautiful garden,"[45] the hymn pictures heaven as a wonderful place, almost like the classical Elysium, with dancing and playing in an eternal summer. It was immediately taken into the Swedish hymnal, but the Norwegian hymnal committee balked at the idea of a hymn that celebrated dancing in heaven, and, more seriously, stated that *all* of our friends and family would be there. Hallqvist noted in an article in the *Svensk Teologisk Kvartalskrift* that even though the Bible did not say we will see our loved ones in heaven, "we can certainly hope we will."[46] She wanted it to be a clear picture of a heaven in which life is utterly new and the old is forgotten. When I asked permission to translate it into English, she was quite insistent that it not have any hint of old words like sin and evil in it. The hymnal committee in both Sweden and Norway worried about how little mention there was of God in the

---

44. Hallqvist, "De skall gå till den heliga staden," *Måne och sol: 1965-1985*, p. 18, tr. Grindal, 1991.

45. Martin Luther, "To John Luther, About June 19, 1530," *LW*, vol. 49, p. 323.

46. Britt G. Hallqvist, "Från en psalmförfattares verkstad," *Svensk Teologisk Kvartalskrift* 60 (1984): 117.

hymn, so Oskar Emrik Natanael Ahlén (1906-1995) wrote the final stanza, with its more biblical language, for use in both of the hymnals. Hovland used this hymn as the ending for his "Pilgrim Mass" ("Pilgrimsmesse") in 1982, and as the beginning theme in his String Quartet, No. 1, Opus 116.

Another hymn she wrote with Hovland was commissioned by Sven Erik Bäck, one of Sweden's most highly regarded contemporary composers, for his son's marriage. Löfström says that the text is both realistic and romantic at the same time.[47]

> God Created Us in Families
> ("Gud har omsorg om vårt släkte")
> Britt G. Hallqvist 1981
> Egil Hovland 1984
> SPB 411
>
> 1. God created us in fam'lies,
>   He has seen our loneliness,
>   He created man and woman,
>   Whom in secret he did bless
>   So that they could find each other
>   Where the spring of life they found
>   Gave them love that they would cherish
>   Like a flower in each one.
>
> 2. God is boundless in his mercy
>   With his maker's fantasy;
>   Both the bird and the suns
>   Are his work, and so are we.
>   When the evening falls around us,
>   And it glimmers toward the night,
>   Then the Lord gives us the power
>   To create and light the light.[48]

Here her verse uses theological concepts of creation and Eden, but it is also very clear in its picture of the nuptials: "When the evening falls around us/

---

47. Löfström, 2nd ed., p. 179.
48. Hallqvist, "Gud har omsorg om vårt släkte," *Måne och Sol: 1965-1985*, p. 62.

And it glimmers toward the night,/Then the Lord gives us the power/To create and light the light." One not only reads in this hymn Luther's theology of marriage, but one can also hear in it a rich appreciation of her own happy marriage.

While the two artists continued their own labors, they also began a more intense collaboration with three family worship services for "small and big children." Hallqvist had written liturgies using what she felt were the six basic parts for Christian services that would engage children: (1) We meet God, (2) We pray for God's help and forgiveness, (3) We pray for other people, (4) We thank God for his gifts, (5) We meet Jesus, (6) We walk with God as we leave. The central point of the service is to help children meet Jesus through one of the Bible stories. The Prodigal Son was the Bible story they used as a basis for their first service. The hymns for these liturgies are still well-known after thirty years. Pastor Karl Hafstad, the pastor at Glemmen church during Hovland's most productive years, who made much of Hovland's work possible, thought the new service was a success.[49]

In 1978, the summer after Hallqvist's husband Sten died, the family liturgy was the main service at the National Church Song Fest in the cathedral in Trondheim at which twelve hundred children participated, singing the processional more than eighteen times. Although Sten had enjoyed two years with Britt G. after their return from Denmark, in 1977, he had a serious heart attack and never really recovered his full health. He died on February 15, 1978. Now Britt G. was alone and turned more and more to Hovland for friendship and collaboration.

It is probably no accident that one of Hallqvist's darkest hymns comes from the time around Sten's illness and death. Although she frequently used images of the suffering and poor in her hymns, the hymn she wrote about God's absence, "God, You Went Away" ("Gud, du gick bort"), is, perhaps, the most desolate and most like other social gospel hymns of its day. She and Frostenson had been reading the hymns of the English hymnwriter Fred Kaan and had seen how he included images of current issues in his hymns. This hymn also deals with the theological notion that God has abandoned us *(deus absconditus)*, something that Swedes like

---

49. Karl Hafstad, "Fornyelsen av barne- og familiegudstjenesten," *Egil Hovland-og korene i Glemmen kirke: Festskrift til Egil Hovland på 70-Årsdagen 18. Oktober 1994* (Fredrikstad: Møkelgaards Trykkeri, 1994), p. 66.

Ingmar Bergman had explored with his films on the silence of God. Hallqvist had herself worked with Bergman on the Swedish versions of Shakespeare's *King Lear* and *Hamlet,* so she was well aware of his convictions and shared his concerns. The hymn, a direct address to the *deus absconditus,* is a complaint and lament. One also hears the language of Bishop John Robinson's "God is dead" theology.

1. God, you have left,
   Gone from the cross,
   Bombers the sword have succeeded;
   Suffering's cross
   Grows every day
   Mostly for those who are poorest.

2. Up into hard
   Darkening space
   Climb all our doubt and our questions:
   God, are you dead?
   How can we live,
   Manage and try to have courage?

3. We would prefer
   Locking our doors,
   Hiding from earth and its chaos.
   Where are you, God?
   Now they all ask:
   Happiness, power, where are they?

4. O Lord, come here
   Living and warm,
   Comfort your flock grown so anxious;
   Follow us, God,
   Out to the world,
   Strengthen us now on our journey.[50]

---

50. Hallqvist, "Gud, du gick bort," *Den Svenska Psalmboken* hymn 592, tr. Grindal, 2005.

Stanza three is particularly interesting with its description, really a confession, of the human condition: rather than wanting engagement with life and God, she sees that "We would prefer/Locking our doors/Hiding from earth and its chaos." Rather than a friend, God in this hymn is a disturber of the peace of the grave, or at least the frozen soul who comes that needs warming up. The idea that God can relieve our anxiety is also a new concept for a hymn, especially in this time when the psychiatrist became the secular caregiver for the soul.

Halleqvist and Hovland's second Bible play was *He Lives Today (Han lever i dag)*. The focus of this service was the story of the parable in Luke 15, the shepherd looking for his lamb, combined with the story of the women coming to the grave on Easter morning, which included a pantomime and a dramatic reading of the text while the choir sang "Where shall the women go?" The hymn that emerged from this drama, "Det var i Soloppgången," is now in the hymnal.

1. One bright and shining morning,
   So very long ago,
   Three women wept with sorrow
   And came into the graveyard
   To look behind the stone.

2. Who was around to help them
   In all their pain and need?
   They could not find a person
   Like him in all creation,
   Their friend who now lay dead.

3. One bright and shining morning
   The three walked toward the grave,
   An angel cried out to them:
   He's living, Christ is risen,
   Come, hurry to the place.

4. He is the shining morning,
   He is the world's true light,
   He warms up those who're freezing,

He follows on our journey
And keeps God's heaven bright.[51]

This Easter hymn, in describing the women coming to the tomb in sorrow and asking who would help them, gives us the somber beginning of the story. The mood of the hymn, however, changes abruptly in the third stanza with the announcement of the angel that changes everything. The last stanza continues the sermon in a kind of rhapsodic cry of the preacher: "He is the shining morning/He is the world's true light." No longer is the sun the morning light, but Christ is now the light. The third line of the fourth stanza also continues Hallqvist's theme of warmth: "He warms up those who're freezing." Warmth against the cold of Scandinavia is also an image for Christ and salvation that works with the weather, but also with the perceived coldness of the people. With the resurrection everything is changed, even the source of our warmth and light.

Their success with these liturgies gave them the idea to produce, in the 1980s, Bible plays ("Bibelspillet"), as they called them, little operettas, or operas, in which children would learn the Bible stories through watching and actually participating in the productions. In early 1980, Hallqvist had asked Hovland whether Norwegian children knew their Bible very well, and he did not think they did. She, herself, was not very sanguine about the situation in Sweden and proposed that they write "Bible plays" that would teach the stories of the Bible in an accessible way to the young, as she had done as a young pastor's wife. *Sing, My Heart*, their first Bible play, performed in 1981, was a dramatic retelling of the story of the ten lepers in Luke 17. After the first performance, the youth choir at Hovland's church begged the pair to write a Bible play that they could perform. This request resulted in "The Man in the Tree," the story of Zacchaeus. Hallqvist attended the premiere in Glemmen church in 1981 and marveled at the unique form they had invented, commenting that it was special for Sweden and Norway to have such a new form of teaching children the gospel. Already by the next year, in 1982, Hallqvist and Hovland were deep into the production of an opera on Joseph and his brothers. This was a pure opera, Hovland said, one that needed costumes and real actors and singers. Over eleven hundred people packed Glemmen church on Little Christmas Eve,

---

51. Hallqvist, "Det var i soluppgången," *Måne och Sol: 1965-1985*, p. 28, tr. Grindal, 2005.

Preaching from Home

ONE BRIGHT AND SHINING MORNING
(*Det var i Soloppgången*)

Britt G. Hallqvist 1975   Egil Hovland 1975

©Norsk Musikforlaget 1975; Translation: Gracia Grindal 2005

Figure 8 "One Bright and Shining Morning."

December 23, that year to see the dramatic retelling of the story. It became one of the more popular of their works. Geir Johannessen, one of Hovland's biographers, reports that the entire city of Fredrikstad had been affected by the production, not only because they had seen or heard it, but also because they had participated in it and learned the story by heart.[52]

Their last Bible play portrayed the life of Noah in three acts, *Noah Finds Land (Noa Går i land)*, which was presented in Glemmen church on October 16, 1988. Johannessen notes in his book that with these Bible plays, Hovland with his music and Hallqvist with her verbal and choreographic inventions had given "the entire country and the North . . . an instructional toolbox in ten parts on how to make the Bible living for young people."[53] All told, they wrote ten Bible plays over the decade.

With many such successes behind them, the two began a larger project, the story of St. Francis of Assisi *(Den lille Fattige)*, which was presented in July of 1993 to great acclaim. Their productions grew larger and larger. That same year, Hovland decided to resurrect an old work, *The Loveliest Rose*, a fairy tale by Hans Christian Andersen, and put it together with a song about Mary, an old Scandinavian carol from the Middle Ages. Hallqvist prepared the libretto for this very successful opera, and it was performed in Glemmen church, once again, but it was much more complicated and professional than the original *Sing, My Heart*. Hæge Aasmundtveit recalled that as his children participated in these dramas and as he watched them, he could hardly believe the richness of *The Loveliest Rose*, compared to the simple choral nature of *Sing, My Heart*. He expressed his gratitude that he had been involved from the first to the last. "On reflection, I see that it was the light from Christ that shone out from the center of the ring to the periphery of the boundaries and shone through everything."[54]

Almost immediately after the success of the first Bible play, Hovland and Hallqvist began to create services, no longer for children only, but also for modern adults. He got the idea for a *Pilgrim Mass (Pilgrimsmesse)* and Hallqvist immediately began writing the text. As Hovland told one of his

---

52. Johannessen, p. 155.

53. Johannessen, p. 167.

54. Hæge Aasmundtveit, "Syng mitt hjerte: Det visuelle bilde i pantomimer og kirkespill Samarbeidet slik jeg opplevde det," *Egil Hovland-og korene i Glemmen kirke: Festskrift til Egil Hovland på 70-Årsdagen 18. Oktober 1994* (Fredrikstad: Møkelgaards Trykkeri, 1994), p. 96, tr. Grindal.

biographers, he had long been interested in the motif of pilgrims, and when he mentioned it to Hallqvist, she very quickly prepared the service. They decided it would be best framed by familiar hymns, beginning with an old Swedish revival hymn by Ahnfelt and Rosenius, "With God and His Friendship" (LBW 371), and ending with "Shall We Gather at the River." After a meditative prelude on the organ and flugelhorn, in came pilgrims who were limping, blind, weary and needy, ready to rest and find food. As they processed, they sang the hymn below, rather like the text of a chorus in a Greek play, expressing their commonly felt situation. This has also become a classic production of Hallqvist and Hovland. It was a service that the entire folk church could identify with, Hovland concluded.[54]

> **We Are a Host of Pilgrims**
> ("Vi är ett folk på vandring")
> Britt G. Hallqvist 1982
> Egil Hovland 1981
>
> 1. We are a host of pilgrims
>   Whose way can be weary and long;
>   We're seeking green grass and still waters,
>   A refuge for prayer and song.
>   A refuge for prayer and song.
>
> 2. We are a host of pilgrims,
>   We're anxious and plagued by our needs,
>   We're longing for strength and some quiet,
>   We gather round wine and bread.
>   We gather round wine and bread.
>
> 3. We are a host of pilgrims.
>   By faith we can glimpse far ahead
>   A home for each wandering pilgrim,
>   A beautiful, blessed land.
>   A beautiful, blessed land.[55]

Also included in this increasingly popular service was the prior pilgrimage hymn, "We Shall Walk through the Gates of the City."

---

54. Johannessen, p. 146.
55. Hallqvist, "Vi är ett folk på vandring," *Måne och sol: 1965-1985*, p. 4, tr. Grindal.

By the middle of the 1980s, Hovland began to think that he as a native of Fredrikstad, where Hans Nielsen Hauge had been born, should write an opera on the life and work of Hauge. He had asked several Norwegian authors to compose a libretto on the life of Hauge and finally persuaded Hallqvist to begin the project. She had at first said no, but then after some thought, remembered that her great-grandfather Lars Wilhelm Henschen had fought against the Swedish Conventicle Act, similar to the Norwegian one that had caused Hauge so much grief. So that winter, Hallqvist, Hovland, and a dramaturge, Ivó Cramer, went to Cramer's apartment in Paris and began planning the opera.

Hallqvist's skill as a translator of operas, plus her work on her own children's operas, had given her a good sense for how to write a libretto. Together, the three artists decided they would not tell the story of Hauge in a consecutive narrative, but rather, they picked several well-known themes from his life that gave the audience insight into his life and work, to avoid having historians quibble about their accuracy or emphasis. His conversion scene in the field as he was plowing on April 5, 1796, well-known in Norwegian hagiography, was not portrayed. What we see mostly is the effect his life had on the nation and its citizens, as well as the church and state. The most touching scene in the opera is the famous event in Hauge's life when some of his followers visited him after he had been thrown into jail in Oslo. They sang outside his window, waiting for some sign that he heard them. Although he could not communicate with them with words, he held up a lighted candle and the light in the window told them he was still alive and listening to them. It was Hovland's idea to use a vesper hymn he had written for another work, *Lysvesper,* to give this scene a musical and textual connection with the introduction of the opera and its ending. Hovland called Lund to ask Hallqvist what she thought. Immediately she agreed and the text "Stay with us" ("Bli hos oss") became the most moving and beautiful moment in the opera. That piece of music is sung frequently at the St. Olaf College Christmas Festival as one of the final numbers.

> Stay with us Lord, stay with us,
> Stay with us, it is soon evening.
> Stay with us, Lord, Stay with us,
> Night is falling.
> Jesus Christ, the world's true light!
> Shine so the darkness cannot overcome it!

> Stay with us, Lord Jesus, it is soon evening,
> Stay with us, Lord Jesus, for night is falling.
> Let your light pierce through the darkness
> And gleam glory on your church!
> Stay with us, Lord, stay with us,
> It is soon evening and night is falling.

Throughout the 1990s, the duo continued their work, although Hallqvist's health began to fail. Still, every time Hovland needed a text he would call her. In the fall of 1996, Hovland remembers, she was getting weaker and weaker. As she realized that death was near, she wanted to return to her childhood summer home by the lake in Visby on her "childhood isle" to see her parents' graves one last time. Hovland became for her a chauffeur and "deacon" *(diakon)*, he said, helping her with everything, as she was barely able to walk, and by the time they left for Lund, she needed a wheelchair most of the time, which was difficult for Hovland, who himself had recently suffered a heart attack and had undergone a bypass operation. Despite this, however, Hovland reported that they had a good time — knowing them, I can imagine it was a magical, but sad, time. They went to the cathedral in Visby, where they met the church warden, who helped them find her childhood home, which was now an office building, and who took them to the family graves. By the end of the tour, Hovland realized, it was their last time together; she had begun her final journey. In November and December she suffered several bouts of pneumonia. In March she came down with her last case of pneumonia and died on March 20, 1997 while Hovland was on the plane to be with her one last time. When he returned to his home in Fredrikstad, he sat down immediately and composed variations on a hymn tune he had written for one of her burial hymns from Ransäter, "God of Earth," which he played at the dinner following the funeral.

God of Earth
"Jordens Gud"

1. God of earth,
   Lord of the heavens,
   Friend of the flowers and children and birds,
   Thanks for the glad happy days that you gave us.
   Thanks for all that you gave our friend.

Figure 9 Egil Hovland with Britt G. Halleqvist in 1993.
Photo: Gunnar Hall Skavoll.

2. God of life,
   Lord of all mercy,
   Light for our friend, bright eternity's light,
   Come to our loneliness, come to our darkness,
   Let us know of your presence there.

3. God who heals,
   Ev'ryone's Father,
   Now we leave our dear friend in your hands.
   Help us each day as we live with our sorrow,
   Each new day help us trust in you.[57]

57. Hallqvist, "Jordens Gud, stjärnornas Herre," *Måne och sol: 1965-1985*, pp. 106-7, tr. Grindal, 1997.

God of Earth

("Jordens Gud, stjärnornas Herre")

(In sorrow)
For a burial

Britt G. Hallqvist 1979
Tr. Gracia Grindal 1997

Egil Hovland 1979

God of earth, Lord of the heavens,
God of life, Lord of all mercy,
God who heals, Ev-'ryone's Father,

Friend of the flowers and children and birds, Thanks for the
Light for our friend, and e-ter-ni-ty's light, Come to our
Now as we leave our dear friend in your hands, Help us each

glad happy days that you gave us. Thanks for
lone-liness, come to our darkness, Let us
day as we live without sorrow, Each new

all that you gave our friend.
know of your presence there.
day help us trust in you.

Text Copyright © Britt G. Hallqvist 1979
Tune Copyright © Egil Hovland 1979
Translation Copyright © Gracia Grindal 1997

Figure 11 "God of Earth."

The funeral was held in Lund Cathedral, considered to be the finest example of Romanesque architecture in Scandinavia, which she had been able to see from her home on St. Annagatan 4 where she and Sten had lived for years, between the cathedral and the university. People filed past her casket, and many of them set a flower beside it. She had left clear instructions that she wanted her biographer, Inge Löfström, a pastor, to officiate at the funeral, not a bishop or any other dignitary. Like Sten, she was cremated. Her remains are now in the Norra church graveyard in Lund. Her most important remains, however, are her writings, especially the hundreds of hymns that she wrote for children and adults in an age that was cynical and unable to believe, as she had been when she first began her writing. Her journey through the twentieth century and its devastations, its increased secularism and loss of faith, shows us how one intellectual came to faith. She showed how to move from theological complications to very concrete and simple pictures of Jesus' life and the heavenly home, which no demythologizing theologian of her day would have countenanced except for the charm of the poetry she used. Yet those simple pictures were what especially appealed to her audience, who seemed to be, more often than not children, or at least the child we all have living within us and the one Jesus commends to us in Mark 10.

Comparing the Work of Sandell and Hallqvist

While the pieties of Lina Sandell and Britt G. Hallqvist seem, at first blush, to be as different as day and night, it is fruitful to compare them. Both began writing poetry at a young age; both spent their lives preparing literature for children; both translated literature from German and English. Both missed their fathers, Lina through a tragic death, and Britt G. through the divorce of her parents. Both thought of themselves as nontheological and much preferred simply to write from their own experiences of Scripture and the faith. Hallqvist reported to her biographer that she was "undogmatic and untheological," saying with what must have been an ironic smile that her old friend and colleague on the hymnal committee, Anders Frostenson, had sent her a long list of theological books for her to read because they had inspired his hymnody and he thought she would profit from them. She read none of them, she said. Lina Sandell grieved when those around her engaged in bitter theological debates that resulted in the split between the Swedish Lutheran and Evangelical Covenant churches. She much preferred learning about the history of mission and the Bible, she said. Both women knew a great deal about the Bible — it was from Scripture that they received most of their inspiration.

Both wrote of the pilgrimage from earth to eternity, Sandell with a clear weariness of this life, Hallqvist with great pleasure in the good things of this world. Sandell, however, had a severe piety with little humor, yet at the same time she had a great joy in the undeserved grace of God. Hallqvist is almost always smiling at the story of salvation, both ironically and with a childlike simplicity. While Hallqvist spoke lovingly of Jesus in her children's hymns, one finds more about the heavenly Father in her more serious hymns, such as the last one, "God of Earth." In many of her works, fathers are always just a bit too good, and God the Father is much more present than his Son, as in the burial hymn "God of Earth." "I pray to God the Father," she had said, "seldom to Jesus."[58] There is an odd consanguinity, however, between the two writers. Lina Sandell's hymnody pictures God and Christ in tones that are very loving and warm — her word might be "sweet" — as does Hallqvist, whose simplicity has its own kind of charm without being sweet. It is very common for Hallqvist to speak of God as warm, as in her "Sun, Moon and Stars." In her darkest hymn about bombs and the violence of the contemporary world, she asks the Lord to come "living and warm." In her Easter hymn, she reports that Christ "Warms up those who're freezing." In a poem about the angels in Lund, she notes that she felt them, something "warm and glowing" in the gray day. That the angels, and thus God, are warm is slightly surprising, given Hallqvist's lack of interest in the Pietist hymns of her predecessor.

Lina Sandell, like many Pietists, was besotted with Jesus as her Bridegroom; she experienced her confirmation as a rapturous wedding with him. Hallqvist would have done nothing of the kind: she had her bridegroom in this life; post Freud, such raptures have faded, at least for now, from the life of Christians with intellectual credentials. Hallqvist is longing for her own father. Lina Sandell, whose father was taken from her in a drowning accident, needed Jesus to be a friend, brother, mother, and bridegroom as much as a father, and for God to be a gracious God whom she credited with sorrows as much as with joys. It was God who had taken her father, her sisters, her nieces and nephews. About that she had no

---

58. Löfström, 2nd ed., p. 201.

doubt. Hallqvist likewise notes that God may do terrible things to get our attention, but she struggles with God as one who abandoned her, rather than one who, as Lina Sandell believed, was the author of all her sufferings. For all that, however, Sandell's hymns have very little of the darker side that we can see in the Norwegians Berthe Canutte Aarflot and Dorothe Engelbretsdatter, which is surprising, given her rather fierce understanding of God's chastening in her own life. Sandell's struggles with the terrors of God seem to have been stilled only by her hymns, which wrested from her own soul and her reading of Scripture a merciful God. God was a vivid reality to Sandell; Hallqvist was looking for God. She did not have to make him merciful, she wanted him to be there, if he existed. We can see this in one of her later hymns, "I Have Never Met an Angel." Such an idea would never have occurred to Sandell, who knew God was there, if not what he was doing, at all times.

1. I have never met an angel,
   Nor have seen the face of God.
   But one gloomy day it happened,
   Ev'rything grew light and broad, light and broad.

2. Yes, I felt it, warm and glowing,
   I stood still and heard a song.
   Far away but close beside me,
   Low and clear, it was not long, was not long.

3. And now I am filled with wonder,
   And the myst'ry leaves me awed.
   Had I heard an angel singing,
   Was it that, or, maybe God, Maybe God?[59]

Hallqvist is the hymn writer of doubt — and wonder. "I do not come because I trust in you." As she grew older, this hymn may not have been her creed, but it spoke to many with its simple proclamation to Christians with little faith and helped them to see God where they had not seen him before. On the other hand, this later song is not wracked with doubt, but

---

59. Hallqvist, "Aldrig har jag mött nån ängel," *Måne och sol: 1965-1985*, p. 4, tr. Grindal.

Figure 12 "I Have Never Met an Angel."

with possibilities. God could well have been in the mist and the fog and then the sunshine of gloomy Lund. It fills her with awe, rather than agony at God's absence. While it is probably not a hymn for a serious church service, it is filled with a kind of ironic delight in God's presence among us.

While Lina Sandell may struggle in her hymns, she does not use irony — which is not a trope of her time — although we can read her fear of abandonment and hints of doubt in some of her hymns. "Lord, do not hide your face from me" ("Herre, fördölj ej ditt ansikte för mig") is a constant theme for Lina Sandell: God is there, although I cannot see him. We could also hear a question in another of her greatest hymns, "Is It True That Jesus Is My Brother?" Sandell begins it, however, with wonder. Her question will be answered with wonder and awe somewhat like the feeling one gets at the end of Hallqvist's angel song. Something in the times allowed Hallqvist to express her doubt in a way not available to Sandell. Moderns prefer "honesty" to loud affirmations of faith that sound to them a bit overblown. No doubt the audience singing their hymns has also made a difference. The nineteenth-century Swedish Christian was not asking the kind of questions the twentieth-century Swede was asking.

Lina Sandell's greatest hymns were written when she was quite young, even a girl. "Children of the Heavenly Father" emerged from her pen when she was sixteen or seventeen, "Day by Day" when she was in her thirties, and "Thy Holy Wings" not long after that. Very little of the prodigious output of hymns from her later years reached such high quality again, although many of those hymns were beloved at the time. Hallqvist's work continued to improve and ripen as she got older. While her earlier hymns are well wrought and worth singing, her collaboration with Hovland brought out in her a more shining and evangelical sound, still with her twinkling bit of humor, what one could call her Lundensian character: an intelligent humor, ironic distance toward herself.[60] Perhaps Hovland's evangelical upbringing in the prayer-house ("bedehus") of Fredrikstad communicated to her that it was possible to have a simple and childlike faith and still be sophisticated and artistic.

One of the more interesting things about Hallqvist's work at this time is her context in Lund among theologians such as Nygren and the angst of the modern world. One would think such a time would call for a

---

60. Jan Mårtensson, "Britt G. Hallqvist, språkets mästarinna," *Serie: Lundaprofiler under tusen år* (Lund: SDS, 1998), p. 132.

hymn writer with very complex hymnody, filled with theological clichés or assertions that would have been clearly contemporary to her. While many of her issues are indeed those that were pressing Christians in the last half of the century, it is not necessary to know these issues in order to read most of her hymns. The ones that are most bound to their times, such as the one about the Cold War, do seem dated, but her hymns about children and Jesus are not, nor are her hymns about heaven.

To the contrary, the hymnody of Hallqvist is clear of such language; in fact, it is, by her own confession, hardly theological at all. As the age grew more and more complex and theology more and more arcane, she continued to write texts that were increasingly simple and direct, easily accessible to children or non-churched citizens of her country. One could say they were childlike in their simplicity, but it would be better to say that she had achieved the second naiveté that Paul Ricoeur recommended, where the simple images of Scripture and our common heritage of language about things spiritual could be used to communicate new spiritual insights into the old faith. Hardly anything in English hymnody is so elegantly done as the hymnody of Hallqvist. Her ability to communicate to the people of her own time with images and narratives from her own time gives her hymns on the whole an appeal to other generations because she was, as Aristotle suggested in his *Poetics,* able to find the "concrete universal" necessary for great poetry. Whether people will be singing her hymns for the next few generations, we cannot tell, but their immediate simplicity may give them a universal popularity. It would be the last thing she would have expected. She was writing for her time, to speak to the modern Christian. Her simple elegance, her ironic, comic view of the world and the faith, are unique to her, as was her ability to deal with big theological issues in extremely concrete ways. In many ways she was the poet of whom modern theologians would have approved. Their attempts at myths were labored, abstract, and, most telling, not very appealing. Hallqvist was able to preach the faith to a time that spurned almost everything from the past and no longer valued it. She achieved what she did by dealing with the basic images of Scripture and her life and giving them to people who had very little idea of the theological concepts of the Christian faith. What is most amazing about her work to me is that in the height of the Bultmannian era and the effort to rid the church of its three-storied universe and demythologize the faith, especially the language of heaven, Britt G. Hallqvist continued populating heaven with delightful images of paradise and children happy and laughing in it. One had to be unbelievably sophisticated to do that, especially as an intellectual in her time without regard for the spirit of the times. After she had won the South Swedish Literary Award, Lars Westman, of the periodical *Vi*, interviewed her for an article. The interview was entitled "She Makes the Heavenly More Human.[61] To say that one of the major hymn writers of a secular country like Sweden could do so in the late twentieth century is remarkable indeed.

---

61. Lars Westman, "Hon gör det himmelske mera mänsligt," *Vi* no. 10 (1996): 32.

CHAPTER 6

Lisbeth Smedegaard Andersen (1934-   )
Bringing Heaven to Earth

"People say it is impossible to write hymns today," Lisbeth Smedegaard Andersen (b. 1934) noted in her book about contemporary Danish hymnody, *Bursting with Song: On the Newer Hymn Writers (Brystefeldt af Sang: om nyere salmedigtere)*,[1] "but like the bumblebee who should not be able to fly, does," so are there contemporary hymn writers in Denmark who write hymns. Lisbeth Alend Smedegaard Andersen, one of Denmark's most prolific contemporary hymn writers, has spent her life proving that it is, in fact, possible to write contemporary hymns. Now a retired pastor in Copenhagen, a graduate of Aarhus University with degrees in both theology and the arts, Andersen shows in both her life and work one who experienced the two worlds of modern women. She married during a time when women were expected to stay at home and raise their children, much like all of the previous hymn writers in this study, but in the middle of her conventional life, she entered into the pastoral vocation in her own right. Andersen is the first in our study of women whose vocation is that of a pastor, preaching in public, rather than from home. She has responded to the vocation in her own way, continuing the tradition of women hymn writers in Scandinavia, but now as one of Denmark's most highly regarded preachers. In fact, she occupied one of Denmark's most prestigious pulpits, Holmen Church, the historic naval church in the center of Copenha-

---

1. Lisbeth Smedegaard Andersen, *Brystefeldt af Sang: om nyere salmedigtere* (Frederiksberg: Materialecentralen: Religionspædagogisk Center, 1989), p. 7.

Figure 1 Lisbeth Smedegaard Andersen.

gen from 1990 to 1997. Over the past twenty years, she has become one of Denmark's leading hymn writers, joining ranks with some of the greatest hymn writers — Sthen, Kingo, Brorson, and Grundtvig — in the very distinguished tradition of Danish hymnody. Like the fine preacher that she is, she is always looking for ways to make the gospel of Jesus Christ present in the lives of secular Danes.

Andersen's Life and Works

Lisbeth was born in Copenhagen, in 1934, where her mother had gone for a trip, but her home was in a small town in southeastern Zealand, called Præstø, some seventy-five miles south of Copenhagen. Lisbeth, whose father was a wholesale dealer for Standard Oil, lived on the eastern Danish coast of the Baltic Sea with its mild climate and green rolling hills until her father was transferred to Herning, in the heathlands of Jutland, in what is known as the Danish Bible belt, when she was seven. Her parents, while not active in the church, taught her to say her prayers and valued the hymns and traditions of the Danish church, which she eagerly imbibed in her early years. The fact that Lisbeth's parents encouraged her to pray and learn the national treasury of Danish hymns that she was also learning in school bore fruit when she began writing poetry while still a young girl.[2] It was not until Lisbeth's last year of high school, however, that she started writing hymns as part of her growing interest in things theological. While she was in high school, she met another student who would become her husband, Jens Smedegaard Andersen.

Because her parents had not thought the education of a girl as important as that of a son, she was not encouraged to go to university but rather to marry. So when they were both twenty, in 1954, Jens and Lisbeth married. While Jens was in the military, the young couple lived in Vordingborg, a small city not far from Præstø, where Lisbeth had grown up. After Jens completed his military duties, they returned to Jutland, so he could attend Aarhus University to study law. To help support their young and growing family, Lisbeth went to school for three months to learn secretarial skills. While she was raising her four children and working as a secretary, she kept up her interest in writing, but did not have time to explore the craft with four children so close in age. In 1972, when the youngest turned five and began kindergarten, Lisbeth resumed her formal education at the nearby Aarhus University in eastern Jutland, on the Kattegat, the body of water connecting the North Sea with the Baltic.

In an interview in the *Jyllandsposten* she reported on some of the difficulties she had encountered on her way toward the degree. A friend had told her that while it was good for her to complete her studies, it really didn't matter very much. The comment was like a bucket of cold water poured on her head, she commented, replying that it was a personal necessity for everyone to finish the life's work they had begun. As a member of a generation undergoing revolutionary change in gender roles, naturally, she found that her life had its difficulties, typical of all mothers trying to balance school and family life. In the interview she noted, "While it was absolutely beneficial, it was probably not always happy for everyone (At det har absolut været til gavn, måske ikke altid til glæde, for alle parter)."[3] Her

---

2. Interview with Lisbeth Smedegaard Andersen, January 9, 2006, Copenhagen, Denmark.

3. Annelise Vestergaard, "Fra hjemmegående husmor til præst for søens folk," *Morgenavisen: Jyllandsposten* (August 12, 1979), p. 2.

studies included languages, history, literature, and philosophy, especially the work of Søren Kierkegaard. At first she had been a bit nervous about beginning school as an older woman among younger students, but she threw herself into her studies, noting that both students and teachers were helpful to her as she began.

Through the 1970s, while she was in school, the hymn explosion that was renewing the staid traditions of hymnody in neighboring Scandinavian countries, with the work of Anders Frostenson and Britt G. Hallqvist in Sweden, and of Svein Ellingsen in Norway, left little Denmark somewhat untouched. Although the Danes observed what was going on in their neighboring countries, their tradition, so heavily influenced by Kingo and Brorson, but especially dominated by Grundtvig, made it difficult for budding young hymn writers to find their voices. The great literary critic of our day, Harold Bloom (b. 1930), in his book *The Anxiety of Influence* (1973), has written about the oppression of a great master on a young writer who has to live under its burden. In order to flourish, Bloom suggests, young writers have to overthrow, in some way, the weight of the earlier writers whose work presses heavily upon them. For Danish hymn writers, the weight was Grundtvig. Only one Danish hymn writer in the twentieth century, Karl Laurids Aastrup (1899-1980), had been able to write hymns that got much attention at all.[4]

One cannot understand Denmark, or Andersen's hymnody, without some sense for Grundtvig's contribution. Nikolai Fredrik Severin Grundtvig (1782-1872), a pastor's son born in Udby, not far from Lisbeth's childhood home in Præstø, came of age during the Enlightenment. He soon realized that its emphasis had put the Danish church in the deep freeze. His feelings about this became clear in his trial sermon in 1810 when he asked the question, "Why has the Word of God fled from the Danish churches?" Although he failed in his attempt to become a pastor, his writings on many subjects began to dominate Danish life and thought. But even more influential were his hymns and revisions of old classic hymns, even as famous as Martin Luther's "A Mighty Fortress," to which he added a fifth stanza for the four hundredth anniversary of the Reformation. Known as the Danish poet of Pentecost, Grundtvig and his theology of the ever present work of the Spirit in daily life have affected Danish church life

---

4. Kirsten Pruzan Mikkelsen, "Salmer til lyst og nød," *Berlingske Tidende* (March 11, 2000, section 2), p. 4.

ever since. Thirty percent of the most recent Danish hymnal, *Den Dansk Salmebog 2003* (DDS), consists of hymns by Grundtvig.[5] It is not uncommon to attend a Sunday morning service in Denmark and have all of the six or seven hymns be Grundtvig's. This is a heavy burden for Danish hymn writers even today, nearly 140 years after Grundtvig's death. He is still so dominant that people have frequently commented to Andersen after singing one of her new hymns, "We have Grundtvig, why do we need any new hymns?" Andersen's coming of age as a hymn writer coincides almost precisely with the first perceived cracking of the hegemony of Grundtvig and his hymns.[6]

Immediately after Lisbeth finished university in 1979 she was ordained. Soon after, she and the family moved to New York City where they lived for a year while Jens studied international jurisprudence at New York University. During that year, Lisbeth served as assistant pastor at the Danish Seaman's Mission in New York City. Before the family left Denmark, *Jyllandsposten*, the Aarhus paper, published an interview with her by Annelise Vestergaard, "From Stay-at-Home Housewife to Pastor for Sailors" ("Fra hjemmegående husmor til præst for søens folk").[7] In it we see her expressing concerns that will be enduring in her work: preaching the gospel to contemporary Danes in images and language that speak to their concerns and world view.

This comes through in her answer to the question of whether or not she had always wanted to be a pastor. Lisbeth described her growing sense of calling to the ministry, something she had not at first envisioned, even though theology had been her first interest. Later, she realized that as she continued her studies and people came to know that she was studying theology, she would be asked questions about faith and religion. As we read the article, we can see how the questions of those around her turned into a calling for her. As she spoke with her interlocutors she came to understand

---

5. The current Danish hymnal of 2003 has 163 hymns by Grundtvig, and 90 which he has edited or revised. So, out of 788 hymns in the entire hymnal, about 30% of all the hymns in it are products of Grundtvig's pen.

6. At a seminar marking the three hundredth anniversary of Brorson's birth in Løgumkloster, Denmark, in 1994, the leader of the seminar, Steffan Arndal, and I both noticed that many speakers, meaning to say "Brorson" would instead say "Grundtvig," as though his was the only name they could think of when speaking of a Danish hymn writer.

7. Vestergaard, p. 2.

that "it was a great undertaking to preach."[8] Since she was a typical Dane, she noted that she became shy or modest when words like "God" or "faith" or "Jesus" came up in the conversation. People would rather tell a dirty story, she realized, than speak of God. She laid this state of affairs at the feet of the clergy as much as the "religious" in Denmark who shunned cards, drinking, and dancing — the typical list of open sins that Lutheran Pietists traditionally had prohibited. What troubled her most, however, was the deep religious hunger of many in the society who, instead of returning to the Christian faith, began to immerse themselves in Eastern mysticism without understanding much about the Christian faith. She felt an urgency to speak to these hungry people about the

> richness we can draw upon in Christianity. We do not need to turn to the east. Christianity, moreover, has the advantage of existing right in the middle of our earthly lives, rather than the eastern religions which tended to shun this earthly life in favor of the next.[9]

Her strong interest in apologetics comes through very clearly in this interview, as well as her debt to Grundtvig's "matchless discovery" *(mageløs opdagelse)* that we are human beings first and Christian second, and that Christ is present in the world for us to see with help from the poets and preachers of the day. This is clear in her answer to the interviewer as to whether or not the church's theology and rituals were alien or inscrutable to contemporary Danes. Lisbeth's answer showed that it was for her a consuming question as she read theology and worked on her preaching. "I want to endeavor in my sermons to expound the text, not explain it away, but expound it in such a way that both I myself and the congregation get something out of the Gospel."[10] We see her trying to think about these issues in regard to the most fundamental elements of the tradition such as the sacraments and even the apparel of the pastor, which could be problems for secular people who had no idea what they meant.

When the interviewer asked whether or not her fear of being old-fashioned in her preaching the gospel to contemporary Danes would keep her from wearing the typical Danish pastor's robe and collar, she mused

---

8. Vestergaard, p. 2.
9. Vestergaard, p. 2.
10. Vestergaard, p. 2.

that at first she had thought the old-fashioned clergy outfit was not helpful, but she had come to see that it gave the minister the authority of the office and she would wear it. "It is not the preacher's unique opinions and beliefs that have first place, but the Gospel."[11] The gown symbolized that "the pastor was the intermediary and announcer of a message that he or she has expounded to the best of their ability."[12] The article concluded with the journalist's amusement that this tiny ("spinkle") woman had been called to serve big strong sailors not known for their devotion to God's word. The interviewer predicted that Lisbeth, during her time in New York, would write some poetry, a vocation in which she had already distinguished herself by winning two first prizes for her verse in the Aarhus student review. "No doubt," the interviewer concluded, "she is clever enough to write occasional songs about and for Danish sailors in New York."[13]

Later, Lisbeth would describe this time as a wonderful year in which she would study hard in English and write an M.A. thesis at Union Theological Seminary under the direction of Professor Tom Faw Driver (b. 1925), a student of Paul Tillich, who held the Paul J. Tillich Chair in Theology and Culture at Union.[14] His interest in the arts, and his deep knowledge of Tillich, proved to be helpful to Lisbeth as she explored Paul Tillich's theology of the arts.

Andersen's Hymns

In 1980, when the family returned to Denmark, Lisbeth took a call as assistant pastor in Risskov, a wealthy suburb of Aarhus, in a beautiful new church right on the shores of an inlet of the Kattegat. While there, she finished a course of study *(bifag)* on the arts at the university.[15] In the meantime, as a pastor, she continued writing hymns and poetry, with the fortunate collaboration of the organist in the parish, Erik Haumann. In 1984,

---

11. Vestergaard, p. 2.
12. Vestergaard, p. 2.
13. Vestergaard, p. 2.
14. Lisbeth Smedegaard Andersen, "Dansk husmors opdagelse i New York," *Aarhus Stiftstidende,* May 20, 1980.
15. What the Danes call a "bifagseksamen i kunst." Although it is difficult to translate these degrees into American academic jargon, we might call it a graduate minor or secondary degree.

when she was fifty, she was appointed head pastor in Risskov parish and published her first book of hymns, *Winterlight and Bramble Blossoms (Vinterlys og tjørneblomst).*[16] In the title we meet two of her most frequent images: "winter light," which has a special character in Denmark, and "thorn blossoms," which she liked because of their connection both to the burning bush at Mt. Sinai and Christ's thorn of crowns.

The collection treats the seasons of the year — New Year, winter, spring, late summer, November; the times of the day; and, finally, the church year, with the traditional festivals of the Danish Lutheran church calendar: Advent, Christmas, the Annunciation, Holy Week, Easter, and Pentecost. She concludes with hymns on the sacraments and meditations on Psalms 90 and 139. These are themes and texts she will frequently use over the next decades. While they are very much in the Danish tradition — they echo Sthen, Kingo, Brorson, and Grundtvig — they also bear her unique stamp.

It is not unusual in Danish hymns to have images of Danish nature and weather, but Andersen uses them very deliberately to create an effect that contributes uniquely to the narration in the hymn. From the very first hymns in this collection we can see the trope that will become her particular trademark: beginning with a description of the weather, time of day, or season in which the actions take place. The following Easter hymns give a clear sense of the trajectory of Andersen's hymns.

Easter Saturday
(An opposition song)

1. The gloomy morning sunrise
   Ris'n from the ocean's end
   Like death gives rise to sorrow
   And gives itself to dread.
   Darkness swallows up the day;
   Nothingness — our morning way.

2. A word from sunny kingdoms
   Is swallowed like the sun

---

16. Lisbeth Smedegaard Andersen, *Vinterlys og tjørneblomst: Salmer* (Herning: Poul Kristensens Forlag, 1984).

Figure 2 Andersen's first pastorate was at Risskov Church.

    And only shrieking blackbirds
    Are waiting round the stone.
    Echoes from Good Friday's night:
    People feel — Abandoned fright.

3. The women's cries are silenced
    In resignation's calm
    And now we see the weakest
    Beneath the ruler's claws.
    His disciples fled away,
    Each one for himself, afraid.

4. For now no borders broken
    To move us toward the day,
    Dejection's brooding flinches
    In hope's complete decay.

"Heaven does not answer us!"
Death now is, where life once was.

The very first images in the hymn give us a footing in the time and place of ancient Palestine; we are immediately on the scene. They are, however, not just neutral images of a time and place; they give us an emotional feel for the morning and what it was like to be there. As she describes the sunrise, rather like a sunset, nature seems to be without hope — as do we. It is a picture of the day in both Jerusalem and Denmark, like many Easter Saturdays, gloomy and dark. The "ocean" is, however, particularly Danish. The sun does not rise out of the sea in Jerusalem, but it does in Denmark and Danish poetry, since most Danes live near water. The weather that she reports for the morning of Easter Saturday helps us understand the disciples on that early morning after the terror of the crucifixion. Andersen frequently begins with the weather because, she says, it is a universal concern for people, especially Danes, whose temperamental climate affects the dispositions of nearly everyone.[17]

While we have no idea what the weather was like on Easter Saturday in Palestine, the biblical accounts of the terror of Good Friday when the sky goes dark use the literary convention critics have called the "pathetic fallacy." John Ruskin (1819-1900), the English critic, defined it as "anthropomorphism," in which inanimate objects in nature react to events with human emotions, such as the "cruel sun" or "weeping clouds." The gospel writers use it most effectively in describing the crucifixion, when the sun goes dark as Jesus dies, or when the curtain in the temple is torn in two. Driver, Andersen's thesis advisor, had written in his *Patterns of Grace* that he had noticed "experience is always intersubjective" and poetry, having to do with what is alive, "has only to do with what meets, addresses, and listens to the poet."[18] Noting that Ruskin had warned his contemporaries against the "pathetic fallacy," Driver dismissed such a worry because poetry was "the original and pervasive form of truth, than which there is no higher."[19] A good poem or story has to have a plausible setting, as well as convincing characters and plot, so that those reading it believe the ac-

---

17. Mikkelsen, p. 4.
18. Tom Driver, *Patterns of Grace: Human Experience as God's Word* (Harper and Row: San Francisco, 1977), pp. 45-46.
19. Driver, p. 46.

THE GLOOMY MORNING SUNRISE
De mørke Morgenrøde

Figure 3 "The Gloomy Morning Sunrise."

count. Without a clear sense of what is "on the walls" where the action is taking place, or what the weather is like, readers may find it difficult to "willingly suspend their disbelief" as Samuel Taylor Coleridge (1772-1834) called it in his *Biographia Literaria* (1817) as they enter into the action.[20]

As Andersen helps us experience ancient Palestine in a concrete way through her images, we enter into the life and times of the disciples who lived with Jesus during his ministry, and as he died and rose again. Through the narrative, she invites us to become believers as we experience the life of disciples through identification with them. This helps us understand for the moment, maybe even believe, the events occurring on that first Easter Saturday, since the disciples probably had feelings very like our own as they encountered these earth-shaking events. The hymn also captures that feeling of a morning after some sorrow has come to us, when, upon first waking, we slowly realize that something has happened that changes everything for us. We wonder if it is our dreams that were bad, and then realize that our dreams were better than the reality into which we are waking. While we are singing the hymn, we become like the disciples.

In the second stanza, the horror grows, as we move from the ominous weather to omens from the animal kingdom. Not only has the day been taken over by night, but the dark, shrieking blackbirds signify the despair and terror of Good Friday. The only living things at the grave are creatures that live off carrion. In the presence of these birds, we shudder, deserted and abandoned as we are. The blackbird in myth signifies death, evil, or the devil. In Luke 17:37, Jesus tells the disciples, in the King James Version of the Bible, "Wheresoever the body is, thither will the eagles be gathered together."

> A word from sunny kingdoms
> Is swallowed like the sun
> And only shrieking blackbirds
> Are waiting round the stone.

Admittedly the blackbirds are not eagles, but both are *scavengers* that gather around dead bodies. Easter Saturday for Andersen is the most terri-

---

20. ". . . it was agreed, that my endeavours should be directed to persons and characters supernatural, or at least romantic, yet so as to transfer from our inward nature a human interest and a semblance of truth sufficient to procure for these shadows of imagination that willing *suspension of disbelief* for the moment, which constitutes poetic faith."

ble day in the life of the disciples because Jesus was dead; his body lay in the grave. Jesus' followers thought everything was over and were not ready for the surprise of Easter morning.

The image of the blackbirds, with their sharp beaks and claws, prepares us for the powers-that-be who are now "baring their claws." Although many treatments of this scene, such as Bach's "St. Matthew Passion," hint at a better morning to follow, this hymn does not. Here everything is as it was before: no boundaries have been broken. The drama seems to be over, nature is brooding, even the women have ceased their weeping, and the disciples have all fled. What we see is a barren spiritual landscape where things are even worse than they were before: death seems to be in charge and their hopes have been dashed. The concluding line — "Death is now where life once was!" — makes us see the closed grave with the sealed stone in front of it, shut against all earthly powers: nature, Caesar, human beings. The hymn ends with the emptiness of the mourners who have left the tomb behind. One is reminded of Driver's comment about poetry and death, "Poetry has to do only with what is alive. In poetry, even death is not dead."[21] Because we know the story of the resurrection, we know things are not as dead as they seem. It is important, however, for Andersen that we feel the hopelessness of that day. While Christians can sing her hymn knowing the end of the story, recapturing the feeling of the disciples on Easter Saturday may serve to give us a better sense of the miracle of the resurrection. Perhaps this is also a picture of many contemporary people who live in a desolate Easter Saturday throughout their entire lives.

One can also see as she paints the scene, like many of the painters she will be writing about later, how the images in her hymns reveal and interpret the story to people who may have never heard the story before, as the stained glass windows of medieval churches became the Scripture of the poor, telling Bible stories to people who could not read them. Perhaps this is Andersen's way of telling these Bible stories to those who have never heard. As the subtitle indicates, this hymn is in opposition, or contrast, to her accompanying Easter hymn, which concludes: "life is now where death once was."

She uses the same techniques in her hymn on the Emmaus text, another biblical text that she frequently treats in her hymnody.

---

21. Driver, p. 45.

Emmaus
(sung to L.M. tune *Gak under Jesu kors at stå*)

1. They quickly left Jerusalem
   In flight from that which frightened them.
   From dawn's first light, the whole day long,
   They bore the loss they lived among.

2. You met them as the long dark night
   Saw moving shadows turn to light,
   And silently you heard them talk
   About their pain at Golgotha.

3. "For we had hoped" — the two confessed
   With souls now cleft by bitterness,
   "The pow'rs that be so brutally —"
   Their hope then flickered hopelessly.

4. Your hand inside your murky dress
   Still bore the wounds of violence.
   But still you took the darkest past
   And made its hidden future last.

5. A stranger, then, you walked with these
   While daylight lit the moss gray trees;
   You opened Scripture up to them,
   It blossomed into faith's new tongue.

6. You walked with them until the eve,
   Then blessed the bread and gave them peace;
   See! There within your nail-pierced hands
   Was life, made flesh at your command.

7. Then they stood up with daring faith
   In spite of dusk, the sunlight's death,
   And ran with joy through night to them
   Who waited in Jerusalem.

This hymn begins with the couple on the road to Emmaus explaining to their unknown companion why they are leaving Jerusalem in dejection. Andersen depicts the scene and the interior moods of the pair, which echo and reflect the light in the early morning. . . . The early morning is dark, like their hopes and dreams. As they flee, one is not sure what it is they fear: the terrors of the crucifixion or their own vulnerability as disciples of the crucified one. When Jesus joins them, they are still in the shadows of the morning, which resonate with the shadows within them. As in Luke, Jesus engages them, listening to the whole story of their despair and fear. The hymn then gives snatches of their conversation:

> "For we had hoped" — the two confessed
> With souls now cleft by bitterness,
> "The pow'rs that be so brutally —"
> Their hope then flickered hopelessly.

This report of a conversation, with its short stops and starts and fragments, especially its doubt, is probably unique to this hymn.

One of the most significant details in the hymn is the nail prints in the hands of the Lord, which he hides inside his dark robe and bears toward the future. Here Andersen uses one of her more frequent tropes, found in the word *bag* ("behind" or "underneath"). That is to say, behind, or underneath, the things we see there are deeper meanings hidden from our sight, but which are real. These are not Platonic symbols, but rather one of her most persistent themes about the hidden things of the faith. Because Jesus is hiding who he is from them, he is able to speak with them as a person with their same vulnerabilities and worries. What the nail prints meant in the past will mean much more when they are brought into the future. These, however, he will not reveal until later. Like the light that is gradually dawning around them, their faith comes into being. While he walks with them as a stranger, he opens Scripture to them — taking the words, imprisoned in letters and a book, and makes them "bloom" into the new language of the faith. He *opened* or *expounded* or *interpreted* the Scriptures to them, Luke says (24:27). Andersen makes his exposition more vivid by using the word *budding,* or *blossoming,* to describe what is happening to them as they listen, a surprising, but true picture of how the language of Scripture blossoms in our beings when it is opened up and expounded.

They see the light, finally, when the sun has set, and Jesus breaks the bread. In his nail-pierced hands, they see "life, created in blood and spirit." Like the paintings of this event by Rembrandt, in which one can see the darkness closing around the pair as evening falls, we see here the light exploding from his nail-pierced hands, which they do not see until Christ breaks the bread. The explosion of light in the hands of Jesus rouses the pair with faith and courage so they now rush back to Jerusalem, after the sun has set, no longer afraid, because they now *have* the light. The last word of the first line, "Jerusalem," is also the last word of the last line, and the same darkness is there, but now they have seen the light and have the "courage of faith." Everything is different now.

Writing Hymns for Contemporary People

About the same time that this book appeared, Andersen wrote an article that appeared in the Nordic hymnological journal *Hymnologiske Meddelelser*, "On the Necessity of Writing Hymns." Here she deals with what will become a continuing frustration to her as she tries to write contemporary hymns because there already were enough good ones. After people had sung her new hymns in church, she reported, they would leave the services with comments that could not be met with a thin skin. One is almost shocked to read how mild and easy-going Danes could be so critical. Once, she reported, a woman came out of church, smiled sweetly, and said, "Well, it wasn't really Kingo. . . ." Andersen wrote that the next time it happened she would respond with a sweet smile and say, "It wasn't my intention to write another hymn by Kingo."[22] The incident did raise the question for her of what contemporary hymns should do. Did the old hymns contain all that could be said about our faith? Her answer was that of a gifted preacher: Although the gospel is the same in every age, its light reveals new facets when exposed to our age, and the sermon must still convey judgment, hope, and promise.[23] As a pastor, she was concerned that when she asked people to sing a hymn in response to the gospel or sermon, she did not want them to sing something that was either too old-fashioned or just

---

22. Lisbeth Smedegaard Andersen, "Om nødvendigheden af at skrive salmer," *Hymnologiske Meddelelser* 13 (1984): 217.

23. Andersen, "Om nødvendigheden af," p. 218.

plain wrong for today. Could modern people, she asked, really sing about their total unworthiness, as they could in Kingo's hymns? She felt that the contemporary person was not overwhelmed by a sense of unworthiness but by fragmentation and the feeling of being split in two by their minds and bodies as they tried to live a whole life in this world. She tried to write hymns that would speak to those who had come to church with their "fragmented and frightened minds."[24] In order to do that, like any good preacher, she needed to find language that was not "foreign, old-fashioned, and far away from life experiences."[25]

She also realized that, as a woman hymn writer and preacher, she could write hymns that could bring out in her retelling of biblical stories new facets from a woman's point of view. For this reason, she found it interesting to consider the feelings of Mary at the Annunciation, Visitation, and Nativity, from the point of view of seeing the angel Gabriel appear and make his announcement to her. As a young mother she understood Mary's fear and her very real temptation to turn away from Gabriel and life in order to remain untouched; at the same time she understood Mary's courage and faith when she assented to bearing the child. Andersen's experience allowed her to see these events with a sympathy not quite possible, she thought, among male hymn writers. She contrasted her own experience with Grundtvig's bombastic version of the Annunciation, "Like lightning Gabriel came in with his greeting," which sounded to her more like Zeus and his lightning bolts.

Musing that more women came to church than men probably because for them children and the faith were more closely knit together, she supposed that women were well aware that the most important things in life cannot be done alone. "One is filled with an unbelievable longing for God, when one is overwhelmed with tenderness and thanksgiving for children." She remembered in her droll way that when she brought her four children to be baptized, she was fortunate not to have known enough theology to have had her "theological blindfolds on." She was very certain that she had not come to the font to have her children born again, but she had come because of her overwhelming sense of care and responsibility for the child, along with her own feelings of weakness, and because she was also

---

24. Lisbeth Smedegaard Andersen, "Vi kommer, Herre, til dig ind," *Hymnologiske Meddelelser* 13 (1984): 220.

25. Andersen, "Vi kommer, Herre," p. 220.

certain that here was something that she needed to share with One greater than herself. This was another reason she thought it was necessary for her to write hymns: to give words to feelings that could not be found in previous hymns. She wanted women to feel that the words they were singing were true to their own experiences. Finally, she concluded, a song of praise was very distant from most people's world view. For her to find words that contemporary people could use to praise God honestly was a responsibility and task of some moment. With some pleasure she noted that not all church people were as opposed to new hymns as some supposed, reporting on a letter she had received from a ninety-three-year-old woman who said we needed new hymns because the "faith is not as simple as it was in the olden days."[26]

The article gives us a glimpse into Andersen's reasons for writing hymns, as well as her concern for clear and relevant proclamation of the gospel so people would understand that the faith had meaning in the present as well as the past. Her indignation, as well as her humor, becomes clear in this piece. As the work to produce a new Danish hymnal by the end of the century proceeded, she continued to write letters of exasperation and ironic humor to get her point across to the antiquarian impulses she felt were too dominant in the Danish hymn book committee.

Her next book, *You Dwell in Our Day: Hymns and Poems 1988 (Du bor i vor Dag: Salmer og digte),* contains probably her best-known hymn, which has the same title. The hymns, written in collaboration with the parish organist Erik Haumann, premiered in May, 1988, at Our Lady Church in Aarhus, a historic church building from the thirteenth century. The diocese paper, *Aarhuus Stiftstidende,* reported that the church was packed with admirers.[27] As Risskov's head pastor, Andersen had moved with her family into the Risskov parsonage on the shore of the ocean, next to the new church. Her star as a hymn writer and preacher was rising, something one of her pastoral colleagues, Kjeld Holm, noted in his review of her new book. Supposing that many of her hymns would eventually end up in a new Danish hymnal, he praised them because they both grew out of the Danish tradition and renewed it at one and the same time.[28]

---

26. Andersen, "Vi kommer, Herre," p. 223.

27. Hanne Stouby, "Danmark er ikke et afkristnet land," *Aarhuus Stiftstidende* (June 5, 1988).

28. Stouby.

You Came to Us Here
(Du Fødtes På Jord)

1. You came to us here,
   A baby who nursed, who felt joy and knew fear,
   You played and you grew up, you laughed and you cried,
   Wherever we live, you have lived, you have died.
   Renew us, we pray,
   Each joyful new day.

2. Each joyful new day,
   Give hope to our struggles through difficult ways,
   Come, show us in spite of the brambles and thorns,
   Abundant great harvests of wheat and of corn,
   Give us daily bread,
   Each morn's dawning red.

3. From birth until death
   We travel assured in the word that you said
   When frightened poor women arrived at the tomb
   And saw winged angels stand guarding the room.
   Then baptized in death,
   They found hope and faith.

4. To give hope and faith
   We bring you our children, baptized in your death,
   And let you receive them and give them new life.
   To live, born again, with new strength in their strife.
   The word which you give
   Grants power to live.

5. We have pow'r to live
   Because of the bread and the wine that you give.
   We come to you weary, and kneel for your grace,
   You lift up your countenance, show us your face.
   We take from your Word
   The peace of the Lord.

6. And so we pray: Lord,
   Come, give us the courage to live by your Word,
   To grow in your love as its glory unfolds
   Till all become one in a hymn to our God,
   Who made his Word clear
   When he sent you here.

As Pastor Holm had predicted, this hymn is in the new Danish hymnal of 2003 (*DDS*, 69) and is well known today. One can see in it the very strong influence of Grundtvig with its theology of the presence of Christ in daily life, telling as it does the story of Christ's incarnation, the crucifixion, resurrection, and the sacraments: our induction into the church and the life of faith through baptism, and our need for nourishment through the sacrament of communion that will give us the strength to tell others about Christ, all because of Christ's incarnation.

The form of the hymn — a chain in which the last word of each stanza is repeated as the last word in the first line of the next stanza until the last stanza, which repeats the first line of the first stanza — shows the interrelatedness of these parts in the story of salvation. In the original version, she ends the chain with a prayer to God to continue to strengthen us in our daily life of faith. (I have translated that version of the hymn, which Andersen has changed in her book.)

The rhetoric of the poem is an address to Jesus. While it is deeply Scriptural, with echoes of many of the important events and images in Jesus' life, it is not on a particular passage of Scripture. She notes in her book on contemporary Danish hymnody, in which she includes a chapter on her own work, that the hymn contains the whole "story of salvation" *(Frelseshistorien)* in a nutshell.[29] The first stanza describes the incarnation and how Christ's being born and being physically dependent on his mother for food and life gave him an understanding of our daily life. The focus on the childhood of Jesus, especially, makes him accessible to the modern person, telling him or her that Christ is now among us, a direct quotation from the language of "dwell" in the first chapter of John, "The Word became flesh and dwelt among us." The Danish is a bit more accurate to the original Greek, which means "tented among" (*tok bolig* — took residence). Because of the incarnation, Christ now lives among us and gives us hope, as the second

---

29. Andersen, *Brystefeldt af Sang*, p. 79.

Figure 4 "You Came to Us Here."

stanza has it, with its images of suffering and modern life, which in spite of the trials and thorns, is graced with a rich harvest that gives us our daily bread and joy. Once again, we see one of Andersen's favorite images, the "thorns" of our daily lives, along with language from the Lord's Prayer — daily bread. The third stanza returns to Christ's life and our reason for the hope we have in the resurrection. Here she uses one of her favorite subjects: the images of the frightened poor women at the tomb, describing it as their baptism into Christ's death and resurrection:

> Then baptized in death,
> They found hope and faith.

With the word baptism *(dåb)*, which wonderfully rhymes with hope *(håb)* in Danish, Andersen refers to the two sacraments: in stanza 4, the infant being baptized into Christ to be newborn into a life with the word of blessing over all our life on earth, and in stanza 5, with its specific reference to the sacrament of Communion. This is the place to come, kneel down, and receive "bread for the journey," as contemporary theologies of the sacrament have said. She finishes the hymn with a rhymed version of the Aaronic benediction that traditionally concludes the Sunday service in the Danish church, ending with a prayer of confidence in God "who came to us here" with his Spirit and Word. Having sung through this entire hymn in a service, one would have learned the essence of the Christian faith and life. The tune, with its chain melody and lilting 6/8 meter and repetition of certain motives throughout its short lines, is accessible to most singers and suits the meaning of the text. In a chapter on her own work in her book *Bursting with Song (Brystefyldt af Sang)*, Andersen described the hymn as not only salvation history, but also the sermon for a regular Lutheran worship service.

In 1990 Lisbeth and Jens moved to Copenhagen so she could take up the work of head pastor and naval chaplain *(orlogspræst)* in Holmen Church, one of the most significant pulpits in Copenhagen, and one of the few structures that survived the many terrible fires that had destroyed much of the old city. When the petite pastor climbed up the stairs into the well-wrought Baroque pulpit from 1662, with its intricate wood carvings, in her Danish robe and clerical ruff, she made a strong impression on the many people who had come to church to hear her vivid preaching and new hymns. At this time, she also began to teach preaching at the Pastoral Sem-

Figure 5 The pulpit in Holmen Church, where Andersen served as head pastor.

inary in the Danish Folk Church's practical pastoral education program, *(Pastoralseminariet i Den danske Folkekirkes praktiske præsteuddannelse)* along with Mogens Lindhardt, one of Denmark's leading homileticians. These years came to be very productive and busy for her as a writer and scholar. One can read in her increasingly frequent newspaper columns and articles, however, how the heavy weight of the Danish tradition of hymnody pressed upon her. As the members of the new Danish hymnal committee began to make their aesthetic and historical prejudices clear, Andersen became increasingly frustrated with their preference for the treasures of Danish hymnody and found their reverent restorations of the older, more archaic language antiquarian. Not surprisingly, she reacted against what she perceived to be fear, on the part of the committee, that the hymns it might choose would not be as durable as the old songs in the Danish treasury of hymns. It is not difficult to see, from today's vantage point, that new hymns were not particularly welcome. For Andersen, this meant that the gospel as it appeared in the hymnal would be more like an archive of Danish literature than the living word.

She responded with a thoughtful article, "Hymn Writing between the Tradition and the Traditional," in *Danske Kirkeliv 1988-1989*. How to emerge creatively from the literary tradition of which hymnody is a part without overthrowing the tradition was the issue. It was clear that if the church used only traditional language and images, the Christian faith and life would seem to have become a mere historical and intellectual curiosity of Danish culture. Quoting Luther, she noted that the hymn was to be God's Word for the people — that meant, given Luther's understanding of preaching, the hymn had to be the "living word" and needed to speak to the day in the language of the day in much the same way that a good sermon was to speak to the moment, not to all time. Whether or not it survived and became a classic was irrelevant to her. For Andersen, by now an acknowledged master of homiletics, the writing of a sermon or hymn involved great care and creativity because she needed to find the right words to communicate the gospel. For contemporary secular Danes that meant the images and words had to be simple, not abstract or theological. Here we see the influence of Frostenson and Hallqvist. For Andersen what communicated the gospel were images.

As a preacher, she had found that it was images, not concepts, which intrigued people. They gave people relevant new associations with the Bible stories they were hearing, maybe for the first time, or had never associated with contemporary life. For her, the vocation of the hymn writer, as it is for the preacher, was to help people see that the God of the Bible was present in their daily lives. This meant that the words had to say in new, understandable, experiential ways something true about sin, grace, forgiveness, and judgment — all in fresh language. Like clichés that finally weary hearers with predictable connections, the old language could be dismissed along with the subject matter as irrelevant. For that reason, she argued, the hymn writer had to find images from the time — as every generation always has had to do — even if those images in their turn would also become dated. Andersen was careful to say that the old, traditional images such as the fountain filled with blood, the bride of Christ, the celestial river certainly had to be regarded, but they did not speak very clearly to the modern person, although all of them could be found, she said, in nature, daily life, family life — and, not least of all, in the Bible. To illustrate her point, she noted that even some of these primal images from nature would have been heard differently in a previous age when most of the people lived on the land and nature was not only a smiling, restful thing, but filled with violence and unpredictability. It was her job to find the right images for today, in order to proclaim God's active presence in our daily lives.

Thus it was not only the images, Andersen argued, that needed to be contemporary, but also the world view of the hymn, which had to be consistent with the world view of today. The baroque generation with its weariness of this world, which is the main theme of Kingo's great hymn "Farewell, Vain World, and All Your Vanities," could hardly speak to the people of the day who valued this world and their sexuality very differently from the people in Kingo's time. Very few people under ninety, she wrote, could hear Kingo's language without puzzlement. While a Danish hymn writer should know the tradition, understand it, and be shaped by it, the hymnist could be so hide-bound that he or she could not find new ways to express these timeless truths.

On the other hand, Andersen was also beset by the modernists who could not bear anything from the old. There were literary scholars around her, she noted, who wanted the new hymns to be altogether new and free, without any form or engagement with the conventions of the past. This was not possible either because the hymn, in its form and context, was meant to support the church service and its preaching. Andersen's comments here deal with one of the true frustrations of the writer living between the innovators and the archivists. She resolved the tension by noting that she was not suggesting one had to choose *between* old and new hymns; it was about choosing old *and* new hymns.[30]

This addressed one of the more consuming and perplexing questions for the hymn writer in the late twentieth century. While the Bultmannians, at their worst, had tried to strip the Bible of its three-story world view and images, they were as much bound by their own time as any age. Tillich, with his call for new symbols, or myths, had presented contemporary hymn writers with this problem as well. What is most interesting about this piece is her conclusion that no age, especially no hymnal committee, could escape either its own time or its own world view. Andersen, however, was able, unlike many others, to take these concerns and find the new imagery that spoke to moderns and was still deeply Scriptural — more like Luther's replacing the pastoral images of Psalm 46 with martial images from medieval Germany rather than translating the images of Scripture into theological propositions, which many preachers and hymn writers had done. In her struggle to speak to her own age with truly biblical language and images, she had come to understand that in order to preach to one's contemporaries one had, in fact, to be bound by one's age. This flies in the face of the commonplace that if we marry the spirit of the age we will be widows in the next. From Andersen's point of view, one cannot *but* marry the spirit of one's age; it is impossible not to. Part of her reason for dwelling on this issue was her perception that the Danish hymnal committee was choosing old hymns over new ones because it was wary of choosing hymns which would not last — an understandable response from learned Danes who were well aware of the mistakes of previous hymnals in their overdependence on Birgitte Boye's hymns.

In 1991, the year after she published a book on the paintings of Rembrandt, Andersen produced a book of meditations, in both hymns and poems, on the stations of the cross, *A Sonnet Wreath of Thorns and Blossoms: Hymns and Poems on the Fourteen Stations of the Cross (Kranse av torne og blomster: salmer og digte over 14 korsvejsstationer)*, which continued her interest in writing formal poetry that challenged her abilities as a poet and showed her to be accomplished in her poetic craft as well as theology.[31]

---

30. Lisbeth Smedegaard Andersen, "Salmedigtning mellem Traditionen og det Traditionelle," *Dansk Kirkeliv* 65 (1988-1989): 75.

31. Lisbeth Smedegaard Andersen, *Kranse av torne og blomster: salmer og digte over 14 korsvejsstationer* (Copenhagen: Anis, 1991).

In the weekend section of the *Berlingske Dagbladet*, Copenhagen's major newspaper, Johannes Værge interviewed Andersen, along with another popular Danish hymn writer, Sten Kaaløm, about their newly published works and on their feelings about how they were being received. Under the headline "Not That We Are Embarrassed by Kingo and Grundtvig" *("Ikke for at genere Kingo og Grundtvig")*, both hymn writers marked the frustration they experienced every time their work was introduced in churches throughout Denmark, where they would meet with almost exactly the same responses — why do we need new hymns when we have Kingo, Brorson, and Grundtvig? Their answers were consistent with what they had said repeatedly from the time they first began writing hymns: Andersen asserted that although our experiences are the same as those of people in the past, they need to be expressed differently in order to speak to modern people. For example, she noted, darkness for the earlier hymn writers was much more frightening than it is today when we can light up almost any place immediately.[32]

In this interview she revealed a new insight about her work: For her, the writing of a hymn was an experience of coming to better understand the biblical text, so that when she was finished reflecting on the text or the theological point she was trying to make, she would be, surprisingly for a learned pastor, "wiser than she had been before writing the hymn!"[33] At the end of the interview, she repeated her impression that modern people were looking at the Christian faith with new interest, and they needed contemporary language for the gospel. "It is important to listen, not simply to bury ourselves in the old forms."[34]

In June, 1994, I met Lisbeth Smedegaard Andersen for the first time at a conference celebrating the three-hundredth birthday of Hans Adolf Brorson in Løgumkloster, a popular retreat center for Danish church people in southern Jutland. During this time, we became good friends, and I invited her to represent the Danish tradition of hymnody at the festival songfest I had planned at Luther Seminary to celebrate the Brorson anniversary. That fall she and her husband came to Washington, D.C., for a sabbatical during which she studied at Wesley Theological Seminary, near

---

32. Johannes Værge, "Ikke for at genere Kingo og Grundtvig," *Weekendavisen: de Berlingske Dagbladet* (May 21, 1993).
33. Værge, "Ikke for at genere."
34. Værge, "Ikke for at genere."

American University, and gathered material for her next book on art: *Icons in Modern Art (Ikoner i moderne kunst)*.³⁵

In late October of 1994, Jens and Lisbeth came to the Twin Cities for a celebration of the Danish hymn tradition, especially the contributions of Brorson, at Luther Seminary. While they were there, Muskego Lutheran Church in Wind Lake, Wisconsin, which had built the first Norwegian Lutheran church in this country, was celebrating its one hundred fiftieth year. Their first pastor, Claus Clausen, was a Dane, and his wife Martha had written the first hymn by a Scandinavian American, "And Now We Must Bid One Another Farewell." As part of the festivities, there was a rededication service for the restored Muskego church, which had been moved to the Luther Seminary campus in 1907. I preached on Psalm 90. Lisbeth and Jens were there for the service. The experience moved Lisbeth to write a hymn on Psalm 90, which is now in the 2003 Danish hymnal (DDS, 717), and is one of her better-known hymns, "I går var hveden moden." Reviewers praise its simple diction and clear language.³⁶

Just Yesterday Was Golden
(I går var hveden moden)

1. Just yesterday was golden,
   Today the woods are white,
   And soon the lark will warble
   Of sun and springtime's light.
   While calling from the graveyard
   The present never ends,
   And outside dust is flying,
   Who knows where it will land?

2. Our days, we learn to number,
   And pray we will endure.
   Our work increases daily,
   For what we are not sure.

---

35. Lisbeth Smedegaard Andersen, *Ikoner i moderne kunst* (Copenhagen: Samleren Forlag, 1996).

36. Lone Vesterdal, "Anmeldelse: Lisbeth Smedegaard Andersen. *Bag Vinger af Løvfald: 21 nye Salmer med 18 nye melodier,*" *Hymnologiske Medellelser* 28 (2000): 266.

The greatest words lose meaning,
Our plans, they fail the light,
We fly the stars of morning
To drowsy evening night.

3. And so on Sunday morning
We come inside again,
The church door opens for us
To welcome an old friend.
We thought the words were worn out,
But now as they are said
We are surprised to hear them
Speak hope and love instead.

4. And so we baptize babies
And hear the wedding vows
And pray that all our loved ones
Are safe in God's hands now.
They taught us to be faithful
And left their legacy
Which gladly we inherit
For all eternity.

5. For when our dreams have failed us
Or fallen by the way,
The shadows seem to lengthen
And bring the end of day,
The church will still be telling
The story of our faith,
Which bears us toward the ending,
Eternal life at death.

Hymns as a Useful Art *(Brugskunst)*

As the Danish Folk Church committee continued its work, the antiquarian and aesthetic tendencies of the committee continued to frustrate Andersen, something she would publicly address in letters to the editor and in interviews in the papers. Peder Balslev-Clausen, editor of *Hymnologiske Meddelelser*, asked her to write an article on her own hymns. The frustrations were also helping her understand the argument more and more clearly. Her article, "Dear Mr. Editor!" ("Kære Herr Redaktør!"), expressed her understandable pique about the way her new hymns had been greeted by the establishment.[37] Not long before the article was written, she had been greeted by someone who shook her left hand asking how it "felt to be among the presumptuous."[38] Despite her irritation, she realized that the comment posed another important question for her about the problem of hymnody in a post-modern world. What kind of art was a hymn? What was its use? Why write contemporary hymns? Were they needed?

This article helped her express more clearly the issue at hand with a kind of "defense of poesy" and a new sense for exactly what kind of art a hymn was. If the hymnal committee had been looking for hymns that would be classics and live through the ages before they could be chosen for a hymnal, the committee would never choose a contemporary hymn. Thus she developed the idea that hymns were what the Danes called *brugskunst*, or a "useful art," which had a practical purpose within the worship service. Written for a certain moment, it might address the ages, as many great hymns do, but that was not the primary purpose of the hymn. If it spoke to the immediate moment it could be used and discarded when it no longer did. While the klieg lights of eternity may make some writers better as they write their poetry thinking of posterity, the glare of this light will not necessarily help a hymn writer who is writing for the occasion at hand. This meant, she saw, that there was not necessarily any *prestige* in the writing of hymns, despite the urgency. She wanted people to hear the gospel. Her own prestige was beside the point. Neither hymn nor the sermon was a "fine" art, although they had similar aims: to interpret and present Scripture in a way the people in the congregation could understand. In like manner a hymn was not the same as a poem, although it shared many of the same conventions. To illustrate her point she referred back to her work on Rembrandt, who had begun his career illustrating Bible stories, but as he grew in his art, he began interpreting the stories using the theology and world view of his day to make a new thing, his own interpretation, one that

---

37. Lisbeth Smedegaard Andersen, "Kære Herr Redaktør!" *Hymnologiske Meddelelser* 26.3 (1997): 111-26.

38. Andersen, "Kære Herr Redaktør!" p. 111.

would give viewers a new thing to contemplate and bring them back into the Scripture. This was also what she was doing as a contemporary hymn writer. She resolved, after understanding this, that she would never write a hymn without first finding the main idea, or theological theme, in the biblical text so that she could present it in such a way that the hymn would help the congregation behold, or see, the biblical story with greater and more relevant richness in their own lives.[39]

In order to demonstrate this, she described how she wrote one of her hymns. While she was taking a walk in a suburb of Washington, D.C., she noticed the remains of a little sparrow in a gutter, some brown leaves from the year before, and a simple shard of pottery from a rather fine pot. As she continued on her way, a line of poetry came to her: "Among sparrow feathers, leaves, and old pottery shards: a broken cup, and dried-up flowers, reminders of yesterday." For her it was merely an interesting poetic line. A hymn was far from her thinking as she contemplated what she had seen. As she continued to think about the images, however, they began to tell her things: how quickly time flies from us; how the cup from which the shard had come had once held liquid, which had slipped away, like time. Time never stands still; the moment, no matter how lovely, passes away. It was a melancholy thought, she observed, and not terribly original. Her theological habit of mind, however, moved her reflections to Easter. The women at the grave discovered this truth on Easter Sunday morning when the angel urged them not to linger, but to go on to Galilee to tell the others of Jesus' resurrection. This was a given in the Christian faith: going forward, not back. In order to do that, however, she realized, we need some little thing, some physical reminder, to give us courage. That had been given to us in a little piece of bread and a few drops of wine. The gospel, which we can taste in the elements at communion, opens our eyes to something bigger, which we call the "mystery of the cross, its enigma, even the enigma of the resurrection."[40] As she thought more and more, she realized that the gospel is made up of little things: scenes from Good Friday, which drew her to realize that life goes deeper than that which comes and goes. It is like the seed which falls to the ground, dies, and one day will bear fruit. This is what love is, she thought. As a mother, she knew that to love her children was also to let them go. Holding on to them would destroy them; only when she let go, or died to her own

---

39. Andersen, "Kære Herr Redaktør!" p. 119.
40. Andersen, "Kære Herr Redaktør!" p. 119.

love, could they flourish. The words from Jesus to Peter (Mark 8:35) came to her: those who would save their lives would lose them. Suddenly, she realized she might have a hymn on her hands, one that had grown out of refuse in a gutter. At first she thought it was nothing, but it had haunted her, until suddenly, something came of it, if not a sermon, a hymn that instructed her readers/singers in the gospel and the rich textures of its meaning.

A Potter's Parable

1. A leaf and sparrow feathers
   And broken shards of clay,
   A dried-up flow'r,
   A shattered cup,
   Are hints of yesterday.

2. They are a fragile witness
   To things we once held dear.
   A hand, a voice
   That sounded once
   And not so long ago.

3. A shadow of dark feathers,
   A dream that never ends.
   So listen! Time
   Like water flows
   Down through our folded hands.

4. It whispers like an echo
   Of things which fell apart,
   And still we have
   Some steps to go
   And yet, and yet, and yet . . .

5. Some bread, some wine can tell us
   Of a life that was destroyed
   Good Friday night on
   Golgotha
   Then rose again in joy.

6. To love is what we live for,
   What we risk our lives to do,
   And if we lose
   Our lives, we'll find
   It's what our love is for.

7. In leaves and sparrow feathers
   And the things that fall and break
   We find the Word
   Eternally
   In every step we take.[41]

When a church musician, Preben Andreassen, asked if she had a text he could set to music, she gave him this text, and suddenly these scattered images became a hymn.

Using this story she contrasted it with what she believed was the concern of the hymnal committee: good taste and lasting literary value. She was certain "Midst Leaves and Sparrow Feathers" would never be used in a hymnal because "the hymnal committee had terribly good taste and a hymnal was a very holy book"; her hymn would never be chosen by the committee since it began with refuse.[42] Still she wondered, in a not-so-gentle jab at the committee, how hymns could be superior to the Bible, which itself contained just such images, as in Jeremiah 18 with its image of the clay and potter. How the hymnal committee could be more "pious" than the Bible puzzled her. It was her opinion that the images from Jeremiah could help us to understand the events of Good Friday and Easter. This little vignette captures both her technique for writing hymns and her frustration at the way in which the experts were treating her hymns — and all contemporary hymns. She then imagined a little picture of what the hymnal committee would look like if only we could see inside the room where they were working: they would very likely be intoxicated on the spirit of the classic Danish hymns from the olden days, each little detail, their pretty pictures. She wondered, had they any idea of what was happening on the outside, and did they know that a hymn was not fine art, but

---

41. Lisbeth Smedegaard Andersen, "En pottemagerens lignelse," *Bag Vinger af Løvfald: 21 nye Salmer med 18 nye melodier* (Frederiksberg: Anis, 1999), pp. 48-49.

42. Andersen, "Kære Herr Redaktør!" p. 125.

useful art, and for today, not all time? Looking for hymns that would outlast the current age was fruitless.

She concluded her argument with a fairy tale by Hans Christian Andersen, "Drop of Water," about the magician Kribble Krabble, who had found a rather violent world in a drop of water when he looked at it through a microscope. He saw thousands of creatures assaulting one another. The violence interested the magician and his friend, "who had no name, which was the best thing about him," and as they looked in on this world they saw one creature with a little bruise on his ear, and they ate him up, as they did a little maiden as well — which the magician without a name thought was very funny, very funny indeed. She concludes that it *was* very funny. "But not very fruitful."[43]

Active Retirement

At the end of 1997, Andersen retired from her position at Holmen Church and moved with her husband to Farum, a northwestern suburb of Copenhagen, where they lived in a typically Danish home surrounded by the flowers Jens liked to cultivate. Soon, because of the long commute to the city and the highway noise, they wearied of suburban living and returned to a third-floor apartment in the center of the city overlooking the King's Gardens, not far from where they had lived before. In an interview, which coincided with her retirement, in the *Kristeligt Dagbladet,* Denmark's most influential Christian paper, she was featured as one of Denmark's leading hymn writers who would surely be represented in the new hymnal. What Andersen stated was most important to her in this interview was the audience: people distressed by the superficiality of life in a world about which they could do little, so they would drink "a glass of red wine and try to forget."[44] What Andersen wanted to write was a hymn that gave contemporary singers something to contemplate that would lead them deeper into the gospel, not its theological "meaning" but a set of images that would give singers something to contemplate further, her enduring concern as a hymn writer. "The language of a hymn," Andersen concluded,

43. Andersen, "Kære Herr Redaktør!" p. 126.
44. Anne-Lise Bjerager, "Salmesang til eftertanke," *Kristeligt Dagbladet* (November 4, 1996).

should create new images in order to create sympathy in the person who reads or sings the hymn. And the language above all should not tie the person to one interpretation.[45]

Two years later, in 1999, Andersen published her next book of hymns *Under Wings of Fallen Leaves: 21 New Hymns and 18 New Tunes (Bag Vinger af Løvfald)*.[46] It is a handsome publication, with a lovely abstract cover in greens and yellows designed by one of the artists she held in high esteem, Maja Lise Engelhardt. Although Erik Haumann had been a steadfast friend and colleague in the setting of her first hymns and had set three of the texts she included in this book, Peder B. Lange, the organist at St. Paul's Church, near the Holmen parsonage in Nyboden where Lisbeth and Jens had lived, set ten of the hymns in the collection. Lange had a good sense for her texts, and his tunes have a sound that is unmistakably contemporary with their references to jazz and folk music. These attracted attention in the community. One rainy fall evening in 1996, I attended a brief service in the neighboring St. Paul's church, where a choir of young girls sang Andersen and Lange's hymns with excitement and interest. They seemed to speak very clearly to the young girls, as well as the congregation assembled there to sing with them.

In this collection Andersen wrote another hymn on Easter Saturday. In the following hymn, written some twenty years after her first published hymn on Easter Saturday, we see her growing skill with the form.

Easter Saturday

1. So easy to condemn him
   When at first the trial began
   With no dissenting voices
   When his sentence was proclaimed.

2. Who thanked him on Good Friday
   For the wounds he had received?
   Who wept when he was sinking
   Under the cross's heavy weight?

45. Bjerager, "Salmesang til eftertanke."
46. Lisbeth Smedegaard Andersen, *Bag Vinger af Løvfald: 21 nye Salmer med 18 nye melodier* (Frederiksberg: Anis, 1999).

3. Who saw the King of Heaven
   Under his crown of thorns?
   And knew that he forgave them
   All, and now all things are his?

4. You know — it's difficult for
   Us, for none can fail to see
   Such violence, and all that blood —
   We let it simply be.

5. It frightened us, we fled it
   As we felt the earth turn cold
   Where Satan found his subjects
   There where unbelief could grow.

6. And children are done crying
   Now, they've put away their toys,
   They weep in rainy weather
   But are silent when it snows.

7. With empty hands we're standing
   Here, our thoughts swirl round and round
   And listen to the darkness,
   But we do not hear a sound.[47]

It is interesting to compare this with her first Easter Saturday poem. The later hymn is written from the point of view of those left behind, not *about* them. Instead of describing the scene from the outside, as she did in the previous hymn, she has now moved us inside the action so we can experience the events in the words of one who was there, describing the crucifixion, long afterwards, in a dramatic monologue. The speaker clearly knows about the resurrection but is still able to give us a feeling of how awful the day felt to him, and, through his images, get us inside the event. The difference this creates in the feelings of the singer is curious. Through the narrative we understand something of what might be called "survivor's guilt" for not doing anything to stop the crucifixion. The sentencing went

47. Lisbeth Smedegaard Andersen, "Påskelørdag," *Bag Vinger af Løvfald*, p. 23.

easily and quickly, and no one really protested; the followers of Jesus felt powerless to do anything against the great powers aligned against them. The third stanza, however, shows us that the narrator remembers the events of the day from the point of view of the resurrection. No one on that day, however, says the speaker, saw that "underneath" *(bag)* the "bloody thorn of crowns" the king of heaven was dying. Scripture, especially the Gospel of John, is quite clear that the glory of the Lord was revealed most fully on the cross, although Jesus' glory was hidden to even his most devoted followers. The voice, however, does not find much to commend in their behavior, when it seemed to them that Satan had won the day. Everything was dead, hope completely gone. For Andersen, as we have seen in her first hymns on this subject, the glory of Easter day cannot be fully appreciated without a full and deep awareness of Easter Saturday. One might think that the singer would say all that is over now since we know what happened the next morning, but the singer does not.

Andersen is too good a theologian to think that Jesus' followers would have, or could have, done anything to change what happened on the cross. Her aim appears to be to make us feel what the followers of Jesus felt like on that Saturday evening: guilty for their complicity in this most terrible event of all. Andersen's hymn has something of Johann Heerman's recognition in his hymn "Ah! Holy Jesus" and his realization that "I, I was the guilty." Her hymn fills us with guilt, not the kind of guilt familiar to the Baroque era, which wallowed in its unworthiness, but a modern kind of anxious regret. The voice is uneasy, suggesting there was something he or she could have done. While moderns stoutly refuse to believe they are responsible for something that happened so long ago, this may help them recognize how it could have happened. This puts them in the passion narrative: the King of Heaven died because of my inaction, not my terrible sin, but still I was there causing the death. This turns the knife in the conscience of the modern — not to have been powerful enough, but to have stood by, and by doing nothing, to have caused the death of Jesus. I am still guilty of allowing it to happen. As I sing it, I feel the unease that Andersen is trying to cause in me, which helps me understand the nature of my complicity in the crucifixion.

Her Easter hymn, "Easter Day," is more of a sermon than a dramatic monologue that begins with some of the hopelessness of "Easter Saturday." The events of Easter morning begin with disappointment and a picture of what the morning was like.

Easter Day

1. They did not sleep that evening
   And were up before the sun.
   Their footsteps echoed softly
   In the early morning dawn.

2. They went with oil and spices
   To his grave but found it bare,
   He'd risen in the darkness
   Long before the light appeared.

3. They came with dried-out spices;
   When they turned and went their way
   The trees burst out in fragrance
   In the place they'd gone to see.

4. The earth was white with flowers
   That had once been dry and bare,
   Now where they stepped were blossoms
   Where no blooms had been before.

5. They left their vases standing
   By the empty grave and trees,
   The alabaster glinted
   When the sun rose from the sea

6. And mildly shone as people
   With their children followed them
   Toward the city's open portal,
   Toward the new Jerusalem.

7. Christ is alive and risen
   And he goes before us now.
   Hear Easter bells are chiming
   In the early morning town.[48]

48. Lisbeth Smedegaard Andersen, "Påskedag," *Bag Vinger af Løvfald*, p. 25.

THEY DID NOT SLEEP THAT EVENING
(De sov kun lidt)

Lisbeth Smedegaard Andersen 1999 **Aksel Kroglund Olesen 2000**
Tr. Gracia Grindal 2006

5. They left their vases standing
By the empty grave and trees,
The alabaster glinted
When the sun rose from the sea.

6. And mildly shone as people
With their children followed them.
The city's open portal,
Toward the new Jerusalem

7. Christ is alive and risen
And he goes before us now.
Hear Easter bells are chiming
In the early morning town.

Figure 6 "They Did Not Sleep That Evening."

The hymn begins, typically for her, with a picture of what the day was like, but our first focus is on the women and their internal state: they had not slept and they are up early, in the gray light of morning, giving us a clear feeling of the sadness with which they come. The language is true to the biblical story — the spices, the women coming to the tomb in the early morning. The surprise comes in the third stanza where, on hearing the good news that Christ is risen and no longer in the grave, they (and we) see a completely new world come into being; suddenly things are so different that nature itself changes. Their spices, the remains of dried flowers, are all truly dead. After the women hear the news, however, the trees rain down flowers, and on the road where the women run, dead, gray stones are now blossoming underneath their feet. They leave the dead spices and oils by the grave, but the sun even changes the alabaster jar so it gleams with light from the grave, as the sun rises, once again from the ocean, as it did in her first Easter hymn. Now, suddenly, the children and people in the town are walking in and toward a new reality: the new Jerusalem into which the Lord is leading us into the morning sunshine of an early Easter morning in Copenhagen.

The poem works in the same way as the miracle of Easter. We begin hearing the old story, in fairly traditional images, but then suddenly, in the light of the resurrection, we are part of those who follow Jesus toward the New Jerusalem, or the eschatological ending, something of a feat of the hymn writer's imagination. As she did in her first Easter hymn, she shows us the event, but here we are in the Easter story in a more intense and imaginative way because it is happening here and now, in our own time and place, not just in Jerusalem. The narrative allows the preacher to give us a new world that we may not have seen before. As every preacher knows, if one cannot bring Jesus from Palestine into the place where one is preaching, the sermon will be dead for those who are listening, something that happened a long time ago and far away. Andersen, through the magic of narrative, makes the events of Easter Sunday happen to the singers as they sing the hymn.

In an article on this hymn, Andersen noted that Easter hymns could only be sung by faith. Since faith is not reason, it would be useless to try to argue people into faith or convert them by reason. She thought that too many Easter Sunday sermons and hymns were overly bombastic as though they were trying to raise Christ from the dead.

Too much is expected by the preachers if they forget that really no one in the congregation is expecting that they will preach Christ out of the grave at approximately 10:35 on Easter morning. He is already risen, and the grave is empty.[49]

At the same time, Easter hymns should express images and ideas for the singers that will continue to work in their minds as they go on in their lives.[50] Since no one actually saw the resurrection, it could only be proclaimed as the angels did to the women. "He is not here; he is risen."

She concluded her article with a short note of how the alabaster jar had appeared in the hymn. She had had a small alabaster jar when she was a child that she loved to hold and feel, noticing that when she held it up to the light, the thin stone would shine with white and gold tints. Later she found out that alabaster had been used in the windows of old church buildings, and the alabaster jar from the anointing of Jesus by the woman before his death was the theme of one of her favorite hymns by Grundtvig. Who knows, she concludes, "maybe they dropped the jar by the grave stone so it shone with light on that first Easter day while the cry went out, Christ is risen!"[51] We can see her craft as she looks for the fundamental theological point of the biblical text. The images and feelings of the characters in the narrative; her knowledge of the rich hymnological heritage that is hers in Denmark; her concern to preach the resurrection to modern Danes using her own experience of an alabaster jar as a child — all of these things work through her mind as she writes a hymn to make it speak in the best way possible to the congregation singing the hymn, so that they have something new to take with them, rather than a theological concept or two about what this all means.

Lisbeth Smedegaard Andersen has continued to write hymns since this last book appeared. Her books on the arts have proceeded from her pen at a startling rate. In the same year that she published *Bag Vinger af Løvfald*, her book *The Myth's Abandoned Houses: Danish Church Art after 1945* (*Mytens forladte Huse: Danske Kirkekunst efter 1945*) (Copenhagen: Samleren, 1999) appeared. While this book is specific to the Danish church and its artists, it is an astonishing piece of work, in which she, once again, teaches her readers

---

49. Lisbeth Smedegaard Andersen, "Påske," *Tema: Opstandelsen fortolknings-historie: Kritisk forum for praktisk teologi* (Frederiksburg) 79 (2000): 92.

50. Andersen, "Påske," *Tema*, pp. 89-93.

51. Andersen, "Påske," *Tema*, p. 93.

not only how to look at contemporary art, but reveals, to her own surprise and ours, how fully the contemporary artist can be engaged with the Christian story, reflecting on it in beautiful new ways for contemporary people. At the same time that she was working on the images for the New Testament, she was also completing a highly regarded book called *The Hidden Face: Essayistic Sermons on the Hidden Face of God in Scripture*.[52] Not long after that, in the fall of 2005, she came out with another cycle of sonnets on the stations of the cross, *Nu lægger vinden sig i verdens haver: en sonnetkrans*.[53]

The increasing regard for her work as a hymn writer in Denmark, and her growing influence on the artists and the church of Denmark, are finally making the hymn establishment take notice. In 2004, Edition Wilhelm Hansen published a book, *Hymns for Morning and Evening*, in which Andersen has five hymns. Intended for use in school and family, the book gathers together the glories of the Danish tradition of hymnody beginning with Sthen up to her own work. Ever since Sthen's book of devotions, *En Liden Vandrebog* (1578), the Danish tradition of hymnody has provided a rich variety of hymns for morning and evening, aids to daily devotions suggested in Luther's *Small Catechism*, made even more significant by Kingo in his first book of hymns for daily devotions. Andersen's contributions are hymns for the beginning and ending of the day, the seasons, and the faith as it is lived in Denmark today.

Evening

1. It's twilight. Sunlight is fading
   Behind all the roofs in the west;
   The remnants of daylight are scarlet,
   The bushes and brambles are glowing,
   They fade in the darkness at last.

2. In houses, noisy or quiet,
   The children are going to sleep.
   God send them the angels to bring them

---

52. Lisbeth Smedegaard Andersen, *Det skjulte ansigt: Essayistiske prædikener* (Copenhagen: Anis, 2005).

53. Lisbeth Smedegaard Andersen, *Nu lægger vinden sig i verdens haver: en sonnetkrans* (Copenhagen: Anis, 2005).

    The dreams that are brilliantly winging
    And bless them with faith and with peace.

3. We sit conversing together
   while sounds all around us die out.
   With love we enjoy one another
   While sharing our joys and our worries
   And thankful for life from our God.

4. But hearts can hide all of their sorrow,
   That no one around us can tell.
   They come back to haunt us at evening
   When something thankfully opens
   The door where the truthfulness dwells.

5. O, Lord, you know all our worries
   For you were yourself born of flesh,
   In you we find refuge, and dwelling,
   You listen so close and so near us,
   And hear all our quiet requests.

6. To you, I give all of my troubles
   And know that my guilt is made right.
   In darkness and quiet I felt it
   Come beating, a heart that is living
   In light under brambles and night.

This shows us how Andersen keeps to the tradition of the Lutheran evening hymn, but also sets it into a contemporary context. The picture of parents sitting and talking while children are falling asleep with dreams sent from God's angels is rather different from the picture of Dorothe Engelbretsdatter's evening prayer, in which she rehearses all the terrible things that could happen at night. Andersen, however, while not filled with Baroque anxieties about sin and death, describes the anxieties and regrets of the day and the need to make a confession "where truthfulness dwells." Handing over her guilt and troubles to God can help her sleep peacefully.

Danes are coming to see that Andersen is preaching new images of the gospel, although not a new gospel, and these images are intersecting

Figure 7 Lisbeth and Jens Smedegaard Andersen before the altar screen in Kingo's church in Slangerup, Denmark.

with their daily lives as Christians. Perhaps they will see soon, but not soon enough, how richly she speaks to them, how deeply traditional she is, even as she reacts to and changes the tradition. Her latest work, *Black on White: A Devotional Book (Sort på Hvidt: Andagtsbog)* combines her considerable gifts as pastor, writer, and patron of the arts, as the book contains black-and-white etchings by some of Denmark's best-known artists for each devotional piece intended for every Sunday and each festival of the Danish church year.[54] In 2006 she completed a new book on the face of Christ in art from the beginning until today, and at present she is finishing a book on the Virgin Mary in art.

Andersen's Impact

The career of this tiny and powerful woman has impacted Danish life and letters from the first, when she first took up her work as pastor in Risskov

54. Lisbeth Smedegaard Andersen, *Sort på Hvidt: Andagtsbog* (Copenhagen: Thaning and Appel, 2006).

in 1980. She is the first of the women I have written about in this book who was trained to be a public theologian and preacher. While the others were very shrewd and understood their own times and vocations quite clearly, we note a difference in Andersen's work, although she is in their tradition. Her public office is that of a pastor and preacher. She understands that she is preaching in her hymns as well as helping people pray. Although she did not spurn theology, as Britt G. Hallqvist did, Andersen can be as simple and disarming as Hallqvist. Andersen is profoundly theological and philosophical but also deeply Scriptural. She has learned from her predecessors and her own preaching that hymns should not contain theological language, because such language does not communicate with moderns. She gives us images that communicate on a much deeper level than ideas and theological principles. Too much hymnody is little more than "rhymed theology," which theologians often prefer because they can understand and control the meanings. However, our most beloved hymns are sermons whose texts have the most vivid images: "Rock of Ages," "What a Friend We Have in Jesus," "A Mighty Fortress Is Our God," "Children of the Heavenly Father," and so on.

One can notice the ironies in Andersen's life as a woman hymn writer in Denmark as well. Dorothe Engelbretsdatter, although a friend and admirer of Kingo, was suppressed by him when he did not include her works in his hymnal, which was used in Denmark and Norway for at least one hundred years. Oddly, Andersen seems to be fighting with the presence of Kingo almost as much as Engelbretsdatter did. Andersen's having to contend with the three "great Danes" in her every moment of life and work as a hymn writer has clearly frustrated her, as suggested by Harold Bloom's *Anxiety of Influence*. It is of interest to see that she has chosen Hans Christensen Sthen as the hymn writer whom she admires the most in the tradition. While Sthen is very good and is the first Danish hymn writer of note, he does not present for her, or any Dane, the heavy weight of the other three, and so one could surmise that she "overthrew" her oppressors — Kingo, Brorson, and Grundtvig — by preferring Sthen.

One can also wonder whether her gender has held her back, even in liberal Denmark, where society is very supportive of the work and life of women. To be sure she did achieve one of the major pulpits in Denmark when she was called to Holmen Church. The progress of her hymns in the Danish church, however, may show another side of that problem. We feel her struggle to find her way as she moved from "stay-at-home housewife" to an influential pastor and preacher in the Danish church. We can see quite clearly that her work is different because she had given birth and been a wife and mother. We hear it in her comment that when she took her children to the font to be baptized, she was not taking them to be born again, but to receive help from a power greater than she was as she faced the awesome duty of bringing them up. I wondered if her unfortunate predecessor Birgitte Boye could have helped her with the long-forgotten hymn on the churching of women, which clearly expressed the terror and joy of bringing a child into this world. Andersen, like Boye, has been looking for some very specific ways in which the church can speak to her own experiences as a woman in the faith. It will be interesting to see how her own hymnody fares in the future Danish church as more hymns flow from her pen.

Like the prince in *Amadeus* who complained that Mozart's music contained too many notes, a Danish pastor remarked, when I asked him what he thought of the images in Andersen's hymns, that there were "almost too many." One hears this from her critics, who may be looking for a controlling image that they can parse theologically. As we have seen, her hymns are quite dense, but that may be, finally, what helps them live. Like Augustine, she understands the necessity of using many signs to communicate with people. In his great book *De Doctrina Christiana*, Augustine writes that communication is not simple — our meaning does not simply go directly into the hearer's mind. Any sermon is best when the preacher uses "a multiplicity of signs," since our listeners do not hear everything the preacher says, and in fact, cannot take in anything unless they take into their own being at least one of the signs the preacher gives them to chew on. When they have taken into their being one of those words, they have "heard" some meager part of what the preacher is saying.

Andersen is very learned: she knows what the theological tradition has to say about Scripture, culture, and life with Christ, and she knows art and literature. Her work with the tradition of Christian art has also helped her to understand that we have no control over what people think of our work, so it had best be rich with signs that free the observer to think one's own thoughts, guided by the Holy Spirit, and behold Christ through these images. Yet, although her learning is deep and wide, her humor and Danish sense of irony help her not to take her work too seriously, even as she is passionate about finding her place in the tradition of Danish hymnody.

Although Andersen notes that she does not think hymns should try to argue or convert their singers, and the image of an Innermission deaconess going into far-off lands with her Jesus is not what one sees when Andersen appears in the huge pulpit of Holmen church in her clerical ruff, ready to preach, it is possible to argue that, from the first until now, everything she has done in her writing, whether hymnody, poetry, or her extensive work on art, is apologetic. She has always had an urgency to show modern Danes that the Christian faith is richly redolent with meaning for life today. Most important, it is true, and she wants her hearers to find some way into it, if not through her hymnody, then through her preaching. In both of these useful arts she has helped her hearers pay gracious attention to God's world around them as they have come to see Christ's saving work, showing them that heaven is there in their midst.

CHAPTER 7

Gracia Grindal (1943-   )
Homemade World

Helen Vendler, the dean of American literary critics, notes in her book *The Music of What Happens: Poems, Poets, Critics* that "each European nation cherishes its poetry . . . as part of the deposit of patriotism, and therefore institutionalizes it in the schools,"[1] or one could add, especially in small nations like the Scandinavian ones. The preceding chapters show that these Scandinavian women hymn writers understood themselves as being part of a homiletical and literary tradition, as well as possible contributors to it. That is not true for American hymn writers, who would find it difficult to think of themselves as coming from or contributing to the canon of American literature. The American hymn writer lives in a much bigger world, one which Vendler describes as incoherent, although another might simply say diverse: The "United States is probably one of the less coherent nations of the world, and poets rightly feel uncertain about their canon, their audience, and their culture."[2] As the American canon of literature continues to expand, young American hymn writers hardly know where to turn in their search for literary advice. Vendler's argument also contains an interesting remark that applies to the situation American hymn writers face: "The ritual and liturgical uses of poetry have so far vanished that it seems unlikely that they will reappear."[3]

1. Helen Vendler, *The Music of What Happens: Poems, Poets, Critics* (Cambridge: Harvard University Press, 1988), p. 35.
2. Vendler, p. 40.
3. Vendler, p. 39.

Figure 1 Gracia Grindal in 2006.

Except, maybe, in American hymns. If they can be regarded as poetry, and even as part of the American literary canon, there is, in churchly quarters, a continuation of the liturgical use of verse. The American hymn writer, often unschooled in the art of poesy, also shares what Vendler called that "national incoherence" while still writing formal "ritual and liturgical" verse, which is, almost by definition, European. This may not be conscious, however. American hymn writers probably learned how to write hymns by imitating the hymn texts they know, not by studying poetic meter and form, a skill rarely taught in school.

Fortunately, hymn tunes by themselves can teach poets how to write hymns. If they want to write words to fit a tune, which most hymn writers do when they begin, they have to provide words that fit the notes exactly. The tune imposes a discipline of form that many contemporary American poets do not learn but must acquire if they are going to find words for a tune. Tunes demand an exact precision of beat and syllables. For the unschooled hymn writer this is a good thing. While there are not many novice hymn writers who are aware of poetic meter or form, or the literary conventions connected with certain kinds of meters, certain kinds of subjects, or the rhetorical purpose of a hymn, these questions tend not to be the first ones asked by novices when they begin writing hymns. They just "look in their hearts and write," probably unconscious that they are using a very strict form with centuries of conventions behind it. Hymns, in the popular imagination, come directly from the heart of God, and if they are in English, they are usually written in the basic English ballad stanza. (A ballad stanza consists of four lines with a rhyme pattern of either abcb or abab. John Newton's "Amazing Grace" is an example.)

The first book published in America, the *Bay Psalm Book* (1640), with its crusty language, shaped psalmody, and thus, hymnody, in this country for many generations. The psalm tradition, naturally, occupies central place in American literature and language, with its flinty determination to present meaning, not art. And yet it was art. Even the *Bay Psalm Book*, probably the roughest of the lot, gets into one's head, even verse as inelegant as its version of Psalm 23:

The Lord to me a shepherd is;
want therefore shall not I.
He in the fields of tender grass
Doth cause me down to lie:

To waters calm me gently leads,
Restores my soul doth he. . . .

David Daniell, in his magisterial book *The Bible in English,* is scandalized by how little the historians of American life and literature understand this, calling this "Bible-blindness . . . puzzling."[4] Whether or not hymn writers in America today know much at all about the *Bay Psalm Book,* any writer of English hymns in America, no matter how naïve or learned, has inherited its forms and traditions. One can hear it thumping along in almost all of the first hymns by beginning hymn writers in America.

American hymns are also a pastiche of the American family's ethnic origins. Somewhere in the back of every family are shreds of particular language hoards, English, Scotch Irish, German, Irish, Scandinavian, Polish, Russian, Yiddish, and now hundreds of other languages that are enriching the American tongue, including Spanish, Mandarin, Japanese, Arabic, and Swahili. Every family has something in its speech that reveals those roots, and whatever they are, they give each young person a slightly different sense of the American song than one would have had without it. For me that other sound came from both of my parents, whose first language was Norwegian, and from the hymnal of the Lutheran Free Church, the *Concordia* (1932), which took as its mission providing its members with the important Lutheran chorales out of Germany, the English hymns, and then the spiritual song tradition from both Scandinavia and the Anglo-Saxon treasury. Its spare but accessible collection of chorales with multiples of Germanic meters, English hymns, and the American gospel song, along with generous helpings of Scandinavian tunes, make up the metrical house in which I live.

Translating a Tradition

My first attempt at writing a hymn came during my very first meeting with the Hymn Text Committee of the *Lutheran Book of Worship* (LBW), in January 1973. Appointed to fill the position of another woman, I had been nominated by two of my college teachers at Augsburg, Gerald Thorson and

---

4. David Daniell, *The Bible in English* (New Haven: Yale University Press, 2003), p. 352.

Leland B. Sateren. On the day we began, in a snow storm in a cheerless motel near the St. Louis airport, I was asked to revise a hymn that had been proposed for a Lutheran version of Key '73, an effort of evangelicals to work for revival in the country. It was probably a test. Each evening I would retire with my latest revision of the hymn and prepare a new, less rough version of the hymn, using all the poetic skills I had learned in my graduate schooling for a Master of Fine Arts degree from the University of Arkansas' creative writing program. Every morning the new verse would be greeted negatively: Too literary, too much art.

Hymnody, the committee assured me, was not poetry. What they wanted was propositional language without dense metaphors. It was a powerful, but inaccurate, lesson that stuck. For a hymn to be modern, the theology had to be modern, as did its images, with nothing from the previous piety, especially not a sweet Jesus, or any hint of the three-storied universe (heaven, earth, hell) decried by Bultmann and his followers. What mattered most was the tune, which had to be a kind of Neo-Renaissance creation, difficult and strong. The idea burned itself into my brain. These men were, after all, my teachers, the experts, I believed as I began editing and retranslating hymns into contemporary English. Not having much with which to counter them, since I was naturally deferent to my teachers and elders, I believed them. It took a long time for me to undo this prejudice and realize that hymns were indeed poetry, but very restricted verse that, because of the tune, and the general nature of the congregation, could not be too artsy or use some of the conventions of great poetry, such as enjambments or metrical variations. The verse had to be very regular and repeated from stanza to stanza. Nor had any one taught me specifically about my own Norwegian-American Lutheran tradition of hymn texts. I had to learn it on my own.

The Hymn Text Committee of the LBW was aware of a "Hymn Explosion" in England that insisted new hymnody needed to be written for modern people. Most of these new hymns were Methodist or Reformed. Contemporary Lutheran hymns were not easy to find except for a few translations from Swedish by Fred Kaan, a Dutch pastor in the Reformed Church of England, who put some of Anders Frostenson's hymns into English. Whether or not we knew of the Hymn Explosion in Scandinavia, we did know there was call for new hymns — of which there were curiously few, especially any with the kind of language the theologians were requesting. In some ways it was an exciting time, as we overthrew old certainties for our own new ones, but in other ways it flattened out the universe of faith. Old hymnody was only to be tolerated because the poor, benighted people in the pews needed it. As a poet and lover of the Tudor prose of the King James Version of the Bible, I felt it was a bitter loss from which the church would not recover, especially since people revising the old language did not have the rotund sense for the language that the Tudor translators had had. Our Bible translators seemed to be mostly interested in meaning, so weaker versions, such as the New English Bible, appeared.

In my distress, I wrote an article in *The Christian Century*, "Lord, Bless This Burning Pit Stop!" It launched my career. It was the reason the Inter-Lutheran Commission on Worship (ILCW) had asked me to be a member of the Hymn Text Committee. The Hymn Society of America asked me to give an address at its annual meeting at Fourth Presbyterian Church in Chicago on these issues related to updating hymn language. It was an incredible honor for such a young person, even though I probably excused it on the basis of a quota — get a woman to speak. It was my pleasure to meet the stars in the current hymnological skies: Erik Routley, Alice Parker, F. Bland Tucker, Jean Lorenzo Porter, and Mary Oyer.

All this time I was working on the Hymn Text committee, revising and updating old translations, since it was part of our commission to do so. It was painful to update old favorite translations by Catherine Winkworth (to whom Lutherans in America owe a great debt: without her there would have been few German chorales available in decent English). Her words "Ah! How long I've panted, ere I ne'er had fainted!" simply did not work in English today, the argument went, but any attempt to modernize them foundered. We were not as good as she was.

Despite this discovery, translation became a refuge for me. I could be fully involved in the poetry of the original poet, regardless of its discarded world view. The de-mythologizers made it difficult for anyone who valued the tradition. So translation became my home. There I could play freely with these rapturous images of heaven, the pearl and jasper, the rivers, the tree, the crystal fountains, while keeping, so to speak, poetically fit through practice. This became most clear to me when I undertook to translate the Queen of Chorales, by Philip Nicolai, "Wie Schön Leuchtet der Morgenstern."

> How lovely shines the Morning Star,
> The grace and beauty of our Lord
> And sweetest branch of Jesse.

King David's Son, of Jacob's line,
A king and groom of royal sign,
Has won our hearts with blessing.
Lowly, holy,
Full of beauty and of duty
Jesus graces
All the earth and starry spaces.

O dearest pearl in heaven's crown,
True God and Mary's human son,
The highest king of any,
My heart names you its sweetest flower,
The fullness of the Gospel's power
More sweet than milk or honey.
So rare and fair,
Sweet hosanna, heaven's manna
For our feeding,
Nourishment beyond our needing.

O Lord, set deeply in our hearts
Like rubies cut with some new art
The flame of this new loving,
When Jesus took our flesh and bone
To make the world his very own.
A gracious rose from heaven
He loved and moved
Through our fearing, ever nearing
Where we waited
Fearing life, the death we hated.

He brought to us a shining ray
And set his love down in our way
More bright than any vision.
And now we see our deepest good
In his pure word and life and blood
More sure than simple fashion.
O keep us deep
In your word, our gracious Lord,

Make us never
Slight the grave you give forever.

O God, our Father, strongest shield
Who thought of us before the world,
And loved us through your sorrow;
In giving up your Son who died,
It was our death we crucified,
A treasure marked with terror.
O praise his way,
Ever giving and forgiving,
He is holy;
Praise him for his death so lowly.

So take the instruments and play
Glad music for the joyful day
Our Savior comes redeeming.
He came to us as Mary's child
And returns to claim his bride,
O sing the Lord's returning!
Singing, ringing,
Jubilation for salvation,
Praise the Father,
For his Son, our loving brother!

A word can scarcely hold this friend,
The world's beginning and its end,
Our Alpha and Omega.
He is the Word and heaven's Son
Who came to end what he began —
The trumpets sound hosanna.
Amen! Amen!
Come, Lord Jesus (see he frees us).
Love surrounds us,
Crowns of light and grace astound us!

This translation of "Wie Schön Leuchtet," however, was not accepted because one of the members of the committee found it "too" sensuous and embarrassing. With that we returned to the old language of Winkworth, slightly updated and made more theological, rather than imagistic.[5] This proved to me once again that even the grand old Lutheran Queen of Chorales had to be sheered of its hopelessly old-fashioned imagery. Images did not matter, theology did. I understood it, hanging around theologians as I had my entire life, but this experience only increased my difficulties as a hymn writer. I knew for sure that if I set out to write a hymn, it would have to be modern and up-to-the-minute, with asphalt and slums in it to be acceptable. Such images did not attract me; I had not seen any hymns with such diction that seemed to be successful. Asphalt and concrete were traditional images of hell, which I could never use in my hymns, even though the contemporary theologian was calling for it.

Paraphrasing the Word

Absent much teaching on what the Lutheran hymn and its poetic conventions were, I found myself most attracted, for obvious reasons, to the Psalter tradition started by John Calvin and his dictum that the Psalter was where God taught us to pray and praise. Paraphrases did not call for originality of expression, only for skill with the verse. My work on the committee had developed in me a disdain for the homiletical and theological hymns that the *Service Book and Hymnal* (SBH) had criticized in its preface as being "manward" not "Godward." Given Augustine's dictum that "a hymn was a song in praise of God," that prejudice seemed correct to me, so I naturally gravitated to paraphrasing psalms, where, as Calvin had written, God teaches us how to praise him. Calvin's idea that originality in praise of God was presumptuous seemed right to me. God knows our hearts. Maybe the problem was a formal one, since trying to write modern hymns in old-fashioned forms seemed to be a contradiction in terms. Isaac Watts' fine eighteenth-century classicism sits heavy on the English hymn still. Adding contemporary diction and images to his forms only made the problem worse. It turned the worshippers' attention to the author of the hymn, whose strain to be modern became the main interest. How original one could be in naming God also became important with the rise of the feminist movement. Both of these efforts re-

---

5. For further reflections on this issue cf. my article "On Translating Hymns: Outrageous Opinions and Personal Regrets," *The Hymn* 37.2 (April 1986).

minded me of what the Puritans said about rhetoric: putting gaudy decorations on the fair face of truth. "God's Word needeth not our polishings" is the wonderful way the *Bay Psalm Book* preface puts it.

Paraphrasing, within these limits, became for me the perfect solution. My work paraphrasing biblical texts caught the eye of the Christian Reformed Psalter Hymnal committee, which had begun working on its own version of the Psalter. They asked me, along with Alice Parker, to come to Westminster Choir College to teach a workshop for them on the paraphrasing of psalms. At the time, I had been struggling with the persistent need for rhymes in English hymns and felt there were few hymn writers who could rhyme well enough to avoid the old traps like "June" and "moon." For a language with so many words, English is extremely poor in words that rhyme. There are very few rhymes in English for some of our most important words: "love" or "hope" or "baptism" or "joy." I tried to develop metrical forms that would break out of the need for rhyme: repetition, refrains, and even nonce stanzas — sets of metrical patterns that I made up, which would break open the sounds of Isaac Watts thumping in our ears. While ultimately unsuccessful, this approach was the only way I could deal with the difficulties, for me, of writing any new hymns. Paraphrasing a psalm was freeing. I started to think that rather than trying to fit the words into the old forms that had been used ever since Calvin, maybe it would be easier to write a modern hymn if I broke the metrical conventions and created a nonce stanza, one that came out of careful attention to the rhythms and language of the original psalm, in much the same way modern painters struggled with the notion of a frame and the meaning It gave their absurd creations. This was an effort doomed to fail, but helpful.

Its main problem, however, was that this nonce form made little emotional or formal sense. So the first line of a text on Zechariah 4 established the meter for the first line of each stanza.

"Not by might, not by power,
but by my Spirit," says the Lord.

"Who are you, oh great mountains?
You shall become a plain," says God.

"I will build a great temple
Upon a stone with seven eyes."

> "The eyes see all our doings,
> They restlessly go to and fro."
>
> "Build my house, take the plummet,
> Do not despise the smallest thing."
>
> God has come, oh great mountains,
> Fall down and wonder at the sight!

Writing in this form loosened my verse a bit as I came to understand both the opportunities and limits of such metrical attempts to break up the conventional forms that were restricting the contemporary hymn. I was not saying anything of my own, either. Like the Calvinists, I relied on the text alone for content. The nonce stanza, not surprisingly, despite my efforts, sounded rather like the indigenous eight-beat ballad line Americans understood. These poems did have the effect of confusing — and maybe liberating — the musicians, who had every bit as much reason to be weary of the old ballad stanza as the form they continued to use, even when it came to setting new hymns. If we wanted new hymnody, maybe we needed new forms as well as new language.

During the 1980s I experimented with some forms like these and found some musicians who understood them and were able to successfully set these nonce stanzas to tunes which could be sung by congregations, more or less. One of my most successful was a version of the Lord's Prayer, taken to some extent from Martin Luther's *Small Catechism*. In writing this I was beginning to access the Lutheran tradition of metrics, more German than English. I was still paraphrasing another text, however. I wrote the text almost in one line, which Mark Sedio figured out how to set to a very nice tune.

> Father in heaven,
> We are truly your children,
> As children we approach you,
> As beloved children we call you by name:
> R/The pow'r and the glory are yours!
>
> Your name be hallowed, by itself it is holy,
> Now make it holy for us

As your Word is taught to us;
Your Word is truth!
R/The pow'r and the glory are yours!

Bring us your kingdom,
Though it comes in its own time,
O let it come in our lives;
As you give your Spirit,
So keep us in faith,
R/The pow'r and the glory are yours!

Your will be finished,
Here on earth as in heaven
And help us do your bidding:
Curb the evil one, Lord,
And keep us in faith.
R/The pow'r and the glory are yours!

Give us bread daily,
As you feed all your children.
O work thanksgiving in us
For your gift which satisfies
All our needs:
The pow'r and the glory are yours.

Save us from trials
So that even when tempted
We will not fall to sinning
Into unbelief or to
Sins of despair:
The pow'r and the glory are yours.

Forgive our sins as
We forgive one another;
O grant us grace to praise you
And to live in love for our
Friends and our foes:
The pow'r and the glory are yours!

> Spare us from evil
> And from all that would harm us,
> And when death comes to take us
> Grant us life eternal and
> Give us your peace,
> The pow'r and the glory are yours!

After the LBW was put to bed, I began to work more intentionally on the poorly translated Scandinavian treasury of hymns with which I had grown up and which had been generally regarded as mawkish or childish by the Germans on the committee. I had by this time become aware of the movement in Scandinavia that had started playing the traditional hymns using jazz organs and saxophones. Not only did this movement bring the old hymns of my youth into new focus for me, but it also connected with the desire in America for more "contemporary" hymnody and worship materials, which I took to be a desire for less "modern" music than had concerned the musicians of the LBW, and more folk music, or at least music that appealed to ordinary people whom the LBW music committee seemed to disregard. They were composing difficult music — meaning good music — they would growl. As they did this, they were essentially attacking the music of America and of their dear mothers — who loved and had promulgated the gospel songs, which the committee regarded as sentimental and too feminine. They wanted strong, masculine music like that from the Reformation or Renaissance, not the feminine music of Robert Lowry or William Bradbury, who, although trained at Leipzig, had written for their audience with a shrewdness that had wide appeal and also made them very rich. The hymns the committee liked and wrote were tough and difficult to sing, not very accessible to the middle-class membership of the mainline church.

In 1981, I left Decorah, Iowa, for two years to attend Luther Northwestern Theological Seminary in Minneapolis and to teach on the side. While there I started teaching my creative writing course but this time for hymn writers. While I taught the course, I wrote a chapter for a book on hymn writing for each session of the class. It became the little book now called *Lessons in Hymnwriting*. Together, my students and I explored the tradition of writing hymns in English, especially as they were developed in England and America, starting with the Calvinists and the paraphrasing of the Psalms. One reason that it was efficient to start with paraphrasing was that it relieved students of having to write creative, original content. They would learn their craft by fitting one psalm into several English forms, learning the ins and outs of several traditional hymn forms in doing so. If they used the same psalm for each form, they could see the ways in which the form changed what was possible in the paraphrase of the material. It was how the English Renaissance poets had learned their craft, and it seemed a good way to teach these budding hymn writers. The first classes had a good number of writers who would go on to make their names as hymn writers and composers, including Rusty Edwards, Marty Haugen, and Mark Sedio. Those were heady days.

I still had not really figured out what it was to write a Lutheran hymn, so I kept on paraphrasing psalms or translating hymns from Danish, Swedish, and Norwegian. As the Evangelical Lutheran Church in America (ELCA) was being formed, I was invited to enter a competition for a hymn that could be used at its founding services. Those of us asked to write were told that we were to use the slogan of the merger, "Come Share the Spirit," a not very felicitous slogan. My hymn was chosen. Like the form of many of my paraphrases, it was a nonce stanza (with a 9.10.9.10.8.8. meter) that I started "Come, Share the Spirit, Christ Has Called Us." Its rhetoric is that of an exhortation, more homiletical than I had been in the past.

1. Come, share the spirit, Christ has called us
   To untold ventures in the life of faith,
   To bring good tidings to the needy
   And tell of Jesus' vict'ry over death.
   Christ speaks and all of life is new,
   God's word is pure and it is true.

2. Come, drown your sins beneath the waters
   Where life is flowing from the granite rock,
   The stone from which our Lord has risen,
   Our only cornerstone and building block,
   Christ speaks and raises from the dead
   All those who hear the living Word.

3. Come, let us tell the Gospel story,
   How God in Christ has given us new birth
   And raises us to live for others,

To speak good news throughout the whole, wide earth,
Christ speaks and life is come again;
It is good news for ev'ry one.

4. Come, God invites us to the banquet
Which ev'ry people will rise up to share,
With shouts of joy and loud thanksgiving
Before the throne of God we will appear.
Christ speaks and bids us sit and dine —
His body, bread, his blood, the wine.[6]

The tune was a typical neo-Renaissance tune, which had all the characteristics of the LBW composers: no real home row, so the pitch was hard to find, syncopation in odd places that made congregations wary. The music did not endear itself to many ELCA members, because of its difficulty. Although the text is not among my favorites now, I realized once again the old truth that it's the tune that makes the difference, not the text. I received over forty different new tunes for it from musicians who liked the text but found the tune forbidding.

Moving from Theology to Imagery

In the summer of 1985, during a meeting of the United Methodist Hymnal committee in Bethlehem, Pennsylvania, which I attended as a consultant, I got to meet several writers and composers from Scandinavia, since the Internationl Arbeitsgemeinschaft für Hymnologie (IAH) was also in session there. In their work I heard a different kind of voice, one I needed to understand. It was a fortunate meeting. In August of 1987, I attended the meeting of the IAH in Lund, Sweden. Here I renewed my brief acquaintance with those I had met in Bethlehem and we became good friends as I made scholarly connections with people whose interests were the same as mine: Britt G. Hallqvist, Svein Ellingsen, Egil Hovland, Inger Selander, and Steffen Arndal, among others, all important to hymnological studies in their homelands. Some of these were scholars deeply familiar with the his-

---

6. *We Are One in Christ: Hymns, Paraphrases, and Translations by Gracia Grindal* (Kingston, N.Y.: Selah Publishing Company, 1996), p. 82.

Figure 2 Norwegian hymn writer Svein Ellingsen. Photo © Morten Krogvold.

tory of pietism and the works of some of my favorite hymn writers: Lina Sandell and Hans Adolf Brorson. Their scholarship gave me a new perspective on my work with hymnody and made it possible for me to study more closely what the Scandinavians, especially the Swedes and Norwegians, were up to in their understanding that new hymns should not use hackneyed theological language, but preferably images and words contemporary people understood. When the Swedish committee distributed its new hymnal, I saw at once something more than the English and American push for contemporary language. Our English hymn writers, such as Fred Kaan, were using contemporary *theological* language in their hymns. The Swedes were using contemporary *images*. The difference is radical. Kaan, a Dutch pastor whose native language was not English, wrote hymns that had always bothered me with their political correctness, theological assertions, and lack of poetic skill. Texts such as his "Help Us Accept Each Other" seemed pedestrian, too theological and hortatory. In addition, his being a non-native speaker of English always seemed to cause a bump or inversion in his grammar — "Each person to embrace" — that did not feel like very contemporary English poetry to me.

> Help us accept each other
> As Christ accepted us,
> Teach us as sister, brother,
> Each person to embrace.
> Be present, Lord, among us
> And bring us to believe
> We are ourselves accepted
> And meant to love and live.

While Kaan had come to know Anders Frostenson's work, he picked up only one part of the new creed: contemporary theology. The hymn is a close paraphrase, in verse, of Paul Tillich's sermon "You Are Accepted." Although there are few images to contemplate in it, it is one of his most frequently anthologized hymns. The Swedes were excited by the attention Kaan had given them and translated some of his work for their hymnal, but it may be that they missed, in English, the lack of images and picked up only his contemporary sound. Their versions of his work seem more successful in Swedish, but that may be the problem of translations. The work of the Swedes Anders Frostenson, Ylva Eggehorn, and Britt G. Hallqvist; the Norwegian Svein Ellingsen; and the Dane Lisbeth Smedegaard Andersen felt different.

I had kept most of Kaan's work from inclusion in the LBW because of his dreary verse. Here among the Scandinavians was an alternative, but I had to struggle for nearly a decade to make it work in English. Kaan's and F. Pratt Green's work did not attract me — rhymed theology with some references to asphalt and concrete, trains and buses, slums and ghettos. The search for new mythologies in which to express the faith had foundered on theology. Theological assertions did not make for very good poetry. About this time I had attended a service where the leader had made us laugh at "Wake! Awake! For Night is Flying," the King of Chorales, because we had all been awake for hours. How could one write a contemporary hymn if biblical images could not be used? What would be left was not poetry. I knew that my own work, now mostly paraphrases of psalms, had nothing much to say, even though I was saying it well. I was too orthodox to leave the biblical witness. The call for new images seemed to call for a new religion. I needed to find a way to transmit the tradition faithfully to a new generation. My trip to Sweden that August, and the meetings in the old Lund University, the hymn festivals in the beautiful Lund cathedral, and the lovely trip out to an old country church in the hills and lakes of Skåne helped me to understand something about hymnody that I would not have learned if I had only studied the English/American tradition of hymnody.

On the bus ride, a couple of Swede-Finns came to me and asked me to quickly translate a hymn by one of their favorite authors. As we rode on the bus through the green fields of Skåne to the lovely, old, white church, they would not accept any of the quick and easy theological phrases I was giving them, until the English images were as close as they could be to the Finnish. I grew impatient, since by then I was, as a poet, captive to the notion that the only thing important about a hymn was its tune. They should be so lucky to get sensible words to sing to the meter, I felt! Since poetry was what one lost in the translation, being accurate seemed unnecessary. As the bus dipped and turned through the verdant fields of Skåne, I learned something but did not understand it very well. My initial work expressed the theology in the hymn — that I need the Lord in order to find rest for my anxieties — but not the imagery of the "salt," "embers," or "dry wells." After a lot of hard work, pressed on by my colleagues on the bus, I came up with this.

O Savior, within Your Keeping

Viola Renvall 1933   Sulo Salonen 1955
(1905-1998)   (1899-1976)

O Savior, within your keeping,
I rest all my loves and fears,
The joy of the loveliest mem'ry,

The salt of the bitt'rest tears.
I cast all my worlds upon you
and wait with my head bent low.
You see I am sunk in darkness,
There's nothing that I can do.

Take all of the dying embers
that flicker in sorrow's breast
And close your hands warmly around them
and give them, O God, your rest
which passes my understanding
— and comes from I cannot say —
it fills up dry wells with water
and brims with it ev'ry day.[7]

For the next decade, I looked forward to these biannual meetings in order to renew my acquaintances with people whose interests and backgrounds were similar to mine and helpful to me in my scholarly work as I tried to understand how the traditions we shared had flowered in this country in English. By this time I thought that my main work would be to translate hymns, since my own work, like a bad English pudding, seemed to have no theme. This was evident in my first book of hymns and paraphrases. While I could be proud of the skill and craft in the verse, I did not have much of my own to say. As the contemporary poet would say, I had not found my voice as a hymn writer. What I was writing did not interest me. My friend Inger Selander, the Swedish hymn scholar, noted that although my hymns were technically skillful, they were old-fashioned, while my sonnets, in a very traditional form, were not. It struck me as true and depressing. She could not say quite why.

Discovering the Lutheran Hymn as Sermon

By this time it was also clear that my expertise as a scholar of the Scandinavian tradition was in no demand by the ELCA hymnal committee putting

---

[7]. Viola Renvall, "O Herre, i dine händer," *Psalm och Sånger*, p. 565 (private unpublished translation).

together the new hymnal of 2007, *Evangelical Lutheran Worship*. At this same time, I was embroiled in theological controversies having to do with Lutheran ecumenism and became part of the movement later known as Word Alone, formed to oppose the adoption by Lutherans of the historic episcopate of the Episcopalians. Lutheran identity and theology had always been important to me, but I had always thought of it as a theological issue, not hymnological or cultural. When the Word Alone Board authorized me to begin thinking about developing a hymn project for our constituency, one that would be traditionally Lutheran, with services that met the criteria Luther had developed in his reform of the Mass, I began to learn things I had not fully understood before. What, in fact, was a Lutheran hymn? I began to look closely at Luther's works, thinking about what he was trying to do in his hymns in order to relate his understandings to the work of the hymnal project that seemed to be developing in my mind. I was astonished. Here I was, over 60 years old, a Lutheran pastor's daughter, a scholar and practitioner of the craft, considered an expert in the writing of hymn texts, and I had not carefully looked at this material, especially its rhetoric. Luther's hymns were, in fact, different from the hymn as Augustine defined it — a song in praise of God. They were sermons, neither praise nor prayer. It clicked for me one day when I heard a speaker marvel at the freedom that Martin Luther, in contrast to Calvin, had shown in his paraphrase of Psalm 46, "A Mighty Fortress Is Our God." The implication was that Luther's freedom, next to the so-called "grubbing literalism" of Calvin, was to be praised. As a long-time admirer of the Calvinist tradition in psalmody, and also of Luther, it struck me as uninformed. I looked back at Luther's work and reread the Confessions to see how they spoke of their reason for writing hymns. I was stunned to see this:

> Ceremonies should be observed both so that people may learn the Scriptures and so that, admonished by the Word, they might experience faith and fear and finally even pray. For these are the purposes of the ceremonies. . . . We also use German hymns in order that the [common] people might have something to learn that will arouse their faith and fear. ("Apology of the Augsburg Confession," [XXIV] "The Mass" 4, p. 258)

For Luther, a hymn was not a *paraphrase* of the Word, it *preached* the Word of God. In other words, a hymn was a sermon, since by his understanding, and Melanchthon's in his *Apology to the Augsburg Confession,* the sermon is the living Word of God, which arouses faith and fear. While a hymn could be both praise and prayer, its primary function, in the Lutheran understanding, was proclamation, which, of course, produces faith.

Like the proverbial magnet under iron filings, I felt all the disparate things I knew about hymns making sense. The "Introduction to Hymns" in *The Service Book and Hymnal* (1958) made it clear that these compilers were moving from hymns that were "manward" to those that were "Godward." They were changing the understanding of what a Lutheran hymn had been. The Lutheran chorale, at its root, had been, in fact, homiletical. Because the hymns had preached the gospel in language the laity could understand, the faith had survived and spread. One of my colleagues has commented that the Lutheran church survived the dreadfully dry and intellectual sermons of the Orthodox period, to say nothing of the Enlightenment, only because of its hymns. Lutherans were singing their faith in their hymns. The apparent drought of edifying literature during the Orthodox period, except for John Gerhard's book *Sacred Meditations,* demonstrates that the faith lived in the richness of its hymnody, the greatest period of Lutheran hymnody. Not surprisingly, these writers knew they should bend their efforts to producing chorales that the people could sing, and as they sang them, soak up Orthodox Lutheran thinking, which would teach them how to face any trial or joy in life. The idea that hymnody was inferior theology, an old charge by theologians, missed the homiletical purpose of the hymn. To be sure, because hymns were poetry, they sometimes eluded rational and theological explanations, but they themselves were beautiful enough to remain in the imagination of the public so they could be recalled for use in difficult times.

This new understanding reoriented my thinking about 180 degrees. No wonder I was unable to write a hymn — being original for the sake of being original in my prayers was not a very interesting calling. Prayer is either help me, help me, or thank you, thank you! To be original in prayer flies in the face of all we know about God, who knows our hearts! Like both Luther and Calvin, I was suspicious of the originality that flowed from the human heart, but I trusted Scripture. It was quite different if the hymn was to preach the gospel so that people could see how God's incarnation among us, his death, and his resurrection worked in daily life: in other words, to speak directly to the singers or congregation, to preach using new images and ideas that were faithful to the text. That I could do!

In fact, contra the words of the *Service Book and Hymnal*, the rhetoric of the Lutheran hymn *should*, in fact, be "manward." The Word of God was for human beings, not God. This was, in fact, how God was trying to get to us, through the Word. The change in the rhetorical direction of the hymn was, not surprisingly, consistent with the change in direction of the Lord's Supper that Lutherans had espoused after Vatican II. Instead of proclaiming the gospel to the congregation, we were now preaching to God about all the things we were doing. It was backwards from what Luther had done when he reformed the Mass and the hymnody of the Lutheran church to be down from God to us. Both contemporary liturgical hymns and praise songs were tedious to me because they were all *about* what we were doing for God, not what God had done for us. Everything started to make sense.

Even the hymns that had originally been written as sermons had been changed to prayers by those who did not want to refer to God in the third person masculine, so they sound oddly like sermons to God. Of course, we should love and help the neighbor, but being given specific actions and political positions to take up was not what I wanted to hear in the hymns I was singing. One of the most popular of these is Jeffery Rowthorne's hymn, to the tune Abbot's Leigh, "Lord, You Give the Great Commission." It contains only one fairly vague image: treasure.

> Yet we hoard as private treasure
> All that you so freely give.
> May your care and mercy lead us
> To a just society.

This language irritated me. The preaching in this hymn comes across as predictable, using as it does the homiletical method of the day: What the text meant, and what it means for us. This stripped the old four-fold interpretation that was second nature to Dorothe Engelbretdatter's generation down to two-fold — the literal historic and the moral. Its predictability and moralistic understanding of the text did not interest me, nor did liturgies straining to be "with it." As W. H. Auden put it in his poem "Doggerel by a Senior Citizen":

> *The Book of Common Prayer* we knew
> Was that of 1662:

> Though with-it sermons may be well,
> Liturgical reforms are hell.[8]

These discoveries began, however, to show a way out: if one could preach the sermon using the Scripture to help us see our own world in a new way, transformed by the gospel, then the hymn could be as creative as it needed to be. As Lisbeth Smedegaard Andersen, like Rembrandt, noted, the work of art, in this case a hymn, should give you a new thing to contemplate that brings you back to Scripture, the Word of God, even as it teases you into thought and helps the singers truly "hear" the Word, or in other words, make something out of the images and ideas in the hymns in their own minds. Furthermore, in understanding the rhetorical intention of the hymn, I now understood the place of originality in the hymn. I had been trying to praise God, or pray creatively, as though Scripture was not very useful. One could feel the strain of this in contemporary American hymns when the poet would add images of atoms, asphalt, or buses. Understanding the rhetorical purpose of a hymn changed everything: I was communicating with an audience of contemporary Christians, not God! When I am trying to make the biblical text relevant by preaching it, the purpose in writing and inventing material for hymns is absorbing. The model is one of preparing a sermon, one that will last in the heads of the people who have sung it.

Writing this book, I have come to see how clearly these women, several without formal schooling, understood their tradition, the forms and meters common to their particular language, and what the Anglo-Saxon poets called their "word hoard," or words that fit with a certain image. They also understood, implicitly, that, like the hymns of their day and heritage, a hymn could be a sermon; in fact, they seemed to prefer it. Lina Sandell, sitting in her little chair beside her preacher father, learning Greek from him so she could read the New Testament, was preparing to preach as well as praise and pray in her hymns. As Vendler makes clear in her book, Europeans understand the conventions and traditions of their poetry, especially one might note, in small countries like the Scandinavian ones, where writers need to learn and treasure their own heritage. Their teachers could transmit this. This is hard for Americans, or even the English-

---

8. W. H. Auden, *Collected Poems*, ed. Edward Mendelson (New York: Vintage International, 1976, 1991), p. 851.

speaking world, to comprehend. On the other hand, while English speakers have inherited a very rich and bewildering tradition of poetry and hymnody, and the English may still be aware of their own particular tradition of "ritual and liturgical poetry," the American hymn writer, like the American poet, lives in an essentially Calvinist or Methodist "home-made world," which Hugh Kerr notes in his book on Ezra Pound. Or as Helen Vendler calls it, *incoherence*. No one explicitly taught me how to write hymns. The first things I learned about English hymnody were the ballad stanza, Isaac Watts, John and Charles Wesley, and then the psalmody of America's founders. This was a good start, but I found it difficult to fit it with the Scandinavian meters lilting in my head, to say nothing of the German Lutheran chorale. The choices of meters alone were bewildering. The definitions of hymns and the genres within hymnody littering the landscape of hymnody textbooks and dictionaries have also been widely varied and very English. If a hymn is a "song in praise of God," as per Augustine, there is no place for the Lutheran chorale with its sermon, as the compilers of the SBH did, in fact, understand. Those rich Scandinavian hymns I had sung, in fairly workmanlike translations in the *Concordia Hymnal*, while sitting in small wooden churches on the North Dakota prairies as the wind slammed against the building, were dazzling with images of the Christian life that populated our imagination as we struggled to live on the bleak prairies and worship in the simple churches the pioneers had built to house their faith. After some years thinking about that sentence in the SBH, I wondered whether they really knew what they were doing by abandoning the homiletical hymn, or were they as oblivious as I?

I now understood what was needed, although I was not sure I could do it. One of the strange things about creativity is that one may very well know what is needed yet be completely unable to do it until the right time or insight comes. It was to happen for me very soon. This new understanding, which many of my readers might regard as rather self-evident, transformed my work. One needs to actually try to do these things, as opposed to simply understanding them in the tradition.

The opportunity came at the 2004 Hymn Society Convention at St. John's University in Collegeville, Minnesota. I had been there to work with some hymn writers who were beginning to paraphrase psalms. Some of us were sitting outside one of the halls, Wayne Leupold among them, when I made the idle comment that I no longer wrote, and probably never had written hymns because of inspiration. If, however, someone asked me to write a text, I could have one before the morning. Leupold turned to me and said, "Well, then, Gracia, would you be willing to write hymns on the common lectionary, all three years?" It was a moment. "Sure," I said, unaware of what it would mean. Although I have never feared work, this was a tall order. In the first place, I have never been an enthusiast for the lectionary, which misses huge swatches of Scripture, but for this challenge I could put that by. Then there was the sheer volume of the hymns needed. At least sixty hymns a year, if not more, to include the extra festival days of the year, a good bit of work! This was July of 2004. I would make it a kind of weekly ritual for writing the hymn, the same as I would a sermon: live with the text through the week and then write the hymn on Saturday evening, after the evening news. Later, in October, Wayne called me and asked if I were still interested. Yes, I was; it had not even occurred to me to refuse the work, although I had no ideas about themes or images beforehand. One thing, however, that I was going to do in these hymns was preach. Wayne remarked, "Preach?" "You'll hardly notice it, but it's what I am thinking of as I write," I concluded. "All right," he answered, to his great credit.

The night before the first Sunday of Advent in 2004, I followed that process exactly. After the ten o'clock evening news, I went downstairs and began thinking about how to preach the text for that Sunday. As I grew to understand more and more the genre of the hymn as sermon, it clarified my thinking about what was possible and what should be avoided. As I have now produced around two hundred and forty hymns in three published and unpublished volumes, and as of this writing have two more well on the way, I am learning more and more about how to write Lutheran hymns for people in the twenty-first century. In addition, studying these women who came before me, I have come to understand even better where I fit into that very definite set of traditions, even as I emerge from the incoherence of my own rich, American experience of poetic diversity. Continuing my labors on Saturday night, I have come to understand more fully what Lisbeth Smedegaard Andersen was doing in her work. It is something I feel myself working toward. Perhaps I came to understand this, suddenly, between the writing of the following texts, the first a fairly theological text, the second a sermon. I count it as a kind of breakthrough, between what my friend Inger Selander would call an "old-fashioned" hymn and a new one. The first hymn reminds me of a Bible campfire song.

Preaching from Home

Pentecost X
Romans 8:26-39; Matthew 13:31-33, 44-52

Help Me, Holy Spirit
(6.5.6.5.D.)

1. Help me, Holy Spirit,
   When I need to pray,
   Help me find expression,
   Intercede for me.
   Make my wordless sighing
   Prayers that God will hear.
   Heed my troubled groaning,
   Bring our Father near.

2. Help me, Holy Spirit,
   Know that God is love
   And to trust the goodness
   Jesus' works have proved.
   Teach me to be thankful
   That God sent his Son
   Here to take the sentence
   For the wrong I've done.

3. Help me, Holy Spirit,
   Fill my anxious heart,
   Show me there is nothing
   Driving us apart,
   Neither past nor present,
   Neither height nor depth.
   Nothing now can shake me,
   Neither life nor death.

4. Help me, Holy Spirit,
   Fill my heart with peace,
   Peace I cannot fathom,
   Peace that gives release.
   Bring me to Christ Jesus,

To the heart of love,
There where I can praise him
In our home above.

While that is competent verse with some nice literary devices and closely follows the biblical text, it is too theological. The next evening, not on my regular schedule, the following hymn came to me. It is on the same lesson, but here it is very different.

> Pentecost Xa
> Romans 8:26-39; Matthew 13:31-33, 44-52

After Singing Hymns of Comfort
(8.7.8.7.D.)

1. After singing hymns of comfort
   We have left the one we love
   Covered over with bright flowers
   On the rich, expensive wood.
   Still the words that we are saying
   Seem as empty as our hearts,
   Even if the sun is brightly shining,
   Life seems overcast and dark.

2. What we cling to is the promise
   Spoken as the pastor stood
   By the coffin as they closed it
   And we felt your presence there.
   Nothing separates us from you,
   Neither life nor cruel death,
   Not the mundane world around us,
   Nothing, neither height nor depth.

3. By the casket blooms a lily
   Weak and fragile from a stone,
   So your promise breaks the iron
   Of the doubt that we have known.
   Spirit, come to us and give us

Words to help us try to pray;
Turn our bitter sighs to morning
And our sorrow into day.

Lisbeth taught me to start a sermon/hymn with a universal perception or feeling to which most of the singers will be able to assent and then to move them into seeing the radical difference the gospel makes in our perceptions of the world. It has made my palette richer, as I come to apprehend that my rhetorical goal has more and more turned to helping people to see what Christ has done for them in their lives through his death and resurrection. The focus is now not on my own creativity, but on how I can use my creativity to speak to contemporary people the gospel of Jesus Christ. Although I try not to write a hymn that does not refer to the death and resurrection of Jesus or does not give us some sense of the eschatological ending into which he brings us by his grace, not every hymn can do everything, so if the hymn has to concentrate on just one thing, I will do so. In some ways, these hymns are harder to write because I have to think all week, not just of the texts, but of what images I can use to preach the texts. This gives me clarity because I have a sense of my rhetorical purpose in writing: My audience is there for me to persuade. Revolutions in a tradition come when a shaper of that tradition takes a five-degree turn on it and sees something completely different and begins to use it.

Conclusion: Learning from Our Foremothers

This new understanding of the rhetoric of the hymn has been like a miracle for me, and it came from writing this book as much as anything. Learning from Dorothe Engelbretsdatter how she used the homiletical techniques of her Lutheran father and husband to preach in her sermons, using her own voice, and from her own point of view helped me use the conventions of Lutheran homiletics I had learned from my own father, a vigorous and creative preacher himself, who knew and loved this tradition of hymnody and used it to great effect in his ministry. Reflecting on the women I have written about in this work, I am struck by how powerful the father has been to most of these hymn writers. Perhaps it shows what a difference a father could make in the life of a gifted young woman who knew without a doubt that she could not be called to be a pastor or preacher except as a writer of hymns. Dorothe was preaching in her hymns in the way her father and husband were preaching in their sermons, although she was not preaching from the pulpit. Her writings show her to be an active part of the civic life of her day. Even though the church did not allow women preachers, her importance to her day and the civic life of Dano-Norwegian literary culture is astonishing. Her acquaintance with Kingo and Dass, her frequent trips to Copenhagen, the capital city of literature in her culture, her association with men of consequence in the world of the court, church, and commerce are considerable. We can also see in her hymns how fully she participated in the world of ideas regnant at the time. As Lila Akslesen has shown in her works on the Baroque in Norway, while Dorothe found much inspiration in Scripture, she also accessed the spiritually edifying works popular in her day: Johan Arndt, Richard Baxter, and others. In addition to her intellectual resources, one can find many artifacts and gems from her own daily life among the ordinary people, especially women. She was not only a product of her own time, but she also wanted to speak to it with all the force she could. Her success in supporting herself through her writing shows that she did very well indeed. She also lived long enough to experience the fate of anyone whose time has passed. Ludvig Holberg's memory of her as an old, somewhat eccentric woman dressed in old Bergen clothes shows us the temporary nature of much art, especially hymns. While many hymn writers will speak to a time, few leap over the constraints of their own age to become classic. We can be happy some did.

Birgitte Boye is perhaps the best evidence for the hymn as *brugskunst*, art written for its own time. We know far less about her than we should. We know nothing of her father's interest in her and very little about her mother. Still, hers is an amazing story of a young woman who, by dint of sheer effort and discipline, mastered the languages of Europe and the philosophical currents of her time, even while raising four children in a somewhat remote coastal area in Denmark. That she did, in fact, gain the kind of influence she had by virtue of the patronage of First Minister Ove Høegh-Guldberg is also astonishing, as is the almost immediate plummet in her reputation, which is difficult to account for, except for the bad reputation of the Enlightenment among Lutherans even today. Her falling star could also be attributed to several men in the church at the time who for some reason, perhaps rank sexism, did not appreciate her work and utterly ignored it in the next hymnal, which suffered an even quicker demise than Guldberg's hymnal, which was kept alive by Norwegians and

Norwegian Americans of the nineteenth century who continued using it until the middle of the century. Her reputation in Danish letters needs refurbishing. She was better than her reputation today would have it.

Berthe Canutte Aarflot is a similar figure in Norwegian hymnody. She had a sense of calling, and she understood the hymnody of her predecessors, especially Dorothe's, whose Bride of Christ imagery, along with her extensive dilations on the weeping Mary Magdalene, appealed much more to Berthe than did the creation theology of Boye. Hans Adolf Brorson, however, was her main teacher with his devotion to the order of salvation and Bride of Christ imagery. Pietists such as Hans Nielsen Hauge in the previous generation influenced her work most directly. Like many of these women hymn writers, she also learned from her father, even though his Enlightenment persuasions seemed not to attract her. While her hymns may seem of secondary importance in a collection of classic Norwegian hymns, her own life and the influence of her hymns at their time testify to the fact that her vision of herself as a preacher and spiritual mentor, which she gained directly from Hauge's movement, was widely accepted and honored in her own day. People at the time obviously needed to hear her sermons and hymns. They were written for a particular audience with whom she shared many ideas about the Christian faith. Although she used the Bride of Christ imagery as much as Brorson and Dorothe, her particular twist on the faith was more directly from Matthew 25, with its waiting maidens and the Last Judgment. Her point, however, was to be ready for the last day. The urgency with which she preached on this theme was still alive during my youth, when countless Norwegian-American Lutheran evangelists came through our area with sermons based almost exclusively on the clock — what if you should die on your way home, or make the basket too late, after the final bell. This theme rings through almost everything Berthe wrote, and her urgency to bring people to a saving knowledge of Jesus Christ, a pure Haugean theme, may seem strange to some Lutherans today, but she stands as a good reminder of a time that lingers in the minds of Lutherans who still believe in personal faith, conversion, and salvation.

Lina Sandell, also a Pietist, and without doubt the most famous and maybe the greatest of these writers, also thought of herself as a preacher through her hymns and work translating, editing, and writing for nineteenth-century Swedes. The fact that her father's friends and colleagues in the ministry had seen her gifts while she was yet a very young girl shows how remarkably gifted she was in the time of a new day for women — we can see as she takes the editorial position in Stockholm and leaves her home that something new is happening in the lives of women. Her ability to use her vocation in such a public role was rather different for women up to that time. Lina Sandell's vocation and career, however, gave her enormous influence over the church at the time. She and Oscar Ahnfelt gave the nineteenth-century revivals a new song to sing that marked especially the Swedes and Norwegians who came to America where they continued to cherish her work and keep it alive. Like her foremothers in hymn-writing, she was attracted to the Bride of Christ imagery and the feminine nature of the Holy Spirit with its wings, but her theme came to be one of preaching the undeserved grace of God. As Rosenius noted, no one could sing of the grace of God like Lina. Like the others, she was deeply biblical and aware also of the corpus of edifying literature cherished by Lutheran Pietists from Johan Arndt, Zinzendorf, and her own colleague, Rosenius. In true nineteenth-century style, however, her doubts and agony over God's love for her were not expressed in the way Britt G. Hallqvist expressed them a century later. It is almost as if Sandell worked to solve the problem of God's mercies before she began writing and then penned her grateful praise in her hymns which ring with a devotion we will not see in our own time. Her hymns have clearly transcended their time, as much because of their melodies as the texts — simple and filled with images which communicate across the ages more directly than theology. It is a remarkable story and well worth telling.

Britt G. Hallqvist, Sandell's direct successor, has many of the same qualities as Sandell with her interest in the biblical story and the teaching of children, but she is of quite another age. Where Lina struggled to believe God was merciful, Hallqvist struggles more over whether God exists, perhaps in a kind of longing for a father whom she did not know well enough. In Hallqvist we see something of a conversion as she enters into the conventional life of the parsonage, even as one who was surprised to find herself there. Her engagement with the philosophical and theological questions of the day are clear in her hymnody, even though she noted that she was not much interested in contemporary theology. She picks up the modern question in her own life in a university community. Her response to the problem was to become simpler and more biblical, taking without cynicism the stories of Scripture on their own merits. Thus her gentle irony and humor come through in most of her work as she grew into a deeper familiarity with Scripture. Raised among the people Schleiermacher would have described as "the cultured despisers," she continued in that milieu all her life, hearing their concerns and doubt, giving them a simpler language with which to pray — contemporary language that was faithful, yet not theological. That she did it in the face of the cynical 1960s is a triumph. Her collaboration with Egil Hovland has left a substantial treasury of work that is now being sifted as the next generation of hymn books is being prepared. Her work will continue to be considered an important contribution to Swedish (and Norwegian) hymnody that, while we cannot know what will endure, since no one has been granted the gift to see what the next age will be like, should continue to give post-moderns words to sing the gospel to others. Her work is to be regarded.

Lisbeth Smedegaard Andersen is still continuing her work as a hymnist, poet, preacher, and writer of edifying books of sermons, devotions, and books on Christian art through the ages. She is the first woman of the six to have trained for the ministry and served as an ordained pastor. In her struggles to find her own way as a hymn writer, and finally, pastor and preacher, we can see little of her relationship with her own father. In many ways, her longing to have a career — rather different from what her parents imagined for her — reflects an entirely different age and situation, with which she dealt courageously and generously. She has also been blessed with a helpmeet in her husband Jens, who is, by her own testimony, her best critic and encourager. We can see from the first, when she began her pastorate in New York City, her eagerness to get her contemporaries in Denmark to hear the gospel in language that connects with them. Her notion of a hymn as *fortolkning*, or an interpretation that tells the gospel story to her contemporaries, is always evident in her works. Through the power of her imagery she is able to bring Christ into modern Copenhagen in unforgettable ways. While she is surely a part of her tradition, she has also had to fight against it in ways the other women, oddly, except for Birgitta Boye, did not have to. The Danish hymnal committee, perhaps with its fears that it would repeat the mistakes of the Guldberg committee, has been fairly unresponsive to her notions about hymnody as of necessity being contemporary and not for all time.

As I have previously noted, Lisbeth has been the one who has taught me some of my most important lessons while I was writing this book: that when one writes a hymn, unlike a sonnet, one is not addressing the klieg lights of eternity but the current audience. In other words, the writer has to humble herself and her aspirations by working to get the gospel message

Figure 3 Lisbeth Smedegaard Andersen, Gracia Grindal, and Jens Smedegaard Andersen in 2004.

across to her contemporaries. To die in that way for the sake of the gospel takes hard spiritual discipline for many a would-be hymn writer today, schooled as they are on the poison of immortality. She has also taught me that one can write thoroughly contemporary hymns without having to drag in the engines of modern industry. While they are part of the landscape and cannot be denied, they are not at the heart of the modern psyche, although they may have caused it. What gnaws at people today is whether or not they matter and whether God, who may or may not exist for them, cares for them. To write a hymn today one cannot assume the same deep and vast biblical knowledge in one's audience as Dorothe did of her biblically besotted Baroque age. Until the time of Britt G. Hallqvist, all hymn writers could assume as part of their culture a deep knowledge of Scripture. Perhaps that is why both Britt G. and Lisbeth have spent considerable time in their hymns telling the biblical stories from inside the psyches of the actors in them. There we discover that they are remarkably like us in their unbelief and worries. In writing hymns for us they help us understand and see the story of Jesus from the inside, a genuinely evangelical approach. While both wrote to a people that have mostly been baptized into the Lutheran faith, they knew that their hearers were generally agnostics and ignorant of the Christian faith, except through some prejudices they may have picked up in their youth. For both of them the apologetic task of the hymn is somewhat new, but they have both used their hymns to preach and teach the faith. Coming as they did from a rich tradition and educated in it, they have continued the tradition and brought it to new and better understandings of the rhetorical role of a hymn in the life of the contemporary church.

America is a nation of immigrants. The many varieties of traditions and cultures that have arrived on its shores number in the thousands, if not hundreds of thousands, and each one enriches and invigorates what Vendler calls our incoherent world of poetry. Even as the classic English forms have been stretched and pushed to accommodate more traditions than they might have been expected to, it is also important to see how dominant Calvin's followers have been in setting down a form for hymnody that overwhelms most of these little traditions a couple of generations after the group has arrived. In the same way that New York City is in some ineluctable way still New Amsterdam with a typical Dutch tolerance for a brawling commercial culture, at the same time, so is the American hymnal, of whichever stripe, still deeply Calvinist and Methodist. Even though Lutherans brought with them from their various countries of origin a rich treasury of chorales and spiritual songs, and even though they worked to include these songs in their subsequent English hymnals in this country, they did not quite fit. Before long their Yankee neighbors with their sturdy Calvinist psalms and the sprightly Methodist hymns of praise, along with other Protestant traditions of song, took over.

Most people noticed that Lutheran hymns were something different because of the tunes, frequently thought to be difficult, alien, and doleful. Almost no one noticed that the Lutheran chorale was a different rhetorical form that did not fit the Augustinian definition of a hymn. If a young American Lutheran were to think of writing a hymn, it would most likely be in the Watts ballad form, even if the young writer had been steeped in the old German or Scandinavian hymns in their original language. Even if she or he thought of writing a text to a Lutheran tune, the notion that a hymn should either praise or pray dominated. Lutherans, should they survive many more generations in this country, will probably continue to use the ballad stanza and the rhetoric of their Calvinist and Methodist neighbors in their hymns. And that is understandable. It is to be hoped that this book, perhaps, can show Americans of all Christian traditions that there is another kind of hymn: the homiletical poem. While these little traditions may not become major contributors to future Lutheran hymnals, they may at least help us see that they are different and have a contribution to make to the whole. They may help us see what a Lutheran hymn has been and possibly give young Lutheran hymn writers, looking to sing a new song, a new grasp of their tradition among the many different forms and traditions already alive and active in this rich and incoherent tradition. The prophecy of Joel, "your sons and daughters shall prophesy" (2:28), still is being fulfilled in these latter days.

Index of Names and Subjects

Aarhus, xii (map, spelled Århus), 275, 277, 288
Aarflot, Berthe Canutte, viii, 53, 70, **113-62**, 265, 348
Aastrup, Karl Laurids, 274
Acts of the Apostles, book of, 55, 58
Ahnfelt, Oscar, viii, 174, 179, 201-5, 207, 258, 349
Almqvist, nee Sandell, Charlotte, 167, 170-72, 180
Almqvist, Augusta, 187
Almqvist, Knut, 170, 174, 180, 187
Andeliga Sånger (Spiritual Songs), 174, 201-3. *See also* Spiritual Songs
Andelige Siunge-Kor, Anden Part, 28, 155
Andersen, Lisbeth Smedegaard, viii, x-xi, 13, **271-317**, 335, 341, 343, 350-51
Andersen, Hans Christian, 147, 257, 304
Andrewes, Lancelot, 52
Anfektelse (Anfechtung), 125-26
Applicatio, 48, 58-59
Arbetärens Vän (The Worker's Friend), 188
Arndt, Johann, 24, 44, 51-53, 58, 62, 68, 133, 161, 169, 347, 349
Auden, W. H., 340
Augustine, 161, 316, 338, 342

Ballad stanza, 321, 329, 342, 352
Balle, Nicolai Endinger, 92, 95, 98, 111

Baptism, 41, 58, 101-2, 165, 211n.88, 290, 292, 328
Barnens vän (The Children's Friend), 187
Baroque, 23, 37, 41, 44, 48, 50-51, 55, 58, 65, 67, 70-71, 73, 292, 295, 313, 347, 351; era, 41, 47, 48, 94, 307; period, 52; piety, vii, 64
Bartholin, Ahasverus, 31, 35
Bay Psalm Book, 321-22, 328
Bayly, Lewis, 24, 64, 68-69
Berg, Carl Oscar, 180-82, 188, 191-92
Bergen, Norway, x, xii (map), 17-18, 21-22, 26, 31-32, 38, 40, 69, 71-72, 78, 88, 124
Bergen's Deborah, 15, 39, 43
Biehl, Charlotte Dorothea, 95, 98
Birch, Hans Jørgen, 40, 78, 80-82, 98-99, 111-12
Bjørnson, Bjørnstjerne, 113, 137
Blake, William, 92, 228
Bloom, Harold, 274
Børnelærdom (Children's Teaching), 125
Boye, Birgitte Hertz, viii, xi, 12, 72, **75-112**, 137, 316, 347-48, 350
Bradstreet, Anne, 25
Brække, Amund Knudsen, 134
Bremer, Fredrika, 168
Bride of Christ mysticism, 157, 295, 348-49
Brorson, Hans Adolph, xi, 25n.20, 54,

Index of Names and Subjects

70, 79-80, 83, 85, 88, 90, 92, 110, 115, 127-30, 137, 158, 204, 272, 274, 275n.6, 278, 297-98, 315, 334, 348
Brinch, Ivar, 127
Brugskunst, 299-300, 347
Budbäraren (The Gospel Messenger), 170, 174, 178
Bunyan, John, 69, 161-62
Buxefolck (trouser folk), 35

Calvin, John, 5, 327-28, 338-39
Caroline Mathilda, 83
Christian IV of Denmark, 18
Christian V of Denmark, 26
Christian VI, 78-80, 83-84
Christian VII, 83-84
Church Book with Music, 76
Clarissa, 81
Coleridge, Samuel Taylor, 282
Concordia Hymnal, The, 117n.5, 342
Contrafecta, 54
Conventicle Law, 119, 122, 166, 175, 202
Copenhagen, xii (map), 18, 22, 24, 27-28, 30-31, 37, 78, 82-83, 85, 87, 91-92, 94, 96, 98, 109, 127, 181, 271-72, 292, 304, 310, 347, 350
Corinthians, First Letter to the, 48, 121

Dano-Norwegian Kingdom, 19-20
Dass, Petter, x, 32, 35, 54, 66-69, 72, 347
DED (Dorothe Engelbretsdatter), 37-39
Den Dansk Salmebog 2003, 275
Deuteronomy, book of, 10, 154, 196, 197
Driver, Tom Faw, 277, 280
Dryden, John, 90
Dutch East India Company, 23

Edwards, Rusty, 332
Ellingsen, Svein, 245, 274, 333, 335
Engelbretsdatter, Dorothe, vii-viii, x, 12, **15-73**, 81, 90, 110, 115, 133, 137, 140-42, 155, 157, 265, 313, 315, 346
Enlightenment, The, 15, 40, 78, 82-84, 87-88, 90, 94, 110, 119, 124, 137, 169n.12, 274, 339, 347
Ephesians, Letter to the, 138
Et Christelight Valet fra Verden og Længsel Efter Himmelen, 38
Ethiopia, 184, 198
Eugenie, Princess, 189-90
Evangelical Christian Hymnal (Evangelisk Kristelig Psalmebog), 72, 76, 95, 111
Evangelical Lutheran Worship (2007), 76, 338
Evangeliska Fosterlandsstiftelsen (EFS), 170, 178, 184, 188, 192, 202-3
Evening prayer, 62, 64, 100n.33, 142, 197, 211n.88, 313
Exempla, 48
Explicatio, 58, 59

Fjellstedt, Peter, 168-69, 173, 189, 211
Fjällstugan, 183
Flacius, Matthias, 129-30
Forklaring, 78
Francke, August Hermann, 79, 161, 166, 169n.12
Franzén, Franz Michael, 109
Frederick III of Denmark, 18
Frederick IV of Denmark, 40, 79
Frederick V, 83, 85
Freylinghausen, Johan Anastasius, 79-80, 201
Fridhem, 189-90
Fröderyd, xii (map), 167, 173-74, 180, 182, 197
Frostenson, Anders, 215, 231, 241, 242-43, 245, 248, 252, 263, 274, 294, 323, 335

Galatians, Letter to the, 138
Geersøn, Christian, 28
Gellert, Christian Furchtegott, 87, 94, 99
Gerhard, John, 40, 339
Gerhardt, Paul, 23, 67, 135, 137, 163, 201, 343
Grundtvig, Nicolai Frederick Severin,

355

Index of Names and Subjects

96, 111, 175, 191, 272, 274-76, 278, 287, 290, 297, 311, 315
Guldberg's Hymnal, 76, 84, 87, 88-89, 91-94, 99, 104, 109, 110, 111-12, 137, 347-48

Hallqvist, Britt G., viii, **215-69**, 274, 294, 315, 333, 335, 349, 351
Hanseatic League, 17
Harboe, Ludvig, 92-93, 95, 104, 109
Hardenbeck, Ambrosius, 19, 22, 25
Hardenbeck, Engelbret, 26
Hardenbeck, Lucas, 22
Hauge, Hans Nielsen, 72, 110, 113, 115-25, 128, 131, 134, 158, 160, 161, 189, 259, 348
Haugen, Marty, 332
Hebrews, Letter to the, 147
Heerman, Johann, 23, 135, 137, 141, 307
Heggtveit, Hallvard Gunleikson, 121
Hemlandssånger (Songs of the Homeland), 163, 202-8, 210
Hersleb, Bishop Peder, 92
Hertz, Herman Michelsen, 80, 82
Hinterlassene Werke von Margareta Klopstock, 85
Høegh-Guldberg, Ove, 72, 84, 88-89, 91-92, 347
Holberg, Ludvig, 15, 40-41, 83, 95, 347
Holmen Church, 271, 292, 304, 315, 317

International Arbeitsgemeinschaft für Hymnologie (IAH), 215, 333
Isaiah, book of, 154

Job, book of, 193
Joel, book of, 2, 121, 353
John, Gospel of, 58, 62
Jönköping, xii (map), 168, 170, 172, 181, 222
Jørgensen, Engelbret, 17
Jyllandsposten, 273

Kaan, Fred, 242, 252, 323, 335
Kalkar, Christian Andreas Herman, 175

Kierkegaard, Søren, 161, 274
King James Bible (1611), 42
Kingo, Thomas Hansen, 15, 23, 28, 30-32, 38-39, 54, 65, 68, 76, 79, 84-85, 92-95, 99, 104-5, 108-10, 115, 126, 133, 137, 155-56, 191, 272, 274, 278, 286-87, 295, 297, 312, 315, 347
Klopstock, Friedrich Gottlieb, 85, 87, 90, 96, 111
Klopstock, Margareta, 85
Korsblomman, 184-85, 196
Korskirken (Cross Church, Bergen), 17

Laache, Niels, 191
Landstad, Magnus Brostrup, 54, 72, 76, 104, 109-10, 156, 204
Leupold, Wayne, 342
Leviticus, book of, 101
Lind, Jenny, 177, 203, 207
Linné, Carl von, 165
Lobwasser, Ambrosius, 40
Lord's Supper, 41, 157, 340
Lübeck, Germany, 18, 22
Luke, Gospel of, 48-49, 51, 88, 100, 130, 146, 147, 170, 254, 255, 282, 285
Luther, Katherina von Bora (Katie), 12, 21
Luther, Martin, vii, 1-7, 9-11, 43, 47, 49, 54, 58-59, 62, 102, 106, 109, 116, 122, 126, 128, 130, 133, 135, 141, 163, 169, 178-79, 195, 227-28, 250, 252, 274, 294, 296, 338-40
Luther Northwestern Seminary, 331
Luther Seminary, St. Paul, MN, 297-98
Lutheran Book of Worship (LBW) (1978), 76, 87, 169n.12, 208, 238, 322
Lutheran Hymnary, The, 72, 75n.1, 209
Lutheran parsonage tradition, vii, 19-21
Lutheran sermon, 41, 47, 50, 55, 58, 160

Magdalene, Queen Sophie, 79
Malling, Anders, 23-25, 82, 88, 92, 97, 111
Maria Church (Mariakirken), 18, 22
Mark, Gospel of, 233, 263, 302

356

Index of Names and Subjects

Mary's purification, 100-101, 104, 109
Matthew, Gospel of, 129, 135, 138, 158, 159, 197, 344-45, 348
Milton, John, 90
Møller, Peder, 24, 73
Monica, Augustine's mother, 26
Moravians, 161, 184, 196
Morgenbladet, 188
Morning prayer, 11, 59, 100n.33, 156-57
Müller, Heinrich, 24, 28, 133
Muses of Helicon and Parnassus, 32
Muskego Church, 298

Nohrborg, Anders, 169
Nonce stanza, 328-29, 332
Nordland's Trompet (The Trumpet of the North), 32

Odencrants, Thor Hartvig, 170-71, 173, 175, 182, 188, 191
Opitz, Martin, 23-25, 219
Order of salvation *(Ordo salutis)*, 80, 93, 117-18, 127-28, 130, 158, 160, 169, 348
Oscar I, 170, 189
Oscar II, 188-90

Palladius, Peder, 102-3, 105-6
Paradise Garden, 58, 62
Paraphrasing Psalms, 327, 332
Parker, Alice, 324, 328
Pathetic fallacy, the, 280
Pericope hymns, 41, 55
Peterson, Per August, 171, 179
Peterson, Hanna, 185
Peterson, nee Sandell, Mathilda. *See* Sandell, Mathilda
Pia desideria. See Pious Desires
Pietism, 79, 82-83, 87, 110, 169n.12, 213-14, 334; Lutheran, 68; State, 79, 83; Swedish, 201
Pietisten (The Pietist), 177
Pilgrimsharpan (The Pilgrim's Harp), 178, 204

Pilgrim's Progress, 69
Pious Desires (Pia desideria), 24, 79, 166
Plüttschau, Heinrich, 79
Poenitentze (repentance), 47
Pontoppidan, Erick, 54, 70-71, 78-79, 81, 83-84, 88, 92-94, 103-5, 108-9, 115, 125, 130-31, 135, 137, 144, 159-60, 166
Practice of Piety, 69
Psalms, book of, 4, 42, 48, 50, 88, 96, 104, 111, 172, 183, 184n.45, 197, 212, 219, 278, 296, 298, 321, 338

Rambach, Johan Jakob, 76, 99, 169
Rauhe House, 181
Renvall, Viola, 336
Revelation, book of, 138, 144, 236
Rhetoric, x, 3, 7, 35, 48, 52, 58, 62, 84, 138, 140, 145, 195, 290, 328, 332, 338, 340, 346, 352; rhetorical, 3, 5-6, 41, 55, 87, 195, 321, 340-41, 346, 352
Richardson, Samuel, 81
Rimbrev (poetic epistles), 24
Rist, Johann, 23, 99
Romans, Letter to the, 155, 195, 344-45
Rosenius, Carl Olof, 170, 173-74, 177-79, 182-83, 185, 191, 211, 258, 349; Movement, 180, 201n.73, 211; Revival, 166, 170, 200
Rostock, Germany, 18, 22, 24, 92
Rowthorne, Jeffery, 340
Ruskin, John, 280

Sandell, Christina, 167, 180
Sandell, Fredrica Engstrand, 166
Sandell, Jonas, 164-67, 169, 171-72, 201, 211, 264
Sandell, Lina, viii, x, 53, 157, **163-214**, 263-65, 267, 334, 341, 348-49
Sandell, Mathilda, 167, 171, 179, 185
Sandell, Nils Johan, 167, 191
Sandell's songs, 208-9, 211, 214
Scott, George, 177, 211
Scott, Sir Walter, 168, 170
Schartau, Henrik, 165, 169n.13, 211

Index of Names and Subjects

Schrader, Johann, 79-80
Scriver, Christian, 135, 161, 169
Sedio, Mark, 329, 332
Seeberg, Gerhard, 115, 118
Sehested, Jens Søthen, 22, 31
Sellergren, Peter Lorenz, 165-66, 201-2
Selvbiografi, 113
Service Book and Hymnal, The (1958), 208-9, 327, 339-40
Shaw, Joseph, 128
Siælens Sang-Offer, 25, 28, 41, 155
Small Catechism, 5n.13, 11, 20, 59, 64, 78-79, 115, 125, 144, 202, 312, 329
Småland, 13, 165, 167, 170, 182, 193, 202, 206
Sor Academy, Denmark, 22
Soul's Offering of Song, The. See *Siælens Sang-Offer*
Spaeth, Harriet Krauth, 76
Spener, Philipp Jakob, 24, 79, 126n.19, 161, 166, 169n.11, 181
Spiritual Choir: Part II, 28
Spiritual Songs, 3, 5, 94, 136, 138, 174, 185, 200-205, 208-9, 214, 217, 243, 352. See *Andeliga sånger*
Storckenfeldt, Aurore, 173
Storckenfeldt, Sigrid, 185
Struensee, Johann Friedrick, 83-84, 87-88, 91, 96
Sunday School Union, 185

Taare-Offer (Tear Offering), 16, 25, 28, 30, 67, 155
Tears and Spring of Comfort, 24
Tegnér, Esaias, 165, 168
Tillich, Paul, 277, 296, 335

Timothy, Second Letter to, 39
Tønder Songbook, The, 79
Topelius, Zacharias, 182-3
Treaty of Westphalia, 18
Trondheim, xii (map), 32, 92, 124, 191, 252
Truth unto Godliness, 78, 144
Twin Kingdoms, 15, 18, 78, 81, 83

University of Halle, 79, 166

Volda, xii (map), 124-25, 162
Von Passow, Anna Catharina, 95
Vordingborg, xii (map), 82, 85, 94, 112, 273

Wadström, Bernard, 170-71, 174-75, 181-82, 192
Wallin, Johan Olof, 109, 201n.73, 212, 243
Watts, Isaac, 327-28, 342, 352
Wennerberg, Gunnar, 186n.45
Wexels, Wilhelm Andreas, 175
Wichern, Johann Hinrich, 181
Wieselgren, Peter, 166, 169, 171, 188, 201n.73, 202
Winkworth, Catherine, 324, 327
Wolcot, John, 89
Wraaman, H. N., 162
Wrangel, Anna, 17, 21
Wudrian Valentin, 24, 40

Young, Edward, 91-92

Zechariah, book of, 328
Ziegenbalg, Bartholomaeus, 79

Index of Books and Hymns

BERTHE CANUTTE AARFLOT

Books

Religious Letters, for the Support and Edification with the Strengthening of Faith, Hope, and Love, with the Addition of Occasional Songs together with Morning and Evening Prayers with Appropriate Songs (Religiøse Breve til Opmuntring og Opbyggelse samt Bestrykelse i Tro, haab og Kjærlighed med et Anhang af Leilighetssange samt en Morgen og Aftenbøn med hosføiede Sange), 157

Selvbiografi, 113, 115n2, 133, 162n

The Soul's Morning and Evening Offering Containing Prayers, Sighs, and Songs for Every Day in the Week Along with Songs for the Four Seasons (Sjælens Morgen = Og Aftenoffer), 155

The Soul's Spiritual Festival of Joy, 156

Troens Frugt: En samling af aandelige Sanger i tvende Dele med tre Tillæg, 133n, 134n, 138n, 140n, 142nn, 143nn, 144n, 145n, 146n, 150nn, 151nn, 152n

Hymns

"By Grace's Short Time" ("Af Naadens korte Tid"), 141

"Come, Friends, and Stand Beside My Gravestone" ("Kom, Venner, hid til Graven træder"), 50n, 146, 148

"Do Not Forget That You Are Dying" ("I som slaa døden hen i glemme"), 152

"In Jesus' Name I Now Prepare to Take My Last Journey" ("I Jesu navn eg no til siste ferd meg reiser"), 115

"Like the Rose Standing in Its Fullest Bloom" ("Som Rosen, der i Blomstring staar"), 149, 150n

"My Days on Earth toward Night Are Turning" ("Min Levedag hen mod sin Aften skrider"), 136

"O Lamb, I See Thee Filled with Wounds" ("O Lam, jeg ser dig fuld af saar"), 115, 144

"O Now Is The Time to Be Hasting and Hurrying" ("Nu er det fornødent at haste og ile"), 139, 140n

"O, You, My Longing and My Pleasure" ("Du min Længsel og Behag"), 142, 142n

"O Thou, Worthy Holy Spirit" ("O du værdig Helligaand"), 144, 144n

"Parents Who Are Grieving Me" ("Forældre, some begræder mig"), 147

"See, How Time Flies" ("Se Tiden, hvor den rinder"), 143, 143n

Index of Books and Hymns

LISBETH SMEDEGAARD ANDERSEN

Books

Bag Vinger af Løvfald: 21 nye Salmer med 18 nye melodier, 298n, 305, 305n, 306n, 308, 308n, 311

Black on White: A Devotional Book (Sort på Hvidt: Andagtsbog), 314, 314n

Bursting with Song: On the Newer Hymn Writers (Brystefeldt af Sang: om nyere salmedigtere), 271, 271n, 292

Du bor i vor Dag: Salmer og digte, 288

The Hidden Face: Essayistic Sermons on the Hidden Face of God in Scripture (Det skjulte Ansigt: Essayistisk prædikener), 312, 312n

Kranse av torne og blomster: salmer og digte over 14 korsveysstationer, 296, 296n

Nu lægger vinden sig i verdens haver: en sonnet krans, 312, 312n

Vinterlys og tjørneblomst: Salmer, 278, 278n

Hymns

"Emmaus" ("Emmaus"), 284

"The Gloomy Morning Sunrise" ("De mørke Morgenrøde"), 278-80, 281 fig. 3

"It's Twilight" ("Det Skumre"), 312

"Just Yesterday Was Golden" ("I går var hveden moden"), 298, 299

"A Potter's Parable" ("En pottemagerens lignelse"), 302, 303, 303n

"So Easy to Condemn Him" ("Påskelørdag"), 305-6

"They Did Not Sleep That Evening" ("De sov kun lidt"), 308, 309 fig. 6

"You Came to Us Here" ("Du fødtes på Jord"), 289, 291 fig. 4

BIRGITTE BOYE

Poems and Plays

David's Psalms in a Free Translation (Davids Psalmer i en fri Oversættelse), 96

Gorm, the Old: A Heroic Play in Three Acts (Gorm den Gamle. Et heorisk Skuespil i tre Handlinger), 96

Melicertes (Play in two acts), 96

Sigrid or Regnald's Death (Sigfrid eller Regnalds Død), 96

Hymns

"Be Filled with Holy Gladness" ("Bliv fuld af hellig Glæde"), 104, 105, 107

"He Is Arisen, Glorious Word" ("Han er opstanden, store Bud"), 75

"Men From the Land of Immortality" ("Mænd fra Uddeligheds Land"), 93

"O! Light of God's Most Wondrous Love" ("O! Lue fra Guds-Kierlighed"), 75

"Prodigious Earth! A Crowded Dwelling" ("Uhyre Jord! Opfyldte Boelig"), 89

"Rejoice, Rejoice This Happy Morn" ("Os er idag en Frelser Fød"), 75

"While Divinity's Gleaming Plays" ("Mens Guddoms Straale spiller"), 19n, 90

DOROTHE ENGELBRETSDATTER

Books

A Farewell from the World and Longing for Heaven (Et Christeligt Valet fra Verden og Længsel Efter Himmelen), 38n, 50

The Soul's Offering of Song (Siælens Sang-Offer), 25, 27, 28, 29, 37, 40, 41, 42n, 53, 155, 167

Index of Books and Hymns

Offering of Tears (Taare-Offer), 16 fig. 1, 25, 28, 30, 67, 79

Epistolary Poems
"Ack! Kingo Is Gone Back to Dust" ("Ach! Kingo blev til Jord igien"), 39, 39n, 56
"Ærbodigst Hilsen med Gud," 26n, 37n
"At jeg for ingen Deel," 19n, 26n
"De rette Enckers Flugt til deris Naadige Dommer i Himmelen," 37n
"Dorothe Engelbretsdatters Responsorium til von Ahnen," 36n
"Effterfölgende Liig-Sang," 39n
"Effterfølgende Grafskrift," 37n
"Er Spurren den Vndschyldt at holde Dantz med Tranen," 22n, 31n
"Liffsens Frste Ærens Konning," 37n
"Longing for Eternal Life" ("Længsel effter det Evige Liff"), 66
"Medlidig Trøst til Jndvaaneren i Bergen over den Jammerlige Jldebrand som Aar 1686," 17, 17n
"Merciful Father and Comforting God" ("Barmhiertigheds Fader og Trøstens Gud"), 38, 38n
"Ned ad helder onse *Mater*," 36n
"NU har den Bergens *Debora*," 39n
"O at jeg snart maa bliffe qvit," 66n
"Oh! Father of Mercies" ("Ah! Miskunds Fader"), 27, 27n
"Paa same Maneer frem Kommen," 36n, 48n
"Recept for en Ord-Gryder," 27, 27n
"Sidste Ære-Mindis," 25, 26n
"Som den Taareful Jød-Jinde," 26, 26n
"Svar til Mester Jens Pedersen," 38n
"Tack til Madame Bladt for Bindebrevet," 36n
"Te Deum nos Laudamus," 39, 40n
"Til Ahasverus Bartholin," 31, 31n, 35n
"Til Hr. Peter Dass, da Bogen følgede med efter Begiering," 34n
"Til læseren," 42n, 44n, 54
"Till een der drømte vi hafde Lagt Kierlighed sammen i Gamle dage, uden tviill," 18n, 36n
"Till Mag; Laurs Thura, Rector i Kiøge," 19n, 31
"Till Præsid: Dyseldorph," 19n

Hymns
"Daylight Dies and Flies Away" ("Afften Psalme, Dagen viger og gaar bort"), 59, 62n, 71, 72, 73, 73n
"Længsel effter det Evige Liff," 66
"Nu da i Jesu Naffn," 65n
"Paa Jorden Fred og Glæde," 55
"Welcome! O Blessed Pentecost" ("Om den Hellig Aands Udsendelse, Velkomme salig Pintze Dag"), 55-57, 57n
"When Earth with All Its Joys Defeats Me" ("Om Verden med sin Glæde sviger"), 73
"When I Behold My Mistakes" ("Naar jeg mine feil vil skue"), 71
"When Jonah Went to Nineveh" ("Strax Jonas kom til Ninive"), 44

GRACIA GRINDAL

Books
Lessons in Hymnwriting, 331
"We Are One in Christ": Hymns, Paraphrases, and Translations by Gracia Grindal, 333n

Hymns
"After Singing Hymns of Comfort," 345
"Come, Share the Spirit," 332
"Father in Heaven," 329
"Help Me, Holy Spirit," 344
"Not by Might, Not by Power," 328

Index of Books and Hymns

BRITT G. HALLQVIST

Books
At the Door of Paradise (Vid Paradisets Port), 238, 238n
Church Songs for Children (Kyrkovisor för Barn), 231
I Will Sing a Song to God (Jag vill sjunga en visa för Gud), 225
Nalle's Poetry (Nalles Poesi), 239
People and Faith (Människor och Tro), 235, 235n
Prayer Book for Children (Bön bok för Barn), 235
Simplified (Förenklat), 223

Poems
"Adam Came First of All" ("Bibelskt ABC"), 235
"I Have Finished Playing" ("Nu har jag lekt färdigt"), 235
"I Walked Through Clay and Reeds" ("Jag gick i lera och i vass"), 239
"I Went One Early Morning" ("Jag stod en tidig morgon"), 228, 238
"I Wonder, said Mrs. Peter" ("Jag undrar, sa fru Petrus"), 240
"The New Song" ("Den Nya Sång"), 236-37
"Post Card" ("Vykort"), 237

Bible Play, Operas
Captive and Free (Fange og Fri), 259
The Little Poor One (Den lille Fattige), 257
The Loveliest Rose, 257
Noah Finds Land (Noa går i Land), 257
Pilgrim's Mass (Pilgrimsmesse), 257, 258
Sing My Heart (Syng mitt Hjerte), 257

Hymns
"The Boy of Bethlehem" ("Pojken, Bethlehem"), 224-25
"Everyone's Rushed" ("Alle har hast"), 230, 232 fig. 5
"God Created Us in Families" ("Gud har omsorg om vårt släkte"), 251, 251n
"God of Earth" ("Jordens Gud"), 260-62, 262n, 261 fig. 11
"God, You Went Away" ("Gud, du gick bort"), 252, 253, 253n
"He Walked the Tearful Highway" ("Han gick den svåra vägen"), 247n, 248-49
"I Have Come Not That I Trust You" ("Jag kom inte hit för att jag tror"), 233
"I Have Never Met an Angel" ("Aldrig har jag mött nån ängel"), 265, 265n, 266 fig. 12
"One Bright and Shining Morning" ("Det var i Soloppgången"), 254-55, 255n, 256 fig. 8
"Stay with Us" ("Bli Hos oss"), 259-60
"Sun, Moon and Stars" ("Månen och Sol"), 245, 247
"Teach Me to Seek You Sincerely" ("Lär mig att bedja"), 243, 244
"There by God's Heav'nly Throne" ("Inför Guds himlatron"), 227
"They Will Walk through the Gates of the City" ("De skall Gå till den heliga Staden"), 249-50, 250n
"Who Is It We See on the Highway?" ("Vem är det some kommer på vägen?"), 226
"Zacchaeus Was a Publican" ("Sackeus var en publican"), 228-29

LINA SANDELL

Books
Childhood Attempts (Barndoms försök af Carolina Sandell), 167

Index of Books and Hymns

Jessica's First Prayer *(Jessicas första bön)*, 185
Library of Christian Biographies, 185
Spiritual Dewdrops (Andeliga Daggdroppar), 170
Spiritual Spring Blossoms (Andeliga Vårblommor), 170

Hymns

"All Day as I Am Working" ("Om Dagen vid mit Arbeide"), 204
"Allt i allom Kristus?" 171
"Are You Living the New Life?" ("Lefver du det nye lifvet?"), 171
"Art Thou Weary and Sad and Dark in Thy Troubled Breast?" ("Är det ödsligt och mörkt och kallt"), 207
"Children of the Heavenly Father" ("Tryggare kan ingen vara"), 163, 170, 192, 193, 194 fig. 4, 206, 208, 209, 210, 211, 267, 315
"Day by Day" ("Blott en dag"), 196, 197, 206, 209, 210, 211, 267
"The Father's Arms Are Open to Receive Us" ("Se, öppen star Gud fadersfamn"), 195
"Great Hills May Tremble" ("Bergen må vika"), 211
"Have You Courage to Follow Jesus?" ("Har du mod at följe Jesus?"), 204
"I'll Never Count All of God's Mercies" ("Jag kan icke räkna dem alla"), 195, 199
"Is It True That Jesus Is My Brother?" ("Är det sant at Jesus är min broder?"), 195, 196, 196n
"Jerusalem" ("Jerusalem"), 207, 208, 209
"Lord, Hide Not Thy Face from Me" ("Herre, fördölj eg ditt ansikte för mig"), 171, 199, 211, 267
"Now I Will Sing of the Mother's Wings" ("Nu vill jag sjunga om modersvingen"), 198
"O, May the Song of Jesus Ring Out" ("O, må Jesus-sången klinga!"), 191, 191n
"O Tender, Gracious Father" ("Du ömma fadershjärta"), 195, 211
"Strait Is the Gate" ("Den port är trång, den väg är small"), 209
"There Is a Time Before All Others" ("Det gifs en tid för andra tider"), 170
"Thousand, Thousand Stars Are Gleaming" ("Tusen, tusen stjärnor glimma"), 171
"Thy Holy Wings" ("Bred dina vida vingar"), 205, 206, 210, 211n
"Thy Kingdom Come, Quickly, O Lord" ("Tilkomme ditt rike, O Herre, vår Gud"), 173

www.ingramcontent.com/pod-product-compliance
Lightning Source LLC
Chambersburg PA
CBHW071146070526
44584CB00019B/2684